Managing Urban Tourism

Stephen J. Page and C. Michael Hall

Prentice
Hall

An imprint of **Pearson Education**

Harlow, England · London · New York · Reading, Massachusetts · San Francisco · Toronto · Don Mills, Ontario · Sydney
Tokyo · Singapore · Hong Kong · Seoul · Taipei · Cape Town · Madrid · Mexico City · Amsterdam · Munich · Paris · Milan

Pearson Education Limited
Edinburgh Gate
Harlow
Essex CM20 2JE

and Associated Companies throughout the world

Visit us on the World Wide Web at:
www.pearsoneduc.com

ISBN 0 130 27286 8

British Library Cataloguing-in-Publication Data
A catalogue record for this book is available from the British Library

10 9 8 7 6 5 4 3 2 1
07 06 05 04 03

Typeset in 10/12pt Sabon by 35
Printed in China
PPLC/01

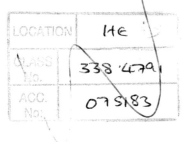

Contents

List of figures

List of tables

List of plates

Preface

This is the fourth book in the 'Themes in Tourism Series' and reflects the continued growth in towns and cities as places and locales for tourism activity and as spaces within which leisure activity is structured and consumed. A cursory scan of the tourism and cognate research literature now indicates that the role of tourism in cities is receiving more attention than ever before. It has moved from a neglected field of social science a decade ago to a position where the importance of urban tourism is now receiving due recognition in a variety of academic fields, not least of which is tourism studies itself, but increasingly it is being seen as a specialised area of destination management and marketing with its own set of concerns and issues. This book therefore seeks to incorporate much of the recent research and scholarship in the field, as well as some of the insights and results of the authors' own studies to provide a contemporary introduction to urban tourism management to the student of tourism. However, we also hope that this book will be of value to those in human geography and urban and regional planning who are now starting to realise the vital role that tourism plays in cities as they position themselves in the increasingly competitive global economy.

This book has its genre in responding to the constant criticisms related to the way in which researchers have approached and analysed the city as a context for tourism activity. Probably the most influential and widely cited study on urban tourism is the seminal paper by Ashworth (1989), which documented both the literature and interest in urban environments. This is an important starting point for a book such as this because when Ashworth (1989) observed an 'imbalance in attention' noting that it is '. . . remarkable because most tourists originate from cities, many seek out cities as holiday destinations and the social and economic impacts of tourism are substantial in urban areas. The failure to consider tourism as a specifically urban activity imposes a serious constraint that cannot fail to impede the development of tourism as a subject of serious study' – it established a challenge for researchers. More importantly, Ashworth (1989: 33) recognised that a 'double neglect has occurred. Those interested in the study of tourism have tended to neglect the urban context in which much of it is set, while those interested in urban studies, itself a rapidly growing focus of academic interest, have been equally neglectful of the importance of the tourist function in cities'. This book returns to this fundamental premise and not only seeks to reconceptualise the way the city is viewed in tourism terms, but also seeks to provide a synthesis of recent advances in research. In fact Page (2000) reiterated Ashworth's (1989) comments, arguing that research has been slow and bogged down by a large proliferation of descriptive case studies and analytically devoid assessments of tourism in individual city environments. These studies have often contributed little to the development of theory or new conceptual frameworks. Therefore, we hope that this fresh and interdisciplinary synthesis of urban tourism as a subject of study moves the research agenda forward by highlighting germane areas of study within the umbrella of cities as places that offer a multitude of opportunities for tourism, leisure and recreational activities. No one book can ever offer a comprehensive review of the field, since specialist areas such as the tourist-historic city and conservation and preservation are covered in Ashworth and Tunbridge's (1990, 2000) seminal work. However, this book is specifically aimed at the undergraduate and postgraduate audience to make tourism in cities a more accessible, integrated and central element of the research and teaching focus for students of tourism and associated subjects such as geography, planning, management and the wider social sciences.

The book assumes no prior knowledge of urban studies or tourism and seeks to distil the essential debates, reviews and state of knowledge and thinking on towns and cities as places for tourism. It seeks to be a rounded and provocative text that sets out potential challenges for both the tourism sector and public and private sector agencies involved in city planning and management. It highlights successes and failures in tourism and develops an understanding of good practice in managing the growing impact and spread of what can broadly be described as the tourism phenomenon. Much of the thinking within this book is informed by both an academic and practitioner involvement with the tourism industry on different facets of tourism planning, development and management as advisors and consultants which blends our academic expertise within a problem-solving and advisory capacity. We hope this will engage you in a critical and ongoing debate about urban tourism, its significance, effects and the challenges it poses for people working, living and experiencing it as a dynamic and ever changing phenomenon in time and space.

Stephen Page   Michael Hall
Stirling   Dunedin

Acknowledgements

This book has its genesis in some of our previous work, particularly Stephen's previous work on urban tourism and urban redevelopment and Michael's in tourism planning and reimaging, and those who are familiar with our writing will find both continuities and new tangents along which we have travelled. However, the development of such a work is not ours alone and we would like to thank past and present colleagues, as well as past and present students for their input and stimulation. In particular, Stephen would like to thank Paul Spoonley for his feedback on the postmodern city and Lynne Tunna at Massey University for typing some of the chapters, tables and assistance with the book. Stephen would also like to thank Charles Johnston at Auckland University of Technology for those very convivial 'research lunches' and fieldwork exploring the postmodernist city, and how the geographer still has a vital role to play in interpreting the urban landscape around us. At the University of Stirling, help and advice was provided by Lynsey, Lynne, Sharon and Sheila at various points in time and their help is gratefully acknowledged. Also, the opportunity to meet and spend time at the University of Groningen in 1999 and to review issues with Greg Ashworth was helpful and informative as was the dialogue with other geographers in the Department of Marketing. Last, but not least, the assistance provided by the Argyll, the Isles, Loch Lomond, Stirling and Trossachs Tourist Board and Scottish Enterprise Forth Valley in discussing urban tourism is gratefully acknowledged.

Michael would like to thank Nick Cave, Ed Kuepper, David Sylvian and Tom Waits as well as a number of academic colleagues who have directly assisted in urban research that has found its way into this book, including Richard Butler, John Jenkins, Alan Lew, Maurice Roche, Dallen Timothy, John Tunbridge, Josette Wells, Allan Williams and Heather Zeppel. Michael's research was also greatly assisted by the granting of an International Council for Canadian Studies/National Capital Commission/National Capital Scholarship which enabled him to spend a month in Ottawa undertaking research on tourism there as well as looking at tourism in urban areas and capital cities in general. The assistance and kindness shown by Francois Lapoint and the rest of the staff at the NCC was invaluable and it is hoped that this book will also be of interest and value to them.

Finally, at a personal level Stephen would like to thank Jo and Rosie, while Michael would like to thank Jody. Both of us realise that without the support and incentive that you all give us, particularly Rosie's excellent proof-reading skills which are coming along very nicely, our work would be considerably more difficult and our leisure not so much fun.

Stephen Page
Stirling

November 2001

Michael Hall
City Rise
Dunedin

Publisher's acknowledgements

We are grateful to the following for permission to reproduce copyright material:

Butterworth Heinemann for figures 1.1 and 1.2 from C.M. Hall and S.J. Page (2000) *Tourism in South and South-East Asia: Critical Perspectives*, reprinted with permission from Butterworth Heinemann; Oxford University Press for table 2.1 from R. Le Heron, L. Murphy, P. Forer and M. Goldstone (eds) (1999) *Explorations in Human Geography: Encountering Place*; Blackwell Publishers for figure 2.1 from M. Dear and S. Flusty (1998) Postmodern urbanism, *Annals of the Association of American Geographers*, 88(1), 50–72, © Blackwell Publishers; Routledge for figure 3.1 from D. Ioannides and K. Debbage (eds) (1998) *The Economic Geography of the Tourist Industry: A Supply Side Analysis*; for table 3.16 and figures 4.4 and 4.5 from D. Pearce and R. Butler (eds) (1999) *Contemporary Issues in Tourism Development*; Office for National Statistics for tables 3.13, 4.1–4.3 and 4.5 from *Focus on London*, National Statistics © Crown Copyright 2000; HOTREC for table 4.7 from http://www.hotrec.org; Elsevier Science for tables 6.2–6.4 reprinted from *Annals of Tourism Research*, 25(3), M. Huse, T. Gustaven and S. Almedal, Tourism impact comparisons among Norwegian towns, 721–38, copyright 1998, with permission from Elsevier Science; Cognizant Communication Corporation for table 6.6 from M. Barker, S.J. Page and D. Meyer (2002) Evaluating the impact of the 2000 America's Cup on Auckland, New Zealand, *Event Management*, 7(2), 79–92.

Argyll, the Isles, Loch Lomond, Stirling and Trossachs Tourist Board for plates 4.1–4.6, copyright AILLST.

In some instances we have been unable to trace the owners of copyright material, and we would appreciate any information that would enable us to do so.

Introduction: cities as places for tourism

CHAPTER 1

Introduction: the city as a place for tourism?

Urbanisation is a global process, described by Johnston (1981: 363) as 'a process by which: first, an increasing proportion of an area's population become concentrated in its statistically defined urban places'. Through the process of urbanisation places, which are described as towns and cities, are created. Neither the process, nor reflection on it, is a new phenomenon. For example, Jones's (1966) synthesis of the geographer's interest in the city highlights the concern with the development of the pre-industrial city through to the industrial city, and in recent years this has also encompassed the post-industrial city. In each case, the city has resulted from a need for people to agglomerate (i.e. to associate close together for productive activities) for economic purposes, to achieve economies of scale in productive activities, to utilise the infrastructure, communication and transport systems that exist which give producers a competitive edge over non-urban producers. Furthermore,

➜ Urbanization is a major force contributing to the development of towns and cities, where people live, work and shop. Towns and cities function as places where the population concentrates in a defined area, and economic activities locate in the same area or nearby, to provide the opportunity for the production and consumption of goods and services in capitalist societies. Consequently, towns and cities provide the context for a diverse range of social, cultural and economic activities which the population engage in, and where tourism, leisure and entertainment form major service activities (Page 1997: 112).

In fact through history, towns and cities have functioned as important locations for tourism activity since ancient times with the accommodation and entertainment function of the pre-industrial city. For example, the development of spas and the rise of the Grand Tour saw tourism focus on urban locations, while the Grand Tour routes on mainland Europe focused on locations with sites of cultural significance often within Renaissance and Classical cities (Towner 1996). In addition, the development of educational tourism in the UK with the rise of the genre of public schools (e.g. Eton, Westminster and latterly Rugby), along with the rise of Oxford and Cambridge Universities, contributed to the development of towns and cities as tourist centres and sites of tourist interest.

Much of the current interest in cities by geographers, sociologists and planners and other social scientists has focused on the role of urbanisation and the consequences for economic, social and political outcomes. The emphasis of research in each discipline and the growing interest in multidisciplinary approaches to urban issues has largely focused on the changing dimensions of cities in modern society and paid little attention to their tourism function. Indeed, Law (1996b: 9) argued that 'Perhaps one reason why urban tourism has been so little recognised is that its evolution does not fit easily into urban growth models'. For example, in models of the pre-industrial city, much of the attention on its growth and development focused on trade, monopolies and military power (Langton 1978). In contrast, the development of the industrial city was based on the rise of the capitalist system of production, the nascent manufacturing industries and the evolution of urban industrial complexes (Lawton 1978). In most of these models and analyses tourism and the provision of leisure and recreational services were absent. Indeed, it is only during the 1970s with the concern associated with cities affected by industrial restructuring induced by deindustrialisation, that the interest in the form and nature of the post-industrial city emerged. As Harvey (1989a) observed, the growing global competition among cities for mobile investment and conspicuous consumption in sunrise service industries such as tourism, meant that many cities were forced to look for a new economic rationale. This previous neglect of the role of cities and their significance as places where service activities such as tourism and leisure are produced and consumed, emerged as a new research agenda focused on the post-industrial city and notions of globalisation, which have made tourism a more visible area for research.

Globalisation, urbanisation and the rise of cities as places for tourism

A great deal of research has emerged in the late 1980s and 1990s on the concept of globalisation and the future form of cities is poignantly summarised in a paper by Peter Hall 'Modelling the post-industrial city'. Hall (1997: 316) argued that

> The new world of the 1990s is a profoundly different world, in at least two senses. First, it is a world in which cities compete in a global economy, seeking constantly to redefine their economic roles as old functions are lost and new

functions are sought to take their place; and while the lost functions are in the goods-manufacturing and goods-handling sectors, the new functions involve the creation and exchange and use of information. Second, it is a world in which cities deconcentrate and spread to become complex systems of cities linked together by flows of people and information; and in which the different con-stituents are likewise involved in a process of shedding old activities while they gain new ones.

One of the main features of this new urban realism is the effect that globalis-ation has had on the form, structure and function of cities internationally. As Peter Hall (1997: 316) explains,

> Globalization . . . has operated to forge a new international division of labour – large multinational corporations, operating in a number of cities around the globe, relocate their operations to the lowest-cost location where it is efficient and effective to operate; corporations, including relatively new arrivals based in industrializing countries, increasingly spread their operations to occupy new markets. The most obvious effect of this, during the 1970s and 80s, was the large scale deindustrialization experienced in many of the developed world's older manufacturing cities, and the growth of new manufacturing cities in industrializ-ing countries . . . Further, all this was associated, somewhat contingently, with the restructuring and relocation of transport logistical centres . . . leading to further job losses and large scale dereliction in the cities.

What this marked for many cities was the move from traditional production-based activities, to a growing emphasis and dependence upon services, especially the more advanced services which deal with the exchange and use of information which Castells (1996a) has termed informational services. The effect on cities and their economies has been profound during the 1980s and 1990s, and has been described by Castells (1996a) as being as significant as the shift from an agrarian to an industrial mode of production in the eighteenth century in Europe. One outcome has been that many towns and cities have repositioned their economic and employment structure to develop the advanced service sector activities such as banking, finance, business services, headquarters, government-based employment and most notably the expansion and development of tourism, especially the cultural and creative industries (Pratt 1998) as well as the hospitality sector.

At a global scale, these changes have affected the hierarchy of towns and cities and their position in global and regional economic systems. This has resulted in the development of a limited number of global cities. These global cities dominate the world economy (e.g. London, New York, Tokyo, Frankfurt, Paris and Los Angeles – see Plate 1.1) and some of the indices used to evaluate which places make up the elite group of world cities include (P. Hall 1997):

- the number of world or regional headquarters of multinational firms;
- numbers of foreign banks and other financial institutions;

Plate 1.1 Los Angeles – a world city which also suffers from congestion and pollution as the haze in this plate shows

- the presence of international agencies;
- cultural indicators (e.g. museums, art galleries, libraries, theatres and opera houses and the number of events they hold);
- the concentration of print and electronic media;
- the number of international tourists hosted;
- indices of connectivity (i.e. the number of direct flights and connections to other destinations; number of air travellers handled; rail connections, especially high-speed links and the extent of national telecommunications traffic).

What is important to note here is the significance of tourism-related indices as indicators of world city status in an economic system where the service sector is the major form of production. This hierarchy is complemented by the proto-global cities which are at the second order level, where cities have a special role within the economic system as centres for government agencies (e.g. Brussels, Strasbourg, Geneva and Rome), for financial institutions (e.g. Frankfurt) and a role in culture (e.g. Milan, Madrid and Vienna). The growth of international trade organisations such as the European Union and North Atlantic Free Trade Area (NAFTA) and ASEAN may also favour certain cities at the expense of others. Linked to this development is what has been termed the rise of megacities in regions such as South East Asia. Here a growing emphasis is placed on an interconnected region (Teo *et al.* 2001) based on export sectors, telecommunication links and the exchange of information leading to a much wider metropolitan agglomeration – the Extended Metropolitan Region (EMR).

The Extended Metropolitan Region as a new tourism location: the Asian experience

EMRs are a new form of urban region which are particularly evident in Newly Industrialised Countries (NICs). This is apparent in Dick and Rimmer's (1998: 2303) assessment that in South East Asia, the growth and development of urban areas has made use of terms such as the third-world city redundant due to the effects of globalisation. In many discussions of cities and their development, a great deal of the attention is placed on the Western European or North American examples, although as Devas and Rakodi (1993) show, South and South East Asia combined accounted for one-third of the developing world's urban population. This population increased by 4 per cent per year between 1970 and 1985. Much of the growth is due to in-migration and the natural growth of the existing population, with the attraction of urban lifestyles and improved economic opportunities in both the formal and informal sectors of the economy (e.g. the casual labour market). Tang and Thant (1994) show that the success of EMRs and their location within the region's trans-national 'growth triangles', which sometimes transcend national borders, illustrate the significance of the inflow of foreign direct investment into South East Asia and regional economic cooperation, notably the role of trading blocs. Therefore such developments impact upon population distribution, further concentrating the workforce in specific areas of economic potential.

The recent Asian Development Bank (1998) report on *The Development and Management of Asian Megacities* highlights the scale of urban and population development in the region. The definition of megacity, as areas of population in excess of 10 million people, has been used by the Asian Development Bank to examine the prospects for the region into the next millennium. The urban population of Asia has increased from 0.4 billion in 1965 to 1.1 billion in 1998, with the level of urbanisation increasing from 22 per cent to 33 per cent over the same period (i.e. the population who are now urban-based). Dixon and Smith (1997) point to the increasing concentration of urban economic activity into larger complexes. They refer to the concept of extended metropolitan regions (EMRs), which represent something different from urbanisation elsewhere in the world because they are driving both regional and national economic growth. In fact Douglass (1995) identifies four patterns of restructuring that are occurring in South East Asia, based on the experience of EMRs such as Bangkok:

- National economic development is being polarised into a small number of core regions.

- Mega-urban regions are emerging (the Asian Development Bank calls these megacities), which are linked through technological, economic and social networks (see Rimmer 1997) to enable a pattern of multinuclear development to occur. Both local and global processes are at work, a feature explored in detail by Gertler (1997) and many of the papers in the recent book by Rimmer (1997) characterised by the localisation/globalisation debate.

- The new EMRs are the focus of the accumulation and circulation of global capital, a feature that has attracted a great deal of attention among economic geographers since the influential work of Dicken (1988). These EMRs are also part of a global pattern of world cities.

- A number of transborder regions are emerging where urban agglomerations cut across national borders (the growth triangles concept) which is highlighted in Figure 1.1. These regions of economic activity are based upon emerging international networks of 'transportational, communicational and decision-making corridors of international development, designed to integrate the region as a whole into the global system of finance, production, trade and consumption' (Dixon and Smith 1997: 15).

Explaining the factors that have promoted the emergence of EMRs is as McGee (1995) argues a function of three processes: globalisation; the transactional revolution and structural change, each of which are discussed by Castells (1996b). In terms of globalisation, national governments have encouraged the export-oriented manufacturing and investment (foreign direct investment, FDI). Through increased labour productivity, the use of flexible labour strategies in the post-Fordist era and the provision of improved 'existing spaces or by creating new spaces to attract these activities . . . states and firms are reshaping the landscape of production within Pacific Asia, with the spatial impact being felt at a variety of levels from the purely local to the emergence of complex growth corridors' (Dixon and Smith 1997: 10).

In terms of transactional costs, the greater use of technology to facilitate decision-making, with information and capital flows transmitted electronically, has meant that many EMRs have developed electronic nodes. The spatial outcome of such developments is that transportation is vital in the connection of the multiple nodes (polynodal) that develop in EMRs, such as a tourism region, multiple business centres, retail districts, port zones and industrial areas. New developments often gravitate towards the new infrastructure routes where new tourism regions can be created. As McGee and Greenberg (1992) recognised, EMRs not only stem from industrial deconcentration, but FDI and new business start-ups seeking new locations fuel this pattern of growth. The third process, that of structural change, illustrates that development planning has been sectoral rather than spatial in its focus, with the focus on export-based growth of which tourism has also been incorporated in the development strategies of many countries. Tourism has been a major beneficiary of the EMR developments not

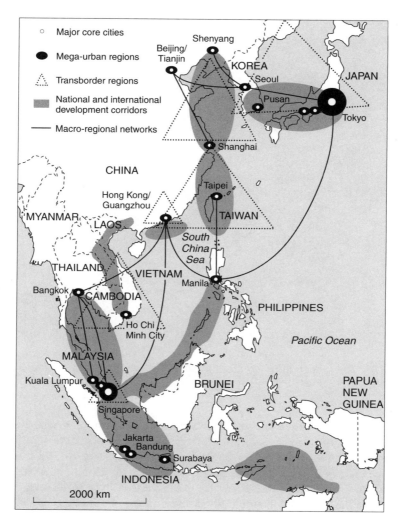

Figure 1.1 Transborder regions and growth triangles in South East Asia
(source: Hall and Page 2000)

only for business travel related to economic development and growth, but also
due to the primacy role of many EMRs in the national urban hierarchy, so that
they also function as the main gateways to the country (see Page 2001 for further discussion of this issue). Given this pattern of growth, many of the urban
and regional planning problems facing South East Asia are likely to be focused
on the growth effects of EMRs.

Figure 1.2, based on the United Nation's (1998b) report *Population of Capital Cities and Cities of 100,000 and more Inhabitants* (http://www.undp.org),

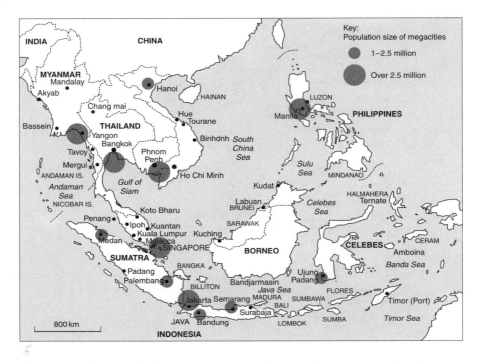

Figure 1.2 The growth in urban areas in South East Asia (source: Hall and Page 2000)

illustrates the scale of the growth in urban areas in South East Asia. Based on the United Nations forecasts of population growth, the population residing in Asian megacities will rise from 126 million people in 1995 to 382 million in 2025 (see Figure 1.2). Of the 20 megacities forecast for growth in Asia, 10 will be in South East Asia. These cities are characterised by a series of problems including: a declining environmental quality, inadequate housing, social alienation and insecurity with a need for comprehensive urban management strategies (see Devas and Rakodi 1993). One of the pressing needs for many of the cities is infrastructure provision, a major concern since these cities play a major role in gross domestic product (GDP). For example, in 1990, the two Japanese megacities (Tokyo and Osaka) were responsible for 36 per cent of the country's GDP. In Bangkok, 37 per cent of Thailand's GDP and in Manila, 24 per cent of the Philippines' GDP. One of the prevailing problems, which has important consequences for tourism, is the impact of megacities on the quality of life of residents and visitors. For example, McGee (1979: 186) indicated that tourism had accompanied urbanisation in South East Asia since,

> At the beginning of the 1960s, most of the large cities of the region received fewer than 100,000 tourists a year. By the mid-1970s many were already receiving more

than half a million visitors a year and the influx of tourists on the cities' economies is significant both in terms of job creation and income generation.

Thus if the quality of life deteriorates, the attraction for visitors will diminish too. Therefore, it is evident that cities throughout the world are undergoing profound changes to their economic rationale and spatial form and tourism is now playing a much more embracing role in many of them explicitly or as part of a complex urban system. For this reason, it is pertinent to focus on cities as tourist destinations because 'The large city as an important tourism destination came of age during the 1980s' (Law 1996b: 1).

Cities as tourist destinations

According to Law (1993: 1) 'large cities are arguably the most important type of tourist destination across the world' and yet urban areas have been greatly neglected in most academic studies of tourism. Indeed, Law (1993: xi) cogently comments, 'Almost every aspect of the life and organization of cities has been described and evaluated, with the apparent exception of tourism'. As tourism has grown as an international phenomenon, it is viewed as a complex process associated with the culture, lifestyles and demand in different societies for holidays and travel. Major components of this process and its effect on urban places remain relatively unknown (Law 2002) and as Law (1992: 599–600) argues, 'the topic of urban tourism is only gradually being recognised . . . most textbooks on tourism make hardly any reference to it. There are only a few articles in the academic literature and some of these are calling for more study'. Although this situation has changed somewhat since 1993, Page (2000: 197) argued,

> Despite recent advances in research . . . progress in research has been slow and bogged down by a proliferation of descriptive case studies and analytically devoid assessments of tourism in individual city environments. These studies have often contributed little to the development of theory or new conceptual frameworks.

The expansion in discretionary leisure time and increased living standards have contributed to the demand for travel, but few researchers have considered the wide-ranging consequences for urban tourism destinations nor of the role that urbanisation plays in the demand for travel itself. The operation and management of this process, whereby people decide to travel to urban destinations, are poorly understood in theoretical and conceptual terms since few researchers adopt an integrated approach towards the analysis of tourism. Although researchers do identify some of the dominant origin and destinations of tourist travel, providing an indication of the patterns and flows of tourists at a global scale, much of the existing research in tourism is based on descriptions of international tourism phenomena. Much of the demand originates from the urbanised and industrialised nations where high levels of disposable income facilitates tourist travel. Identifying the destinations that tourists visit is more complex. In addition to the demand for international tourism, Pearce (1987) identifies the significance of domestic tourism, which in statistical terms is estimated to be four times greater in volume than international travel. Domestic tourism is the movement of people within their own country for the purposes of tourism, whereby they spend at least one night away from their home area. More recently, the boundaries between tourism and recreation have become even more blurred as day-tripping has come to be recognised as a significant tourism phenomenon, particularly in urban areas and their recreational hinterlands (Hall and Page 1999).

A notable feature of these patterns of tourist travel is the significance of urban destinations, which serve as gateways for tourist entry to the country (see Plates 1.2 and 1.3), as centres of accommodation and a base for excursions to rural areas as well as destinations in their own right. It is significant within the context of recent trends in tourism, since many countries such as the UK have experienced a rapid expansion in the demand for short break domestic and international holidays to urban destinations. Therefore, urban areas are not simply places where populations concentrate together with economic activities, cultural life and the control of political power. Urban places are also

Plate 1.2 Auckland, New Zealand promotes its gateway and downtown location – the heart of the City – in a highly visual and dynamic manner with a tourist bus service

Plate 1.3 Culture is an important element of the urban tourism function of cities as illustrated by the built heritage in Madrid, Spain

assuming a greater role as centres for tourism activity in their own right and in the wider processes of tourism within countries and regions (Plate 1.4).

How does one attempt to explain this phenomenon? One approach is to consider the nature of tourism research and the extent to which its development has impeded the specialisation of research into areas such as urban tourism.

Tourism research: the search for a focus

Although a number of books now exist that examine international tourism from different perspectives such as management science (e.g. Witt *et al.* 1991), politics (Hall 1994) and geography (e.g. Hall and Page 1999, 2002), it is apparent that major gaps exist in our understanding of the processes contributing to tourism (i.e. its growth, development, operation and management) and the way it functions in different environments, particularly urban areas. Existing knowledge of urban tourism is limited in general terms because of the way in which tourism has developed as an area of study, typically as a sub-discipline of other social science subjects in the 1970s and early 1980s. Alternatively, it could also be viewed as a branch of the tourism industry and its desire to

Plate 1.4   History is a very important determinant of the value of urban tourism, as illustrated by the town of Toledo in Spain, which functioned in bygone years as an administrative capital and now is an urban heritage destination

improve the calibre and quality of its existing and future personnel. Indeed Faulkner and Ryan (1999: 3) argue that

> The growth of tourism management as a field of research is a reflection of the emergence of tourism as a major sector of the global economy, which is itself a manifestation of the widespread transition to post-industrial society. In this sense, the relatively recent development of our field can be construed as a response to changing industry, government and community needs, and perhaps as a consequence of this, tourism research has arguably assumed a more applied orientation than many of the more traditional disciplines. The other outstanding feature of tourism as a field of study is its tendency to draw on theoretical and methodological insights from many disciplines.

This has meant that tourism has lacked the direction and unity in research that one often associates with other social science subjects (Hall and Page 2002). For this reason, it is useful to explore the nature and purpose of research in tourism to examine the extent to which its diversity actually contributes to its fragmented nature, thereby constraining research on specialist areas such as urban tourism.

What is research?

Defining the purpose of research is a far from easy task, because it is undertaken for various reasons. Research, regardless of subject area, is intended at a rudimentary level to discover something new and to advance our understanding of the subject or topic under investigation. In the case of academic research, publication of research findings produces the information and material for the future development of the subject, thereby establishing new paradigms (i.e. a new focus for the subject) and a new agenda for research. Arguably, tourism does not yet exist as a social science discipline in its own right, and researchers usually approach the analysis of tourism with their own disciplinary perspective. As Faulkner and Ryan (1999: 3) argued, 'The reliance of tourism research on virtually the full range of social science disciplines is emphasised . . . where the contribution of traditional disciplines, such as Geography, Economics, Psychology, Sociology, Anthropology and History, is recognised'. Hall (2002a) argues that the growth of bodies such as the International Academy for the Study of Tourism and the Tourism and Travel Research Association, both general in their scope, and numerous academic journals, e.g. *Annals of Tourism Research, Journal of Travel Research, Tourism Management* and *Current Issues in Tourism*, and more specific, e.g. *Journal of Sustainable Tourism, Journal of Travel and Tourism Marketing, Tourism Geographies, Tourism Economics* and *Journal of Ecotourism*, suggest that tourism is becoming recognised as a legitimate area of study in its own right and possesses many of the characteristics of a discipline:

- a well-established presence in universities and colleges, including the appointment of professorial positions;
- formal institutional structures of academic associations and university departments; and
- avenues for academic publication, in terms of books and journals. Indeed, 'It is the advancement of knowledge – through the conduct of fundamental research and the publication of its original findings – which identifies an academic discipline; the nature of its teaching follows from the nature of its research' (Johnston 1991: 2).

In fact P. Pearce (1993: 26) raised the question 'is tourism, the study area, somehow more than the sum of its parts (such as economics, geography, marketing, business, management, psychology) or (will it remain) simply a composite of these separate contributions?' The implication is that tourism may never develop as a discipline in its own right, remaining a multidisciplinary field of study. This may be one factor that has contributed towards the absence of cohesion in the analysis of tourism, a feature reinforced by the structure of tourism research (see S.L.J. Smith 1989 for a fuller discussion of this issue). One of the main practical uses of tourism research is to facilitate data collection for industry, undertaken by academics and practitioners as well as market research, to understand the needs and motivation of visitors together with other forms of research.

Within the context of tourism, Veal (1992) identifies three types of research in leisure and tourism:

1. *Scientific research*, where specific rules, conventions and routines exist to follow particular models of thought. The use of prior logical reasoning and an understanding of scientific principles is implicit in this approach and theories and concepts may be tested to assess their validity in an abstract or applied manner.
2. *Social science*, where researchers use the research methods and traditions developed within social science to examine issues which often have a human dimension. In this context, the study of people often means that the behaviour, actions, attitudes and their relationship to tourism are studied.
3. *Applied research* occurs where research is focused on the solution of a specific problem in a planning, management or policy-oriented context.

One can sub-divide these categories of research into a number of commonly used approaches to research:

- *Explanatory research*, where the investigation of a theme sets out to consider why something happens or occurs, which is often based on observations and social survey work as a basis to explain some phenomenon.
- *Evaluative research*, whereby the study considers the policy, management and decision-making functions or policy issues within organisations associated with the tourism process.

These different forms of research coexist within tourism and therein lies one of the major problems for the development of tourism as an area of study. With researchers adopting a disciplinary approach rather than a range of distinct tourism methodologies in the study of tourism, research remains fragmented and methodologically unsophisticated. This has meant the emphasis has tended to be on results rather than methodology, restricting the development of distinctive research methods and approaches which could be identified as the hallmark of the tourism researcher. Such criticisms have been frequently echoed by many of the leading researchers in tourism, most recently by P. Pearce (1993). Yet it is only recently that such criticisms have been taken seriously, as tourism searches for a purpose and direction following its massive expansion as a subject of study at vocational, degree and postgraduate study in the late 1980s and 1990s. The 1990s appear to have been a decade in which the subject began to reach a state of maturity as more researchers became concerned with the search for an intellectual rigour, purpose and methodological acceptance within social science without compromising the applied and vocational nature of tourism studies. As Ryan and Page (2000: ix) argued under the 'heading of tourism studies, one cannot fail to acknowledge that within the last decade – perhaps even the last five years – significant changes have occurred in the range of methodologies and research paradigms being adopted by researchers'.

The scattered nature of tourism literature, spread across a disparate number of sources, complicates matters. Aside from general textbooks, tourism material is published in a number of mainstream academic journals (i.e. *Annals of Tourism Research*, *Tourism Management*, *Journal of Sustainable Tourism*, *Current Issues in Tourism* and *Journal of Travel Research*) and periodic reviews of the literature and there are now over 80 journals regularly publishing tourism-related material. Ad hoc publications, such as special issues of non-tourism journals and occasional publications and monographs, also contribute to the dispersed nature of tourism research. One useful abstracting source, which provides a contemporary review of current research in tourism – the *CAB Leisure, Recreation and Tourism Abstracts* – tends to confirm the diverse location of tourism publications as do other non-tourism databases. In this respect, understanding the focus and direction of current research in tourism is difficult. One consequence is that specialised research on topics, such as urban tourism, have not developed as major areas of study, despite their overwhelming significance in international and domestic patterns of tourism. One notable development in 1999 was the launch of a new market intelligence journal by Travel and Tourism Intelligence – *City Reports*, which contains reviews of tourism in major world cities and the current trends and issues facing the tourism sector. This represents a growing recognition of the paucity of current and valid tourism data for decision-makers within the tourism industry and certainly reaffirms the significance of urban tourism as a valid area to study.

Urban tourism: the existing literature

It is apparent from a preliminary assessment of the tourism literature that 'research on the structure of tourism in urban areas is relatively recent . . . [and] . . . there are very few studies of urban tourism. The majority of the work is ideographic in nature and has come from Europe and the United Kingdom' (Pearce 1987: 178). Pearce's prognosis on urban tourism can be updated quite readily from Page's (2000) more recent review of the state of knowledge where:

> The 1980s saw the emergence of new and popular research areas in tourism, and urban tourism was no exception to this. One indication of the growing interest in this area was the proliferation of journal articles and, during the 1990s, a range of mainstream texts and edited collections of books on urban tourism . . . Probably the most influential and widely cited study on urban tourism is the seminal and classic study by Ashworth (1989) which documented both the literature and interest in urban environments (Page 2000: 197).

Ashworth's (1989) seminal study 'Urban tourism: an imbalance in attention' serves as a good starting point for research on urban tourism, though its contents need not be reiterated here. Ashworth (1989: 33) asserts that 'a double neglect has occurred. Those interested in the study of tourism have tended to neglect the urban context in which much of it is set, while those interested in urban studies . . . have been equally neglectful of the importance of the tourist function in cities'. A subsequent review by Ashworth (1992a) reaffirms the case for studying urban tourism and provides a useful rationale for its study:

> urban tourism exists as a sufficiently distinct activity and . . . can be studied apart from other aspects of tourism or aspects of the urban environment. Urban tourism is sufficiently important either as a particular group of tourism activities or in the role such tourism does, or might play within the broader context of cities (Ashworth 1992a: 3).

It is also evident from the publication of tourism textbooks (e.g. Shaw and Williams 1994) and more specialised monographs (e.g. Law 1993) that urban tourism is receiving increased attention by researchers. In fact, Shaw and Williams (1994) argue that criticisms of the neglect in attention are not as valid in the early 1990s owing to the increasing academic and political attention paid to urban tourism as a spur to economic and urban environmental regeneration (Plates 1.5 and 1.6). But Page (2000) disputes these assertions claiming that

Plate 1.5 In San Francisco, the reuse of Alcatraz as a tourist attraction has built on the fascination with 'dark tourism' and contributed to urban regeneration in the waterfront area

Plate 1.6   The San Francisco Maritime Museum is one element in the development of an urban tourism cluster to regenerate the waterfront area

Urban tourism research has also suffered from a range of seemingly novice researchers attempting to write on the subject area, which appears simple, uncomplicated and well suited to descriptive case studies. One might argue that this problem has become sufficiently acute during the 1990s and that one has to question whether sufficiently theoretical and conceptual development has taken place in the area to justify the delineation of urban tourism as a sub-field of tourism studies (Page 2000: 198).

One can also question Shaw and Williams's (1994) argument in a number of other respects. First, urban regeneration is a highly specialised area of study which sometimes has a tourism or leisure outcome. Second, if the literature and research on urban tourism are now becoming established and are no longer neglected, it is surprising that Shaw and Williams (1994: 207) argue that when analysing tourists within urban areas a '. . . somewhat limited literature on visitor activity in urban areas' exists. Thus, while interest has focused on the significance of urban tourism as one approach to stimulate economic regeneration, it has not led to the rapid development of an urban tourism literature that is widely disseminated beyond specialist reports, journal articles and monographs. As a result, urban regeneration has formed the focus of a significant range of research that has subsequently emphasised the benefits of tourism development as a strategy for redeveloping redundant spaces in older industrial cities (Mansfeld 1992; Law 1993). One exception to this is the theoretically derived research by Mullins (1991) (which is discussed in more detail in Chapter 2). Law's (1993, 1996a) syntheses of urban tourism may be a major step towards establishing urban tourism as a focus for research with a concern for large cities, but it is evident that many gaps still exist in the literature and our understanding of this complex phenomena remains partial and incomplete. Indeed Law (1996b: 1) claims that '. . . the scale, importance and significance of tourism in cities is often not recognised'. The main conceptual problem this raises is a simple one: the urban tourism system and subsystems existing within cities are complex and not easily explained without a thorough understanding of the interrelationships that exist between the constituent parts. Indeed, recent research on the nature of contemporary human mobility highlights the importance of seeing the interrelationships between urban areas and leisure, day-tripping, tourism, educational and migrant activity (Williams and Hall 2000, 2002).

Despite the fact that urban tourism research has developed in the 1980s and 1990s, one can identify early concerns related to the significance of tourism in cities in the recreational research by Stansfield (1964), which was symptomatic of the reluctance of researchers to examine tourism in an urban context because of the difficulty of disaggregating the tourist and non-tourist function of cities (excluding resort towns) (see Mazanec 1997a). As a result, a range of studies cited in previous reports (e.g. Ashworth 1989, 1992a; Page 1989a,b; Page and Sinclair 1989; Ashworth and Tunbridge 1990, 2000) provide evidence of work undertaken on tourism in an urban context, though much of the research is in inaccessible or dated sources. Furthermore, the existing literature does not necessarily imply that urban tourism exists as a distinct area of tourism studies. Thus, research has often been based on case studies of particular locations which are descriptive and contribute little to the theoretical or methodological understanding of urban tourism. For this reason, one is led to consider Ashworth's contention as to whether an urban tourism exists, and if so, what is meant by the term.

Does an urban tourism exist?

According to Ashworth (1992a) tourism in urban environments has not led to the development of a distinct 'urban tourism': moreover, research is focused on tourism in cities. One explanation for this strange paradox is that tourism in cities is not a distinctive attribute which is associated with the main function of the city. Many other economic activities are seen by planners, commercial interests and residents as the main rationale for the city: a place that meets both service requirements of people, commerce and industry and also fulfils a residential function. One can argue that tourism is not viewed by most urban geographers, sociologists and planners as a serious area of study since urban regeneration has been the main focus for many urban tourism studies by geographers and planners (e.g. Hoyle and Pinder 1992) and a growing interest in place-marketing in the 1990s (e.g. Ashworth and Voogd 1990a; Gold and Ward 1994; Gold and Gold 1995; Ward 1998). More specifically, because the demand and supply aspects of tourism in cities is entwined with other urban functions, planners, commercial interests and local governments rarely perceive tourism as a significant element within the urban economy (with the exception of resort towns). It is viewed more as an adjunct to the way in which the city operates, as an ephemeral phenomenon which is seasonal in character and transitory.

Therefore, why should planners and researchers be concerned about the effects of a transitory activity, when competing demands for resources and time mean that efforts can be put to better use elsewhere? Such attitudes have meant that the collection of detailed data on the 'urban tourist', the activities they undertake in the destination and their effect on city environments, has frequently been overlooked in both applied and academic research. In fact Law (1996a: 251) confirms this in the argument that 'Nearly all studies of urban tourism reveal how little is known about the impact of the activity on cities . . . There is relatively little detailed research on the negative impacts of tourism in cities'. In essence, planners may view urban tourism as a managerial activity but as visitors have always come to an area, the need to manage and attract tourists is not always high on the agenda. Even so, in the academic literature 'Probably the most researched area within tourism in cities is the focus on what can be categorised as management, planning and policy' (Page 2000: 199) epitomised by the two studies by Murphy (1997) and Tyler *et al.* (1998). In contrast, the modelling and forecasting for urban tourism destinations has remained within the domain of a small number of specialist economic forecasters (e.g. Mazanec 1997a). Even so, the supply aspects of urban tourism remain among the most researched features (e.g. C.M. Hall 1992; Hall and Hamon 1996; Oppermann *et al.* 1996; Cockerell 1997; Bramwell 1998; Heung and Qu 1998; Hughes 1998; Pearce 1998).

Thus, a vicious circle exists: because of the neglect of research on urban tourism, the public sector does not see the necessity of detailed research to understand the urban tourist. Therefore, researchers have access to very limited sources of data, making research difficult where large-scale funding is unavailable to generate substantive sources of primary data using social survey techniques (e.g. face-to-face interviews with tourists, residents, planners and local government officials). How can this book contribute to a better understanding of urban tourism? At this point Ashworth's (1992a) comments on the way forward for the development of urban tourism are useful, as they highlight the range of issues which need to be addressed. He argues that the development of an

> urban tourism requires the development of a coherent body of theories, concepts, techniques and methods of analysis which allow comparable studies to contribute towards some common goal of understanding of either the particular role of cities

within tourism or the place of tourism within the form and function of cities (Ashworth 1992a: 5).

For this reason, it is pertinent to consider the ways in which one might conceptualise urban tourism.

Urban tourism: approaching a nebulous concept

Conceptualising why tourists seek cities as places to visit is one starting point in trying to understand this phenomenon. Clearly any detailed examination of why tourists visit specific places requires an analysis of the social psychology of tourist behaviour, especially tourist motivation (P. Pearce 1982, 1993: see Chapter 3). But at a general abstract level, one can argue that tourists are attracted to cities because of the specialised functions they offer and the range of services provided. Shaw and Williams (1994) provide a useful explanation of the significance of urban areas in tourism. They argue that such areas have a geographical concentration of facilities and attractions which are conveniently located to meet tourists' and residents' needs alike. Furthermore, they suggest that tourism in urban areas is a diverse, affecting phenomenon in three different ways that affect the way in which researchers examine such places. First, urban areas are heterogeneous in nature, meaning that they are different and diverse when considered in terms of their size, location, function, appearance and heritage. It is this feature that makes the study of urban tourism so interesting because no two destinations are identical and yet they are characterised by a common denominator – tourism. For researchers and planners, the challenge is in understanding of how to develop planning strategies that accommodate and manage specific types of tourism in their locality. Second, the sheer scale of urban areas and the different functions they simultaneously provide make them multifunctional and complex to understand. Last, urban tourist functions are 'very rarely solely produced for, or consumed by, tourists but by a whole range of users' (Shaw and Williams 1994: 201) although the work on tourism urbanisation discussed in Chapter 2 does question this proposition in a theoretical context. In many countries, the gateway function provided by the capital or major city for incoming and outbound tourists, due to the location of transport terminals (e.g. airports) in or near the urban area, reinforces the tourist function for many urban areas (Page 1999) (Plate 1.7). In this context, tourists cannot avoid moving through these environments when travelling.

In conceptualising the different ways one might view urban tourism, Ashworth (1992a) identifies three approaches:

1. *The supply of tourism facilities in urban areas*, where the categorisation and inventories of facilities by geographers has led to research on the distribution

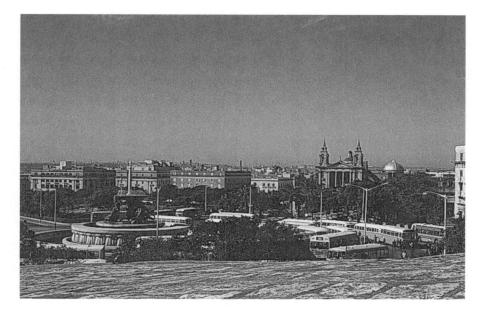

Plate 1.7   In Valetta, Malta, the bus terminal is a tourist and resident transport hub which is used to connect the tourist and non-tourist areas together as part of the island's transport network. This reinforces the primacy of Valetta as the major urban tourism location and capital city of the small island

of hotels, restaurants, attractions, shopping, nightlife and other tourist-related services. These approaches have also utilised the traditional approach of urban ecological models to produce regionalised descriptions of urban tourism patterns. More recently, the facility approach has been developed a stage further with the use of the term 'product' as an attempt to package together many of the discrete facilities identified on tourism inventories, to highlight the diversity and variety of tourism resources available to potential visitors.

2. *The demand for urban tourism*, where research has largely been descriptive to establish who visits urban tourist destinations, why they visit, the patterns and behaviour of tourist activities, and the ways in which such destinations are perceived by visitors.

3. *Policy perspectives on urban tourism*, generated by planners and the private sector, which are not widely disseminated and restricted to those organisations who generate the studies or who have a vested interest in the tourism sector.

Even so, Law (1996b) argues that urban tourism is a chaotic concept given the wide range of contexts in which it is applied. Operationalising the concept – urban tourism – is clearly problematic according to Law (1996b), who prefers to use it only to refer to large cities, a theme debated in more detail in Chapter 2. What this issue raises is the extent to which an organising framework can be developed to understand the complexity of urban tourism as a series of inter-related constructs and elements which can then be disaggregated and analysed within this book. For this reason, attention now turns to a systems approach.

Analysing urban tourism: a systems approach

To understand the complexity and relationships that coexist within urban tourism, one needs to develop an analytical framework that is capable of synthesising the multiplicity of factors, processes and issues affecting the process of urban tourism in different contexts. The objective of developing such a framework should be to encompass the total tourist experience of urban tourism which incorporates a range of disciplinary perspectives of urban tourism. One methodology used by researchers to consider tourism is a systems approach, where the complexity of the real world situation can be rationalised in a simplified model to try and understand how different elements fit together (C.M. Hall 2000). This is developed more fully in Page (1999a) in the context of tourist transport and developed here in Figure 1.3. One of the key principles underpinning this approach is to reduce the complexity of urban tourism into a number of constructs and components which highlight the interrelated nature

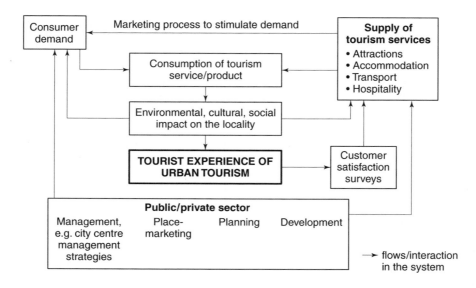

Figure 1.3   A systems approach to urban tourism (source: Page 1995a)

of different factors affecting the system. Such an approach also accommodates the multidisciplinary nature of tourism studies, whereby the broader issues and interrelationships can be synthesised into one framework regardless of approach or discipline.

Leiper (1990) suggests that a system is a set of elements or parts that are connected to each other by at least one distinguishing principle. In this instance the urban tourism phenomenon is the distinguishing principle which forms the focus of the system. Laws (1991: 7) develops the systems idea a stage further by identifying the key features of a tourism system:

- the inputs (e.g. the supply of tourism products and tourism demand);
- the outputs (e.g. the tourist experience of urban tourism);
- external factors conditioning the system (e.g. the business environment, consumer preferences, political factors and economic issues).

The external factors exert a degree of influence on the nature of the system, and where these factors have a strong effect on the system it can be termed an 'open' system, since the tourism inputs are not the only factors affecting it. Conversely, where external factors exert a limited influence, the system is 'closed'. To examine the links between different elements in the system, one can consider the nature of the 'flows' between the various components, where specific relationships may exist. For example, if a flow is in one direction only, then the relationship is often seen as a cause and effect (i.e. factor A affects factor B). However, if the flow is in both directions, a reciprocal relationship exists whereby the two factors are interrelated and influence each other.

A systems approach also allows one to trace the effect of different issues as well as identifying where improvements need to be made in the overall urban tourist experience. One important concept to consider at this point is the distribution channel used by researchers in marketing and operations management. This allows one to directly trace the flow of the product or service through a system from the point of production to consumption. Such an approach adopts a process-oriented approach to the analysis, operation and management of different issues. In operations management, tourism could be conceptualised as a process, and therefore the object of a systems approach would be in understanding and managing the process. In the case of urban tourism, this involves the human activities, communications between different elements in the system and the effect of tourists on the system.

Therefore, urban tourism needs to be conceptualised as a service encounter and experience (see Page 1999 for a fuller discussion of the term 'service' and its significance in tourism research) which has:

- a high degree of customer involvement;
- a simultaneous supply component;
- inconsistent demand, which varies according to seasonality;
- an intangible product which is often consumed.

Some of these elements are specifically urban in a multifunctional city, since it is the diverse urban area that can provide the intensity of resources to facilitate such an encounter. Thus, the concept of tourist service is important because it provides a focus for the analysis of the visitor's experience of urban tourism.

The structure of the book

This book sets out to examine the international phenomenon of urban tourism and its significance as a process affecting urban areas which poses many opportunities and problems for the development, management and functioning of such destinations. Having briefly outlined some of the main features of the literature and the systems approach towards the analysis of urban tourism, it is pertinent to outline how the book is structured. It is not intended to be a comprehensive review of urban tourism: this is clearly not possible nor feasible for an introductory book. The book is designed to provide the reader with a clear understanding of the operation of urban tourism in different localities, some of the general similarities and differences in relation to the process of urban tourism and the systems developed to exploit and manage it in different tourist environments. One underlying objective is to raise awareness of the international significance of urban tourism and to develop a more integrated approach towards the study of urban tourism than has hitherto been the case. It does not adopt an explicitly theoretically determined approach, such as that advocated by Mullins (1991), although theoretical propositions underpinning certain dimensions of urban tourism research are discussed.

The book does pursue a more general assessment of urban tourism, emphasising the importance of an interdisciplinary approach towards its analysis. One useful way of conceptualising the scope and extent of this book is through a systems model of the process of urban tourism and some of the interrelationships which exist. The tourist experience is the central feature (Figure 1.3) together with the interaction of different components in the system. This is probably best documented by focusing on the structure of the book which begins by examining the principal inputs – the demand and supply features of urban tourism – and then proceeds to investigate other elements and relationships within the system. The effect on the main output – the tourist experience of urban tourism – indirectly forms the focal point for other chapters to illustrate how improvements to this outcome can be implemented by modifying some of the principal inputs.

Chapter 2 considers the recent development of theoretical debates on urban tourism and the growing interest in trying to understand the nature and form of the postmodern city as a tourist destination. This is followed in Chapter 3 by an analysis of the demand for urban tourism generated by visitors in terms of the locations which visitors seek and the difficulty of quantifying the scale and extent of this activity. The chapter then goes on to discuss how different forms of tourist motivation lead to discrete and interrelated reasons for visiting urban locations. In Chapter 4, the supply of tourism facilities is examined as a basis for an assessment of how different agencies and organisations influence and affect the provision of services and infrastructure for urban tourism. In Chapter 5, the role of the visitor as a central component of the tourist city is examined, focusing on the behaviour and actions of visitors and how their activities are structured in time and space. The intersection between supply and demand is used to describe how the patterns and processes of tourist use of areas and districts of cities creates specific forms of activity spaces. This raises the issue of the impact of urban tourist development and the need to develop approaches to understand the effect of the supply and demand in various localities. Therefore, Chapter 6 considers the methodological problems associated with examining the impact of urban tourism to illustrate the effects of urban tourism in various contexts.

As a consequence of highlighting the impact of urban tourism, Chapter 7 considers the role of tourism planning and management as a natural corollary of urban tourist development. This is followed in Chapter 8 by a discussion of the significance of place-marketing of urban tourism, particularly the trend towards the promotion and reimaging of towns and cities not only for tourism purposes, but also for economic redevelopment. This leads to a discussion in Chapter 9 of the role of tourism as a tool for economic regeneration in urban environments, particularly as a mechanism for urban renewal in inner-city districts and waterfront locations. In particular the role of events as a means to link place-marketing and urban redevelopment strategies is highlighted. Finally, Chapter 10 identifies some of the strategies and action needed to maintain a quality urban tourist experience and the future issues associated with urban tourism in the new millennium.

Questions

1. To what extent is urban tourism an established area of study within tourism research?

2. What does Ashworth (1989) mean by an 'imbalance in attention' in the study of towns and cities within tourism studies?

3. Why are cities an important issue to study within a tourism context?

4. What is the value of a systems approach to the analysis of urban tourism?

Further reading

Ashworth, G. (1989). 'Urban tourism: an imbalance in attention', in C. Cooper (ed.) *Progress in Tourism, Recreation and Hospitality Management*, Volume 1, London: Belhaven, 33–54.
This is a good review of the state of urban tourism research in the late 1980s and remains the most frequently cited article by most tourism researchers who examine urban tourism.
Ashworth, G. (1992). 'Is there an urban tourism?', *Tourism Recreation Research* 17(2): 3–8.
This is an interesting overview of urban tourism.
Page, S.J. (2000). 'Urban tourism', in C. Ryan and S.J. Page (eds) *Tourism Management: Towards the New Millennium*, Oxford: Pergamon, 197–202.
This is a useful synthesis of progress in research since the two studies by Ashworth (1989, 1992).
Shaw, G. and Williams, A. (1994). *Critical Issues in Tourism*, Oxford: Blackwell.
This is a good starting point for those interested in a geographical approach to urban tourism.

Urban tourism: concepts, theory and reality

CHAPTER 2

Introduction

The development of urban tourism in the period since the late 1970s has to be viewed against long-term economic and structural changes in the nature of capitalism, as Chapter 1 indicated. This has resulted in a transformation from an industrially based to an information technology-based, post-industrial (sometimes called post-Fordist) form of capitalism which is now very evident in the nature of urban places. At the same time, since the 1980s globalisation in the international space economy has produced an increasingly transnational, multipolarised, interactive and highly interdependent world economic system. The significance of these macro-economic processes for urban places is reflected in the declining economic autonomy of the individual city, and arguably the nation-state. This is because post-industrial technology both facilitates a decentralised pattern of economic organisation at a global scale, where capital operates transnationally and has a preference for new centres of production where the competitive advantage no longer relates to conventional location theory (Dicken and Lloyd 1978). Instead, a new global–local dynamic has emerged, combined with the de-industrialisation of many existing urban centres. Post-industrial restructuring and a pursuit of increasingly mobile forms of capital to invest in the new sunrise service industries of the late twentieth and early twenty-first centuries, particularly those related to consumption, now characterise urban places. In this respect, many national and local governments have recognised the long-term nature of the processes of economic reorientation necessary to restructure and reorientate urban places in a national space economy. It is against this background that many governments have promoted tourism as a major stimulus for regional and local economies. Yet as Roche (1992: 582) argued,

> In addition to its effects as a growth industry tourism also often requires significant and lasting improvements in urban infrastructures and facilities . . . It

is assumed that urban tourism can induce a modernisation of the local economy and, through its effects on local morale and outside image, that it can positively influence outside and local investment and local labour productivity.

Yet these supposed changes that urban tourism is expected to induce also require changes in local politics to generate the environment attractive to capital, and may lead to new urban tourism developments in former waterfront areas that become contested landscapes (see Doorne 1998). No longer do capital cities and regions have a monopoly on specific forms of production in the global space economy, and this is particularly true in the case of urban tourism with the growing competition for visitors. In the post-industrial era, examples of what Roche (1992) calls micro-modernisation in specific cities to develop urban tourism have been politically divisive, generated conflict and often subject to local corporatist arrangements, such as the Urban Development Corporations in the UK with their waterfront redevelopment schemes (Page 1987; Page and Fidgeon 1989; Page and Sinclair 1989). This has given rise to a renewed interest in urban tourism because changes in the production function of cities (i.e. the supply) need to be situated in the context of not only these changes in the political economy of places, but changes in consumption and employment (i.e. demand). Urban tourism has directly benefited from shifts away from mass marketing and mass consumption to more 'flexible consumption and niche marketing (short breaks, special events and shopping as a pastime), places have sought actively to create themselves not only as locations of investment opportunity, but also places of consumption to capitalise on the lucrative tourism/leisure market' (Meethan 1996: 323).

At the same time, Davis (1999) observed the rise of the privatisation of public space in the city, what Sorkin (1991) has called the end of public space in the city. The new private space, created from redevelopment and investment by the public and private sector, has created cities as places of entertainment (Davis 1999), where the media and entertainment by transnational corporations create new leisure and tourism opportunities. In fact Davis (1999) has also commented on the rise of *Entertainment Retail*, a new form of media-based development in many American shopping malls as retail investors seek to derive new forms of consumer spending. Entertainment Retail is typified by the development of fast-moving entertainment complexes such as IMAX and Iwerks which 'break the cocoon of home entertainment' (Davis 1999: 444) with the consumption of media in public spaces. Yet even many of these new entertainment spaces are carefully controlled, often gated, providing a safe and secure area with surveillance cameras in themed space. As Davis (1999: 454) concluded: 'In these new spaces, the core cultural ideas are not only embodied by products, they *are* products. Citizens are collapsed into consumers, and loyalty is a technique that expands the bottom line . . . the media conglomerates are knitting our everyday lives more tightly into spectacle by remaking places'. Thus, the contemporary city is undergoing profound economic and social change which indirectly and directly affects, shapes and develops a tourist experience of place that is a complex amalgam of place, space and culture.

This chapter seeks to explore some of the processes and explanations that underlie the evolution and development of urban tourism within an advanced capitalist society in the early twenty-first century. While urban tourism *per se* is not a new activity for cities, towns and coastal resorts that exhibit urban characteristics (i.e. the agglomeration of people, services and infrastructure; Jakle 1985), it is the nature of what Roche (1992) calls the 'new urban tourism' based on the consumption of places in a post-industrial society that assumes so much significance. Indeed, arguably urban tourism may be perceived as a parody of modern day society and a reflection of the way in which the supposed 'leisured society' spends and consumes its affluence and time. For example, Meethan (1996: 324) recognised that

> tourism involves the visual consumption of signs and increasingly, simulacra and staged events in which urban townscapes are transformed into aestheticised spaces of entertainment and pleasure . . . Within these places of consumption . . . a variety of activities can be pursued, such as promenading, eating, drinking, watching staged events and street entertainment and visually appreciating heritage and culture of place.

It is this preoccupation with consumption, such as the purchase of tangible services and souvenirs, that is embodied in the new urban tourism where places seek the economic and cultural advantage and has led critics such as Hewison (1987) to challenge the basic tenets of heritage interpretation – that places have been commodified in pursuit of a populist appeal.

To understand the development of the 'new' urban tourism in advanced capitalist society (Roche 2000), this chapter commences with a discussion of tourism and urbanisation, emphasising the importance of globalisation as a process shaping urban tourism. The issues raised by this debate are followed by a critique of the prevailing literature on tourism urbanisation and Hannigan's (1998) *Fantasy City* and the implications for urban tourism destinations are considered. This is followed by an analysis of post-modernism and the form of tourism cities. Lastly, a series of models of urban tourism are explored as a basis for attempting to explain the dynamics of change and the form of the tourist city in the twenty-first century.

Tourism and urbanisation: globalisation

At a global scale, almost 46 per cent of the world's population live in urban areas and by the year 2030 this is set to rise to 61 per cent. Accompanying these changes, as later chapters will show, is the growing significance of urban places and their space for the consumption of tourism and leisure experiences. One of the underlying processes shaping these consumption-related activities is the impact of globalisation, as distinct from the concept of global cities introduced in Chapter 1. While global cities operate as 'nodes' in the global economy, they are localised environments in which higher-order service activities and corporate headquarters are located. In effect, these global cities are 'centres of information . . . centres of innovation and places in which key actors can establish networks of contacts and monitor changes in markets and products' (Murphy 1999: 313). In contrast, globalisation is the associated process whereby the globalised production and network system is extended to areas across the world. The dynamics of this global economy according to Castells (1996a) are the networks, which are constantly evolving and depend upon advanced telecommunications systems to operate.

Globalisation has two distinct elements which one needs to understand in relation to urban places. The first is the way in which the globalisation process produces new forms of economic activity within a city, and the spatial forms and distribution of production within the urban landscape. Castells' (1996a) work is instrumental in explaining the new role of cities in the post-industrial era in relation to 'economic, political and cultural networks that now determine and dominate global production' (Spoonley 2000: 189). The second is the way in which globalisation produces or reproduces a multinational/internationalised global capitalism. This interest in the supply issues has been concerned with the hallmark symbols and expressions of globalisation – the standardisation of production and consumption in many aspects of city life. Ritzer (1996) discussed this in terms of the McDonaldisation of production and consumption, with the 'Golden Arches' of McDonald's acting as a metaphor for the way globalisation now affects society and the urban environment.

McNeill (1999) reiterated the 'need for more nuanced and detailed analysis of the effects of globalisation on the world's cities', within the discussion of globalisation as a process which is uneven in its effects in time and space. This also challenged the homogenisation thesis of Ritzer (1996). In fact, McNeill (1999: 145) established that Ritzer's main thesis of homogenisation as one: 'Whether through a straight forward penetration of local markets by "global products", the proliferation of out-of-centre shopping malls, the edge cities, or the "Disneyfication" of historic city centres, there are grounds for believing that this is an urban corollary to the "McDonaldisation" thesis'.

Thrift (1997) argued that the range of experiences available in the contemporary city has increased, with a range of locally differing consumption and lifestyle cultures. He concluded (1997: 141) that our experience of place has thickened rather than thinned, with the impact of globalisation. However, in the built environment, architecture and the urban periphery (i.e. edge city) is increasingly being viewed as a standardised environment (e.g. out of town shopping malls). Harvey (1989a) poignantly described the modern city with its architecture as a no-frills style which was rational, based on efficient urban plans and large-scale development. In contrast, the postmodern city was characterised as a palimpsest of past forms, superimposed upon each other. Many of the new urban spaces in the postmodern city were described by Harvey (1989a) as architecturally shaped to provide organised spectacles in the attempt to generate high-quality appealing images of place, often serially reproducing successful models developed elsewhere. In this context, it reflects the pursuit of attracting people and consumption activities, as advanced capital emphasises images, reconstructions and staged events as part of encouraging conspicuous consumption. What McNeill (1999) alluded to was that globalisation has not necessarily led to a cultural imperialism in the European urban environment, taking on an indigenised form in specific locations to retain an element of distinctiveness. In a tourism context, the regionalisation of wine and food are two such elements embodied in the consumption landscapes of the new urban tourism as a means of enhancing and seizing opportunities proffered by globalisation (Hall and Mitchell 2000). In other words, interpreting the impact of globalisation on urban environments requires one to be 'sensitive to place-specificity in an epistemological sense. In methodological terms, it requires attention to how the global is understood locally' (McNeill 1999: 147).

According to Dear (1994), the development of geographical research on postmodernism during the 1980s and 1990s highlighted its significance for urbanism (Dear 1999) and that the postmodern city has a number of defining characteristics (Dear and Flusty 1999). The postmodern city is characterised by the global–local connections (Lake 1999), a ubiquitous social polarisation (Jackson 1999) and a reterritorialisation of urban processes where the hinterland now organises the centre (Dear and Flusty 1999). These changes to the space within postmodern cities are highly contentious and subject to continued discourse as researchers explore the validity and wider application of such debates on the form of the postmodern city (Hall 1997; Murphy 1999). Therefore, how has globalisation manifest itself in wider changes affecting the evolution of urban places?

The capitalist city in transition: post-industrialism vs postmodernism?

There is a great deal of debate in the sociological literature on urbanism relating to the nature of the city in the late twentieth and early twenty-first centuries. The term 'post-industrial city' is one that is associated with changes in the social structure of the city related to wider developments in the economy, particularly the impact of technology on occupational structure (Hall 1999). One of the principal changes is the expansion of services, particularly personal and human services. This has also been accompanied by increased participation in the labour force by women. While post-industrial analyses tend to focus on economic and technical factors, there is a growing interest in the use of the term 'postmodern city'.

The postmodernists emphasise the cultural dynamics of society utilising the theoretical constructs that characterise postmodern society as fast-moving and technologically sophisticated, where vast amounts of information are available and knowledge is a prerequisite for accessing information, employment and wealth. Society is also characterised by a fascination with consumerism, where consumer goods and media images play a major role in the everyday life of urbanites (Davis 1999). The mass consumption of goods gives way in postmodern society to hierarchies of taste (niche markets), where reality and simulation blur and are characterised as a stage in late capitalism (Table 2.1). What Mansfeld (1999) highlights in Table 2.1 are the three underlying

Table 2.1 Characteristics of the postmodern epoch

Modernity (c.1750–1970s)	Postmodernity (c.1970 onwards)
Technological superiority and progress celebrated	Technological superiority and progress challenged
Sameness, universalism	Difference, diversity, discontinuity, fragmentation
Search for absolute knowledge	Belief in relative knowledges
Depth and essence	Surface, hyper-reality
Rules and regulation of style	Pastiche, collage and spectacle
Belief in real, authentic world that exists outside our knowledge of it	Idea of independent authentic reality challenged; the relationship between the 'real' and how this is represented is not simple or straightforward
Mass production of commodities (i.e. in large batches and runs) for consumption by mass markets	Niche production of commodities occurring in short runs and small batches specifically for consumption in differentiated markets
Production of objects economically and politically significant	Consumption and reproduction of images economically and politically significant (rise of social movements connected to patterns of consumption)
State power, welfarism and intervention	Decline of state power, individualism and enterprise
Goal of individuals is concerned with satisfying wants	Goal of individuals is attaining desires through symbolic meanings through material possessions and images of possessions.
Emphasis on character	Emphasis on self and bodily representation
Identity formed in relation to sphere of production (e.g. work) and collectively based identities have a degree of stability	Identity formed in relation to sphere of consumption (e.g. leisure) and individualised fragmented, multiple, shifting and contradictory identities of subject.

Source: Mansfeld (1999: 330).

processes that characterise postmodernism and the fascination with consumption, commodification, social division and new forms of everyday life.

In Urry's (1995: 1–2) analysis of places as sites for consumption, he concurs with much of the literature on the postmodern city in that

> First places are increasingly being restructured as centres for consumption, as providing the context within which goods and services are compared, evaluated, purchased and used. Second, places themselves are in a sense consumed, particularly visually. Especially important in this is the provision of various kinds of consumer services for both visitors and locals. Third, places can be literally consumed: what people take to be significant about a place . . . is over time depleted, devoured, or exhausted by use. Fourth, it is possible for localities to consume one's identity so that places become almost literally all-consuming.

What the sociologists highlight in the debates on the postmodern city is the significance of the economic basis of cultural transformations that have occurred between the modern and postmodern epoch. It is both the spatiality of these cultural transformations and the impact on the urban dweller and visitor that attract a great deal of interest. Most notably it is the creation of cultural industries that embody the arts, leisure and tourism as complex and diverse postmodern phenomena to be consumed in the city that characterise the 'new urban tourism'.

In contrast, geographical research by Dear and Flusty (1998), based on the analysis of the Los Angeles (LA) urban agglomeration, devised a range of theoretical propositions that were mirroring wider urban changes in the socio-geographic composition and space of US cities. While Soja (1989) recognised Los Angeles embodied the spatial fragmentation inherent in post-Fordism, with a flexible, disorganised regime of capital accumulation, more wide-ranging postmodern series of changes were occurring. Within a growing postmodern literature on urbanism, a new range of buzzwords has been coined to describe elements of the urban landscape based on the Los Angeles experience, including the following:

- *Privatopia*, the 'quintessential edge-city residential form . . . a private housing development based in common-interest development' (Dear and Flusty 1998: 55).

- *Cultures of heteropolis*, based on the cultural diversity arising from ethnicity and minority populations and a socio-economic polarisation reflected in racism, inequality, homelessness and social unrest.

- *The city as a theme park*, a feature epitomised in Hannigan's (1998) *Fantasy City* discussed later in this chapter.

- *The fortified city*, with residents' preoccupation with security and safety where 'fortified cells of affluence' are juxtaposed with 'places of terror' where the police attempt to control crime.

- *Interdictory space*, where spaces in the postmodern city are designed to exclude certain people and activities through their design.

- *Historical geographies of restructuring* on which the LA schools have focused in understanding deindustrialisation and reindustrialisation based on the information economy and globalisation–localisation debates focused on the region. Soja (1996) identified six types of restructuring that affected the LA metropolis 1925–1992 including:

  - *Exopolis*, where hyper-reality based on theme parks such as Disneyland, create a copy of an original that never existed in reality; it is an image.
  - *Flexicities*, with the growing flexibility of capital and deindustrialisation that coincides with the rise of the information economy.
  - *Cosmopolis*, referring to the globalisation of LA and the region's emergence as a world-city. This is accompanied by not only the multicultural diversity of the city, but an urban restructuring that generated three specific geographic forms – (i) *the splintered labyrinth*, where the social, economic and political polarisation are a dominant characteristic of the postmodern city; (ii) *the carceral city* where a new 'incendary urban geography brought about by the amalgam of violence and police surveillance' (Dear and Flusty 1998: 58) exists; and (iii) *simcities*, which are new ways of seeing the LA urban form.

In the postmodern city, Dear and Flusty (1998: 65) argued that 'The concentric ring structure of the Chicago School [e.g. Burgess 1925] was essentially a concept of the city as an organic accretion around a central, organising core. Instead, we have identified a postmodern urban process in which the urban periphery organises the centre within the context of a globalising capitalism'. What Dear and Flusty (1998) identified was a 'Keno capitalism' to describe the process whereby urbanisation is a random set of opportunities for capital. A more parcelled approach to land development without reference to the urban core in evolving pattern of consumption spaces has developed. What results in Dear and Flusty's (1998) model of Keno capitalism and postmodern urban structure (Figure 2.1) is a 'noncontiguous collage of parcelised, consumption-oriented landscapes devoid of conventional centres yet wired into electronic propinquity and nominally unified by mythologies of the disinformation super-highway' (Dear and Flusty 1998: 66). As a result, their analysis of the post-modern city proposed four broad and overlapping themes:

- *The World City* concept and globalisation.
- *The Dual City* where social polarisation is a dominant element.
- *Altered spaces*, with urban change and the reconfiguration of communities and space and new cultural space in the city.
- *The Cybercity*.

Dear and Flusty (1998: 67) also acknowledge that none of these overlapping themes adequately explains the urban outcomes that one observes in the

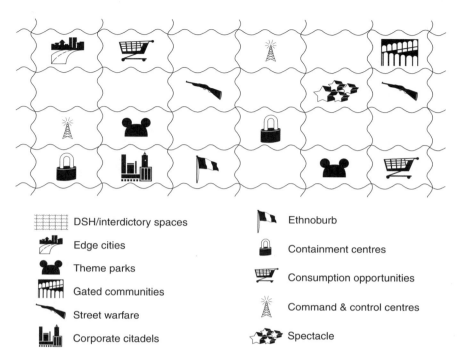

DSH/interdictory spaces

Edge cities

Theme parks

Gated communities

Street warfare

Corporate citadels

Ethnoburb

Containment centres

Consumption opportunities

Command & control centres

Spectacle

Figure 2.1 Keno capitalism: a model of postmodern urban structure (source: Dear and Flusty 1998)

postmodern city. What is apparent is that the processes of urbanisation and the postmodern urbanism constitute a power element that is directly shaping tourism and leisure spaces in cities and a greater theorising is needed to understand it in a global and comparative context. Indeed, Ravenscroft *et al.* (2000) concluded that the promotion of leisure enterprises in town centres as part of the 'evening economy' questions the logic of these developments in smaller provincial towns which may only be delaying the inevitable economic restructuring of the area rather than a wider development of café culture and eating out society, in part, promoted by urban tourism and leisure spending.

What emerges in any discussion of the capitalist city in transition is that societal change is occurring in a globally interconnected world (see Teo *et al.* 2001 for a discussion in relation to South East Asia). It is the world system that transcends the nation-state, with flexible systems of production located in different spatial contexts. For the postmodern city, space becomes heterogeneous, with a diversity of architectural styles in the built environment. Aside from the production of services and experiences, the city is a patchwork of symbols and opportunities for consumption. As Murphy (1999: 302) remarked:

> While consumption is significant within the postmodern city, it needs to be remembered that the places or sites of consumption are manufactured or created

spaces. Shopping malls, hypermarkets, multiplexes, planned communities, water-front spaces, museums and cybercafes are all products of service, property and entertainment industries. Indeed it has been argued that the new urbanism is akin to a giant theme park.

But what needs to be emphasised in a consumption context is that many of the urban landscapes in postmodern cities can be consumed only by those who have the means to do so. As Spoonley (2000: 177) observed, 'If cities are the powerhouses of global change, they also produce some of the worst problems of contemporary social and economic life' which are exacerbated in the post-modern city by extreme variations in wealth. Yet many of the new commun-ities that embody and encapsulate this wealth have become defended spaces owing to the image of wealth and the culture of fear associated with such affluence (see Plate 2.1 on San Francisco). As a result, Cybriwsky (1999) has recognised an accompanying trend in public and private space, with surveil-lance of space to address concerns of urban fear. Many of the highly organised spaces, such as shopping malls and precincts of cafés, are constructed land-scapes to allow conspicuous consumption. Much of the surveillance is based on closed-circuit television in urban centres in the United Kingdom, the United States (Fyfe and Banister 1996) and Japan. Indeed, cities such as New York recognise that to attract tourists, the city environment needs to be perceived as

Plate 2.1   The evolution of gated communities in the urban environment has been a major feature in North American cities as shown in this shot of San Francisco, California

safe. A campaign between 1995 and 2000 by New York City to address fear of crime by visitors and to clean up the city streets led to a 28 per cent increase in visitor numbers in 1995–98 to 36.7 million visits, generating US$15.6 billion in tourist spending. Therefore, the postmodern city is an evolving entity, where advanced capitalism is defining many elements of the built environment in pursuit of the consumption ideal in a post-industrial society. Tourism is without any doubt one of the defining features of the postmodern city: tourism is a complex form of postmodern life, with sociologists seeking to understand its meaning, construction and incorporation into the everyday leisure lives of the populace (see Urry 1991).

What capital has recognised in post-industrial society, in the creation of redundant spaces and landscapes in the inner city, on former production-oriented sites (e.g. waterfronts) and within former commercial districts, is that the edict of leisure spending can fuel the development of new landscapes of production. The development process recognises the power of the consumer and consumption patterns, so that urban leisure experiences and trends in society (i.e. the growth in eating out in cities) can harness new consumption opportunities if created in the postmodern context. While the debate on Ritzer's (1996) homogenisation thesis has highlighted many of the principles inherent in the development of the shopping mall (see Chapter 6 for more detail), there is also the trend towards heterogeneity in the new landscapes of consumption. In the era of the niche, specialised pattern of consumption, the urban dweller and worker, the leisure traveller and the tourist are all sophisticated consumers seeking both the homogenised and heterogeneous experiences in their lifestyles: Thrift's (1997) thickness analogy is a useful concept to explain the diversity that characterises the postmodern city. This translates directly into the domain of tourism and the city because the pursuit of new economic forms of production to replace the employment lost through deindustrialisation and the restructuring of localities has made tourism a fundamental element of most cities' economies. Whether this has been a deliberate policy by political decision-makers, where corporatist models of development have been pursued to promote rapid redevelopment, or has been a wider process of refocusing by capital within cities at a global–local scale is debatable. What is clear is that tourism and leisure development to meet a wide range of consumption needs now characterises cities worldwide. If globalisation has been attributed to the emergence of world cities, it is also pertinent to argue that this has generated a homogeneous and heterogeneous process: the role of the capital is central to the creation of 'the new urban tourism' in the urbanscape of the twenty-first century. In most cities, urban tourism is characterised by the homogenised symbols and presence of the multinational hotel chain (e.g. Quality Inn, Sheraton, Radisson), global hospitality brands (e.g. KFC, McDonald's, Pizza Hut, Starbucks and other franchises) juxtaposed with the heterogeneous examples of the locally or regionally distinctive products for consumption. This global–local relationship is also reflected in the mix of capital and entre-preneurship in the tourist city, where the elements of supply (production) seek

Plate 2.2 In a small way, this producers' market in Boulogne, France, is an attempt to harness both local and day-trip visitors from England as part of the spectacle of the old town on a Saturday with live animal sales and rural produce

Plate 2.3 In terms of consumption in the urban environment, tourist information on the range of possible options for tourist spending is an important prerequisite as reflected in Auckland's new Visitor Information Centre next to the America's Cup Village

to add a level of diversity, local identity and imagery which competes for the increasingly mobile leisure expenditure of residents, excursionists, business travellers and the tourist. Consumerism is now ensconced in contemporary society as a cultural form and as Mullins (1999: 253) argued

> Tourism presents itself as a major avenue for people to satisfy the cultural imperative to consume . . . Of course, not everyone has the financial means to become a tourist, but for those who can afford it, an international network of cities is emerging to satisfy their demands. The globalised middle class has played a central role in establishing the relationship between consumerism and tourism. The high disposable incomes of middle-class men and women and their predisposition to consume a variety of goods and services set them apart as major players in domestic and international travel.

This is one explanation of the increasingly sophisticated reproduction of place images by the marketeer in the postmodern city, where place promotion is a spatial transmission of consumption-oriented advertising to attract the increasing mobile forms of leisure spending (Plates 2.2 and 2.3). Mullins (1991) recognised this specific form of consumption in relation to tourism and leisure which is focused on the pursuit of pleasure as the central component. This pleasure-seeking is part of a constant search for the 'new, different, bigger and better pleasures, with services being either collectively packaged as spectacles and festivals (e.g. theme parks), or available as numerous individual services ranging from concerts to purchased sex, and from sports to holiday accommodation' (Mullins 1991: 231). In some contexts, tourism is assuming the primary rationale for some cities and the result is what has been described as tourism urbanisation. For this reason, attention now turns to the phenomenon of tourism urbanisation.

Tourism urbanisation

Mullins (1994) described tourism urbanisation as a new urban form and yet the advent of mass tourism in Europe in the nineteenth century arguably led to the rapid construction of towns and resorts for holidaymaking and day-trips, with capital shaping the nature and form of these resort complexes. What is new, and what characterises the 'new urban tourism' is the scale, complexity and diversity of consumption experiences which now exist in urban landscapes built specifically for tourism and leisure.

Mullins (1991: 326) explained the phenomenon of tourism urbanisation as '. . . cities providing a great range of consumption opportunities, with the consumers being resort tourists, people who move into these centres to reside for a short time . . . in order to consume some of the great range of goods and services on offer'. The purpose of consumption is pleasure-related. Taking Mullins' (1991) lead, a number of other studies have explored the phenomenon of tourism urbanisation in the United States and the most notable, by Gladstone (1998), is discussed later.

What Mullins (1991: 330) recognised was the 'consumption compounds' in the postmodern city where the city resident and tourist alike gather in purpose-built precincts for fun and pleasure to consume the goods and services available. Specialised compounds exist, namely pleasure spaces packaged for specific groups (e.g. the arts for elites). In the built environments, the process of tourism-led redevelopment has also created consumption opportunities in neighbourhoods that have been recommodified. This is intrinsically and inexorably linked with tourism and leisure opportunities for cultural consumption and pleasure in what might be described as nouveau riche environments aimed at middle-class consumers. In this respect, cultural and social transformations in the postmodern city are occurring in relation to and independent of tourism and leisure processes which have both global and distinctively local expressions in each urban locality. This creates new urban landscapes with a tourism fascination to the observer or consumer of the symbols and images of the new urban environment. Yet to the resident, these new urban environments have a different social meaning. Mullins (1991: 331) claimed that 'tourism urbanisation . . . can be said to be an urbanisation based on the sale and consumption of pleasure', and identified the following characteristics, so that where tourism urbanisation exists it is:

- geographically different, in that the observed patterns of development and land use do not coincide with those characteristics in the urban ecological models of urban geography discussed earlier;

- symbolically different, with various images and symbols used to promote the tourist function, using the natural and built environment as positive images for the consumption of pleasure, often associated with place-marketing (see Plate 2.4);

- characterised by rapid population and labour force growth;

- distinguished by flexible forms of production, meaning that their economies are organised significantly around private sector employers and high rates of unemployment arise from the flexible work practices and insecure nature of the labour market;

- dominated by state intervention which has a 'boosterist' tendency, whereby local government indirectly invest in the local infrastructure (physical – roads and basic services; social – schools and welfare functions; and cultural – the arts and leisure) with a view to encouraging further inward investment, often using state funded quangos such as Tourist Boards and development agencies (Page 1993a, 1994a), a characteristic feature of the postmodern city;

Plate 2.4   To promote the Auckland region as an events destination, Tourism Auckland placed event billboards at Auckland Airport to highlight the major events on a monthly basis under the slogan of 'Eventful Auckland' as part of a campaign for place-marketing to position the destination in an Australasian context

- associated with a mass and customised consumption of pleasure, with vast investment by developers in integrated resort complexes in coastal and inland areas (e.g. Center Parcs in Europe) and vast attraction complexes in or near urban centres of population (e.g. theme parks such as Disneyland);

- characterised by a socially distinct resident population which has a high degree of transient people as temporary workers, high levels of unemployment, with residents openly opposed to the social, cultural and environmental impact of development on their locality. This often gives rise to a local conservation lobby and antagonistic views towards developers seeking to exploit the market opportunities for further tourism development in such locations. Planning restrictions are one local response favoured by conservative minded groups, while those associations favouring progress and development see the positive benefits of local economic development.

The empirical validity of the tourism urbanisation thesis has been developed on the analysis of the Gold Coast and Sunshine Coast and a number of Australian cities. What Mullins' (1991) analysis is predicated on is the notion of specialised resort development for a particular form of tourism. Conceptually,

Table 2.2   Typology of urban forms of tourism

- Capital cities (e.g. London, Paris and New York) and cultural capitals (e.g. Rome)
- Metropolitan centres and walled historic cities (e.g. Canterbury and York) and small fortress cities
- Large historic cities (e.g. Oxford, Cambridge and Venice)
- Inner city areas (Manchester)
- Revitalised waterfront areas (e.g. London Docklands and Sydney Darling Harbour)
- Industrial cities (e.g. nineteenth-century Bradford)
- Seaside resorts and winter sports resorts (e.g. Lillehammer)
- Purpose-built integrated tourist resorts
- Tourist entertainment complexes (e.g. Disneyland and Las Vegas)
- Specialised tourist service centres (e.g. spas and pilgrimage destinations such as Lourdes)
- Cultural/art cities (e.g. Florence)

Source: Page (1995a).

Mullins' (1991) analysis only deals with one of the types of tourism in cities shown in Table 2.2. Indeed, it does not deal with the existence and role of tourism and leisure consumption in the broader genre of cities.

Tourism urbanisation in the United States

Following Mullins' (1991) seminal study of tourism urbanisation, Gladstone (1998) examined the same concept in the United States, identifying two basic types of urbanisation: the sun, sea and sand resort and the capital-intensive attraction-based city. What Gladstone's (1998) study is useful in addressing is the development of research on tourism in cities in the United States, with Zelinsky (1973) and Stanback's (1985) observation that certain cities or regions were devoted solely to tourism. Within the United States, Gladstone (1998) identified employment in entertainment and recreation services in metropolitan statistical areas (MSAs) and used location quotients. Four MSAs had three times the national average of employment in tourism-related employment (Atlantic City, Las Vegas, Orlando and Reno). While the Orlando pattern of employment was explained by Disney and non-Disney tourist attractions, the other three resorts were casino gambling locations. These localities were termed *Tourist Metropolises* by Gladstone (1998). A further nine MSAs (Daytona Beach, Fort Myers, Fort Pierce, Lakeland, Los Angeles, Naples, Panorama City, Sarasota and West Palm Beach) had employment in the tourism-related sector of 30–150 times the national average. With the exception of Los Angeles, each MSA was in Florida, and Gladstone (1998) termed these *Leisure Cities*.

Gladstone (1998) examined the social structure of US tourist cities, observing that tourist metropolises are larger than leisure cities and have a smaller white population, more service workers and fewer retirees. Tourist businesses in the metropolises are on average larger, while smaller businesses play a much greater role in leisure cities. Gladstone (1998) recognised the limitations of Mullins' (1991) tourism urbanisation model, since only one tourist metropolis in the United States (i.e. Atlantic City) was in a coastal area, with gambling enabling the resort to stem the city's economic decline in the 1970s. All the remaining tourist metropolises had inland locations. The similarity between Mullins' (1991) Australian tourist cities and the US examples lay in high rates of population and employment growth, particularly in the flexible production system. In contrast to Australia, US tourism urbanisation has high per capita incomes and lower levels of poverty, with leisure cities more closely resembling Mullins' (1991) Australian model. All tourist cities were racially segregated and a 'high spatial concentration of poor people. Like most urban areas in the United States, central cities are consistently the poorest part of the metropolitan area' (Gladstone 1998: 16), with African-Americans who are disproportionately located in central city areas more likely to live in poverty than the white population. In line with Mullins' (1991) model, American leisure cities were deemed to be more boosterist than tourist metropolises measured in terms of local government employment.

In the United States, both tourist metropolises and leisure cities were located in the sunbelt (i.e. areas in the Southern States of America which were never major manufacturing centres). What Gladstone (1998) points to in explaining these two different types of tourism urbanisation are the following:

- Their previous histories, with tourist metropolises established primarily to attract tourists whilst leisure cities were fuelled by the influx of retirees, second homers and tourists.

- The tourist metropolises rely on the capital-intensive attractions to attract a market while leisure cities use lifestyle, climate and environment. The tourist metropolises use a manufactured experience and the entertainment complex to attract visitors.

- Tourist metropolises also have a business structure that reflects a corporate culture and the dominance of transnational corporations (e.g. the Holiday Inn, Hilton, MGM) and specialist entertainment corporations (e.g. Universal and the Disney Corporation).

What Gladstone's (1998) study is useful in identifying is the growing specialisation of urban functions in the United States in terms of the postmodern city and tourism. Tourism urbanisation may fit the examples of resorts developed specifically for tourism, but does not explain the form and nature of tourism in the postmodern city. For this reason, attention now turns to a recent conceptualisation by Hannigan (1998) – *Fantasy City*.

Hannigan's *Fantasy City*

One of the most interesting and balanced analyses of the postmodern city and the role of tourism and leisure is associated with Hannigan's (1995) initial survey and subsequent publication of *Fantasy City* (Hannigan 1998). What Hannigan (1998) observed was that at the end of the nineteenth century in America, a new commercial culture emerged in urban areas based on leisure and entertainment. Of particular importance was the emergence of new sources of capital, the new entertainment entrepreneurs – the 'merchants of leisure' – to lure a wide cross-section of society in the industrialised city. Such forms of recreational entertainment including the theatre and theme parks were enshrined in popular culture. What is interesting in Hannigan's analysis in a tourism and leisure context was that aside from the major urban centres such as New York, Chicago and San Francisco, the downtown area had little to attract the day visitor or tourist. What Hannigan observed was that the cultural industries of many downtown areas reported lower sales and revenue in 1958 compared with 1945 and the post-war period saw the demise of North American downtown areas as sites of leisure consumption. What this signified was the demise of the urban entertainment district with a focus on the suburbs and recreation and tourism opportunities outside of urban areas (e.g. the drive-in).

It was mainly during the 1980s that the public and private sectors in many downtown areas embarked on urban revitalisation projects, with investment and capital attracted to flagship destination projects. Although some of the origins of tourism and leisure projects can be found in the 1970s when festival markets were developed to attract consumer activity in downtown areas, in tourism terms these were insufficient to expand the visitor base to the downtown areas in North American cities. They were supplemented by a range of 'special activity generators' (i.e. sport arenas, stadia, casinos, entertainment complexes) which were able to attract tourists and day-trippers (Robertson 1995) and to compete with the suburbs. Alongside these strategies for urban revitalisation, shopping and dining out underpinned the consumption experiences while culture and entertainment complemented urban regeneration, especially in the formation of cultural and entertainment districts. During the 1990s, entertainment re-established itself as a dominant theme in the burgeoning entertainment economy of many cities. What Hannigan (1998) focused on was consumption in the contemporary American city, which was not a new phenomenon, but its cultural significance and its construction into entertainment experiences in themed environments were new. This led to the development of fantasy experiences packaged in safe, reassuring and predictable environments such as theme parks.

Hannigan (1998) identified six defining characteristics for Fantasy City:

1. *A focus on themocentricity*, namely that it is based on a scripted theme.
2. *The city is aggressively branded*, reflected in the place-marketing strategies and product range.

3. *Day and night operation is a common feature*, unlike shopping malls which are largely daytime operations.
4. *Modularisation of products*, where a diverse array of components are assembled to produce a wide range of experiences.
5. *Solipsisicity*, where the city is economically, culturally and physically detached and isolated from surrounding neighbourhoods in a City of Illusion.
6. *Postmodernity*, where the city is constructed around the technologies of simulation, virtual reality and the thrill of the spectacle. The city draws a major source of inspiration from the Disney model, which is widely imitated. The Disney model merges the concept of the motion picture and amusement park into a fantasy world using technologies that create conditions of hyperreality. Soja (1989) has termed such creations 'post-modern agglomerations' with their antendent concerns for globalisation.

From the leisure and tourism perspective, many powerful business interests have recognised these trends as part of the growth sector for the future. Critics of the entertainment value of formerly dry and uninspiring museum exhibits in the commodified 'heritage industry' (see Hewison 1987) have voiced concern at urban attractions being transformed into living heritage that are seen as lacking authenticity, accuracy and integrity. Instead they were seen as part of the crass commercialisation of the Fantasy City concept. Goldberger (1996) criticised Fantasy City for its creation of new landscapes of leisure based on urbanoid environments, where cloning and reality were distorted by the eradication of the former living city in downtown areas.

City authorities have seized upon the urban regenerative effects of Fantasy City for inner cities which lost many former productive functions, as conspicuous consumption creates a controlled, organised and measured urban experience. However, theme parks, which are part of the Fantasy City experience, have been criticised as the high-technology playgrounds of the middle classes, of little benefit to local communities. What is clear is their role in the liminality of the tourist experience, where pleasure and thrill-seeking in postmodern cities is a traded commodity (Ryan and Hall 2001).

An interesting perspective proffered by the French sociologist Bordieu (1984) interprets the patronage of theme parks as part of the acquisition of cultural capital: 'been there, done that', which confers status in the postmodern society. In fact Christiansen and Brinkerhoff-Jacobs (1995) progress this argument a stage further, suggesting that the architects of Fantasy City are creating a new kind of experience for the consumer. In the context of theme parks, the consumer is requiring a constant and technologically dazzling level of amusement incorporated into their repertoire of cultural capital (see Plates 2.5 and 2.6). Yet Rojek (1993) observed that an important element in the packaging of the fantasy experience is the provision of a safe, reassuring and predictable environment termed the 'recurrence of reassurance'. This is part of what Ritzer (1996) has termed the *McDonaldization of society* based on the

Plate 2.5 In terms of cultural capital, visiting Disneyland and the Disney experience is interpreted as one element of the Fantasy City product

Plate 2.6 The 'must do' activities within even postmodern cities can be based on heritage experiences, such as the tourist riding the San Francisco cable cars as popularised in North American media and film footage of the city and its scenic streetscapes

principles of efficiency, calcability, predictability and control epitomised in the theme park environment. A further element is the easy to decipher signs, the standardised behaviours and limited human interactive experiences. Although critics may be concerned that in the postmodern city we may be amusing ourselves to death (Postman 1985), these developments are not confined to Europe and North America. The development of theme parks in Asia-Pacific are emerging as a hybrid form of globalisation, given their replication of development from other parts of the world (see Teo *et al.* 2001).

Although Ritzer (1996: 32) argued that theme parks such as Disneyland are 'a world of predictable, almost surreal orderliness', Hannigan (1998) pointed to the organisational model adopted by globalised brands and sites of consumption based on new modes of thematic representation. The globalised themed consumption of the entertainment city also mutually converges with four major consumer activity systems: shopping, dining, entertainment and education, which are interconnected by transport (see Plate 2.6). Hannigan (1998: 89) describes these in terms of 'three new hybrids which in the lexicon of the retail industry are known as shopertainment, eatertainment and edutainment'. Shopertainment is part of the interaction of leisure shopping (see Chapter 3), fantasy fun and the pleasure of consumption. Eatertainment is where the interaction of play and eating combine and are both a pleasure and source of gratification with themed restaurants such as the Hard Rock Café. Lastly, edutainment is where educational and cultural activities are joined with technology and entertainment such as in the new national museum of New Zealand in Wellington Te Papa. According to Dalyrymple (1999):

> One leaves Te Papa knowing no more than when one entered it. If one has the mentality of a child of limited intelligence and curiosity, one might have been amused or kept out of trouble for a while, but nothing more. There are, surely, other institutions, which require no public subsidies, to achieve that limited (and limiting) end.
>
> Only one question filled my mind as I left Te Papa. Who is the correct kind of person to run it?
>
> Certainly not a curator, because no detailed knowledge of any subject is necessary. A casino owner, perhaps, or the manager of an amusement arcade. Te Papa is the institutional exemplar of the lowest common demoninator turned into official cultural policy, and stands as a terrible warning to the rest of the world.

Yet many of these themes and trends described by Hannigan (1998), initially in the downtown area, have also spread across the urban environment, particularly to the urban fringe. Garreau (1991) described 'Edge City' on the urban fringe which has challenged the notion of the urban core as the location of the city's cultural industries. In the post-war American city, many entertainment functions located in suburbs, but what Garreau (1991) pointed to was the move to the urban fringe, socially and spatially excluding inner-city users without the means of transport to access suburban developments. This contributed to a geographical isolation and social exclusion from the new leisure consumptive activities in the urban fringe.

Hannigan's (1998) review highlights some of the dynamics of urban change in the development of tourism and leisure in the postmodern metropolis, with a focus on entertainment. What it is useful in explaining is the evolution of the tourism and leisure elements of the industrial and post-industrial American city, highlighting geographical changes in the use of leisure and tourism spaces in the city over a 100 year period. It questions some of the assumptions made by Mullins (1991) on tourism urbanisation because tourism and leisure have undergone a series of changing fortunes. Yet consumption per se is not just a postmodern phenomenon in the city. What is different in the postmodern context is the cultural embodiment of consumption in the everyday lives of residents and visitors to the city. In the postmodern city, tourism and leisure consumption does not exhibit the spatial fixity that geographers have sought to model. A more complex series of relationships exists and, based on the discussion of tourism in the postmodern city, attention now turns to developing a model of tourism in the postmodern city.

Modelling tourism in the postmodern city

Within the literature on urbanism, an urban ecological modelling tradition developed in the 1920s with Burgess' (1925) model of the social structure and form of Chicago. This urban ecological model has had a major impact on the development of urban studies, as sociologists and geographers have debated the merits of simplifying the reality of urban form to a series of constructs, labels and ideas on cities. If the objective of models is to simplify reality and provide a framework for academic discourse, then they serve as a useful tool to critically examine the processes affecting urban places. Within the tourism literature, geographers have examined cities and places to develop models that integrate tourism into other patterns of economic activity. Within the literature on urban tourism, the dominant paradigm has been shaped by the urban ecological model of Burgess to illustrate how tourism has been added to an evolving landscape. Probably the most influential work has been by European geographers (e.g. Jansen-Verbeke 1986; Ashworth 1989; Jansen-Verbeke and Lievois 1999) in relation to the historic city. Using spatial-analytical techniques, these researchers have highlighted how landscapes of consumption that have been created as heritage resources have been commodified, packaged and sold to visitors.

If one builds on these studies, and develops many of the elements of the postmodern city, particularly the emergence of tourism and leisure as activities that coexist in juxtaposition to other productive activities, then a number of spatially specific forms of consumption can be identified. While critics of models may well argue that the postmodern city is too complex to disaggregate, simplify and reduce to a number of consumption-specific elements, it is a starting point for a more spatially informed analysis of the city. What makes the modelling process useful is that the static impression presented by a two-dimensional hypothetical model has to be viewed against the following context:

- The postmodern city is in a constant state of flux as capital redefines the nature, form and extent of consumption experiences for residents, workers, day-trippers and tourists. The postmodern urban landscape is one undergoing a constant re-evaluation, redevelopment and re-imaging to compete for consumption expenditure.

- The tourism and leisure landscapes in the postmodern city are only one facet of a mosaic of social and cultural forms that have been created through time and illustrate diversity and coexistence with a range of other activities (i.e. housing and employment).

- The tourist city is not necessarily a distinct spatial entity that the visitor can easily recognise: it is a patchwork of consumption experiences, spatially dispersed and often grouped into districts and zones (e.g. the entertainment zone) with symbols, a unique language and range of icons to differentiate the experience of place consumption. In this respect the tourist city is a series of sub-systems interconnected by the pursuit of pleasure, the consumption experience and the defining characteristic – the use of leisure time.

- In time and space, capital competes within and between cities so that the tourism sector is constantly evolving, with a complex set of interactions between the processes of globalisation and localised expressions of local identity, culture and constructions of place.

- The tourist city is predicated on a series of primary attractions and an infrastructure that is utilised by non-tourists.

- Traditional concepts in urban ecological models which were spatially contingent upon the socio-economic structure of the city have been replaced by a mosaic of new socio-geographic forms such as the middle class and gentrification, the reuse of inner-city and waterfront areas, the development of 'Edge City', the rise of 'Fantasy City' and a spatial recognition of the city to accommodate these new elements.

- In highlighting the tourism elements of the postmodern city, any model has to suppress many of the other dynamic elements of the postmodern city so that the tourism and leisure elements dominate. In reality, tourism is subsumed and integrated into the postmodern city and while it may be a dominant element in those localities actively promoting its virtues, it is one aspect of the form of the city.

Figure 2.2a, based on the discussion of the postmodern city and the elements one can discern in the built environment are indicated in this hypothetical example. A number of distinctive features emerge. The city is not primarily dominated by the industrial production patterns of the Central Business Dis-

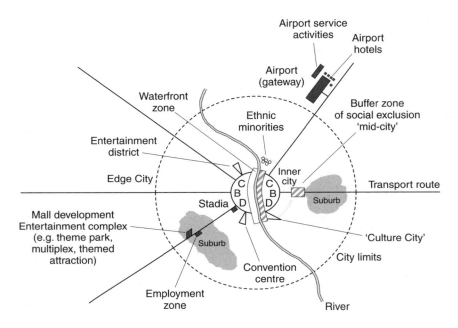

Figure 2.2a   Tourism, leisure and the postmodern city

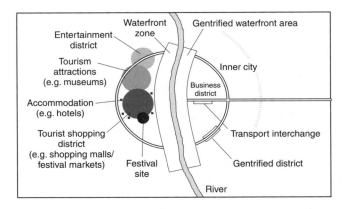

Figure 2.2b   Tourism, leisure and the postmodern city: the inner city dimension

trict (CBD), transport and production functions such as port activity, industrial zones and industrial agglomerations. Instead, a more complex pattern of socio-economic activity exists. The CBD contains the production functions associated with service sector activities and urban revitalisation has transformed the waterfront area. The process of gentrification is at work in and around the inner-city districts while a series of zones or clusters of interconnected tourism and leisure activity (Figure 2.2a) exist (e.g. the entertainment zone, 'culture' city) which are elaborated in more detail in the enlarged area (Figure 2.2b). The defining elements of the postmodern city in downtown locations are also shown in Figure 2.2b. What complicates the pattern for urban ecologists is the evolution of space-extensive developments in Garreau's (1991) Edge City, with mall development, Fantasy City and a series of entertainment functions in out-of-town locations within suburbs. Since employment may also coexist with suburban development, the postmodern city is characterised as multinodal, with a cluster of tourism and leisure related activities in out-of-town locations (e.g. the airport and Edge City). In contrast the downtown area has a range of consumption functions that are culturally, spatially and socially defined and differentiated from Edge City (Figure 2.2b).

Since social exclusion, inequality and a polarisation of social groups characterises postmodern cities, in tourism terms it gives rise to a buffer zone (Figure 2.2a) which may isolate the inner city from Edge City and give rise to a mid-city zone for inner-city residents, if they do not have the means of transport they are socially excluded, or means to consume the experiences available. Although the inner city is near to the downtown area, the creation of landscapes of consumption appealing to visitors and the new middle classes may also further socially marginalise the inner-city population from the tourist landscapes and certainly epitomises the 'new urban tourism'.

In a cross-section of the postmodern city and the new urban forms, Figure 2.3 highlights the changes that now have to be encapsulated in conventional models of the city from the post-war 'modern' period. In this respect, attempting to theorise tourism in the postmodern city is very much dependent upon an understanding of consumption (Urry 1995). This is one of the defining characteristics of tourist space in the postmodern city, and for this reason an understanding of tourists, the sociology of their use of the city (see Urry's 1990 *Tourist Gaze*) and consumption habits are a good starting point. This has to be understood in relation to the role of capital, particularly actors and developers (see Hannigan 1998 for more detail) to understand how the supply of tourism opportunities have been framed to maximise the consumption of pleasure. While the models presented in Figures 2.2a and b and 2.3 are by no means definitive, they do begin to engage the researcher in a more holistic analysis of how tourism and the postmodern city coexist and interact to generate an economic activity structured around the production and consumption of pleasure in leisure time. The spatial dynamics of patterns of consumption by tourists is by no means easy to disaggregate from the complexities of urbanism, although it provides a preliminary attempt to model tourism–city relationships.

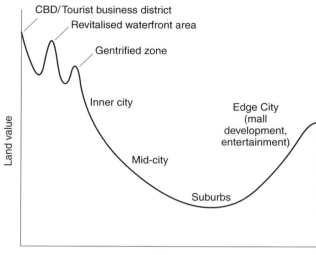

Figure 2.3 Cross-section of the postmodern city: space, place and location

Conclusion

This chapter has shown that a fundamental distinction needs to be made between what Mullins (1991, 1994, 1999) described as tourism urbanisation, which has remained virtually unchallenged within the tourism literature to date with the exception of Gladstone's (1998) research. Mullins' (1991) arguments on tourism urbanisation may well apply to a limited number of contexts where tourism is the sole rationale for economic development, such as resort complexes and associated urbanisation. But by themselves, Mullins' (1991) framework and Gladstone's (1998) useful analysis do not help to identify the defining characteristics of tourism in the postmodern city. This is because the spatial form of tourism and leisure activities represents a complex amalgam of interconnected zones or elements, which are not necessarily spatially grouped in one area and which reflect a wide range of economic, political and cultural forces at work in the shaping of the city. It also reflects the cultural complexity of defining what is meant by urban tourism, with the use of consumption as the defining term, with specific elements in the urban landscape defined, created and subsequently consumed. For this reason, many postmodern analyses of the city have been content to describe facets of these elements of the new urban tourism which is culturally diverse and complex to understand and explain. Traditional models that are spatially derived do not necessarily convey the mosaic of tourism and leisure consumption experiences within the postmodern city. This requires a greater theoretical concern for the fascination that people have with consumption in urban places as a use of their leisure time. It is very much dependent upon a multidisciplinary evaluation of the city and a better understanding of what Urry (1995) described as 'Consuming Places'. Cities are consuming places for tourists, visitors and residents alike. Many of the themes discussed in this chapter will be returned to in later chapters to elaborate upon specific themes introduced here.

Questions

1. What are the main features of Mullins's (1991) 'tourism urbanisation'? How does Gladstone's (1998) research fit in with Mullins's thesis?
2. What is the significance of consumption in explaining urban tourism?
3. How does the analysis of postmodernism assist in explaining the significance of tourism in cities?
4. What are the defining features of tourism in the postmodern city?

Further reading

The literature on the postmodern city is complex, jargon-laden and scattered across a number of social science disciplines. Very few tourism articles or books address this issue. A useful starting point is:

Urry, J. (1995). *Consuming Places*, London: Routledge.

Mullins, P. (1999). 'International tourism and the cities of Southeast Asia', in D. Judd and S. Fainstein (eds) *The Tourist City*, New Haven: Yale University Press, 245–60. This is a useful study which raised the issue of the postmodern city.

Gladstone, D. (1998). 'Tourism urbanisation in the United States', *Urban Affairs Review* 34(1): 3–27. This is a good critical review of tourism and urbanisation in the United States, evaluating Mullins's (1991) work and its application to North America.

Zukin, S. (1996). *The Culture of Cities*, Oxford: Blackwell. This is an interesting assessment of the cultural dimensions of cities in the postmodern environment and the way in which capital has utilised consumption opportunities in North America to develop new landscapes.

CHAPTER 3

The demand for urban tourism

Introduction

As noted in Chapter 1 the demand for tourism in urban areas has traditionally been a poorly understood element of the tourism system, a feature recognised by Blank and Petkovich (1987: 165) who argued that 'urban tourism is almost certainly among the most misunderstood and underestimated of all tourism types. It suffers from underestimation – sometimes even unrecognition'. The issue of underestimation is certainly a perennial problem facing planners, policy-makers and researchers because the scale and extent of urban tourism in large cities means that even sample surveys of visitor numbers may be notoriously under-representative of the totality of urban tourists. Accurate information on the demand for urban tourism is critical for service providers, planners and those businesses associated with the tourism industry to ensure that they meet the needs and requirements of tourists. One of the major challenges for the tourism industry is to attempt to balance the supply of services, products and infrastructure with the actual demand for such goods (see Bull 1991 for a fuller discussion of the concepts of supply and demand). Without adequate information, the day-to-day management of urban tourism will be difficult for planners and providers, as they will find it difficult to establish priorities for attracting, promoting and developing the market for urban tourism. This is a problem that is compounded by the heterogeneous nature of urban tourism. According to Shaw and Williams (1994: 207), 'within the somewhat limited literature on visitor activity in urban areas, two main perspectives can be identified. One concerns the types of users and visitor motivation, while the other, with an even smaller research base, examines visitor behaviour in the city'.

Shaw and Williams's observation provides an important focus for this chapter, the purpose of which is to examine the nature of tourist motivation as a basis to establish why tourists choose to visit different destinations and the complex reasons associated with selecting urban areas. For this reason, a general introduction to the demand for urban tourism is followed by a discussion of tourist motivation to explain the context in which travel to urban destinations occurs. This is followed by a review of the international data sources which may be used to gauge the scale of demand for urban tourism. Following this assessment, the different types of tourists who choose to visit urban areas are discussed.

The demand for urban tourism

Establishing the reasons why tourism develops in a given city and why tourists choose to visit the place or region is normally considered under the term 'demand' and has traditionally been the remit of the economist in terms of analysis. As Sinclair and Stabler (1997: 15) explain, demand at the aggregate level where the

> large numbers of tourists and the scale of their expenditure have considerable effects on the income, employment, government revenue, balance of payments, environments and culture of destination areas. A fall in demand can bring about decreases in living standards and rises in unemployment, while increased demand can result in higher employment, income, output and/or inflation and may threaten environmental quality and sustainability.

What this illustrates is that a fundamental understanding of demand is vital to the immediate and long-term prosperity and sustainability of the destination. At the macro-level, Uysal (1998) identified three determinants of tourism demand:

1. Exogenous factors associated with the business environment.
2. Socio-psychological factors associated with the decision-making of travellers.
3. Economic factors such as income, price and the elasticity of tourism products.

These factors are summarised in Figure 3.1 which outlines the factors that contribute to the overall pattern of demand. It is these factors that are often the focus of tourism demand studies where specific elements of demand are examined (Hall and Page 2002). For example, the common measures used to examine tourism demand in this context are:

*   number of visitor arrivals;
*   tourism expenditure or receipts;
*   length of stay at the destination as part of a single or multiple destination trip;
*   travel propensity indices, which commonly refers to a region or country by the population within it (Uysal *et al.* 1995).

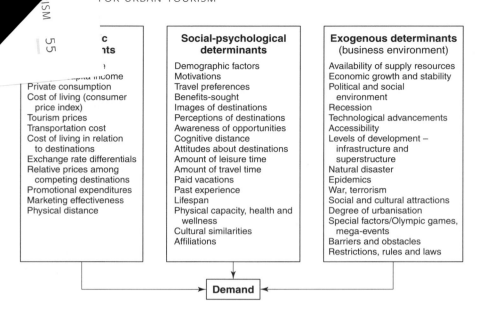

c **its**	**Social-psychological determinants**	**Exogenous determinants** (business environment)
......income Private consumption Cost of living (consumer price index) Tourism prices Transportation cost Cost of living in relation to destinations Exchange rate differentials Relative prices among competing destinations Promotional expenditures Marketing effectiveness Physical distance	Demographic factors Motivations Travel preferences Benefits-sought Images of destinations Perceptions of destinations Awareness of opportunities Cognitive distance Attitudes about destinations Amount of leisure time Amount of travel time Paid vacations Past experience Lifespan Physical capacity, health and wellness Cultural similarities Affiliations	Availability of supply resources Economic growth and stability Political and social environment Recession Technological advancements Accessibility Levels of development – infrastructure and superstructure Natural disaster Epidemics War, terrorism Social and cultural attractions Degree of urbanisation Special factors/Olympic games, mega-events Barriers and obstacles Restrictions, rules and laws

Demand

Figure 3.1 Determinants of tourism demand (source: Uysal 1998)

Ryan (1991) discussed the economic determinants of tourism demand that are associated with the purchase of an intangible service, usually a holiday or tourism service, which make up an experience for the tourist (see Chapter 1). But what is meant by the 'tourist experience'?

The tourist experience of urban tourism

According to Graefe and Vaske (1987), the 'tourist experience' is the culmination of a given experience which can be influenced by individual, environmental, situational and personality-related factors as well as the degree of communication with other people. It is the outcome (or output if viewed in a system framework) that researchers and the tourism industry constantly evaluate to establish if the actual experience met the tourist's expectations. In other words, the 'tourist experience' is a complex amalgam of factors that shape the tourist's feelings and attitude towards their visit. Yet as tourism motivation and consumer research suggest, it is almost impossible to predict tourist responses to individual situations but a series of inter-related impacts may affect the tourist's experience (Figure 3.2). For example, high usage levels of tourism resources may lead to overcrowding and this may diminish the visitor experience, although the results from the recreational literature are inconclusive on this issue. In essence, when the carrying capacity (see Chapter 6) or the ability of a site to sustain a given number of visitors is exceeded, overcrowding results, which may detract from the tourist experience for some visitors. This

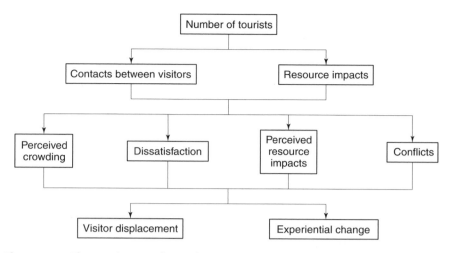

Figure 3.2   The tourist experience (source: Page 1995a)

emphasises the need to understand both the views of groups and individuals, since some people have a low tolerance threshold for an overcrowded site while others are less affected by similar conditions. However, as research has shown, increased use levels may raise the potential for conflict although 'research on all types of impact depicted in Figure 3.2 [sic] shows that the effects of increasing use levels on the recreation/tourist experience can be explained only partially, at best, as a function of use level' (Graefe and Vaske 1987: 394).

Ultimately, the individual's ability to tolerate the behaviour of other people, levels of use, the social situation and the context of the activity are all important determinants of the actual outcome. Thus, evaluating the quality of the tourist experience is a complex process which may require careful consideration of the factors motivating a visit (i.e. how the tourist's perception of urban areas makes them predisposed to visit particular places), their actual patterns of activity and the extent to which their expectations associated with their perceptions are matched in reality (see Ryan 1997 for a more detailed analysis of the tourist experience). Within any analysis of the tourist experience, the one area that assumes a great deal of significance is tourist motivation.

Tourism motivation

Ryan (1991) emphasises the significance of psychological determinants of demand in explaining some of the reasons why tourists travel and their selection of particular destinations. Although there is no generally accepted theory of tourist travel, a range of tourist motivators exist (P. Pearce 1982). According to Moutinho (1987: 16) motivation is 'a state of need, a condition that exerts a push on the individual towards certain types of action that are seen as likely to bring satisfaction. In this respect Cooper *et al.* (1993: 20) rightly acknowledged that 'demand for tourism at the individual level can be treated as a consumption process which is influenced by a number of factors. These may be a combination of needs and desires, availability of time and money, or images, perceptions and attitudes'. Not surprisingly, this is a complex area of research. Ryan's (1991: 25–9) analysis of tourist travel motivators (excluding business travel) identifies the following reasons commonly cited to explain why people travel to tourist destinations for holidays. These include:

- wish fulfilment;
- shopping;
- a desire to escape from a mundane environment;
- the pursuit of relaxation and recuperation functions;
- an opportunity for play;
- the strengthening of family bonds;
- prestige, since different destinations can enable one to gain social enhancement among peers;
- social interaction;
- educational opportunities.

While a range of motivators can be identified, it is possible to classify tourists according to the type of holiday they are seeking and the experience they desire. For example, Cohen (1972) distinguished between four types of tourist travellers:

1. *The mass tourist*, on a package holiday who is highly organised. Their contact with the host community in a destination is minimal.
2. *The individual mass tourist*, who uses similar facilities to the organised mass tourist but also desires to visit other sights not covered on organised tours in the destination.
3. *The explorers*, who arrange their travel independently and who wish to experience the social and cultural lifestyle of the destination.
4. *The drifter*, who does not seek any contact with other tourists or their accommodation, seeking to live with the host community (V. Smith 1989).

Clearly, such a classification is fraught with problems, since it does not take into account the increasing diversity of holidays undertaken and inconsistencies in tourist behaviour (P. Pearce 1982). Furthermore, the classification also fails to acknowledge the complexity of urban tourism. As Shaw and Williams (1994: 201) observed, 'urban areas of all types act as tourist destinations, attracting domestic and international visitors, including holidaymakers, as well as those on business and conference trips'. Other researchers suggest that one way of overcoming this difficulty is to consider the different destinations tourists choose to visit, and then establish a sliding scale similar to Cohen's (1972) typology, but which does not have such an absolute classification. How does this affect the identification of the tourists who visit urban areas?

Urban tourism destinations need to recognise what economic, social and psychological factors are stimulating the demand for visits, and how different types of travellers' preferences are reflected in the choice of various destinations and specific activity patterns. One important study that reviews the different approaches and models used to analyse tourist motivation is that of P. Pearce (1993). It established a blueprint for tourist motivation, but notes that

> tourism demand should not be equated with tourism motivation. Tourism demand is the outcome of tourists' motivation, as well as marketing, destination features and contingency factors such as money, health and time relating to the travellers' choice behaviour . . . Tourism demand can be expressed as the sum of realistic behavioural intentions to visit a specific location . . . [which is] . . . reduced to existing travel statistics and forecasts of future traveller numbers. Tourist motivation is then a part rather than the equivalent of tourist demand (P. Pearce 1993: 113).

It is important to emphasise Pearce's comment that tourism demand cannot be simply equated with tourism motivation. This makes a convincing case for examining tourist destination choice in the context of urban tourism if destinations are to understand their markets. Pearce's (1993) influential work in this field indicated that in any attempt to theorise tourist motivation one must consider the following issues:

- the conceptual place of tourism motivation;
- its task in the specialism of tourism;
- its ownership and users;
- its ease of communication;
- pragmatic measurement concerns;
- adopting a dynamic approach;
- the development of multi-motive perspectives;
- resolving and clarifying intrinsic and extrinsic motivation approaches (after P. Pearce 1993: 18).

To date no all-embracing theory of tourist motivation has been developed that has been adapted and legitimised by researchers in other contexts. This is largely due to the multidisciplinary nature of the research issues identified above and the problem of simplifying complex psychological factors and behaviour into a set of constructs and ultimately a universally acceptable theory that can be tested and proved in various tourism contexts. As a result, Cooper *et al.* (1993: 20) prefer to view the individual as a central component of tourism demand to understand what motivates the tourist to travel. Their research rightly acknowledges that:

no two individuals are alike, and differences in attitudes, perceptions and motivation have an important influence on travel decisions [where] attitudes depend on an individual's perception of the world. Perceptions are mental impressions of . . . a place or travel company and are determined by many factors which include childhood, family and work experiences. However, attitudes and perceptions in themselves do not explain why people want to travel. The inner urges which initiate travel demand are called travel motivators (Cooper *et al.* 1993: 20).

If one views the tourist as a consumer, then tourism demand is formulated through a consumer decision-making process, and therefore one can discern four elements that initiate demand:

- *energisers of demand* (i.e. factors that promote an individual to decide on a holiday);
- *filterers of demand*, which means that even though motivation may exist, constraints on demand may exist in economic, sociological or psychological terms;
- *affecters*, which are factors that may heighten or suppress the energisers that promote consumer interest or choice in tourism; and
- *roles*, where the family member involved in the purchase of holiday products decides on the where, when, how and cost of the holiday.

These factors underpin the tourist's process of travel decision-making.

For this reason, tour operators selling holidays to urban destinations need to recognise the complexity of tourist motivation and the preferred locations tourists seek to visit. More specifically, the tourism industry in urban areas receiving visitors and the tour operators will need to understand the range of motives and expectations of certain types of traveller, since the level of service they provide will need to match the market and the requirements of travellers. This is essential if the 'tourist experience' is to be a favourable one. Operators need to understand not only the dimensions of demand, but also the market segments and the behaviour and expectations of consumers which they will need to accommodate in providing a high-quality tourist experience (see Ryan 1995). For this reason, attention now turns to the data sources available to gauge patterns of demand for different destinations.

Data sources on urban tourism: a paucity of material?

The analysis of tourism, tourists and their propensity to travel and previous travel patterns is 'a complex process . . . involving not only the visitor and his movements but also the destination and host community' (Latham 1989: 55). What statistical information on urban tourism is available? How is it gathered? And who publishes it? One immediate problem that confronts the researcher interested in tourism as a global phenomenon is the absence of international statistics that monitor every aspect of tourism. Although there are industry-specific studies that monitor the volume of travel, these are often confidential to organisations and one is forced to refer to tourism statistics since they are more comprehensive and consistent, providing an insight into:

- tourist arrivals in different regions of the world and for specific countries;
- the volume of tourist trips;
- types of tourism (e.g. holidaymaking, visiting friends and relatives and business travel);
- the number of nights spent in different countries by tourists;
- tourist expenditure on services.

Latham's (1989) excellent study on tourism statistics is essential reading, since it provides a useful insight into the complex process of assessing the general patterns of demand for tourism. Studies by Jefferson and Lickorish (1991), Veal (1992) and Page *et al.* (2001) document the procedures associated with the generation of tourism statistics, which often use social survey techniques, such as questionnaire-based interviews with tourists at departure and arrival points. These surveys often form the basis for calculations by tourism organisations who estimate the volume of tourism for specific countries, regions and individual localities.

Unlike other forms of social survey work, tourists are a transient and mobile population. This poses many problems in relation to which social survey method and sampling technique one should use to generate reliable and accurate statistical information, to ensure that it is representative of the real world. Owing to the cost involved in undertaking social surveys, it is impossible and impractical for organisations to interview all tourists travelling on a specific mode of transport. A sampling framework is normally used to select a range of respondents who are representative of the population being examined. While there are a number of good sources which deal with this technical issue (see S.L.J. Smith 1989; Veal 1992), it is clear that no one survey technique and sampling framework is going to provide all the information necessary to enable managers and planners to make decisions related to planning and service provision. It is possible to discern three common types of tourism surveys:

1. Pre-travel studies of tourists' intended travel habits and likely use of tourist transport.
2. Studies of tourists in-transit, or at their destination, which provide information on their actual behaviour and plans for the remainder of their holiday or journey.
3. Post-travel studies of tourists once they have returned to their place of residence which provides for studies of what they actually did and their reflections on the travel experience.

Clearly there are advantages and disadvantages with each approach. For example, pre-travel studies may indicate the potential destinations that tourists would like to visit on their next holiday, but it is difficult to assess the extent to which holiday intentions are converted to actual travel. In contrast, surveys of tourists in transit or at a destination can only provide a snapshot of their experiences to date rather than a broader evaluation of their holiday experience. Yet retrospective post-travel studies incur the problem of actually locating and eliciting responses from tourists which accurately record a previous event or experience. Each approach has a valuable role and individual operators and tourism organisations use the approach appropriate to their information needs.

International data sources

The most comprehensive and widely used sources of tourism statistics that directly and indirectly examine international tourist travel are produced by the World Tourism Organization (WTO) and the Organization for Economic

Table 3.1 International tourist arrivals and receipts worldwide 1989–98

	1989	1990	1991	1992	1993	1994	1995	1996	1997	1998
Arrivals (millions)	426	458	464	503	518	553	568	600	620	635
% annual change	8.02	7.45	1.25	8.37	3.09	6.75	2.74	5.48	3.33	2.51
Receipts (US$billion)	221	268	278	314	323	353	403	438	436	439
% annual change	8.31	21.03	3.66	13.00	3.03	9.13	14.29	8.57	−0.14	0.28

Source: WTO (1999) World Tourism Highlights, http://www.world-tourism.org

Table 3.2 International arrivals and tourism receipts 1997 and 1998 by WTO tourism region

	Tourist arrivals		% change		Tourist receipts (US$ million)		% change	
	1997	1998	98/97	97/96	1997	1998	98/97	97/96
World	619,574	635,134	2.5	3.3	438,165	439,393	0.3	0.1
Africa	23,190	24,679	6.4	5.9	9,018	9,612	6.6	3.3
Americas	118,887	122,682	3.2	1.7	118,855	119,965	0.9	5.7
East Asia Pacific	88,207	86,629	−1.6	−1.1	76,387	68,598	−10.2	−6.8
Europe	369,803	381,076	3.0	4.7	220,494	228,856	3.8	−0.8
Middle East	14,833	15,035	1.4	5.3	9,135	8,022	−12.2	10.8
South Asia	4,834	5,033	4.1	9.0	4,276	4,340	1.5	8.3

Source: WTO (1999) World Tourism Highlights, http://www.world-tourism.org

Cooperation and Development (OECD) (see Pearce 1987, 1995 for a more detailed discussion of these sources). National governments also compile statistics on international tourism for their own country (in-bound travel) and the destinations chosen by outbound travellers. The WTO publishes a number of annual publications which include the *Yearbook of Tourism Statistics* (published since 1947 as *International Travel Statistics*, then as *World Travel Statistics*, and now as *World Travel and Tourism Statistics*). This has a summary of tourism statistics for almost 150 countries and areas with key data on tourist transport and includes statistical information in the following order:

- A world summary of international tourism statistics.
- Tourist arrivals.
- Accommodation capacity by regions.
- Trends in world international tourism arrivals, receipts and exports.
- Arrivals of cruise passengers.
- Domestic tourism.
- Tourism payments (including international tourism receipts by countries calculated in US$ millions, excluding international fare receipts).
- Tourist transport (tourist arrivals from abroad by mode of transport).
- Tourism motivations (arrivals from abroad and purpose of visit).
- Tourism accommodation.
- Country studies which examine the detailed breakdown of tourism statistics collected for each area, including tourism seasonality.

The availability and accessibility of such data have also been improved with the development of general websites such as www.world-tourism.org which lists all the data sources, reports and press releases of the WTO. It also provides an online statistical subscription service for regular users of its data. The WTO press releases also provide regular updates on global and regional tourism trends which are useful snapshots of inbound tourism by region and destination. (An illustration of the typical data available to researchers is outlined in Tables 3.1 to 3.7.) In addition to the WTO, the OECD produces

Table 3.3 The tourism balance (receipts–expenditure) by WTO regions 1989 and 1997

Region	1989 US$ million	1997 US$ million
Americas	8,149	35,289
Europe	12,463	14,952
Middle East	780	3,815
Africa	828	2,043
South Asia	849	1,825
East Asia Pacific	−4,300	484

Source: WTO (1999) World Tourism Highlights, http://www.world-tourism.org

Table 3.4 Trends of international tourism receipts by WTO region: average annual growth rate 1989–98

Region	Increase 1989–98 (US$ billion)	Average 1989–93	Annual 1994–98	Growth rate (%) 1989–98
Africa	5.1	8.7	8.7	8.8
Americas	59.8	10.9	5.9	8.0
East Asia Pacific	34.4	12.0	2.0	8.0
Europe	113.0	9.0	6.5	7.9
Middle East	3.5	6.1	5.8	6.6
South Asia	2.4	7.9	9.0	9.1
World	218.2	9.9	5.9	7.9

Source: WTO (1999) World Tourism Highlights, http://www.world-tourism.org

Table 3.5 International tourist arrivals by region 1989–98

Region	1989	1990	1991	1992	1993	1994	1995	1996	1997	1998
World										
Arrivals (millions)	426.5	458.2	464.0	502.8	518.3	553.3	568.5	599.6	619.6	635.1
% annual change	8.0	7.4	1.2	8.4	3.1	6.7	2.7	5.5	3.3	2.5
Africa										
Arrivals (millions)	13.8	15.1	16.2	18.0	18.5	19.1	20.3	21.9	23.2	24.7
% annual change	10.5	9.0	7.6	11.3	2.8	2.9	6.6	7.8	5.9	6.4
Americas										
Arrivals (millions)	87.0	93.6	96.7	103.6	103.6	106.5	110.6	116.9	118.9	112.7
% annual change	4.7	7.6	3.3	7.1	0.0	2.8	3.8	5.7	1.7	3.2
East Asia Pacific										
Arrivals (millions)	47.8	54.6	56.4	64.2	71.2	76.8	81.4	89.0	88.0	86.6
% annual change	1.6	14.3	3.4	13.8	10.8	7.9	5.9	9.4	−1.1	−1.6
Europe										
Arrivals (millions)	266.3	282.9	283.0	302.4	310.1	334.3	338.5	353.3	369.8	381.1
% annual change	10.5	6.2	0.1	6.9	2.5	7.8	1.3	4.4	4.7	3.0
Middle East										
Arrivals (millions)	8.6	9.0	8.4	10.9	11.4	12.8	13.5	14.1	14.8	15.0
% annual change	1.4	4.6	−6.6	30.5	4.4	12.3	5.6	4.3	5.3	1.4
South Asia										
Arrivals (millions)	3.0	3.2	3.3	3.6	3.5	3.9	4.2	4.4	4.8	5.0
% annual change	6.5	3.9	3.2	9.9	−2.0	10.1	8.6	5.6	9.0	4.1

Source: WTO (1999) World Tourism Highlights, http://www.world-tourism.org

Table 3.6 World's top 20 tourism destinations

Rank			Countries	Arrivals ('000s)
1990	1995	1998		1998
1	1	1	France	70,000
3	3	2	Spain	47,749
2	2	3	United States	46,395
4	4	4	Italy	34,829
7	5	5	UK	25,750
12	8	6	China	25,073
8	7	7	Mexico	19,810
10	11	8	Canada	18,825
27	9	9	Poland	18,820
6	10	10	Austria	17,352
9	13	11	Germany	16,511
16	12	12	Czech Republic	16,325
17	18	13	Russian Federation	15,810
5	6	14	Hungary	15,000
14	17	15	Portugal	11,200
13	16	16	Greece	11,077
11	14	17	Switzerland	11,025
19	15	18	China, Hong Kong, SAR	9,575
20	22	19	Netherlands	9,102
24	20	20	Turkey	8,960

Source: WTO (1999) World Tourism Highlights, http://www.world-tourism.org

Table 3.7 Hotel and accommodation capacity: thousands of bed-places and market share

Region	Bed-places ('000s)			Market share (%)		
	1980	1985	1997	1980	1985	1997
Europe	8,542	8,637	11,731	52.5	47.3	40.0
Americas	6,436	6,933	9,346	39.5	38.0	31.8
East Asia Pacific	763	1,694	6,726	4.7	9.3	22.9
Africa	269	525	835	1.7	2.9	2.8
Middle East	141	254	400	0.9	1.4	1.4
South Asia	126	198	310	0.8	1.1	1.1
Total	16,277	18,241	29,347	100	100	100

Source: WTO (1999) World Tourism Highlights, http://www.world-tourism.org

Tourism Policy and International Tourism in OECD Member Countries. Although the data collected are restricted to 25 countries, the publication deals with other issues such as government policy and barriers to international tourism.

International data on urban tourism

Tourism statistics collated by the OECD and the WTO are largely based on the information that governments supply to them in relation to the criteria set out by each organisation. Despite the existence of the WTO and OECD data sources, which document different aspects of domestic tourism, neither organisation collects data that directly assess urban tourism. For this reason, one must look to more specialised international sources to identify patterns, trends and the associated impact of urban tourism. This is supported by Shaw and Williams (1994: 212) who argued that 'unfortunately it is difficult to document the scale and importance of urban tourism in a comparative context, since few statistics exist'. Even so, a number of valid sources exist which are reviewed later, combined with the former journal published briefly by Travel and Tourism Intelligence (now owned by MINTEL) – *City Reports*, which identify the scale and volume of tourism in selected tourist cities. The result is that researchers have to revert to individual locations and tourism organisations (e.g. National and Regional Tourism Organisations – see Pearce 1992 for a discussion of these organisations), city governments and commercial bodies who have a vested interest in assembling market intelligence on urban tourism (see Touche Ross 1991). For this reason, it is pertinent to consider the types of data available in WTO and OECD publications which may be used as an indirect measure of the scale and volume of urban tourism that can be supplemented by more in-depth studies.

One important indicator recorded by the WTO and the OECD is the amount and use made of tourist accommodation by domestic and international tourists in relation to the occupancy and volume of usage. But what relevance does this have to establishing estimates of urban tourism? Within the tourism literature, accommodation is normally regarded as a 'supply-side' variable (Bull 1991; Page *et al.* 2001), but its use can be regarded as indicative of the aggregate demand generated by tourists. Therefore, if one makes the assumption that serviced tourist accommodation (e.g. hotels and guest houses) has a tendency to locate in urban areas (Ashworth 1989), it is clear that tourists will stay in locations where accommodation is available. In fact tourist accommodation is the main source used by Shaw and Williams (1994) to illustrate the scale of tourism in major European cities. Of course, there are many situations where hotels locate outside urban areas (e.g. country house hotels and similar establishments in rural areas) but the combination of serviced accommodation in tourist cities, seaside resorts and specialised resorts makes an overwhelming case for arguing that accommodation tends to locate close to urban areas in relation to tourist demand and volume (the locational characteristics of hotels is dealt with in more detail in the next chapter).

Accommodation provides the base for tourists staying in one location for a holiday or travelling on a package or itinerary to visit other urban places on a predefined circuit (Pearce 1987), although the weakness of using serviced accommodation as an approximation of demand is that it may not capture those tourists staying with friends and relatives and camping. Therefore, while not being able to identify the precise patterns of urban tourism for individual countries from WTO and OECD data, it is possible to look at the patterns of arrivals to individual countries (i.e. arrivals at frontiers and gateways) and to compare those statistics with tourist use of accommodation. Admittedly, a proportion of tourist use of accommodation will be non-urban in some cases but a significant proportion will be urban and this is a useful starting point for the assessment of the scale of urban tourism. This provides researchers with initial estimates of the likely scale of urban tourism and is a starting point for more detailed investigation of the situation in individual countries and their urban tourist destinations, if appropriate data exist. The example shown in Table 3.7 provides an illustration of the recent patterns of tourist demand as measured by tourist accommodation.

The international scale of urban tourism demand

Among the most useful studies that examines the availability of data on urban tourism is Cockerell's (1997) analysis of the situation in Europe. Cockerell (1997) recognised that information on urban-based business travel was notoriously difficult to monitor, since it was often associated with a range of non-tourism functions and more specific activities located in towns and cities due to their central place functions in regions and countries, notably the meetings, incentives, conferences and exhibitions (MICE) market. The specialist nature of the facilities and infrastructure required for such business means they are frequently located in urban areas to make use of complementary facilities such as accommodation, transport hubs (i.e. airports) and the wider range of tourist attractions to provide the wider context for MICE venues.

Within a European context, Cockerell (1997) indicated that comparative data on urban tourism rarely exist owing to the different survey methodologies, sampling techniques and inconsistency in the use of terminology or agreement on what an urban tourist is. For example, many European surveys do not consider the day trip and excursion market as a pure form of urban tourism, and therefore exclude them from surveys. Yet these markets are major users of towns and cities for leisure, recreation and tourism activities (see Hall and Page 1999 for a fuller discussion of the tourism–recreation continuum). The problem of recognising users of urban tourism is compounded by the manner in which national surveys of tourism fail to recognise that many coastal resorts are in fact urban tourism destinations. Furthermore, researchers have also overlooked a number of fundamental geographical concepts. For example, many trips to towns and cities are multidestination in character – people visit more than one city on a trip. This seemingly simple concept is evident from tourism geography. Forer and Pearce's (1984) study of coach tours in New Zealand recognised that distinct tourist circuits existed in time and space, structured around organised tourist itineraries, a feature subsequently analysed by Woo and Page (1999) in relation to Korean tourists' urban travel patterns in New Zealand. Each study highlighted the pivotal role of urban places in the activity patterns and daily programmes of touring. Similarly, Forer and Page's (1998) spatial modelling of tourism flows in Northland, New Zealand, identified the role of:

- tourist itineraries and urban-based visits;
- circuit tourism where urban places were important service centres and locations for activities;
- the dominance of urban centres, even where non-urban holidays were taken in coastal areas where holiday homes (bachs) existed;
- multi-destination trips within the region, structured and influenced by road patterns, the available attractions where a mix of rural and urban destinations were often visited in one day;
- day trips and excursion traffic from the main New Zealand city – Auckland – which is both a seasonal but dominant market (Commons and Page 2001).

What these examples illustrate is that urban tourism is a complex phenomenon to understand from a demand perspective once a researcher moves from examining isolated examples of specific towns and cities to considering the dynamics of tourism demand in a wider spatial context. In this respect, urban tourism is methodologically complex to model if one wants to understand how different destinations are linked in a system of visitation and demand. Urban visits and tourist use of towns and cities are multifaceted and structured around different motives, and destinations do not exist in isolation. They are complementary and complete in the wider context of tourist travel patterns and the experience of tourism. The analysis and understanding of these features of tourism demand and the interrelationships with urban places is what the geographer is well suited to (Hall and Page 2002). The difficulty in constructing an analysis of urban tourism demand with a number of temporal and spatial dimensions beyond an individual location is solely dictated by the availability of data.

Cockerell (1997) pointed to the only pan-European data source – *The European Travel Monitor* (ETM). The section on city trips only refers to the holiday sector, ignoring business and VFR travel (visiting friends and relations) and only including international trips involving a minimum stay of one night. A number of other data sources, including academic studies (e.g. Mazanec 1997b) and research institutes in Paris, namely the *Instit National pur la Recherche dans les Transports et leur Sécurité* (INRETS) and the Venice-based *Centro Internazionale di Studi sull'Economica Turistica* (CISET), have generated research data on urban tourism demand.

The European Travel Monitor and urban tourism

In 1996, the European Travel Monitor (ETM) found that Europeans made 33 million city trips abroad; 23 million of the trips were long holidays of four nights or more, and 10 million trips were short breaks of one to three nights in duration. Although nearly 30 per cent of city trips were short breaks, this appeared to be the most significant type of European short break, reflected in the wide range of packaged and unpackaged options. In the late 1990s, this phenomenon was given an artificial boost by the establishment of low-cost airlines in Europe, particularly those in the UK such as Go, EasyJet and Virgin, and discounted fares offered by established carriers such as Ryanair, British Midland and KLMUK. Many of the additional trips generated by low-cost airlines and new infrastructure options such as the Channel Tunnel and Eurostar Service have been short-break oriented, leisure-based and targeted at key urban centres in secondary destinations which complement the established primary tourist cities (e.g. London, Paris, Amsterdam, Geneva, Brussels and Madrid).

The fact is that many urban holiday trips are secondary trips, complementing the traditional summer long annual holiday which is coastal-based. The factors behind the rise of secondary urban trips (excluding the attraction of cheap low-cost airfares) include a number of structural changes among the European travelling population:

- Increased holiday and leave entitlements.
- The availability of public and national holidays which encourage 'long weekends' that are ideal for short breaks.
- Rising prosperity from double income families with greater disposable income.
- Changing perceptions of travel with relative reductions in price convenience and the availability of transport options, making it a social, psychological and recreational necessity.
- Time–space compression, where improvements in transport technology (e.g. the advent of the high-speed trains and the development of regional air services outside the main national gateway) have made access to destinations for short breaks a reality, avoiding multiple-travel options to national airports.

In terms of the main outbound markets, the ETM found that five origin markets generated 54 per cent of all trips, with almost 25 per cent generated by Germany. This is shown in Table 3.8 where the market potential of Germany is still to be fully realised. Cockerell (1997) supported this assertion, referring to a survey in early 1997 by Urlaub and Reisen which indicated that at least 17 per cent of the German population took at least one city break in 1996 (in Germany and overseas). The main demand for this product was heavily represented by the 20–39 age group without children who were in the upper income group. The second largest market in 1995 was the former Soviet Union,

Table 3.8 European city trips[a] by leading markets, 1995

Market	Total trips	% of market share	% booked through trade
Germany	8.1	26	51
CIS[b]	2.5	8	28
UK	2.2	7	67
Italy	2.1	7	57
France	1.9	6	59
Spain	1.6	5	61
Switzerland	1.5	5	46
Belgium/Luxembourg	1.4	5	32
Netherlands	1.3	4	56
Poland	1.2	4	31
Austria	1.0	3	48
Sweden	1.0	3	57
Finland	0.8	3	76
Denmark	0.5	2	61
Norway	0.5	2	64
Total (incl. others)	31.0	100	52

[a] Estimates of holiday trips only – excludes business travel and visits to friends and relations (VFR).
[b] Russia, Belarus and Ukraine.
Source: European Travel Monitor (ETM) cited in Cockerell (1997: 49).
© Travel and Tourism Intelligence

particularly the three countries of Russia, Belarus and the Ukraine in the Commonwealth of Independent States.

In a French context, the former annual survey of urban travel conducted by the Institut National de la Statistique et des Etudes Economiques (INSEE) found that between 1981 and 1992 urban leisure travel doubled. The proportion of short break travel increased from 35 per cent to 50 per cent of the total in the same period. In 1994 INRETS analysis of transport and urban tourism estimated the total volume of city trips (of at least one night) at 124 million a year, generating 370 million nights, of which 60 per cent were short breaks. The INRETS survey was unique because it analysed all forms of travel and found that VFR accounted for 35 per cent of trips, business travel 10 per cent and holiday trips 33 per cent while special events and shopping each accounted for 6 per cent. Of these trips, 73 per cent were undertaken by car and 21 per cent involved hotel accommodation.

The ETM found that 50 per cent of trips to urban destinations were booked through the travel trade (e.g. travel agents, online or by telephone), with a strong relationship with packaged products especially in countries with poor access. On mainland Europe, independent travel to stay in and visit city destinations is more common.

Table 3.9 illustrates the dominant destinations for city trips, where London dominates the pattern. The major weakness with Table 3.9 is that it only

Table 3.9 Hotel arrivals and bed-nights in some of Europe's favourite cities, 1995

City	Arrivals (million)	Bed-nights
London[a]	23.7	100.0
Paris	11.3	24.8
Rome	5.4	12.8
Prague[b]	5.2	NA
Madrid	4.3	8.4
Munich	3.1	6.1
Florence[c]	2.6	5.9
Barcelona	3.1	5.7
Vienna	2.0	5.0
Brussels[d]	NA	3.3
Copenhagen	NA	3.1
Budapest	1.2	3.0
Oslo	NA	2.0
Frankfurt	1.0	1.8
Geneva	0.7	1.6

[a] Figures from the London Tourist Board are not strictly comparable
 as they include arrivals in all other forms of accommodation as well as hotels.
[b] Based on actual figures for Jan.–Sep.
[c] Based on actual figures for Jan.–June.
[d] 1994 data.
Source: Cockerell (1997: 53).
© Travel and Tourism Intelligence

enumerates tourists of European origin and does not consider other visitors. When one refers to accommodation for selected tourist cities in Europe in 1995, these statistics provide an indication of how difficult it is to harmonise urban tourism statistics and to establish acceptable measures.

Harmonising urban tourism statistics

According to Wöber (1997b: 26)

> research in [sic] tourism is usually based on accommodation statistics, results from sample surveys of guests, accommodation providers or other experts, or estimates achieved by grossing up procedures using other statistical sources. Even elementary tourism data like nights, arrivals, number of beds, number of accommodation establishments, occupancy rates or length of stay may vary significantly between cities.

Therefore, to derive data on international patterns of urban tourism requires cities to conduct research using identical surveys and methodologies, while standardising the terminology such as city, tourist, hotel, expenditure and trip. Since the reality of the situation is a multiplicity of different research studies and data lacking consistency, one has to work within the confines of what is available.

In the mid 1990s, Wöber was commissioned by the Federation of European Cities Tourist Offices (FECTO) to examine the harmonisation of city tourism statistics (Wöber 1997b, 2000). This represents one of the major methodological breakthroughs in attempting to harmonise urban tourism data in Europe (see http://tourmis.wu-wien.ac.at for FECTO data site). What Wöber (2000) explained was the process by which the majority of European cities received their accommodation statistics from official registrations of accommodation establishments among 72.8 per cent of the 83 cities involved. Some 15.8 per cent of city statistics were derived from sample surveys of visitors, while a further 9.2 per cent were derived from national or regional tourism statistics. Of the 83 participating European Cities Tourist Offices, 93.5 per cent had time series data (i.e. historical data) on overnight stays and 83.8 per cent had visitor arrival statistics. Although a certain degree of statistical manipulation of the data was possible, Wöber (1997b) also explored the methodological problem of establishing missing data values in the time series statistics to estimate values from different data sources thus:

$$L = \frac{N}{A}$$

and

$$O = \frac{C}{N}$$

where

L = average length of stay
N = number of bed-nights
A = number of arrivals
O = average occupancy rate per year
C = annual bed capacity

Source: Wöber (2000: 57)

However, the calculation of missing values may not be possible in some cities where missing data for a number of categories of information exists. What Wöber (2000) explored was the value of combining a conventional database system with an expert system (Moutinho *et al.* 1996). The outcome of this approach – the tourism marketing information system (Tour Mis) – has been maintained by FECTO and the Austrian National Tourist Office (see http://tourmis.wu-wien.ac.at) – and the results for FECTO members are contained in Table 3.10. Clearly this example of a pan-European project highlights

Table 3.10   Domestic and international visitor arrivals and bed-nights in selected urban tourism destinations in 1995 based on FECTO data

Destination	Visitor arrivals	Bed-nights	Duration of stay
Aachen	270,000	707,000	2.6
Aix-en-Provence	m-d	1,336,000	m-d
Amsterdam	m-d	6,584,300	m-d
Athens	2,057,479	4,689,178	2.3
Augsburg	263,000	416,000	1.6
Baden-Baden	244,000	771,000	3.2
Barcelona	3,090,000	5,674,580	1.8
Basel	314,457	606,080	1.9
Berlin	3,166,000	7,529,639	2.4
Bern	235,903	448,839	1.9
Bonn	491,245	1,037,372	2.1
Bordeaux	m-d	913,295	m-d
Bratislava	353,851	724,878	2.0
Bregenz	119,242	223,017	1.9
Bremen	484,753	896,212	1.8
Brussels	m-d	3,302,099	m-d
Budapest	1,636,909	4,327,671	2.6
Cagliari	129,000	290,000	2.2
Cologne	1,362,255	2,622,685	1.9
Copenhagen	m-d	3,080,000	m-d
Dijon	526,655	750,953	1.4
Dublin	m-d	m-d	m-d
Dubrovnik	m-d	m-d	m-d
Dusseldorf	1,088,768	2,163,253	2.0
Edinburgh	2,190,000	9,700,000	4.4
Eisenstadt	16,336	30,069	1.8
Florence	2,512,459	6,455,060	2.6
Frankfurt	1,794,636	3,174,009	1.8
Freiburg	330,024	623,426	1.9
Geneva	292,835	2,119,892	2.3
Genoa	432,941	1,058,200	2.4
Gent	211,000	404,000	1.9
Glasgow	1,500,000	6,900,000	4.6
Graz	246,420	479,439	1.9
Hamburg	2,271,694	4,164,533	1.8
Heidelberg	488,720	781,469	1.6
Helsinki	1,106,840	1,914,561	1.7
Innsbruck	598,277	1,005,526	1.7
Karlsruhe	260,854	501,678	1.9
Klagenfurt	140,703	327,575	2.3
Lausanne	260,000	623,000	2.4
Leipzig	434,008	1,042,568	2.4
Linz	295,000	542,000	1.8
Lisbon	1,477,784	3,267,760	2.2
Ljubljana	140,950	313,192	2.2
London	22,611,000	103,300,000	4.6
Lubeck	357,837	825,370	2.3

Table 3.10   (cont'd)

Destination	Visitor arrivals	Bed-nights	Duration of stay
Lucerne	m-d	m-d	m-d
Luxembourg City	308,948	683,043	2.2
Lyon	1,558,038	2,375,675	1.5
Madrid	4,281,000	8,371,630	2.0
Malta	1,115,000	10,919,000	9.8
Manchester	3,300,000	11,000,000	3.3
Mannheim	m-d	m-d	m-d
Marseille	m-d	m-d	m-d
Milan	2,532,402	6,004,656	2.4
Moscow	991,577	5,439,358	5.5
Munich	3,080,923	6,126,930	2.0
Munster	357,373	1,169,385	3.3
Nice	m-d	m-d	m-d
Olomouc	107,507	171,942	1.6
Oslo	1,300,839	2,101,578	1.6
Padua	377,500	825,500	2.2
Paris	11,345,751	24,813,248	2.2
Prague	1,805,286	5,104,409	2.8
Regensburg	251,084	485,041	1.9
Rome	554,849	13,346,206	2.4
Rostock	288,648	724,247	2.5
Salzburg	831,000	1,570,000	1.9
San Sebastian	m-d	m-d	m-d
Zaragoza	648,219	1,164,283	1.8
Sintra	71,640	189,580	2.6
St Etienne	m-d	m-d	m-d
St Gallen	77,000	181,000	2.4
St Polten	43,239	87,946	2.0
Stockholm	m-d	m-d	m-d
Stuttgart	807,323	1,554,000	1.9
Tarragona	233,010	349,550	1.5
Toulon	m-d	m-d	m-d
Trier	447,200	447,258	1.0
Venice	1,355,361	2,944,329	2.2
Verona	m-d	m-d	m-d
Vicenza	135,882	409,064	3.0
Vienna	2,806,057	7,049,710	2.5
Warsaw	1,341,000	2,048,000	1.5
Wurzburg	337,866	586,127	1.7
Zagreb	259,936	642,148	2.5
Zurich	938,149	1,791,000	1.9

Note: m-d = missing data; see Wöber (2000) for a discussion of the statistical generation of missing values for destinations.
Source: Modified from FECTO (2000) data.

the role of industry organisations such as FECTO in promoting the imp
of urban tourism in Europe. Wöber's (2000) modelling of urban tou
Europe indicated that it was a relatively stable phenomenon. In the
1984–90, the majority of European cities experienced a growth in overnight
stays in accommodation (i.e. bed-nights). After 1991, the impact of an economic recession in Europe led to a stagnation in demand for a number of the
83 cities analysed. By 1995, most cities had achieved a full recovery (see Table
3.10 for 1995 data), although in 1996, visitor numbers dropped by 1.9 per
cent.

Wöber (2000: 64) found that

> The most important generating countries are Germany, the United Kingdom,
> France, the United States, Italy and Spain. Each of them generated more than 10
> million overnights in 83 European cities. The German and Japanese markets
> show a promising development, whereas for the UK, surveyed cities recorded a
> considerable drop in demand between 1987 and 1991. In recent years, the
> Japanese market was one of the most dynamic in European cities and its poten-
> tial for further growth is still promising.

Those countries with between 3.4 and 10 million overnight stays in European
cities were: Sweden, Australasia, Switzerland, Belgium, the Netherlands, Den-
mark, Austria and Norway. Less important markets which generate less than
3.4 million overnight stays were Greece, Canada, Belgium, Poland, Finland
and Hungary.

What emerged from Wöber's (2000) innovative study was that FECTO
members designed a standardised questionnaire for visitor surveys with economies of scale by deriving comparative data. This will assist urban marketers
to understand more fully the market volume and visitor mix in a European
city context. Therefore, in view of the significance of understanding these issues,
attention now focuses on market segmentation techniques.

The identification of urban tourists: market segmentation

Market segmentation is the process developed within marketing to identify
whether

> people with similar needs, wants and characteristics are grouped together so that
> an organisation can use greater precision in serving and communicating with its
> chosen customers. Market segmentation, then, is a two-step process of . . . decid-
> ing how to group all potential tourists (the market segments) and . . . selecting
> specific groups from among these (target markets) to pursue (Mill and Morrison
> 1992: 423).

In other words, market segmentation assumes that various tourist segments exist with different needs, and those tourists in different segments have common characteristics, which enables the tourism industry to develop a product or service that is likely to appeal to these groups. As Middleton (1988), Holloway and Plant (1989) and Kotler and Armstrong (1991) have shown, the process of market segmentation is part of the strategic planning process in tourism marketing in relation to identifying the type of market one is dealing with.

Within the literature on tourism marketing, various approaches can be used to segment the market (S.L.J. Smith 1989) and these use a number of bases to identify the market. To segment the tourist market for products or services, one needs to agree that a potential market exists. Once this assumption is agreed, the marketer usually seeks:

- to measure the value and volume of the market;
- to assess the geographical distribution of the tourist market in different locations or regions, and how it will be reached through marketing and promotion, as well as its likely effectiveness;
- to establish whether the market segments are large enough to support a marketing campaign, or if the segments can be combined with other markets to establish a critical threshold for a financially viable campaign;
- to examine if the market is durable, and to establish whether the attributes of the destination or product are sufficiently distinctive to stand the test of time and the efforts of competitors;
- to consider the competitive advantage of the service provider or destination in its target market.

There are different research methods employed by consultancy companies and marketing and advertising agencies as well as tourism operators to implement the process of market segmentation. Two of the most commonly used techniques are forward segmentation and factor and clustering techniques:

- *Forward segmentation* is where the marketer predetermines the basis for segmentation using existing research data, reports and studies of tourist behaviour. A particular base is used (e.g. geographical origin of visitors or purpose of visit) to establish the likely market. In the case of urban tourism, a short break brochure targeted at North American visitors to Venice may emphasise the cultural and historic appeal of the destination as a particular characteristic in identifying this market segment.

- *Factor and clustering techniques* apply sophisticated statistical techniques on existing sources of tourism data from visitor surveys and tourist intention surveys (i.e. where and why they intend to visit a particular location on their next holiday). For example, the survey information is coded to establish a number of variables and input into a powerful statistical package such as

SPSS-PC (see Ryan 1995 for a fuller discussion of the technique and methodology). The statistical technique is selected to cluster the variables around a series of common themes. The usual outcome is the identification of common groupings of tourists according to their behaviour, preferences and activities. A good illustration of this can be found in Clark *et al.* (1993) in the context of British package holidaymakers and health problems they experienced in Malta.

Mill and Morrison (1992) suggest that there are a range of approaches one can use in market segmentation which include the following:

- *Demographic or socio-economic segmentation,* which occurs where statistical data such as the census are used together with other statistical information to identify the scale and volume of potential tourists likely to visit an urban area. Key factors such as age and income are important as these are important determinants of the demand. For example, the amount of paid holidays and an individual or family's income have an important bearing on demand. Holloway and Plant (1989) highlight the value of social class in identifying the spending potential of tourists. In the UK, the Institute of Practitioners in Advertising use the following socio-economic grouping:
  A   Higher managerial, administrative or professional;
  B   Middle managerial, administrative or professional;
  C1   Supervisory, clerical or managerial;
  C2   Skilled manual workers;
  D   Semi- and unskilled manual workers;
  E   Pensioners, the unemployed, casual or lowest grade workers
  (after Holloway and Plant 1989).
  There are a number of variants on this classification, but they tend to have one common purpose in relation to tourism: to group people according to their income potential and propensity to spend discretionary time and income on travel (see below for a discussion of discretionary time). For example, in the UK those people in categories A and B account for 40 per cent of the market for short breaks and visits to heritage and cultural attractions (Holloway and Plant 1989). Although one cannot predict the destinations and urban locations of potential tourists from such classifications, they do help to segment the market for urban tourism when the group behaviour and activities of such people are examined. However, an important facilitating factor (and constraining factor when there is an absence of it) is leisure time and annual holiday entitlement.
    The availability of time for travel is a significant factor which conditions the potential for tourist trips. Researchers normally express the amount of time available for tourist trips as *discretionary time* – that time remaining after one has fulfilled daily obligations such as working, sleeping, shopping,

housework and childcare. In the context of urban tourism, both the daily and weekly amount of time available for leisure trips to urban areas and the annual holiday entitlement of different groups helps to shape the potential demand for urban tourist trips. As most tourism analysts note, the amount of leisure time and annual holiday entitlement in Westernised countries has risen since 1945 and this has helped fuel a growth in these forms of activities. Although there is often a tendency by tourism researchers to distinguish between leisure time for weekend recreational or day trips and annual holiday entitlement used for short breaks (a holiday of up to three days) and long holidays, it is the individual or family's predisposition towards using leisure or holiday time for specific activities that affects the outcome – visits to urban areas.

The growth of consumer spending associated with tourism and leisure expenditure now competes with other forms of discretionary spending in advanced industrial societies. It is important to note that urban areas in Europe benefited from the growth in short break holidays in the 1980s and 1990s, as such spending by people in groups A, B and C1 is reflected in second and third holidays. Yet criticisms of using socio-economic data as predictors of tourist segmentation has meant that there has been a trend towards including the concept of life cycle into the segmentation process. This is a combination of a household's marital status, age, children and ages which is incorporated with the socio-economic data. It assists the marketer in identifying those groups that have the most disposable income for tourism and leisure spending, typically when they reach middle age, have no children at home and have paid off a mortgage.

- *Product-related segmentation* occurs where the tourist market is identified in relation to the product available and the demand for it. One difficulty with this approach is that other aspects of consumer behaviour are often introduced from other forms of segmentation such as psychographic approaches.

- *Psychographic segmentation* is often introduced to complement more simplistic approaches based on socio-economic or geographic data. It involves the complex process of using socio-economic and life-cycle data to predict a range of consumer behaviours or purchasing patterns associated with each stage (see Table 3.11). This is further developed by examining the psychological profile of consumers to establish their traits or characteristics in relation to different market segments. The VALs (Value and Lifestyles) research conducted by the Stanford Research Institute in North America used socio-economic data, the aspirations, self-images, values and consumption patterns of Americans to establish nine lifestyles that people could move through. This has been followed by other forms of lifestyle segmentation in consumer behaviour research to reduce the complex reality of the market for products and services into a series of identifiable groupings.

Table 3.11   A traditional family life cycle

Stage in life cycle	Buying or behaviour pattern
1. Bachelor stage: young, single people not living at home	Few financial burdens; fashion opinion leaders; recreation oriented; buy basic kitchen equipment, basic furniture, cars, equipment for the mating game, holidays.
2. Newly married couples: young, no children	Better off financially than they will be in near future; highest purchase rate and highest average purchase of durables; buy cars, refrigerators, cookers, sensible and durable furniture, holidays.
3. Full nest I: youngest child under 6	Home purchasing at peak; liquid assets low; dissatisfied with financial position and amount of money saved; interested in new products; buy washers, dryers, TV, baby food, chest rubs and cough medicines, vitamins, dolls' prams, sleds, skates.
4. Full nest II: youngest child 6 or over	Financial position better; some wives work; less influenced by advertising; buy larger-sized packages, multiple-unit deals; buy many foods, cleaning materials, bicycles, music lessons, pianos.
5. Full nest III: older couples with dependent children	Financial position still better; more wives work; some children get jobs; hard to influence with advertising; high average purchase of durables; buy new, more tasteful furniture, auto travel, non-necessary appliances, boats, dental services, magazines.
6. Empty nest I: older couples, no children living with them, head in labour force	Home ownership at peak; most satisfied with financial position and money saved; interested in travel, recreation, self-education; make gifts and contributions; not interested in new products; buy holidays, luxuries, home improvements.
7. Empty nest II: older married couples, no children living at home, head retired	Drastic cut in income; keep home; buy medical care products that improve health, sleep and digestion.
8. Solitary survivor, in labour force	Income still good, but likely to sell home.
9. Solitary survivor, retired	Same medical and product needs as other retired group; drastic cut in income; special need for attention, affection and security.

Source: From Wells and Gubar (1986) cited in Mill and Morrison (1992).

- *Geographical segmentation* is commonly used to assess the catchment and accessibility of the destination to each market and their propensity to travel. Such approaches are frequently used by organisations such as the London Tourist Board to establish which markets to target for promotional campaigns overseas. Table 3.12 provides a geographical segmentation for urban tourists for London in 1998.

- *Purpose of trip* is used to segment markets to distinguish between a number of simple categories of tourists such as day-trippers, business travellers and visiting friends and relatives (see Table 3.13).

Table 3.12   Geographical origin of international visitors to London in 1991 and 1998

	1991 (%)	1998 (%)
USA	19.0	21.4
France	9.1	16.1
Germany	8.9	8.8
Italy	5.2	5.2
Netherlands	4.8	4.6
Japan	4.7	3.5
Spain	4.1	3.5
Sweden	4.4	3.3
Australia	3.4	3.1
Belgium	2.7	3.0
Other countries	33.6	33.5
Total visits (millions)	9.2	13.5

Source: modified from the International Passenger Survey, Office for National Statistics.

Table 3.13   Purpose of trip to London by international and domestic visitors in 1991 and 1998[a]

	Overseas visits		Domestic visits	
	1991 (%)	1998 (%)	1991 (%)	1998 (%)
Holiday	49	50	41	27
VFR	16	17	31	53
Business/conference	23	22	21	16
Other	12	11	6	4
Total visits[b] (millions)	9.2	13.5	6.6	11.6

[a] Staying one night or more.
[b] Total visits include visits made by residents of the Irish Republic, but percentages are based on figures which exclude them.
Source: Office for National Statistics (2000: 105). *Focus on London*, based on the International Passenger Survey and United Kingdom Tourism Survey sponsored by the National Tourist Boards.
© Crown Copyright

- *Behavioural segmentation* is a relatively recent approach to defining markets. It has been used in recent years by airlines to highlight frequent flyers and the particular marketing potential for cultivating a group of customers to maintain brand loyalty for a product by offering service enhancements where frequent use is made of the service.

- *Channel of distribution segmentation* is used where other organisations (e.g. intermediaries) can assist in marketing the product to a distinct group of clients. Here the marketer needs to establish who makes up the target market and what type of distribution channel to use. The most commonly used outlet for the marketing of short city breaks are travel agencies who receive a commission on the sale of products and services. These points are summarised in Table 3.14 which identifies the variables one needs to consider in any form of market segmentation.

Within marketing, positioning has also emerged as a complementary technique to segmentation techniques examining the position of tourism products in the marketplace, particularly urban tourism. This focuses on the users'

Table 3.14   Attitude questionnaire used for positioning of six European city destinations

Can you please indicate how much you think each city offers of the benefits listed below.
Use a scale from 1 to 6 where 1 offers nothing at all and 6 very much.
It does not matter if you have not visited the cities yet or that you do not know them very well. What counts is your impression of them.
Please fill in every space.

	Vienna	Prague	Budapest	Barcelona	Paris	Venice
1. Quality and type of accommodation						
2. Entertainment facilities						
3. Ambience of the city						
4. Cultural resources						
5. Attractiveness of price levels						
6. Accessibility of tourist amenities						
7. Accessibility of the city						
8. Location of the city						
9. Originality of the city						
10. Welcoming attitude of the local population						
11. Shopping facilities						
12. Quality of food and beverages						

Source: Grabler (1997b: 104).

cognitive elements and perception of destinations in a competitive context. For this reason, attention now focuses on positioning.

The positioning of European tourism cities: perceptions and consumer behaviour

Grabler (1997a) examined the development of positioning in tourism research as a technique to visualise consumers' perceptions, using the availability of new techniques such as correspondence analysis (Calantone et al. 1989; Gartner 1989; Feng and Page 2000; Bentley et al. 2001) to combine both strengths and weaknesses of urban tourism and visitor perception in a multidimensional context. Grabler (1997a) employed perceptual mapping techniques for six European tourist cities, combining the preferences of respondents. The underlying hypothesis that Grabler (1997a) set out to examine was that the more favourable the perception of a city, then the higher the visitor preferences for that destination, based on the earlier research by Goodrich (1978). Although much of the early research in this area used factor analysis, discriminate analysis and multidimensional analysis, the development of correspondence analysis for use with nominal data offers a new tool for researchers as used by Grabler (1997a).

According to Grabler (1997a: 103)

> The main determinants for the perception of cities are the product familiarity (knowledge) and the origin of the respondent. This is a further indicator of product knowledge and a more general indicator of the awareness, but it includes information of different perceptions due to national differences. It is known that country or regional images may differ according to the geographic distance of the respondents. Other main variables influencing the perception of different cities are consumer characteristics such as previous travel experience, demographics or lifestyle

which have also been examined by Manrai and Manrai (1993). As a result, the attitude model posits that perceptions of cities are likely to influence the preferences, intentions to visit and the ultimate decision to visit a city. What perceptual maps help to explain using correspondence analysis are the different segments and their preference structures.

Grabler (1997a) selected Vienna, Prague, Budapest, Barcelona, Paris and Venice as a sub-set of European competitors which was examined in Grabler et al. (1996). Some twelve attributes were identified and incorporated in a questionnaire (Table 3.14) using a six-point Likert scale. Regardless of knowledge of each city, respondents were asked to evaluate each city, providing an attribute-based image (see Echtner and Ritchie 1993 for more detail), where all elements in the survey are assumed to be of importance to respondents. The

initial description of survey respondents, who comprised equal
German and British tourists, indicated that Germans liked the a
city followed by the attractiveness and price when going on a city t
and entertainment were of less importance. For the British responuents, unc
importance of food and beverages, the ambience and cultural resources were
the most important factors. Shopping and entertainment were also the least
important for the British visitor. Using factor analysis, the basic facets of the
destination (i.e. infrastructure) and image appeal emerged as the two key factors. A series of perceptual maps highlighted the German's greater product
knowledge, which was likely to be a function of geographical proximity to
most of the destinations. The relative position of each city was then examined.

Grabler (1997b) found that three dimensions affect the preference formulation, where the image appeal is of a greater significance than infrastructure
elements. Image appeal emerged as the main driver of demand, where

> Both price/friendliness and infrastructure can be regarded as 'hygiene factors' that
> must not drop below a certain limit. However, they do not heavily influence the
> liking of a city. Nevertheless, they strongly determine the perception of the cities.
> In general, the importance ratings determine the preferences for particular cities
> more strongly than the perceptional [sic] ratings. The perception of the cities are
> relatively homogeneous. This has clear implications for city marketing. Individual
> segments do not perceive the cities significantly differently. The differences in the
> preferences can be attributed to the needs and values of the segments. This means
> that the marketing manager has primarily to detect those segments for which
> the city offers the attributes which fit the needs of consumers. This calls for a
> thorough refinement of the segmentation procedures applied in marketing urban
> tourism destinations.

The destination image and that which is marketed need to be constantly
evaluated (Lawton and Page 1997), since Bramwell and Rawding (1996)
examined the effectiveness of marketing strategies to target specific sources of
demand.

Having outlined the principles and methods used to identify segments and
the position of urban tourism destinations, attention now turns to the development of a typology of urban tourists, since the previous discussion has highlighted the different types of visitors to urban areas.

Towards a typology of urban tourists

Any assessment of 'who visits' and 'why they visit' urban areas requires one to
develop a typology of urban tourists. According to Blank and Petkovich
(1987), there are a number of important points to consider when attempting to
assess why visitors seek urban tourist destinations, a number of which were
examined in Chapter 1. These are:

- cities are places of high population density, with the result that there is a high propensity to visit friends and relatives;
- urban areas are often the focal point of tourist–transport interchanges and termini;
- the concentration of commercial, financial, industrial and producer services in urban areas acts as a focus for different people to visit cities for employment-related purposes such as conferences, exhibitions, business travel, etc.;
- cities provide a wide range of cultural (see Rinschede 1986, 1990; Jackowski and Smith 1992; Nolan and Nolan 1992), artistic and recreational experiences.

Yet Blank and Petkovich (1987) also argue that while visitors may have a major purpose for visiting urban areas (e.g. for business), they may undertake other activities related to the attractions and facilities in urban destinations. In other words, it is not simply the case that tourists visit such areas for a single purpose. Visits may be motivated by a range of factors. However, for the purposes of developing an initial typology of tourist visits, one has to examine the principal force motivating such a visit.

There have been various attempts to construct typologies of tourists visiting urban areas. For example, research in North America by Blank and Petkovich (1987) identifies the motivating factors associated with visits to urban areas in terms of:

- visiting friends and relatives;
- business/convention;
- outdoor recreation;
- entertainment and sightseeing;
- personal reasons;
- shopping;
- other factors.

Their research noted that the significance of each factor varied by destination and its attraction. Yet this does not deal with the more complex methodological problems of distinguishing between urban tourists. As Jansen-Verbeke (1986: 88) noted, visitors can be distinguished according to 'their place of residence and . . . motives for visiting'. Much of the data relating to visitor demand and motivation for visiting urban areas are based on questionnaire-based research focused on individual locations. It forms part of a wider spectrum of urban tourism research and a range of studies in North America (Blank and Petkovich 1987), the Netherlands (e.g. Jansen-Verbeke 1986; Ashworth and Tunbridge 1990) and the United Kingdom (initiated by local authority and tourist boards) have highlighted a range of commonly cited motives (Table 3.15). But, as Jansen-Verbeke (1986) rightly acknowledges, urban tourists are only one set of visitors using the city because day visitors and residents also

Table 3.15 A typology of urban tourists

- Visiting friends and relatives
- Business travellers
- Conference and exhibition visitors
- Educational tourists
- Cultural and heritage tourists
- Religious travellers (e.g. pilgrims)
- Hallmark event visitors
- Leisure shoppers
- Day visitors

Source: Page (1995a).

have distinct uses for the city. A notable study by Burtenshaw *et al.* (1991) confirmed this finding and identified functional areas within the tourist city which expresses the relationship between the supply and demand for urban services (Figure 3.3). In other words, different visitors to cities have a wide range of motivating factors shaping their visit which emphasises the significance of motivation research to understand the different groups of users. Burtenshaw *et al.* (1991) identify both the demand from users including:

- city residents;
- city-region residents;
- visitors seeking pleasure from their visit;
- conference visitors;
- people working within the city

and the resources the users use including:

- historic monuments;
- museums and galleries;
- theatres and concert halls;
- night clubs and the red-light area;
- cafés and restaurants;
- shops; and
- offices in which the workers undertake their employment.

As a result, urban tourists are but one set of users in the multifunctional city which comprises the 'historic city', the 'cultural city', the 'business city', the 'sport city', the 'nightlife city', the 'leisure shopping city' and the 'tourist city'. The latter embraces all of the other functional cities and their resources (see Chapter 5).

What is clear from existing studies is that the multifunctional nature of tourist cities complicates any attempt to develop a complex typology or taxonomy of users. As emphasised above, devising a simple classification of users based on a single motive for visiting is straightforward until the functional

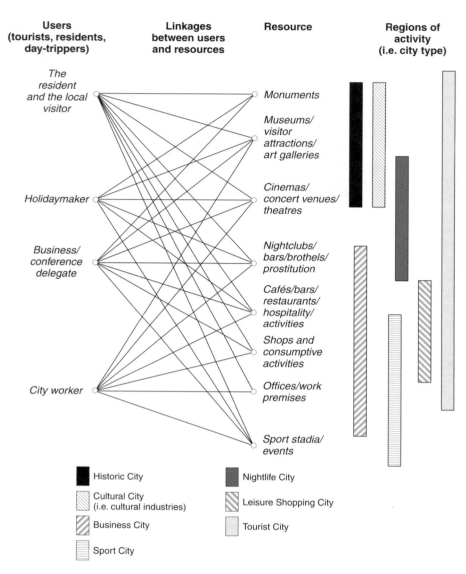

| Users (tourists, residents, day-trippers) | Linkages between users and resources | Resource | Regions of activity (i.e. city type) |

Figure 3.3 Functional areas in the tourist city (source: modified and developed from Burtenshaw *et al.* 1991)

areas in cities noted by Jansen-Verbeke (1986), Ashworth (1989) and Burtenshaw *et al.* (1991) are acknowledged. In other words, simple labels such as 'tourist', 'day-tripper', 'excursionist' or 'business traveller' are descriptive and assume that the use of services and facilities is for one specific purpose.

Although the market segmentation approaches discussed above can also be descriptive and 'may appear superficially similar in their division of actual or latent users into categories . . . these are based upon the actual nature of the use itself rather than any general characteristics of groups of users' (Ashworth and Tunbridge 1990: 119).

Therefore, a segmentation approach is a useful starting point in developing a classification of urban tourists in the multifunctional tourist city. Ashworth and Tunbridge (1990) develop the approach in terms of the consumer market and motives of visitors using concepts such as the 'purchasing intent' of visitors, the attitudes, opinions and interests of users of specific urban tourism products and the frequency of use. Clearly, the most important issue is the distinction between use/non-use of specific tourism resources within tourist cities and it is useful to introduce their initial division of users of urban tourist areas in terms of:

- intentional users (those motivated by the character of the city);
- incidental users (those who see the character of the city as irrelevant to their use).

By imposing a geographical component to their analysis, Ashworth and Tunbridge (1990: 120–21) also recognise the importance of residents and day visitors in the urban system, thereby identifying four specific types of user in the context of the tourist-historic city:

1. Intentional users from outside the city region, who may be holidaymakers staying in the city or outside it using the city for excursions – *tourists* and in the case of these resources quite specifically *heritage tourists* (see Graham *et al.* 2000).
2. Intentional users from inside the city-region, making use of the city's recreational and entertainment facilities or merely enjoying its historic character while engaging in other activities – *recreating residents*.
3. Incidental users from outside the city-region, which would include most business and congress visitors and those on family visits – *non-recreating visitors*.
4. Incidental users from inside the city-region, the most numerous group being ordinary residents going about their ordinary affairs – *non-recreating residents*.

This typology can be refined for other urban destinations since it recognises the significance of attitudes and the use made of the city and its services rather than the geographical origin of users as a fundamental starting point in the segmentation. Yet as Ashworth and Tunbridge (1990) observe, the difficulty in operationalising such an approach is the tendency for tourists to classify themselves according to the principal reason for visiting the destination while, in reality, any destination will have a range of users akin to the classification above. Nevertheless, Ashworth and de Haan's (1986) study of users in the tourist-historic city of Norwich, based on the self-allocation of the most important reasons for visiting Norwich, supports their multimotivation argument on the diverse uses made of the city by visitors. Even so, among holidaymakers only 50 per cent were intentional users of the historic city while variations existed in the day visitor, business traveller and shoppers' use of the historic city. In terms of the motivation for visiting urban areas, a Dutch survey (NIPO 1990; after Jansen-Verbeke and Lievois 1999) ranged the motives for visiting cities thus:

- sightseeing;
- museums and other attractions;
- shopping;
- visits to friends and relatives;
- wining and dining;
- pub visit.

A study by KPMG (1993), which assessed image building as a determinant of destination choice focusing on 10 European destinations, concluded that the following factors determine the image of place:

- ambience/liveliness of the place;
- the cultural and historic heritage;
- museums;
- tourist attractions;
- cultural activities;
- price;
- security;
- restaurants;
- public transport.

These factors are combined in Table 3.16 which examines the pull factors associated with urban tourist trips, highlighting the fact that urban tourism is deeply embedded in the urban system rather than as a discrete activity.

The multimotivation and multifunctional hypothesis developed by urban tourism researchers emphasises the different purposes and complexity of tourist behaviour in such locations. It is a major development within the urban tourism research to encourage a more complex approach towards the demand and motivation for such visits.

Identifying user groups within an urban environment and their diversity, however, assumes that the demand for visits and activities has no temporal dimension. However, the reality is that the major problems for tourism destinations is the issue of seasonality, which is now examined.

Table 3.16 Pull factors for city trips

General pull factors	Specific pull factors
1. Unique and interesting	Lots to see and to do An interesting place Unique experience
2. Cultural attractions and sightseeing	Well-known landmarks Interesting architecture Noted for history Excellent museums and galleries Interesting local people Different culture and way of life Local customs and traditions
3. Entertainment	Exciting nightlife Exciting shopping Live music Theatre and arts Interesting festivals and events
4. Food and accommodation	Good hotels Sophisticated restaurants Typical cuisine

Source: Jansen-Verbeke and Lievois (1999: 88).

Seasonality in urban tourism demand

Seasonality is a dominant element of tourism demand which is characterised by the peaks and troughs of the demand expressed for particular destinations and their facilities. These peaks and troughs can occur over a long time period (e.g. a year or longer), a short time period (known as periodicity) or in relation to specific activities (e.g. a special event such as the America's Cup yachting event – Plate 3.1). Seasonality in tourism measures fluctuations in demand at the destination and in the use of its facilities, infrastructure and attractions (Cooper *et al.* 1993). Among the most comprehensive studies of seasonality in tourism is BarOn's (1975) study of 16 countries over a 17 year time span and the recent study by Baum and Lundtorp (2001). Butler and Mao (1997: 9) argued that

> The limited literature on seasonality in tourism has several foci, including the relationship of seasonality to demand and visitation; seasonality in specific locations; the economic effects of seasonality, including employment; and attempts to mitigate the levels of seasonality. Little of this literature deals with concepts or theory (Hartmann 1986), or with definitions, causes or problems of measurement, although limited attention has been paid to seasonal variations in types of visitors.

Plate 3.1   Auckland's redeveloped Viaduct Basin prepared for the America's Cup event in 1999–2000

Cooper *et al.* (1993) identify two types of seasonality: additive and multiplicative. Additive seasonality refers to the addition to demand at certain points in the year due to seasonal effects. Multiplicative seasonality, however, refers to the proportional increase or decrease in demand at certain times of the year, which is the dominant form of seasonality. The cycle of seasons (BarOn 1975; Patmore 1983) is thought to be one of the main explanations of seasonality, where weather and climate and the rhythm of the seasons determines the comfort levels for outdoor participation in tourism, recreation and leisure (Commons and Page 2001). In addition, BarOn (1975: 2) identified institutionalised seasonality, where holidays are conditioned by vacation periods in schools, universities and other places of work. In fact, Bull (1995: 4) claimed that 'tourism has one of the most highly seasonal patterns of demand for any product'. Indeed, many early studies in tourism geography (see Hall and Page 1999) focused on the seasonal and temporary nature of tourist movements from urban industrialised areas of Northern Europe to the Mediterranean in the summer season, conceptualised by Christaller (1963) as the 'pleasure periphery'.

Butler and Mao (1997: 10) produced an interesting representation of the factors influencing seasonality in tourism, where a further complication to understanding its dimensions relates to its variance in both time and space (i.e. it affects different tourist cities in different ways); Figure 3.4 summarises these factors. Butler and Mao also illustrate the dynamics of tourism seasonality in

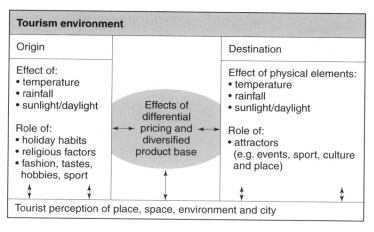

Figure 3.4   Factors affecting seasonality in urban tourism (source: after Butler and Mao 1997)

Figure 3.4. This shows that the interaction of supply, demand and modifying processes helps to explain spatial variations in seasonality. Butler and Mao (1997) identify three types of seasonality in destinations:

1. One-peak seasonality, often associated with coastal resorts and the main summer season or the winter for ski resorts (Plate 3.2).
2. Two-peak seasonality, where two seasons may exist in one year (summer and winter).
3. Non-peak seasonality, which is mainly associated with urban environments, where the centre is non-seasonal in nature but the global seasons of international and domestic visitors may create seasonal patterns of demand.

In existing studies of demand and seasonality (e.g. Murphy 1985), large cities such as London have less pronounced patterns of seasonality than many other types of tourism destination. The continuous operation throughout the year means that urban areas have very little seasonal fluctuation in demand compared to rural or coastal areas. This is often one argument advanced to justify the development of urban tourism because employment opportunities offer more stability for employees. Yet even within urban areas, it is likely that sectoral variations exist in terms of seasonality (Yacoumis 1980) and Shaw and Williams (1994: 155) observed that 'temporal polarisation has the effect of reinforcing spatial polarisation'.

One of the main reasons why urban destinations suffer a lower degree of seasonality is related to the all-year round operation of attractions that are less climatically dependent (e.g. museums, art galleries, historic buildings, leisure

Plate 3.2 Queenstown, South Island of New Zealand: this destination experiences one-peak seasonality with a summer and winter ski season, with its access to the local ski fields and role as a major service centre for adventure tourism activities in the area

shopping, entertainment and hospitality). Indeed, in inclement climates some developers have built enclosed shopping malls such as the West Edmonton Mall, Canada (Finn and Erdem 1995).

Although some urban centres do experience a degree of sectoral seasonality, often related to the geographical origin of visitors, the tourism industry can respond in a number of ways:

- by making changes to the existing product mix;
- through market diversification;
- by differential pricing to facilitate demand;
- through state initiatives such as the staggering of school holidays.

According to BarOn (1999: 2) 'market segments have different seasonality and varied responses to price and other incentives . . . changes may occur [in a destination's seasonality] over the years, due to [unprompted] differential growth of market segments with different seasonality'. What is clear is that

> seasonality has remained a difficult phenomenon to overcome, despite intensive efforts, which suggests the problem is more complex than is often thought. Most efforts to reduce seasonality in demand have concentrated upon the destination

areas rather than the consumer . . . In general these attempts have not been very successful in increasing visitor numbers in the off-peak seasons (Butler and Mao 1997: 20)

which has often increased visitors in the peak season too.

Although the diversity of attractions has helped to increase the all-year-round appeal of urban tourist centres, the accommodation sector faces not only annual but monthly and weekly fluctuations. The demand for business travel during the week has led many hotel chains to offer price reductions for weekend occupancy to reduce the seasonality problem. With the growth of short break holidays in Europe, this is certainly a major boon for the accommodation sector in urban areas if they can match client demand with the availability of appropriately priced supply.

Conclusion

This chapter has indicated that understanding the demand for urban tourism is not a simple mechanistic exercise related to statistical analysis of tourist visits to destinations. The absence of urban tourism statistics at international and national levels in most countries means that most research has emphasised the significance of individual case studies rather than the scale and volume of urban tourism at an international and national scale. Although some useful preliminary approximations of tourism demand can be gauged from the use of accommodation, this approach is not without its problems. Furthermore, it is not appropriate simply to equate demand with aggregate statistics when the motivation and use made of tourist facilities offer many insights into tourist and non-tourist interaction in the urban environment. In fact, the arguments put forward by Ashworth and Tunbridge (1990) criticise simplistic attempts to reduce urban tourists to static classifications which do not incorporate:

- the multifunctional nature of the tourist city;
- the existence of different groups of users within any tourist city;
- the different use made of tourist resources by visitors;
- the multimotivational nature of visits by urban tourists.

The example of Lourdes (Rinschede 1986, 1990) and the brief discussion of the distinction between tourist and pilgrim highlights the importance of considering these key points in any analysis of urban tourism. This suggests that the effective analysis of urban tourists requires one to consider the behaviour and activity patterns of tourists, which is partly conditioned by their motivation and the availability of tourist facilities within different cities. For this reason, the next chapter considers the supply of urban tourism services and facilities and use made by different types of visitors.

Questions

1. What sources of data are commonly used as an approximation of urban tourism demand?

2. What techniques can be used to examine urban tourism markets?

3. What are the problems associated with the use of typologies of urban tourists?

4. How can researchers assess the role of seasonality in urban tourism contexts?

Further reading

Bywater, M. (1993). 'The market for cultural tourism in Europe', *Travel and Tourism Analyst* 6: 30–46.
This is a good comprehensive article that focuses on the market segments for a specific form of tourism that has an urban bias.
Cockerell, N. (1997). 'Urban tourism in Europe', *Travel and Tourism Analyst* 6: 44–67.
This is a very good introduction to the overall patterns of urban tourism at a pan-European scale.
Nolan, M.L. and Nolan, S. (1992). 'Religious sites as tourism attractions in Europe', *Annals of Tourism Research* 19 (1): 68–78.
This is a useful overview of religious sites as tourism attractions in Europe, particularly the role of towns and cities as the location of sites and shrines.
Ryan, C. (1995). *Researching Tourist Satisfaction: Issues, Concepts, Problems*, London: Routledge.
This is by far the best book available on tourism research and methodology.

Supply issues in urban tourism: the production of tourism services

CHAPTER 4

Introduction

In the last chapter, the issue of tourist motivation was considered in relation to some of the approaches used to identify the market for urban tourism. Yet the fundamental question – why do people visit urban areas? – is not easily reduced to simple classifications of motives among visitors. The diverse range of activities users engage in within individual cities complicates the use of typologies of visitors since 'people may visit cities for business including conferences and exhibitions, and also to see friends and relatives' (Law 1993: 68). At a general level, Law (1993) also argued that an urban area's reputation and attractions may be significant in influencing the tourists' visit (KPMG 1993). This means that visitors may often have a preconceived notion or perception of the 'tourist experience' or service encounter they expect. In other words, tourists and other visitors are not passive agents within the t̲ ̲ ̲ ̲ ̲ ̲ ̲ ̲ that exists in urban areas (see Figure 1.3), as they have views o̲ ̲ ̲ ̲ ̲ ̲ ̲ ̲ ̲ ̲ ̲ ̲ ̲ ̲ ities and products they may consume. Shaw̲ ̲ ̲ ̲ ̲ ̲ ̲ ̲ ̲ ̲ ̲ ̲ ̲ ledge that the production and consum̲ ̲ ̲ ̲ ̲ ̲ ̲ ̲ ̲ ̲ ̲ approaches to the analysis of tourism since̲ ̲ ̲ ̲ ̲ ̲

- *production* is the method by which a c̲ ̲ ̲ ̲ ̲ ̲ ̲ are involved in the supply of tourism s̲ ̲ ̲ ̲ are delivered to consumers; and
- *consumption* is how, where, why and̲ ̲ ̲ ̲ ̲ ̲ ̲ tourism services and products.

Law (1993) expands upon these simple n̲ ̲ ̲ ̲ ̲

in many respects tourism is the geography of consumption outside the home area; it is about how and why people travel to consume . . . on the production side it is concerned to understand where tourism activities develop and on what scale. It is concerned with the process or processes whereby some cities are able to create tourism resources and a tourism industry (Law 1993: 14).

While production and consumption have been the focus of the more theoretically derived explanations of urban tourism (e.g. Mullins 1991), such approaches raise conceptual issues related to how one should view production and consumption in the context of urban tourism. According to Jansen-Verbeke and Lievois (1999: 83–4), the development of urban tourism, particularly the supply aspects, has been influenced by the following factors:

- Increasing leisure mobility in society and a growth in urban-based trips (Cazes and Potier 1996).

- A 'reaffirmation of urban attractions' (Jansen-Verbeke 1998), with a renewed interest in heritage settings (Prentice 1993; Herbert 1995), cultural events (Bywater 1993), cultural facilities (Richards 1996a,b,c) and increased opportunities for shopping and amusement.

- New infrastructure, such as hotel expansion, entertainment and shopping are replacing traditional urban functions, reiterating the arguments from Chapter 2 on the changing role of cities, as 'leisure cities' develop.

- In spatial terms, leisure and tourism functions are taking up a greater proportion of public and private urban space.

The purpose of this chapter is to address how one can examine the relationship between production and consumption in terms of the supply of products, services and facilities as a means of understanding why tourists visit urban areas. Both the tourists' consumption (often expressed as the demand – dealt with in Chapter 3) and the products and services produced for their visit (the supply) form important inputs in the overall system of urban tourism (as discussed in Chapter 1 and shown in Figure 1.3) and integrating demand and supply is a major challenge for managers (Jansen-Verbeke 1997). To provide a logical framework for the chapter, the concept of the urban area as a *leisure product* (Jansen-Verbeke 1986) is introduced. The chapter examines the different components of the supply features in urban tourism, and to provide an understanding of the complexity of the interrelationships between illustrations are included from one major world tourist city – ation is also directed to the various elements of Jansen-Verbeke's oduct, with reference to *tourist facilities* and the *conditional* prior to examining these issues, the debates over tourism sidered.

Urban tourism and the concept of 'production'

While Shaw and Williams (1994) review the concepts of production and consumption, it is pertinent to critically examine Britton's (1991) innovative research in this area since it provides a theoretical framework in which to interpret tourism production. Within tourism production systems there are:

- economic activities designed to produce and sell tourism products;
- social groups, cultural and physical elements included in tourism products as attractions; and
- agencies associated with the regulation of the production system.

In Zukin's (1995) seminal study on the *Culture of Cities*, the emphasis on culture assumes both a visual and a symbolic meaning in cities as it is utilised to link consumption spaces with tourism. What Zukin (1995) acknowledged was the transformation of cities, public and private space and the processes creating specific forms of urban consumption for tourism. In a spatial context, the manifestation of these processes in producing tourism landscapes were documented by Sant and Waitt (2000) in relation to Sydney. What emerged in their conceptualisation of the city was a series of 'anchors' in tourist spaces which included:

- the heritage city;
- retail districts;
- an integrated waterfront;
- Chinatown;
- a gay triangle;
- sin city.

In a theoretical context, Britton (1991: 455) argued that the tourism production system was 'simultaneously a mechanism for the accumulation of capital, the private appropriation of wealth, the extraction of surplus value from labour, and the capturing of (often unearned) rents from cultural and physical phenomena (especially public goods) which are deemed to have both a social and scarcity value'. The production system can be viewed as having a division of labour between its various components (transport, accommodation, tour operators, attractions and ancillary services) as well as markets (the demand and supply of tourist products) and regulatory agencies (e.g. industry associations) as well as industry organisations and structures to assist in the production of the final product. This manifests itself spatially in tourist landscapes of consumption as the example of Sydney illustrated.

The tourism industry is made up of a range of separate industry suppliers who offer one or more component of the final product which requires intermediaries to coordinate and combine the elements that are sold to the consumer as a discrete package. Both tour operators and travel agents have a vital role to play in this context, when one recognises the existence of a supply chain. What this emphasises is the variety of linkages that exist and the physical separation of roles and responsibilities to the supply chain. While information technology may assist in improving communication and coordination between different components associated with the production of tourism, other developments (notably horizontal and vertical integration) assist in addressing the fragmentation of elements within the supply system. Strategic alliances also assist in this regard, since suppliers in one part of the system are dependent on those either upstream or downstream. Therefore, there is pressure on suppliers to exert control over other suppliers through transaction arrangements (i.e. through long-term contracts, vertical and horizontal integration) as well as through commissions, licensing and franchising. The two most powerful organisations in this respect are national airlines and tour wholesalers (also known as tour operators).

Britton (1991) also indicated that the state has a fundamental role to play in encouraging industry groups to meet and coordinate problem-solving, such as reducing critical incidents (Bitner *et al.* 1990) in the supply chain. In addition, the state makes a major contribution in terms of funding the marketing of regions and destinations via national and regional tourism organisations (Pearce 1992) so that place promotion takes place (Ashworth and Voogd 1990b; Page 1995a; C.M. Hall 1997) (see Chapter 8). The state may also offer inducements to underwrite major supply inputs where territorial competition or development may not otherwise occur, particularly with respect to urban regional development and rejuvenation (Hall and Jenkins 1995).

One of the interesting areas on tourism supply issues in urban areas is labour supply and markets (see Shaw and Williams 1994 for a good synthesis of the literature). In the tourism business, many workers simultaneously provide and are part of the consumed product. Britton (1991) pointed to the role of capitalist social relations in the production of tourist experiences, although such experiences cannot easily be characterised as tangible elements of tourist supply. This poses major difficulties for capital, where quality of service is easily influenced by personal factors, the behaviour and attitude of staff, as well as by the perception of the consumer in relation to their expectations, values and belief system. One result is that much of the demand for labour is not necessarily recognised through formal qualifications, but through personal qualities, which leads to an undervaluing of labour. In an urban context, Zukin (1995) highlighted the changes induced by service activities in tourism environments such as Disneyland where the enhancement of the consumption experience is a predominant characteristic. Add to this the fact that the labour willing to supply such skills is often casual and female (and often with a local ethnic component), the tourism labour market is characterised by ethnic and gender divisions and relatively poor employment conditions exist relative to other sectors, although there are notable exceptions in permanent posts at theme parks such as Disneyland and Disneyworld (Zukin 1995). For example, in the Australian context, the Industry Commission (1995: 21) characterised the tourism workforce as follows:

- it is, on average, young;
- it is characterised by female, part-time employment;
- it has more casual and part-time than other industries, but the majority of hours are nevertheless worked by full-time employees;
- it is poorly unionised;
- it is relatively low-skilled work;
- the hours of work are sometimes considered unsociable;
- the pay is relatively low;
- it is a mobile workforce with high turnover rates; and
- the workforce has low levels of formal educational qualifications.

Thus to understand some of these components of the tourism production system requires one to comprehend the concepts related to capital–labour relations, the business environment associated with the competitive strategies of enterprises, economic concepts (e.g. transactions analysis), product differentiation, international business as a mode of operation and global markets, along with basic business and marketing concepts. Within a capitalist production system, this is essential so that one can understand how each component in the tourism production system operates (i.e. how it develops products, generates profits and competes with other businesses; and how social groups and places are incorporated into the production system), so that the production system and spatial relationships which exist can be fully understood. In fact, Pratt (1997) explored the production system concept a stage further by introducing the *cultural industries production system* (CIPS). Within a tourism context, his research extended earlier arguments by Myerscough (1988) that the production and consumption of cultural events, artefacts and resources are of vital significance to the tourism industry. In a UK context, Pratt (1997) identified one sub-group – consumption – in which nightclubs, libraries, museums (Tufts and Milne 1999) and art galleries were key elements of the urban tourism product (Hughes 2000). In fact, employment in this sub-group in the UK in 1991 was 68,500 employees, and much of it was urban-based, having increased by 38 per cent in 1984–91 with a strong presence in London. What Pratt's (1997) analysis highlights is the tautological and semantic problem of precisely delineating the scope, extent and composition of the urban tourism production system which is why it is useful to examine methods of conceptualising tourism supply issues.

Conceptualising tourism supply in cities

One of the most poorly researched areas in tourism remains the supply-side of the industry (Sinclair and Stabler 1991). However, in the context of urban tourism, a well-established approach developed by Jansen-Verbeke (1986) is to

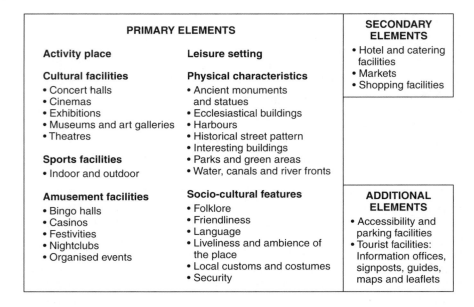

Figure 4.1   The elements of tourism (source: Page 1995a, modified from Jansen-Verbeke 1986)

view the urban area as a 'leisure product' (Figure 4.1) which comprises **primary elements** including:

- a variety of facilities that can be grouped into:
- an *activity place*, thereby defining the overall supply features within the city, particularly the main tourist attractions (P. Pearce 1991);
- a *leisure setting*, which includes both the physical elements in the built environment and the socio/cultural characteristics that give a city a distinct image and 'sense of place' (see Walmesley and Jenkins 1992 for a discussion of this concept) for visitors;

and **secondary elements** that consist of:

- the supporting facilities and services that tourists consume during their visit (e.g. hotel and catering outlets and shopping facilities) which shape the visitor's experience of the services available in the city;

as well as **additional elements** that consist of:

- the tourism infrastructure which conditions the visit, such as the availability of car parking, tourist transport provision and accessibility and tourist-specific services (e.g. Visitor Information Centres and tourist signposting).

Shaw and Williams (1994: 202) rightly argued that 'while such an approach allows a systematic consideration of the supply side of urban tourism, it is not without its difficulties. For example, in many cities, the so-called secondary elements of shops and restaurants may well be the main attractions for certain groups of visitors'. Nevertheless, the supply-side variables within the context of the urban tourism system need to be analysed to understand the interrelationships between the supply and demand for urban tourism and the interaction between the consumers and the products. In this respect, it is also useful to identify what aspect of the 'leisure product' urban tourists consume; some may consume only one product (e.g. a visit to an art gallery) while others may consume what Jansen-Verbeke (1988) terms a 'bundle of products' (i.e. several products during their visit or stay such as a visit to a theatre, museum and a meal in a restaurant).

Jansen-Verbeke (1986) examined this concept within the inner-city tourism system to identify the nature of tourists visiting the inner city and the organisations responsible for the promotion of the inner city as an area for tourists to visit. The role of organisations promoting urban areas for tourism is discussed in more detail in Chapter 7, but to explain Jansen-Verbeke's (1986) analysis it is useful to consider the relationship that she believes exists between the product, tourist and promoter. Promoters affect the relationship in two ways:

1. They build an image of the inner city and its tourists' resources to attract potential tourists.
2. The promotion of the inner city also leads to direct product improvements (see Conforti's 1996 interesting analysis of ghettos as tourism attractions).

Consequently, the model Jansen-Verbeke (1986) constructs (Figure 4.1) illustrated how different elements of the inner-city tourism system are interrelated and the significance of the inner city as a leisure product. Within this context, there has been a growing interest in heritage and cultural resources as one distinct product that can be developed in the central area of cities.

According to Jansen-Verbeke and Lievois (1999), there is a synergy between the conservation of urban cultural resources and their transformation into tourism products since the interdependence is a two-way process (see Garrod and Fyall 2000 for a discussion of the elements which are perceived to be important in heritage attractions) (Plates 4.1, 4.2 and 4.3). The capital costs of conservation mean that tourist revenues are essential to ensure their viability and preservation where public funds are limited (Garrod and Fyall 2000). Likewise, the tourism industry needs cultural resources (Ashworth 1993) to develop niche products in relation to urban tourism (see Caffyn and Lutz 1999 for an example of developing a heritage product in multi-ethnic cities). Not only do these products add value to the urban tourism experience (Page 1997), but there is a recognition in a public policy context that European urban heritage can be utilised as a vehicle for economic development. The EU's programme on cultural values (e.g. RAPHAEL) developed a pilot project on 'Art

Plate 4.1 Following the popularisation of the Stirling District in the *Braveheart* film, not only have visitor numbers to the city and attractions grown but historical sites and relict features in the landscape have been enhanced, as in the case of Stirling Bridge, Stirling Castle and the Wallace Monument commemorating William Wallace: Stirling Bridge (© AILLST)

Cities in Europe', based on 42 cities in 15 countries aimed at 'strengthening the symbiosis between cultural heritage and tourism by application of new information technology' (Jansen-Verbeke and Lievois 1999: 88). What this illustrates is the value of cultural resources for tourism product development (Moscardo 1996), particularly in historic cities (van der Borg *et al.* 1996; Ashworth and Tunbridge 2000) and in a more generic context (Graham *et al.* 2000). There is no doubt that 'cultural and heritage resources in particular play a key role in the development of urban tourism' (Jansen-Verbeke and Lievois 1999: 89) although there is no consensus on what exactly cultural and heritage tourism are (Prentice 1993). At a demand level, it is evident from studies of tourist motivation that examine cultural, historic and archaeological artefacts in the urban environment that there is a fascination with the past, where the morphology and relic features generate a palimpsest landscape that needs to be

Plate 4.2   Stirling Castle has witnessed a doubling of visitor arrivals in recent years following *Braveheart* (© AILLST)

reconstructed. This provides an opportunity to discover and relive the past in the historical and geographical imagination.

The role of the public and private sectors in urban tourism

Pearce (1989: 32) observed that the

provision of services and facilities characteristically involves a wide range of agents of development. Some of these will be involved indirectly and primarily with meeting the needs of tourists, a role that has fallen predominantly to the private sector in most countries [the Eastern bloc is the exception]. Other agents will facilitate, control or limit development . . . through the provision of basic infrastructure, planning or regulation. Such activities have commonly been the responsibility of the public sector with the government at various levels being charged

Plate 4.3   The Wallace Monument, built in the nineteenth century by public subscription and part of the *Braveheart* experience and itinerary in Stirling (© AILLST)

with looking after the public's interest and providing goods and services whose cost cannot be attributed directly to groups or individuals.

This illustrates the essential distinction between the role of the private and public sector in the provision of services and facilities for tourists.

The private sector

The private sector's involvement in tourism is most likely to be motivated by profit, as tourism entrepreneurs (Shaw and Williams 1994) invest in business opportunities. This gives rise to a complex array of large organisations and operators involved in tourism (e.g. multinational chain hotels – Forte and the Holiday Inn) and an array of smaller businesses and operators, often employing less than 10 people or working on a self-employed basis (see Page *et al.* 1999). If left unchecked, this sector is likely to give rise to conflicts in the operation of tourism where the state takes a laissez faire role in tourism planning and management.

The public sector

In contrast to the private sector, the public sector involves government at a variety of geographical scales and may become involved in tourism for various reasons (Pearce 1989; Hall 1994; Hall and Jenkins 1995). These include the following:

- *Economic reasons*:
  - to improve the balance of payments in a country;
  - to encourage regional or local economic development;
  - to diversify the economy;
  - to maintain or increase income levels;
  - to maintain or increase state revenue from taxes;
  - to generate new employment opportunities or maintain existing ones.
- *Social and cultural reasons*:
  - to achieve social objectives related to 'social tourism' to ensure the well-being and health of the individual are protected, as illustrated by the former Soviet Union's network of spas and holiday centres for workers;
  - to promote a greater cultural awareness of an area and its people (see Chang 2000 for a discussion of tourism in Singapore's 'Little India' district and Chang and Yeo's 1999 analysis of Singapore's New Asia campaign to communicate local culture).
- *Environmental reasons*:
  - to undertake the stewardship of the environment and tourism resources to ensure that the agents of development do not destroy the future basis for sustainable tourism development.
- *Political reasons*:
  - to further political objectives as illustrated by the Franco government in Spain in the 1960s where it promoted the development of tourism to broaden the political acceptance of the regime among visitors;
  - in the context of the less-developed world, Jenkins and Henry (1982) argue that the state should have a role in controlling the development process associated with tourism;
  - in socialist countries (e.g. Albania and Cuba), the state has maintained a dominant role in tourism to ensure that forms of development are consistent with its political ideology.

In many cases, the state's involvement is to ensure a policy of intervention so that political objectives associated with employment generation and planning are achieved, although this varies from one country to another and from city to city according to the political persuasion of the organisation involved. The public sector's role is also evident from national government funding of tourism promotion among national tourism organisations. In addition, the establishment of public sector regional and local organisations (e.g. tourist boards) advise on planning, promotion and development, although the trend among developed countries in recent years has been to encourage the private sector to play a greater role in funding these activities. Pearce (1989: 44) rightly acknowledged that

> the public sector then is by no means a single entity with clear-cut responsibilities and well-defined policies for tourist development. Rather, the public sector becomes involved in tourism for a wide range of reasons in a variety of ways at different levels and through many agencies and institutions . . . [and] . . . there is often a lack of co-ordination, unnecessary competition, duplication of effort in some areas and neglect in others.

Analysing the supply and distribution of urban tourism services and facilities

According to Ashworth (1989) one of the most frequently used approaches towards the supply of urban tourism is the descriptive research by geographers based on inventories and lists of the facilities and where they are located. In view of the wide range of literature that discusses the distribution of specific facilities or services, it is more useful to consider these approaches and concepts as they derive generalisations of patterns of urban tourism activity. For this reason, two aspects are considered: the tourism business district and tourism attraction research.

The tourism business district

Within the literature on the supply of urban tourism, Ashworth (1989) reviewed the 'facility approach' which offers researchers the opportunity to map the location of specific facilities, undertaking inventories of facilities on a city-wide basis. The difficulty in such approaches is that the users of urban services and facilities are not just tourists, as Chapter 3 emphasised. Therefore, any inventory will be only a partial view of the full range of facilities and potential services tourists could use. One useful approach is to identify the areas in which the majority of tourist activities occur and to use it as the focus for the analysis of the supply of tourism services in the multifunctional city. This avoids the individual assessments of the location and use of specific aspects of tourism services such as accommodation (Page and Sinclair 1989), entertainment facilities such as restaurants (S.L.J. Smith 1989) and nightlife entertainment facilities (Ashworth *et al.* 1988) and other attractions. This approach embraces the *ecological approaches* developed in human geography to identify regions within cities as a basis to identify the processes shaping the patterns.

The ecological approach towards the analysis of urban tourism dates back to Gilbert's (1949) assessment of the development of resorts, which was further refined by Barrett (1958). The outcome is a resort model where accommodation, entertainment and commercial zones exist and the central location of tourism facilities were dominant elements. The significance of such research is that it identifies some of the features and relationships that were subsequently developed in urban geography and applied to tourism and recreation. The most notable study is Stansfield and Rickert's (1970) development of the recreational business district (RBD). This study rightly identifies the multifunctional land use of the central areas of cities in relation to the central area for business (central business district, CBD). Meyer-Arendt (1990) also expands this notion in the context of the Gulf of Mexico coastal resorts while Pearce (1989) offers a useful critique of these studies. The essential ideas in the RBD have subsequently been extended to urban tourism to try to understand the location and distribution of the range of visitor-oriented urban functions in cities.

Burtenshaw *et al.*'s (1991) seminal study of tourism and recreation in European cities deals with the concept of the Central Tourist District (CTD) where tourism activities in cities are concentrated in certain areas. This has been termed the Tourism Business District (TBD) by Getz (1993a: 583–4) who argues that it is the

> concentration of visitor-oriented attractions and services located in conjunction with urban central businesses (CBD) functions. In older cities, especially in Europe, the TBD and CBD often coincide with heritage areas. Owing to their high visibility and economic importance, TBDs can be subjected to intense planning by municipal authorities . . . The form and evolution of TBDs reveal much about the nature of urban tourism and its impacts, while the analysis of the planning systems influencing TBDs can contribute to concepts and methods for better planning of tourism in urban areas.

Therefore, TBDs are a useful framework in which to understand the components of urban tourism and how they fit together. Figure 4.2, based on Getz's (1993a) analysis of the TBD, is a schematic model in which the functions rather than geographical patterns of activities are considered. This model illustrates the difficulty of separating visitor-oriented services from the CBD and use of services and facilities by residents and workers. Yet as Jansen-Verbeke and Ashworth (1990) argue, while tourism and recreational activities are integrated within the physical, social and economic context of the city, no analytical framework exists to determine the functional or behavioural interactions in

Core attractions	CBD functions	Services
Natural	Offices	Transport to
Heritage	Retail	Access within
Cultural	Government	Catering
Events	Meetings	Accommodation
Shopping		Information
Conventions		

Figure 4.2 The tourism business district (source: Page 1995a)

these activities. They argue that more research is needed to assess the extent to which the clustering of tourism and recreational activities can occur in cities without leading to incompatible and conflicting uses from such facilities. While the TBD may offer a distinctive blend of activities and attractions for tourist and non-tourist alike, it is important to recognise these issues where tourism clusters in areas such as the TBD. Even so, the use of street entertainment and special events and festivals (Getz 1991) may also add to the ambience and sense of place for the city worker and visitor. By having a concentration of tourism and non-tourism resources and services in one accessible area within a city, it is possible to encourage visitors to stay there, making it a place tourists will want to visit. However, the attractions in urban areas are an important component in the appeal to potential visitors. Yet the problem with these conventional models of tourism supply features in cities is that they do not adequately incorporate new urban processes, such as the postmodern city with its multiple nucleated centres where urban tourism may be present in a range of areas aside from the conventional downtown area.

Tourism attractions

Attractions are an integral feature of urban tourism, which offer visitors passive and more active activities to occupy their time during a visit. They are also a key component of Jansen-Verbeke's (1986) 'primary element' (Figure 4.1). Recent studies have adapted descriptive analyses of specific types of attractions (e.g. Law 1993) rather than exploring their relationship with urban tourists. Lew (1987: 54) acknowledges that 'although the importance of tourist attractions is readily recognised, tourism researchers and theorists have yet to fully come to terms with the nature of attractions as phenomena both in the environment and the mind'. As a result, Lew's (1987) study and Leiper's (1990) synthesis and conceptual framework of 'Tourist Attraction Systems' remain among the most theoretically informed literature published to date. Lew (1987) identifies three perspectives used to understand the nature of tourist attractions:

1. *The ideographic perspective*, where the general characteristics of a place, site, climate, culture and customs are used to develop typologies of tourism attractions, involving inventories or general descriptions. For example, the use of Standard Industrial Classification codes (SICs) are one approach used to group attractions (see S.L.J. Smith 1989). These approaches are the ones most commonly used to examine tourist attractions in the general tourism literature.
2. *The organisational perspective*, in contrast, tends to emphasise the geographical, capacity and temporal aspects (the time dimension) of attractions rather than the 'managerial notions of organisation' (Leiper 1990: 175). This approach examines scales ranging from the individual attraction, to larger areas and their attractions.
3. *The cognitive perspective* is based on 'studies of tourist perceptions and experiences of attractions' (Lew 1987: 560). P. Pearce (1982: 98) recognises that any tourist place (or attraction) is one capable of fostering the feeling of being a tourist. Therefore, the cognitive perspective is interested in understanding the tourists' feelings and views of the place or attraction.

The significance of Lew's (1987) framework is that it acknowledges the importance of attractions as a research focus, although Leiper (1990) questions the definition of attractions used by many researchers. He pursued the ideas developed by MacCannel (1976: 41), that an attraction incorporates 'an empirical relationship between a tourist, a sight and a marker, a piece of information about a sight'. A 'marker' is an item of information about any phenomenon that could be used to highlight the tourist's awareness of the potential existence of a tourist attraction. This implies that an attraction has a number of components, while conventional definitions consider only the sight (Leiper 1990: 177). In this respect, 'the tourist attraction is a system comprising three elements: a tourist, a sight and a marker' (Leiper 1990: 178). Although sightseeing is a common tourist activity, the idea of a sight really refers to the nucleus or central component of the attraction (Gunn 1972). In this context a situation could include a sight where sightseeing occurs, but it may also be an object, person or event. Based on this argument, Leiper (1990: 178) introduces the following definition of a tourist attraction as 'a system comprising three elements: a tourist or human element, a nucleus or central element, and a marker or informative element. A tourist attraction comes into existence when the three elements are interconnected'. On the basis of this alternative approach to attractions, Leiper (1990) identifies the type of information that is likely to give meaning to the tourist experience of urban destinations in relation to their attractions.

These ideas are developed more fully in Leiper's model of a tourist attraction system (Figure 4.3), breaking the established view that tourists are not simply 'attracted' or 'pulled' to areas on the basis of their attractions. Instead, visitors are motivated to experience a nucleus and its markers in a situation where the marker reacts positively with their needs and wants. Figure 4.3 identifies the linkages within the model and how tourist motivation is influenced by the information available and the individual's perception of their needs. Thus, it is only once:

- a person with tourist needs,
- a nucleus (a feature or attribute of a place that tourists seek to visit), and
- a marker (information about the nucleus)

become connected together that an attraction system develops.

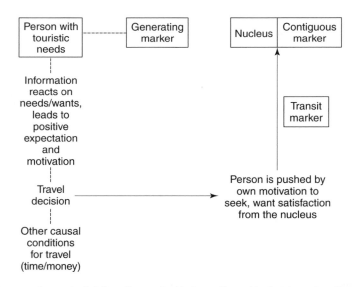

The *generating marker* is information received before setting out for the place where the nucleus is located; the *transit marker* is information received en route; the *contiguous marker* is at the nucleus. The diagram depicts how 'attractions' really operate: the tourists are literally 'attracted', 'pulled' or 'magnetised', but are motivated to experience a nucleus and its markers when a marker reacts positively with needs and wants.

Figure 4.3   A model of a tourism attraction system (source: Page 1995a after Leiper 1990)

Jansen-Verbeke and Lievois (1999) examined the tourism attraction system in Leuven, Belgium, through a spatial analysis of the locational patterns of heritage buildings and complexes. Buildings were weighted to create a morphological positioning index to take account of the distance of buildings and their position in relation to landmarks. It permits the identification of clusters/core areas and how they are constructed in the mental maps of tourists. Heritage sites/buildings with a high 'marker' value were selected while a hierarchy of landmarks was established from promotional literature. What Jansen-Verbeke and Lievois (1999) produced as a conceptual model of the functionality and morphological position of buildings and heritage clusters is illustrated in Figure 4.4. What emerged from the model was that 'There is a clear gradation between heritage clusters which function as core elements in the urban tourist product, both by their morphological characteristics and positioning and by their accessibility, and tourist function and heritage buildings which are not integrated, neither spatially nor functionally, in a cluster' (Jansen-Verbeke and Lievois 1999: 96–7). Therefore, heritage resources as attractions are an integral element of the urban system (see also Chapter 5).

Jansen-Verbeke and Lievois (1999) also utilised their research to develop the generic concept of the tourist opportunity spectrum in an urban context – the Urban Tourist Opportunity Spectrum. This is a modification and development of Clarke and Stankey's (1979) Recreational Opportunity Spectrum and the subsequent modification in tourism by Butler and Waldbrook (1991). In an urban context, the Urban Tourist Opportunity Spectrum (UTOS) is the range of opportunities which the visitor has access to, comprising core and secondary elements as illustrated in Figure 4.5. This UTOS is shaped by a range of factors (Jansen-Verbeke and Lievois 1999), namely:

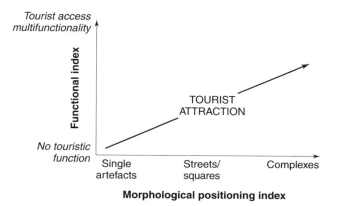

Figure 4.4 Tourist attraction of heritage clusters in a historic city (source: Jansen-Verbeke and Lievois 1999)

Urban tourist opportunity spectrum
=
**Accessibility to a
range of urban facilities and
environmental characteristics
of potential interest and use for tourists**

Core elements of the
cultural tourism product
=
main pull factors for cultural tourists
high marker value
*Heritage buildings and complexes,
museums, monuments, events, theatres, etc.*

+

Secondary elements
(added value to the tourist
experience and image)
*Pubs, restaurants, street markets
and shops, etc.*

Figure 4.5   Urban tourist opportunity spectrum (source: Jansen-Verbeke and Lievois 1999)

- accessibility of the destination area;
- internal access within the destination;
- the availability of alternative activities to meet the needs/preferences of a wide range of user groups;
- the ability to combine a range of activities within a specific time–space budget (i.e. the ability to undertake a wide range of activities in a set time and space framework);
- the spatial configuration of the city, where trails, networks and signposting encourage a wide range of activities structured around attractions/events;
- functional synergies between different urban services and fixed facilities;
- the level of interaction between different types of tourist activities.

In the context of Leuven, the spatial analysis of urban tourist activities in the historic city by Jansen-Verbeke and Lievois (1999: 100) was a significant methodological breakthrough since it moved beyond tourist mental mapping of the city to understand the tourist action space of visitors, especially their time–space paths using Geographical Information Systems (GIS). The outcome of their research was that pre-city visits were based on a mental map of the city with single buildings acting as 'markers'. Post-visit, it was apparent that the visitors had a wider appreciation of heritage clusters and a general awareness of the UTOS, with potential for further visits to explore the city's attractions.

This theoretical framework based on the tourism attraction system has a great deal of value in relation to understanding the supply of urban tourism resources for visitors. Firstly, it views an attraction system as a sub-system of the larger tourism system in an urban area. Secondly, it acknowledges the integral role for the tourist as consumers – without the tourist (or day-tripper) the system would not exist. Thirdly, the systems approach offers a convenient social science framework in which to understand how urban destinations attract visitors, with different markers and nuclei to attract specific groups of visitors. For this reason, attention now turns to the supply of attractions in one world city – London – to examine the scope, extent and nature of the London tourism attraction system.

London's tourism attraction system

There is little doubt that

> For the tourist, the day-tripper, or local resident, London offers a vast array of attractions and activities: celebrated cultural establishments, famous buildings and architecture, the West End theatre quarter, parks and promenade areas, many different kinds of shopping, pub and club areas, as well as specific attractions . . . [mean that any] visit to the city will almost certainly involve the use of a combination of these facilities. Unfortunately, in many cases it is simply not known how often a particular facility has been frequented' (Bull and Church 1996: 161).

Herein lies the problem for tourism researchers: the data that exist nationally highlights London's pre-eminence as the leading centre receiving large volumes of tourist visits but at the micro-level, data are less than satisfactory. The problem begins when seeking to understand the dynamics of the tourism attraction system within London, particularly the changing characteristic of visitation to attractions. As Trew (1999: 58–9) argued 'London's top attractions are dominated by traditional, ever popular sights, the majority of them owned by various trusts and religious bodies, central government departments or local authorities. Of London's 15 attractions that receive over one million visitors a year, seven are museums and art galleries', emphasising the significance of Myerscough's (1988) and Pratt's (1997) cultural industries debate focused on consumption in urban areas. In a London context, the cultural industries as tourist attractions comprise a key element of the tourist product, many of which are icons in their own right among international visitors.

In a historical context, Bull and Church (1996) examined attendances at principal London attractions between 1978 and 1991, documenting fluctuations in some categories, partly associated with the charging regime employed, while other attractions have enjoyed constant growth. The recession in the UK in the early 1990s may have impacted on domestic visits to London attractions and budget cutbacks in school visits. A slump in West End theatre attendances in the early 1990s, with a drop from 11,321,288 in 1990 to 10,905,395 paid attendances in 1991 also occurred, though with over a third of attendances by overseas visitors (Reid 1994) since the London Arts Board (1994) acknowledged that 45 per cent of arts attendances were the main reason for visiting the city. In recent years, the visits to attractions has, in part, reflected the wider trend in visitor arrivals in London (Table 4.1).

Table 4.1 Numbers of and expenditure by visitors[a] to London

	Numbers (millions)		Expenditure (£ million)[b]		Average expenditure (£)	
	Overseas visitors	Domestic tourists	Overseas visitors	Domestic tourists	Overseas visitors	Domestic tourists
1990	10.3	7.0	4,227	680	410	97
1991	9.2	6.6	3,924	720	427	109
1992	10.0	7.0	4,152	640	415	91
1993	10.2	7.2	4,850	875	475	122
1994	11.3	8.6	5,205	1,005	461	117
1995	13.0	10.4	6,336	880	488	85
1996	13.4	12.2	6,509	935	486	77
1997	13.5	14.6	6,449	1,040	478	71
1998	13.5	11.6	6,736	1,055	499	91

[a] Staying one night or more.
[b] At current prices. Expenditure by domestic tourists is rounded to the nearest £5 million.
Source: International Passenger Survey, Office for National Statistics; United Kingdom Tourism Survey, sponsored by National Tourist Boards.
© Crown copyright

Table 4.2 Top tourist attractions by number of visits, 1998[a] ('000's)

Ranking	Attraction visits	Total	Ranking	Attraction visits	Total
1	British Museum	5,620	11	Victoria and Albert Museum	1,110
2	National Gallery	4,770	12	London Zoo	1,053
3	Westminster Abbey	3,000	13	National Portrait Gallery	1,017
4	Madame Tussaud's	2,773	14	Royal Botanic Gardens	1,000
5	Tower of London	2,551	15	Royal Academy of Arts	913
6	Tate Gallery	2,181	16	Hampton Court Palace	605
7	St Paul's Cathedral	2,000	17	National Maritime Museum	474
8	Natural History Museum	1,905	18	Imperial War Museum	472
9	World of Adventures	1,650	19	Rock Circus	455
10	Science Museum	1,600	20	Photographers' Gallery	400

[a] The number of visitors to the London Dungeon in 1998 is not available. In 1995, there were 610,000 admissions.
Source: London Tourist Board.
© Crown copyright

Figure 4.6   Spatial distribution of visitors to London's top 20 tourist attractions in 1998 (source: London Tourist Board)

Table 4.2 lists the number of visits to London's top 20 tourism attractions which reaffirms the significance of heritage and cultural resources. Figure 4.6 illustrates the spatial distribution of visits to London attractions in 1998 which is dominated by the City of Westminster and the geographically coterminous districts (i.e. London boroughs) of Camden and Kensington and Chelsea. The new millennium has also seen a range of new investments in two major attractions, opened in 1999: the Millennium Dome at Greenwich (subsequently closed in 2001) and the London Eye on London's South Bank, a 135-metre high observation wheel with panoramic views of London. Although both attractions were plagued with problems in early 2000, the Millennium Dome suffered major financial crises and fell short of expected visitor arrivals. Yet these two attractions also have to be viewed against investment directed at the arts and leisure since 1994, with the proceeds of the National Lottery invested in different projects. This has a high degree of relevance for the production and consumption of London's cultural industries (see Pratt 1997 for more detail), since 28 per cent of the lottery proceeds are currently divided into six funds:

- The Arts Council;
- The Film Council;
- The National Lotteries Charities Board;
- The Millennium Commission;
- The National Heritage Memorial Fund;
- Sport England and the New Opportunities Fund.

Between 1994 and December 1999, £2.1 billion had been allocated to organisations based in London from the six funds. This comprised 5,700 grants, of which the majority were for under £100,000. Some 190 were over £1 million and 30 were awarded £10 million or greater, which accounted for 55 per cent of the total amount awarded as illustrated in Table 4.3. In geographical terms, 548 grants were awarded to Islington, but the greatest value of grants (£892 million) for 469 grants were awarded to the City of Westminster. The London borough of Camden received 526 grants totalling £186 million. In contrast, outer London boroughs such as Kingston-upon-Thames received £3.6 million for 65 projects and Hillingdon with 44 grants totalling £2.9 million. The significance of London's cultural industries and cultural infrastructure is evident from the projects listed in Table 4.3, particularly museums, art galleries, theatre and the performing arts. Not only has this added to the wider attraction system for tourists, but has improved the facilities used by the 22,103,000 London attendees at theatre (40.4 per cent), art galleries/exhibitions (29.2 per cent), plays (28.9 per cent), pop/rock concerts (24.7 per cent), classical music (15.8 per cent), opera (10.5 per cent), ballet (9.5 per cent), jazz (9.2 per cent) and contemporary dance (6.9 per cent). However, the distribution of grants has also reinforced the pattern of attraction development in London's central tourist district – the West End of London, with its dominance of the cultural industries sector.

Tourist facilities

Among the 'secondary elements' of the leisure product in urban areas, four components emerge as central to servicing tourist needs. These are:

- accommodation;
- catering;
- shopping;
- conditional elements.

Table 4.3 National Lottery grants[a] over £10 million made to organisations in London

Fund	Recipient	Purpose	£ million
Millennium	New Millennium Experience Company Limited	The New Millennium Experience	449.0
Sport	English National Stadium Trust	English National Stadium Wembley	120.0
Art	Royal Opera House	Restoration and refurbishment	55.0
Millennium	Tate Gallery	Tate Gallery of Modern Art, Bankside	50.0
Art	Royal National Theatre Board	Improvement and plant modernisation	31.6
Millennium	British Museum	The British Museum Great Court	30.0
Millennium	Royal Botanic Gardens, Kew	The Millennium Seed Bank	29.9
Art	Sadler's Wells Foundation	Redevelopment of Sadler's Wells Theatre	28.5
Heritage	Heather Trust For The Arts	Gilbert Collection, Somerset House	28.3
Art	Royal Opera House	Supplementary to main application	23.5
Heritage	Science Museum	Construction of the new 'Wellcome Wing'	23.0
Art	Royal Academy of Dramatic Art	To purchase and redevelop building	22.8
Art	Royal Albert Hall	Redevelopment of Albert Hall	20.2
Heritage	Corporation of the Hall of Arts and Sciences	Royal Albert Hall Development	20.2
Heritage	Tate Gallery	Centenary Development, Tate Gallery	18.8
Art	English Stage Company	Restore and enhance facilities	15.8
Heritage	British Museum	Education and Information Centre	15.1
Heritage	Victoria and Albert Museum	Victoria and Albert Museum British Galleries	15.0
Art	London Borough of Newham	Creation of a new arts centre	13.7
Sport	London Borough of Newham	New East Ham Leisure Centre	13.5
Heritage	Imperial War Museum	South West Infill Development	12.6
Art	Shakespeare Globe Trust	Reconstruction of theatre	12.4

Table 4.3   *(cont'd)*

Fund	Recipient	Purpose	£ million
Millennium	London Borough of Tower Hamlets	Creation of Mile End Park	12.3
Heritage	National Maritime Museum	Neptune Hall Project	12.1
Heritage	National Portrait Gallery	NPG Centenary Development	11.9
Heritage	Council of the Museum of the Port of London and Docklands	Museum in Docklands	11.0
Heritage	Somerset House Ltd	Somerset House Restoration	10.3
Sport	London Borough of Hackney	Clissold Leisure Centre	10.0
Millennium	Action with the Communities in Rural England (ACRE)	21st century halls (162 sites)	10.0
Arts	British Film Institute	'IMAX' cinema	10.0

[a] All grants up to 30 December 1999.
Source: Department for Culture, Media and Sport.
© Crown Copyright

Accommodation

Tourist accommodation performs an important function in cities: it provides the opportunity for visitors to stay for a length of time to enjoy the locality and its attractions, while their spending can contribute to the local economy. Accommodation forms a base for the tourist's exploration of the urban (and non-urban) environment. Accommodation is not only a major element of the urban tourism economy, but forms a basis for associated activities such as conferences and conventions (Plate 4.4). For example, Warf (2000) indicated that New York received in excess of 24.2 million overnight stays, of whom 6.4 million were overseas visitors and a further 18 million day visitors a year. Zelinsky (1994) also observed that New York received 830,000 participants a year for 690 scheduled conventions. As a result, tourism contributed US$20 billion to the New York region's economy and generated 265,000 jobs. The tendency for establishments to locate in urban areas is illustrated by the typical patterns of urban hotel location in European cities (Ashworth 1989; also see the seminal paper by Arbel and Pizam 1977 on urban hotel location). The importance of infrastructure and accessibility means that when hotels are built to serve specific markets (i.e. the exhibition and conference market will need hotels adjacent to a major conference and exhibition centre as Law 1988 emphasised) they will locate near to the optimum site.

Plate 4.4   The University of Stirling with its location in an eighteenth-century country estate operates as a conference venue, with an estimated £10 million contribution to the local economy (© AILLST)

The accommodation sector within cities can be divided into serviced and non-serviced sectors (Table 4.4). Each sector has developed in response to the needs of different markets, and a wide variety of organisational structures have emerged among private sector operators to develop this area of economic activity. As Pearce (1989) noted, many large chains and corporations now dominate the accommodation sector, using vertical and horizontal forms of integration to develop a greater degree of control over their business activities. Integration usually consists of:

- *horizontal integration*, whereby hotel chains or franchising arrangements allow the accommodation sector to expand or acquire the business from other operators;

- *vertical integration*, where one organisation seeks to diversify into other areas of activity. For example, in the 1970s and 1980s, it was commonplace

Table 4.4 Market segments and associated types of accommodation

Market segment	Serviced sector		Non-serviced sector (self-catering)	
	At destination	**Along routes**	**At destination**	**Along routes**
Business, convention and non-leisure travellers	City/town hotels Resort hotels with meeting facilities Educational establishments Private clubs Serviced apartments	Motels Inns Airport hotels	Self-service apartments Some educational establishments	Self-service motels and motor lodges
Leisure and holiday travellers	Resort hotels Guest house/ pensions/bed and breakfast Homestays City/town hotels Some educational establishments Serviced apartments Serviced backpackers	Motels Bed and breakfast Inns Farmstays and homestays	Apartment hotels Condominia Resort villages Holiday camps Caravan/chalet parks Gîtes Cottages Villas Self-service apartments Self-service motels	Designated stops for caravans, tents, recreation vehicles Backpacker and youth hostels Self-service motels and motor lodges

Source: after Middleton (1988).

for state-owned airlines to have a chain of airport or city-centre hotels for its customers (e.g. AerLingus in Ireland had the Copthorne Hotel chain until their sale to realise the company's assets).

In terms of understanding the supply and demand for this type of facility, it is useful to focus on one specific example – London, as it reinforces the need to possess good data to assess the demand and supply for urban tourism (a useful set of studies that focus on the issue of tourist accommodation can be found in Goodall 1989).

Tourism accommodation in London

As a global destination for international tourists and a wide range of domestic tourists (Table 4.5), London performs a major role as a centre for commercial accommodation. Wöber (2000) observed the significance of London's accommodation sector, since it is the main source of statistics for gauging the scale and significance of visitor arrivals, and as a data source, it has been problem-

Table 4.5   Origin of overseas visitors[a]

	Visits to London (%)		Visits to the United Kingdom (%)	
	1991	**1998**	**1991**	**1998**
USA	19.0	21.4	15.6	17.9
France	9.1	10.1	12.6	12.0
Germany	8.9	8.8	13.5	11.9
Italy	5.2	5.2	4.8	4.9
Netherlands	4.8	4.6	6.5	6.8
Japan	4.7	3.5	3.1	2.5
Spain	4.1	3.5	4.2	3.8
Sweden	4.4	3.3	3.3	3.0
Australia	3.4	3.1	3.2	2.8
Belgium	2.7	3.0	3.5	3.8
All other countries	33.6	13.5	17.1	25.7
Total visits (=100%)	9.2	13.5	17.1	25.7

[a] Staying one night or more. Ranked according to percentage of visits to London in 1998. Excludes visits made by residents of the Irish Republic.
Source: International Passenger Survey, Office for National Statistics.
© Crown copyright

atic compared to the way other destinations collect arrival data (see Page and Sinclair 1989; Cockerell 1997). Bull and Church (1996) traced the evolution of accommodation in London, where the metropolis had 44,000 bedrooms in 1966 in hotels and other forms of accommodation, with 80,000 bedrooms by 1970. By 1974, London possessed 1,400 accommodation establishments with 130,000 bed-spaces, of which 76 hotels of at least 200 rooms existed. These changes were documented in the seminal study by Eversley (1977) and during the 1980s, the number of establishments stabilised and actually declined, particularly in the bed and breakfast sector. Although this decline in establishments at the lower end of the serviced accommodation scale continued into the 1990s, larger chain hotels have continued to develop. The result is that the number of bed-spaces rose to 137,844 in 1989, dropped to 136,691 in 1996, and rose to 150,419 in 1999.

The accommodation stock as measured by the London Tourist Board and Convention Bureau (LTBCB) accommodation register is in a constant state of flux due to: temporary closures for refurbishments, the closure of bed and breakfast units, the expansion of units to add new bed-spaces, and the development of new properties. London's existing accommodation stock is a function of its historical antecedents and a series of policy initiatives in the 1970s, which fuelled its growth. The 1969 Development of Tourism Act provided grants for hotel room construction up to 1973. Eversley (1977) also observed that in the early 1970s, this policy initiative contributed to a further 62 hotel schemes awaiting approval in Central London. This situation changed dramatically in the 1980s, since in the decade 1973–83, only 10 large hotels were added to the accommodation stock with a further net decline by the early 1990s (Bull and Church 1996). The 1980s and early 1990s were an era of overcapacity, reflected in Table 4.6, though confidence in the smaller hotel sector continued to grow. This led to a growth in the total number of hotels in London 1986–92 of 10 per cent to 477. This figure had stabilised by 1999 at 476 hotels, although bed-spaces grew 9.12 per cent between 1989 and 1999.

Yet these aggregate patterns of accommodation conceal changes in the spatial dynamics of accommodation provision and development in the capital. In 1974, the pattern of hotel and other accommodation was 'spatially concentrated in the three centrally located boroughs of Westminster, Kensington and Chelsea and Camden' (Bull and Church 1996: 160). The only other outlier was Hillingdon with its airport hotels to service Heathrow Airport. In Bull and Church's (1996) assessment of the situation, by the mid-1990s they claimed that the locational pattern of hotel capacity was very similar to the 1970s. This situation began to change in the late 1990s, starting a change in the pattern of provision. In 1989, Westminster, Kensington and Chelsea and Camden had 55.26 per cent of accommodation establishments and 74.75 per cent of bed-spaces. In 1999, this had dropped to 51.45 per cent of establishments and 71.03 per cent of bed-spaces. For this reason, it is pertinent to explore these changes in more detail, since Bull and Church (1996: 161) recognised a spatial change occurring on the outskirts of the city. A second important cluster grew to rival and then exceed Hillingdon. This was Croydon 'resulting from the pursuit of out-of-town sites with easy access to the M25 orbital motorway, Gatwick Airport and other routeways into London accessible by rail'. Figures 4.7 and 4.8 show that a large number of inner and outer London boroughs saw the stock of establishments contract between 1989 and 1999. Yet this was accompanied by a rise in bed-spaces (Figures 4.9 and 4.10) ensuring a continued supply to compensate for smaller establishments withdrawing from accommodation provision or turning over a more lucrative income (e.g. housing the homeless and refugees – see Page and Sinclair (1989) who observed that 11,000 rooms were used to house London's homeless in the late 1980s) and this situation has certainly continued into the new millennium.

What emerged in the period 1989 to 1999 was a greater geographical spread of bed-spaces to outer London locations with access to two markets: the central London market by rail and alternative airports such as London Gatwick and London City Airport (see Page and Fidgeon 1989). The pattern of change is shown in Figure 4.11 where Westminster recorded a 7.71 per cent drop in bed-spaces, which may be a temporary or long-term phenomenon. In addition, a number of areas with inner-city characteristics saw the number of bed-spaces contract (e.g. Brent, Barking and Dagenham, Hackney, Haringey, Wandsworth) as well as outer London locations (e.g. Enfield, Hounslow,

Table 4.6 Tourism accommodation in London 1989–99

London boroughs	Total accommodation establishments 1989	Total bed-spaces 1989	Total accommodation establishments 1996	Total bed-spaces 1996	Number of hotels, motels, inns and guest houses 1999	Number of bed and breakfast establishments 1999	Total accommodation establishments 1999	Total bed-spaces 1999
Barking and Dagenham	3	37	1	29	1	–	1	29
Barnet	40	1,015	22	915	8	19	27	1,253
Bexley	6	258	9	551	4	7	11	605
Brent	31	1,262	17	972	4	13	17	993
Bromley	20	536	14	350	8	13	21	663
Camden	106	16,730	91	18,185	52	65	117	23,121
City of London	1	281	2	774	1	–	1	316
Croydon	53	2,145	42	2,381	20	31	51	2,531
Ealing	47	1,194	27	909	10	22	32	2,229
Enfield	11	403	6	385	4	3	7	433
Greenwich	25	582	11	394	7	35	42	610
Hackney	31	1,417	11	633	4	8	12	689
Harrow	17	888	17	952	8	13	21	962
Hammersmith and Fulham	44	3,549	29	3,766	14	14	28	4,973
Haringey	19	463	14	509	4	12	16	444
Havering	6	371	7	435	8	2	10	601
Hillingdon	22	8,727	24	10,409	20	7	27	11,504

Table 4.6 *(cont'd)*

London boroughs	Total accommodation establishments 1989	Total bed-spaces 1989	Total accommodation establishments 1996	Total bed-spaces 1996	Number of hotels, motels, inns and guest houses 1999	Number of bed and breakfast establishments 1999	Total accommodation establishments 1999	Total bed-spaces 1999
Hounslow	34	1,883	27	1,950	11	16	27	1,303
Islington	22	2,490	13	2,302	9	7	16	2,852
Kensington and Chelsea	189	23,609	141	23,021	71	83	154	25,843
Kingston	20	615	12	560	5	4	9	437
Lambeth	32	544	7	189	4	6	10	1,358
Lewisham	19	600	14	713	2	24	26	947
Merton	16	378	14	478	5	10	15	468
Newham	9	355	6	213	3	3	6	213
Redbridge	14	516	12	481	6	8	14	548
Richmond	30	1,088	24	786	11	60	71	1,250
Southwark	9	838	9	2,011	7	7	14	2,137
Sutton	9	182	8	454	4	4	8	413
Tower Hamlets	2	1,568	2	2,573	2	–	2	2,435
Waltham Forest	5	288	9	437	6	3	9	523
Wandsworth	17	307	4	188	3	6	9	243
Westminster	465	62,725	314	57,486	150	173	323	57,883
Total for London boroughs	1,374	137,844	960	136,691	476	678	1,154	150,419

Source: from various sources.

Kingston and Newham), although most of these areas had a relatively small proportion of total bed-spaces in 1989 and 1999.

The most significant changes occurred in Camden (38.2 per cent growth), Hammersmith and Fulham (40.12 per cent), Havering (61.99 per cent), Hillingdon (31.82 per cent), Lambeth (149 per cent), Lewisham (57.8 per cent), Southwark (155 per cent), Sutton (126.9 per cent), Tower Hamlets (55.29 per cent) and Waltham Forest (81.59 per cent). This illustrates two major changes to the locational pattern of bed-spaces in London. Firstly, a geographical spread south of the River Thames in Central London due to policy and planning constraints on further development in the West End. This emerging process was observed by the LTBCB (1993: 38), where 'there has been an encouraging trend to locate outside of the core area'. This is not a surprise for analysts, since Page and Sinclair (1989) examined the Touche Ross (1988) report that argued that 'The building of new hotels within the existing major areas of tourist accommodation will not be feasible due to high development costs and planning restrictions on further expansion' (also see Bull 1997). Such restrictions reflect local authority concern over the increases in traffic and congestion accompanying the growth of tourism and the loss of residential land to commercial uses' (Page and Sinclair 1989: 128). Thus, the central tourist district has expanded beyond the traditional 'West End' pattern with a further 6.3 per cent of bed-spaces now located in the geographically coterminous areas of Southwark, Hammersmith and Fulham and to the east of the City of London in Tower Hamlets. The Tower Hamlets location may seem an odd location given the major socio-economic deprivation juxtaposed within the borough, but hotel development has occurred by expansion of provision in the existing hotels.

The 4.8 per cent growth in bed-spaces in Greenwich at the foot of London Docklands and adjacent to the attraction cluster in Greenwich (e.g. the National Maritime Museum and Royal Observatory, the *Cutty Sark* and River Boat tours and London Dome during its brief opening) has seen the number of establishments rise from 25 in 1989 to 42 in 1999, while the bed-space stock has grown from 582 to 610. This modest growth has also been encouraged by the recent opening of the Jubilee Line Underground Line and Docklands Light Railway extension into the region. Further afield, the pattern of out-of-town hotel development has continued apace in Croydon (17.99 per cent growth), Bexley, Sutton, Havering and Waltham Forest as each has access to the M25. This reflects the emergence of a new form of transit or axis tourist, particularly the business traveller, which led to the rise of budget hotels in some of these areas to meet a new market generated by the M25 in outer London.

Catering facilities

Ashworth and Tunbridge (1990) note that catering facilities are among the most frequently used tourism services after accommodation by visitors to urban areas. For example, of the £15 billion of overseas and domestic tourist spending in the UK in 1990, nearly £2 billion is estimated to be on eating and

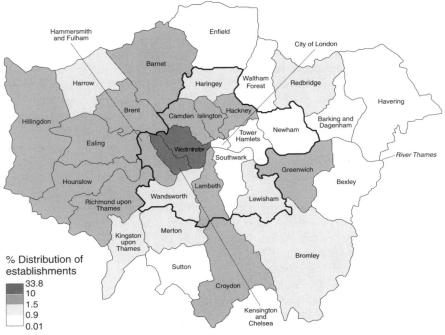

% Distribution of
establishments

- 33.8
- 10
- 1.5
- 0.9
- 0.01

Total number of establishments – 1,374

Figure 4.7 Distribution of accommodation establishments in London in 1989 (source: Page 1989c)

drinking (Marketpower 1991). Bull and Church (1994) suggest that one way of grouping this sector is to use the SIC which comprises:

- restaurants;
- eating places;
- public houses;
- bars, clubs, canteens and messes;
- hotels and other forms of tourist accommodation.

Using the products that this sector produces, they further sub-divide the groups into:

- the provision of accommodation;
- food for immediate consumption.

While there is considerable overlap between the two sectors, there are organisational links between each sector as integration within larger hospitality organ-

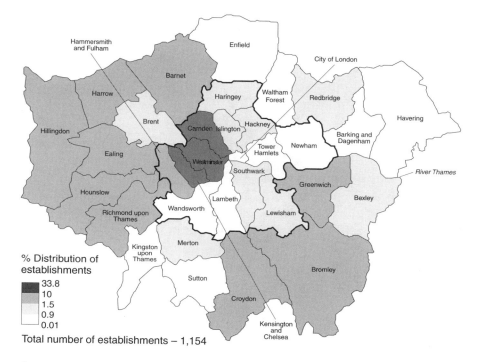

Figure 4.8 Distribution of accommodation establishments in London in 1999 (source: London Tourist Board data)

isations (e.g. the Forte Group), with their subsidiaries offering various products. In the context of urban tourism, one of the immediate difficulties is in identifying specific outlets for tourist use, as many such facilities are also used by residents. Therefore, tourist spending at such facilities also has to be viewed against total consumer spending in this sector. In 1989, Marketpower (1991) found that total consumer spending in the UK on alcoholic drinks and meals outside the home totalled £15 billion. Extracting tourism and leisure spending from this amount can be only an estimate. Tourist use of catering facilities varies according to the specific service on offer, being located throughout cities, often in association with other facilities (S.L.J. Smith 1983). Many catering establishments in cities reflect local community needs and tourism complements the existing pattern of use. Nevertheless, Ashworth and Tunbridge (1990: 65) acknowledged that

> restaurants and establishments combining food and drink with other entertainments, whether night-clubs, discos, casinos and the like, have two important locational characteristics that render them useful in this context: they have a distinct tendency to cluster together into particular streets or districts, what might be

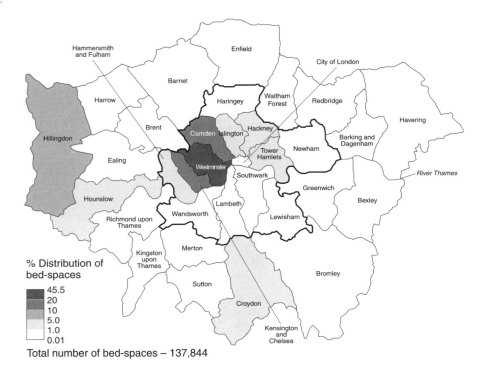

Figure 4.9 Distribution of accommodation bed-spaces in London in 1989 (source: Page 1989c)

termed the 'Latin-quarter effect', and they tend to be associated spatially with other tourism elements including hotels, which probably themselves offer public restaurant facilities.

At a European scale, HOTREC (2000) indicated that the hotel, restaurant and café sector in Europe contributed 6 per cent to EU GDP. Much of the infrastructure associated with this sector is urban-based (including resorts at coastal and in mountain locations) and arguably, it is the single largest component of the tourism industry (since hospitality is often subsumed under this category – see Lashley and Morrison 2000 for a debate on this issue). As a result, HOTREC (2000) argued that it employed over 50 per cent of all employees in the tourism sector, accounted for 50 per cent of turnover with 6 million employees in 1.5 million businesses across the EU. This reflects the concentration of facilities and hotels in Europe (46 per cent of the worldwide hotel capacity). Some 99 per cent of hotel, restaurant and café businesses are small and medium-sized enterprises (SMEs), with 95 per cent employing fewer than

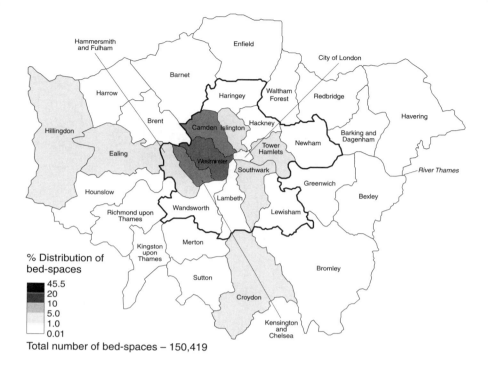

% Distribution of bed-spaces

- 45.5
- 20
- 10
- 5.0
- 1.0
- 0.01

Total number of bed-spaces – 150,419

Figure 4.10 Distribution of accommodation bed-spaces in London in 1999 (source: London Tourist Board data)

10 people (see Evans 1999 for a discussion of SMEs in tourism in London). This sector employed approximately 4 per cent of the EU workforce, of whom over 50 per cent were women (see Sinclair 1997 for a discussion of gender issues in tourism) and around 20 per cent of workers in this sector are self-employed, with 54 per cent possessing only a basic school level education. The problem this poses relates to training, service standards and quality management, an issue recently raised in Scotland's *A New Strategy for Scottish Tourism* (Scottish Executive 2000) for the wider tourism sector.

HOTREC's (2000) data on European establishments in the hotel and restaurant sector illustrates the dominance of restaurant and café sectors (Table 4.7). This is also reflected in the patterns of employment where restaurants and cafés are major employers. The contribution of tourism and leisure spending to this sector is part of a global development in a café culture, and conspicuous consumption in urban areas (Mansfeld 1999). These new consumption spaces display the growing sophistication of consumers in taste, style with food and wine

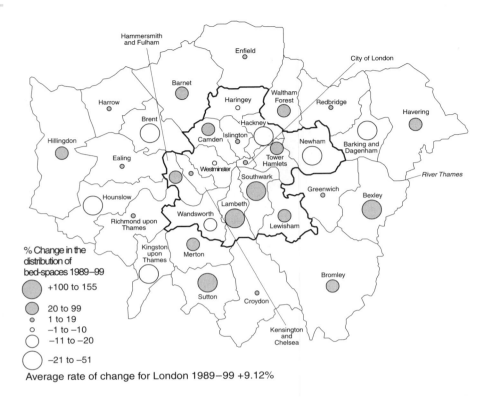

% Change in the distribution of bed-spaces 1989–99

- +100 to 155
- 20 to 99
- 1 to 19
- −1 to −10
- −11 to −20
- −21 to −51

Average rate of change for London 1989–99 +9.12%

Figure 4.11 Percentage change in the distribution of bed-spaces in London 1989–99 (source: Page 1989c and London Tourist Board data)

tourism, new established elements of an urban lifestyle and tourism/leisure experience which Zukin (1995) has called domestication of the urban environment by cappucino.

In a regional context where a number of urban centres and a rural hinterland are juxtaposed – Scottish Enterprise Forth Valley (SEFV) (see Figure 4.12) in Scotland – recognised the significance of these new elements in tourist expenditure in the UK. SEFV covers the central Scotland region to the north of Glasgow and Edinburgh, and covers the three local authority areas of Falkirk, Stirling and Clackmannanshire. It is also the location of the first Scottish National Park (see Figure 4.12) where three towns will act as tourist hubs and urban service centres in the SEFV area (i.e. Stirling, Callander and Aberfoyle). The region contains 277,000 people, almost 5 per cent of the Scottish population and the SEFV workforce is approximately 107,000 people. Tourism generates approximately £165 million direct revenue for the area, mainly focused on the existing urban honeypot of Stirling and a number of other locations such as Callander (Plate 4.5).

Table 4.7 The number of hospitality establishments and employees in Europe

	Establishments					Employees				
	Hotels	Restaurants	Cafés	Canteens	Others	Hotels	Restaurants	Cafés	Canteens	Others
Austria	1,797	21,500	9,600	800						163,300
Belgium	3,000	22,544	27,343			14,748	53,099	19,087		
Switzerland		200			25,000	97,000	3,000			
Denmark	481	7,866	2,441	2,802		11,831				22,088
France	30,255	99,212	50,192			185,000	384,000	90,100		
Finland	1,100	4,700	6,200	1,700		18,500	26,000	12,500	10,400	
Germany	40,041	108,677	69,068	6,399		301,000	527,000	209,000	26,000	
Italy	34,000	90,000	150,000			245,000	450,000	300,000		
Spain	26,388	58,886	213,987			158,536				
UK	40,000	100,000	80,000	16,000		330,000	320,000	350,000	120,000	461,300
Portugal	2,002	9,932	41,310			27,000	82,000	105,000		
Norway	1,274		231	604	3,316	16,400				
Ireland	1,072	2,571	8,694				40,667	1,600	1,500	16,700
Netherlands	2,895	19,181	19,396	2,866		32,520		76,239		
Sweden	1,700	9,000	1,200			25,000	50,000		20,000	271,000
Total	186,005	554,269	679,662	31,171	28,316	1,462,535	1,935,766	1,163,526	177,900	1,097,688
Overall total					1,479,423					5,837,415

Source: HOTREC (2000), http://www.hotrec.org

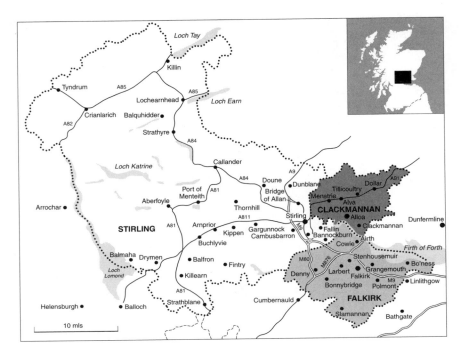

Figure 4.12 The Forth Valley area (source: Scottish Enterprise Forth Valley)

In 1997, overseas tourists were spending 15 per cent of their average daily expenditure on food and drink and 19 per cent on shopping in the SEFV area. This illustration of consumption was much more pronounced among day-trip visitors to the region, where 26 per cent of those taking a day-trip from home spent their daily expenditure on food and drink. This rose to 38 per cent for those people taking a day-trip as part of a holiday. The tourism businesses within the region with a restaurant/food/hospitality dominate the pattern of tourism development, with many visits and expenditure urban-focused. As a result, in the Forth Valley area, tourism businesses are estimated to employ around 8,270 full-time equivalent jobs (Table 4.8), a growing proportion of the region's service sector. Even this example illustrates that in a mixed region, where rural–urban tourism products exist, the urban centres (e.g. Stirling) serves a major central place function and service centre role, with the rural places and destinations interconnected with the urban hierarchy in the region.

Furthermore, a British Tourist Authority report (1993) suggested that the quality of food and service in Britain has improved in recent years (a feature that is highly debatable!): food can be a persuasive ingredient in Britain's over-all tourist appeal, particularly in urban areas. Nevertheless, the report sup-

Plate 4.5   The Rob Roy Centre, Callander, Scotland: this Visitor Centre and Information Centre is themed on the local associations with Rob Roy and local heritage (© AILLST)

ported the reform of Britain's Sunday trading laws and licensing hours, as well as the investment in upgrading the language skills of tourism and hospitality workers, in pursuit of improvements to customer service. As the report suggested, even if the quality of food may have improved, tourist perceptions still lagged behind the reality of provision in many urban areas, illustrating the significance of this element is the 'tourist experience' of urban areas. Catering facilities also have a predisposition to cluster within areas where shopping is also a dominant activity to benefit from the throughput of customers.

Tourist shopping

The English Historic Towns Forum's (1992) study on retailing and tourism highlighted many of the relationships between

> tourism and retail activity [which] are inextricably linked to historic towns with three-quarters of tourists combining shopping with visiting attractions . . . The expenditure is not only on refreshments and souvenirs, as might be expected, but also on clothing and footwear, stationery and books (English Historic Towns Forum 1992: 3).

Table 4.8 Tourism business in the Forth Valley

Business type	Number of businesses
Restaurants	252
Bars, nightclubs	160
Hotels with restaurants	147
Sporting activities	89
Travel agents/tour operators	40
Hotels without restaurants	30
Sport arenas	27
Libraries	26
Recreational activities	20
Self-catering and short-stay accommodation	17
Camping and caravan sites	16
Museums	15
Botanical gardens, nature reserves	3
Youth hostels	2
Total number of tourism businesses	844
Total number of businesses in the Forth Valley	6,242

Source: Scottish Enterprise Forth Valley (2000) http://www.scottish-enterprise.com/forthvalley/

The study also emphasises the overall significance of the environmental quality in towns which is vital to the success of urban tourism and retailing (Plate 4.6). In fact the report argues that, 'for towns wishing to maintain or increase leisure visitor levels, the study reveals a number of guide lines. For example, cleanliness, attractive shop fronts and provision of street entertainment are all important to tourists' (English Historic Towns Forum 1992: 3).

Unfortunately, identifying tourist shopping as a concept in the context of urban tourism is difficult, since it is also an activity undertaken by other users such as residents (Kent 1983). The most relevant research undertaken in this field, by Jansen-Verbeke (1990, 1991), considers the motives of tourists and their activities in a range of Dutch towns. She made a number of interesting observations on this concept. However, the range of motives associated with tourism and leisure shopping is complex: people visit areas due to their appeal and shopping may be a spontaneous as well as a planned activity. Even so, the quality and range of retail facilities may be a useful determinant of the probable demand for tourism and leisure shopping: the longer the visitor is enticed to stay in a destination, the greater the likely spending in retail outlets.

One important factor that affects the ability of cities to attract tourism and leisure shoppers is the retail mix – namely the variety of goods, shops and presence of specific retailers. For example, the English Historic Towns Forum (1992) notes that over 80 per cent of visitors consider the retailing mix and general environment of the town the most important attraction of the destina-

Plate 4.6 Tourist and day-tripper spending, particularly in the Christmas season, makes a major contribution to the scale and range of retail services provided in tourist towns such as Stirling, reflected in the investment by retail developers in indoor mall facilities such as The Marches (© AILLST)

tion. Although the priorities of different tourist market segments vary slightly (Turner and Reisinger 2001), catering, accessibility (e.g. availability of car parking, location of car parks and public transport), tourist attractions and the availability of visitor information shape the decision to engage in tourism and leisure shopping. The constant search for the unique shopping experience, especially in conjunction with day-trips in border areas and neighbouring countries (e.g. the UK cross-channel tax-free shopping trips from Dover to Calais) are well-established forms of tourism and leisure shopping.

The global standardisation of consumer products has meant that the search for the unique shopping experience continues to remain important. The growth of the North American shopping malls and tourist-specific projects (see Getz 1993b for more detail) and the development in the UK of out-of-town complexes (e.g. the MetroCentre in Gateshead and Lakeside at Thurrock, adjacent to the M25) have extended this trend. For example, in the case of Edmonton Mall (Canada) Jansen-Verbeke (1991) estimated that 10 per cent of the total floor space is used for leisure facilities with its 800 shops and parking for 27,000 cars. Finn and Erdem (1995) describe West Edmonton Mall (WEM) as a mega-multimall (MMM) given its scale, since the developer of WEM claimed such a development attracted nine million tourists a year. The political significance of such statements is that

> they have been used to try to obtain regional and local government subsidies or tax concessions for MMMs in Edmonton. . . . The Mall of America reportedly received US$160 million in concessions from city and state governments, as well as US$80 million in taxes set aside for road building. New York State was reported to have offered about US$400 million in incentives to have Triple Five build a US$1.2 billion MMM at Niagara Falls, rather than in Southern Ontario (Finn and Erdem 1995: 367).

What Finn and Erdem (1995) calculated was that approximately 1,885,000 travellers are estimated to have spent US$112 million on shopping at WEM in 1986, US$88 million on food and accommodation, US$26 million on other goods and US$227 million while in Edmonton. Applying methods of economic analysis, such as multipliers (see Chapter 6), 13,800 jobs were supported by WEM. Their study concluded that WEM attracted 3.3 million visitors in 1990, generating US$179 million in income and 4,220 jobs. Even though local and tourist visits generated approximately 5 million visits a year, it remained lower than the 9 million. However, what WEM shows is that it is rated highly as an attractor of urban tourism and leisure visits and certainly rivals many of the leading tourism attractions in capital cities.

Such developments have been a great concern for many cities as out-of-town shopping has reduced the potential in-town urban tourism in view of the competition it poses for established destinations. The difficulty with most existing studies of leisure shopping is that they fail to disentangle the relationships between the actual activity tourists undertake and their perception of the environment. For this reason, Jansen-Verbeke (1991: 9–10) distinguished between intentional shopping and intentional leisure shopping in a preliminary attempt to explain how and why tourists engage in this activity; she also suggested that several criteria need to be considered to distinguish between intentional shopping and intentional leisure and tourism in relation to the following:

- *Behaviour pattern of visitors*
    - trip length – short, possibly longer;
    - length of stay – limited or rather unplanned;
    - time of stay – a few hours during the day, an evening, a full day;
    - kinds of activity – window shopping, intentional buying, drinking, eating, various leisure activities, cultural activities, sightseeing;
    - expenditure – goods, possibly some souvenirs, drinks, meals, entrance fees to leisure facilities.
- *Functional characteristics of the environment*
    - wide range of retail shops, department store, catering, leisure and other facilities, tourist attractions, spatial clustering of facilities;
    - parking space and easy access;
    - street retailing, pedestrian priority in open spaces.

- *Quality of the environment*
  - image of the place, leisure setting, display of goods on the street, street musicians and artists;
  - accessibility during leisure time, including weekends and evenings;
  - aesthetic value, image of maintenance and safety;
  - architectural design of buildings, streets, shops, windows, sign boards, lighting;
  - social effective value, liveliness of the open space;
  - animation, entertainment, amusement and surprise.
- *Hospitableness of the environment*
  - social, visual, physical;
  - orientation, information, symbolism, identification.

According to Mansfeld (1999) shopping as a consumption activity has assumed a new significance in urban areas, especially now that globalisation and capital investment in shopping malls are becoming commonplace in the retail landscape. The evolution of shopping malls as commercial entities in pursuit of profit are now commonplace in towns, cities and the urban fringe (Edge City) where the threshold of population (residents and visitors) is sufficient to support such a development. Mansfeld's (1999) cultural analysis of the mall as a cultural form of production is useful in explaining how contemporary capitalism is now responding to tastes and fashion, just as the café culture is a complex reflection of new leisure practices. A great deal of interest has been shown in the development of West Edmonton Mall in Canada as a reflection of postmodernity. It represents a landscape of spectacle, fantasy, pastiche and artificial creations of new shopping environments. To encourage the throughput and circulation of shoppers, malls often have an anchor tenant at each end of the development, interspersed with precincts, lifts and escalators to encourage the flow of shoppers. Much of the shoppers' activity is subject to surveillance by cameras to assist in the exclusion of undesirable elements. Many malls have distinct gender appeal, with retailers targeting women as primary purchasers of goods, making leisure shopping in these locales a significant form of consumption in the contemporary urban tourism destination.

For many cities, finding the right mix between shops, leisure facilities and tourist attractions to appeal to a wide range of visitors and residents involves a process of development and promotion to attract investment in town centres. So why is tourism and leisure shopping attracting so much attention among planners and researchers?

One immediate reason is the potential for using shopping as a marketing tool by the tourism industry in towns and cities. The English Historic Towns Forum (1992) emphasises this relationship, as 75 per cent of visitors to the cities surveyed combine tourism and shopping. But what changes are occurring and how is tourism and leisure shopping changing in the new millennium?

Only certain shopping centres have the essential ingredients to be promoted as tourism and day-trip destinations. The image and manner in which these places are promoted is assuming growing significance (see Chapter 8 for a fuller discussion of place-marketing). Historic cities in Europe have many of the key ingredients in terms of the environment, facilities, tourism attractions and the ability to appeal to distinct visitor audiences. Many successful cities in Europe have used tourism and leisure shopping to establish their popularity as destinations as a gradual process of evolution. In particular, improvements to town centres by city authorities (e.g. town centre management – see Page and Hardyman 1996) have acted as catalysts to this process by:

- establishing pedestrian precincts;
- managing parking problems and implementing park-and-ride schemes to improve access and convenience;
- marketing the destination based around an identifiable theme, often using the historical and cultural attractions of a city;
- investing in new and attractive indoor shopping galleries, improving facades, the layout and design of the built environment and making the environment more attractive. The English Historic Towns Forum (1992: 12) identified the following factors associated with environmental improvement which tourism and leisure shoppers deemed important:
  - the cleanliness of the town,
  - pedestrian areas/pavements which are well maintained,
  - natural features such as rivers and parks,
  - the architecture and facades/shopfronts,
  - street furniture (seating and floral displays),
  - town centre activities (e.g. outdoor markets and live entertainment).

One illustration of the effect of specific factors that tourists may view as important is evident from the Tidy Britain Group's qualitative study of the cleanliness of capital cities in Europe and the conditions at major tourist sites. The survey examines litter levels and environmental problems, awarding points for cleanliness. While the results of such surveys may be highly variable, owing to the sampling methodology used, London featured as the overall winner in relation to the criteria used. Although Berne's 'Bear Pit' emerges as the most clean tourist site among those locations surveyed (while Athens Syntagma Square came bottom of the league), the environment around other facilities visited and used by tourists (e.g. shopping streets, railway stations and parliament buildings) provide additional insights into the environmental quality of those areas which tourists also visit. Although it is difficult to place a great deal of store by ad hoc and random surveys such as the Tidy Britain Group, it does illustrate the point that cleanliness, litter and the perceived quality of the local environment may influence tourist views, particularly those seeking to visit shopping streets in major capital cities such as Oxford Street (London), Puerto del Sol (Madrid), Rue de Neuve (Brussels), Kalverstraat (Amsterdam), Bahnhof Platz (Berne), Ermou (Athens), Boulevard Haussman (Paris), Kurfustendamm

(Berlin) and Via del Corso (Rome). The impressions that shoppers form of the environmental quality of urban areas may also influence other potential visitors as word-of-mouth communication is a powerful force in personal recommendation of shopping areas. However, as safety of the visitor is also paramount in the urban environment, Carr's (2001) study of gender differences in young tourists' perceptions of danger within London is an interesting insight into this highly topical area, a feature also examined by Barker (2000) and Barker *et al.* (2002) within a New Zealand context in relation to the America's Cup in Auckland. What Barker *et al.* (2002) found was that the design of an environment that had the safety of the visitor in mind and policed in a prominent and visible manner provided an opportunity for leisure activities in a new tourism environment. Yet at the same time, evidence from downtown Auckland on crime and victimisation observed the displacement of criminal activities to an area which was noticeably less policed and so impacted upon tourist and leisure retailers, highlighting the need for a safe environment for leisure spending.

Changes that alter the character of the town, where it becomes more tourist oriented, are sometimes characterised by the development of speciality and gift/souvenir shops and catering facilities in certain areas. However, as Owen (1990) argued, many traditional urban shopping areas are in need of major refurbishment and tourism may provide the necessary stimulus for regeneration (see Chapter 9). Developments such as theme shopping (Jones Lang Wooten 1989) and festival marketplaces (Sawicki 1989) are specialised examples of how this regeneration has proceeded in the UK and North America.

The new millennium, therefore, would seem to be set for tourism and leisure shopping development to further segment markets by seeking new niches and products. Jansen-Verbeke (1991) describes the 'total experience' as the future way forward for this activity – retailers will need to attract tourism and leisure spending using newly built, simulated or refurbished retailing environments with a variety of shopping experiences. Keown's (1989) experience is that the opportunity to undertake a diverse range of retail activities in a locality increases the tourists' propensity to spend. However, the growing saturation of retailing provision in many industrialised countries may pose problems for further growth in tourism and leisure shopping due to the intense competition for such spending. Urban tourism destinations are likely to have to compete more aggressively for such spending in the new millennium. This is reflected in the increased investment in tourism infrastructure among shopping mall owners as towns and cities compete more for the mobile leisure spending at a local, regional, national and international level.

The conditional elements: transport and urban tourism

The last feature that Jansen-Verbeke (1986) views as central to the city's 'leisure product' are the conditional elements, such as transport, physical infrastructure and the provision of signposting. Transport is a vital element in the development of tourism, since it facilitates the mobility of people and the creation of tourist, leisure and recreational trips from an origin area to a destination, and mobility within the destination, depending on its size, morphology and the access permitted (see Page 1999 for a fuller discussion of the tourism–transport relationship). Within the context of urban tourism, a great deal of interest has been directed towards the understanding and analysis of tourist mobility and the pressures this poses for urban areas in terms of visitor flows, the demand for space to accommodate cars, coaches and other forms of transport. This has also produced conflicts with local residents, workers and tourists, where competition develops for space to accommodate vehicles, sometimes leading to restrictive or expansive measures to try to harmonise the needs of these users. Transport in many urban destinations can also be a constraining factor, where the scale of the city, its attractions and products are not adequately interconnected by efficient transport and signposting to encourage the visitor to visit the wider city environment. This leads to what is invariably observed as tourist bunching, crowding or spatial congregation in the most accessible honeypot locations and a lack of dispersion to the wider urban environment. In other words, inadequate transportation provision may prevent cities offering the wider attributes to the visitor and, therefore, congregates urban tourism in a limited number of districts as opposed to allowing a wider range of resources and activities from reaching their tourist potential (Plate 4.7).

The significance of transport as a mode of travel to allow visitors to access urban areas is evident in the case of London, where 73.2 per cent of the 13.5 million international arrivals in 1997 arrived by air. Some 52.7 per cent arrived at London Heathrow, illustrating the significance of urban centres as gateways. A further 12.6 per cent of arrivals were at Gatwick, with an additional 7.9 per cent arriving via London Stansted, London City Airport and Luton Airport. The emphasis on air access for many urban destinations and their perceived accessibility to the central city area has led London to approve a fifth terminal at Heathrow Airport and plans are afoot for further runways in south-east England. This leads to the second role for transport in urban tourism visits: the need for gateway terminal access to the central tourist district, with public and private transport options (car, taxis, shuttle buses/coaches and dedicated rail links).

Costly methods of transferring and connecting visitors arriving at a gateway to a tourist district remains a highly contentious issue in many destinations. Indeed, the example of London is a case in point with the expensive fares charged by the licensed Black Cabs between Central London and Heathrow Airport that certainly tarnishes London's image as a value for money and welcoming tourist destination. Awkward terminal design and the absence of an East–West rail link in London makes tourist transfers difficult and unattractive by public transport. In contrast, many secondary urban destinations outside gateway regions receive many of their visitors by road. For example, Manete *et al.* (2000: 14) cite the following visitor arrivals by road: Rimini (80 per cent),

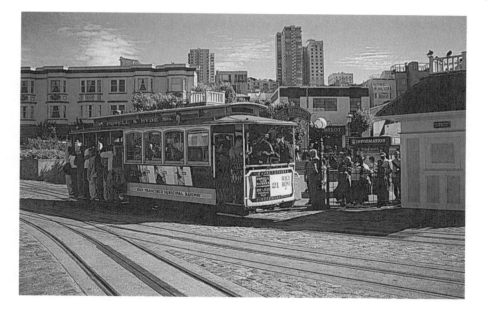

Plate 4.7 The San Francisco nineteenth-century cable car not only acts as an attraction in its own right but connects the waterfront with a number of downtown areas and many of the tourists boarding this service had queued for 2–3 hours just for a 20 minute ride on this historic 'must do' activity on a public holiday

Canterbury (56 per cent), Barcelona (46 per cent), Glasgow (41 per cent), Paris (40 per cent) and Amsterdam (35 per cent). Coach travel is important for historic cities such as Jerusalem (52 per cent), Toledo, Spain (35 per cent) and Paris (17 per cent). Rail transport plays a major role for arrivals in Amsterdam (45 per cent), Rome (34 per cent), Paris (25 per cent), Canterbury (21 per cent) and Glasgow (10 per cent).

This is complemented by the third role for transport in urban tourist trips – mobility within urban areas. The London Tourist Board found that 91 per cent of international visitors used the London Underground during their visit in 1997 and 51 per cent used London's bus routes. In contrast, 30 per cent of international visitors used taxis to travel within the capital, 23 per cent used suburban trains and between 11–15 per cent utilised the hop on–hop off sightseeing buses. Only 4 per cent of visitors used the Dockland Light Railway, while 12 per cent travelled in a friend's car at one point during their trip. This reaffirms the integral role of public transport systems in tourist cities which have an adequate visitor market to justify the operation of public transport. However, as Page (1999) noted, many transport operators are not attuned to the diversity of their visitor markets and the fact that they carry tourists in

addition to residents and commuters. In the case of London, the ageing infrastructure and current maintenance problems facing many sections of the
London Underground, which is 100 years old and used by two million travellers a day, poses an intractable problem for policy-makers and planners.
Upgrading it to a 'world city standard', in line with Tokyo, Madrid or Paris,
has proved impossible, and as Trew (1999: 52) acknowledged, a 'patch and
mend philosophy' is inadequate to accommodate annual growth of passengers
(8 per cent in 1998). The result is a lengthening of journey times to accommodate service interruptions, signal failures and antiquated equipment.

Public–private partnerships (PPPs) are the favoured solution of the existing
Labour government for London Underground Limited to take forward plans
for attracting £13 billion in investment to the network over the next 15 years to
remedy decades of under-investment in the system as the lifeblood of London.
The main controversy over this investment approach is whether it is a new
form of privatisation and sale of assets and the extent to which private companies can successfully operate mass rapid transit systems such as the London
Underground following the Railtrack debacle in the UK, which collapsed
in insolvency in October 2001. It is ironic that one of London's attractions –
the Underground system – is now proving to be a negative element for travel
in London, while the potential of the River Thames as a mode of transport
remains under-exploited and neglected after the ill-fated closure of the River
Bus Scheme in the 1990s. Only a range of Sightseeing River Tours currently
utilises the River Thames' potential between Westminster and Greenwich,
rather than its latent potential as a tourist transport and commuter corridor.

In many urban tourism destinations, accessibility has to be weighed against
problems of congestion on arterial routes leading to the central tourist district
and multinucleated destinations such as in large cities like Los Angeles,
where the freeway dominates resident and tourist travel. This is sometimes
accompanied with congestion and over-use of the inner city by car-users which
conflict with the pedestrian flows. These problems are accentuated by the
existence of seasonality in visitor arrivals and the need to manage excursionist
traffic such as coach-borne visitors. Congestion also generates additional pollution from vehicles. Some cities, such as Groningen in northern Holland, are
virtually car-free and cycling towns to protect the historic city and in other contexts, the public sector has implemented a range of general actions to manage
traffic, including:

- limiting private car use by payment parking methods;
- park-and-ride schemes to promote private car traffic switching to public
  transport at key locations outside the city centre;
- reorganisation of the road network;
- the development of cycling and pedestrian tracks to reduce traffic congestion, noise, pollution and to improve the quality of the urban environment
  for residents and visitors alike;
- tourist coach control systems for managing organised groups; and

- enhancement of local and gateway networks, with direct public transport services.

One interesting example of the application of urban transport measures to address tourism can be found in Manete *et al.* (2000), who provide case studies of Amsterdam, Barcelona, Canterbury, Glasgow, Jerusalem, Paris, Rimini, Rome, Toledo and the Alpine region – North Tyrol – Salzburg.

What emerges from the existing, but limited, literature on the interrelationships between transport and urban tourism is the need for more active management measures to address many of the issues raised above. It is also vital to have transport infrastructure to connect the tourist with opportunities for sightseeing and to explore the destination. In the case of London Docklands, it has taken almost two decades for the transport infrastructure to be developed to a level where the East of London is better connected to the principal tourist districts in West London. The failure to integrate the Dockland transport infrastructure with plans to develop the region's tourism potential (Page and Fidgeon 1989; Page and Sinclair 1989) has directly impacted upon the geographical diffusion of visitors as reflected in the dominance of visits to the capital's major attractions discussed earlier. This is also reflected in the pattern of tourism-related employment in London, where employment is heavily concentrated in West London, with the majority of jobs in Westminster (70,000), Camden (over 20,000), Kensington and Chelsea (nearly 17,000) and Hammersmith and Fulham (16,000). Other important concentrations, including Hillingdon with Heathrow Airport, contribute to the location of employment (Bull and Church 1996). What Bull and Church (1996: 167) recognised was that 'between 1981 and 1991 . . . East London also performs relatively badly. Most of the boroughs recording significant job losses, such as Barking and Dagenham, Hackney, Newham and even Greenwich' had low rates of employment in tourism. In terms of England's most deprived districts in 1988, Newham ranked second (after Liverpool), with Hackney fourth, Tower Hamlets sixth, Southwark eighth, Islington tenth, Greenwich eleventh, Lambeth twelfth, followed by Haringey, Lewisham, Barking and Dagenham. This has profound implications for tourism when one considers one of the objectives of the LTBCB (1993: 2) strategy was 'to contribute in particular to urban renewal, raising incomes and the provision of employment in those parts of London which will benefit most'.

Transport infrastructure has certainly hindered the geographical dispersion of tourism to the East of London, despite the recent development of the promotional agency TourEast. To date, tourism is a missed opportunity in East London, which contains many of London's most deprived boroughs and concentrations of deprivation, often juxtaposed in direct contrast to gentrified inner-city redevelopments. Although new attractions such as the London Dome undoubtedly created a short-term employment boost in East London, combined with the Jubilee Line underground extension, tourism employment and development remains limited despite the production of tourism strategies by many boroughs. The absence of transport infrastructure prior to the late 1990s deterred tourism developers from imaginative products and plans to open up East London as a new tourist destination in London. The existing nucleus of activity in and around Greenwich has attracted additional investment and development, including the London Dome. But the East London boroughs have not benefited from increased benefits from tourism despite the wider dispersion of tourism from the existing West London concentration. In this respect, transport infrastructure and a lack of tourism-related employment opportunities linked to tourism development have failed to make any significant inroads on the multiple deprivation which exists in many East London boroughs. In the London-wide context, the benefits of tourism remain spatially polarised, with development and visitor spending heavily concentrated in the boroughs, with the accommodation attractions and easy access to central London. Tourism has failed to generate a wider distribution of wealth and employment for London's population to alleviate deprivation and unemployment. While this may reflect a mismatch of skills and employment needs for the tourism industry, it is evident that an absence of tourism development in East London has largely been infrastructure-related. With hindsight, a strong social argument could have been made for the London Dome development to be located across the river in East London so that it acted as a catalyst for further tourism and leisure-related development in a locality where multiple deprivation is a constant problem, and employment generation through service activities could provide a new impetus for the area.

Conclusion

This chapter has examined a range of issues and concepts associated with the analysis of tourism supply issues. The 'leisure product' concept developed by Jansen-Verbeke (1986) provides a convenient and meaningful framework in which to explore the supply of different components in urban tourism destinations that influence visitors and provide opportunities for activities. Yet even this framework is not without its problems. Some researchers question the approaches one might adopt towards the analysis of different aspects of urban tourism supply. The public and private sectors each have distinct roles to perform, although there is growing evidence of public–private sector partnerships to expand and improve the provision of services and facilities for tourists, day visitors and residents alike. However, these partnerships should not be seen in isolation from the global and local factors affecting urban tourism destinations.

This chapter argued that it is not simply the case that tourists visit urban areas because of the attractions and facilities available. The supply of services and essential tourism infrastructure is part of the tourism system that researchers can construct to analyse the functional links and activities tourists undertake in specific destinations. While this chapter discussed the different elements of tourism supply, in reality the elements coexist and interact to produce an identifiable 'bundle' of services and facilities. Therefore, it is impossible to isolate any one element of the supply as the main determinant of tourism in a specific location. Although some elements may appear dominant (e.g. attractions), without a well-developed infrastructure and network of services and facilities for tourists, tourism may fail to develop to its full potential. Yet where tourism develops as a successful enterprise, supported by the private and public sector, a variety of impacts occur in given locations which affect the tourists' experience of the destination and environment. For this reason, the next chapter examines visitors to urban areas.

Questions

1. How would you develop a framework to analyse the supply of tourism services in urban areas?

2. What is the value of the tourism business district as a framework for analysing the location and interrelationships between tourism and non-tourism services in the central area of cities?

3. How would you go about decentralising tourism development in London? What social and economic objectives would guide your decision-making?

4. What is the role of transport in the development of urban tourism?

Further reading

Ashworth, G. and Tunbridge (2000). *The Tourist – Historic City: Retrospect and Prospect*, Oxford: Pergamon.
This new edition of a classic text explores many of the tourism issues in relation to heritage, the historic city, its preservation and conservation.
Bull, P. and Church, A. (1996). 'The London tourism complex' in C. Law (ed.) *Tourism in Major Cities*, London: International Thomson Business Press, 155–78.
This is one of the few studies of tourism in London and although it is dated in terms of statistics, the principles and arguments it develops are still relevant for the new millennium.
Goodall, B. (ed.) (1989). Tourism Accommodation: Special Issue, *Built Environment* 15(2): 72–158.

This dated set of papers is a good introduction to tourist use of accommodation in towns and cities.

Jansen-Verbeke, M. (1994). 'The synergy between shopping and tourism: the Japanese experience' in W. Theobald (ed.) *Global Tourism: The Next Decade*, Oxford: Butterworth-Heinemann, 347–62.

This is a good assessment of the relationship between shopping and tourism.

CHAPTER 5

Visitors in cities: activities and attractions

Introduction

The previous two chapters looked at the supply and demand dimensions of urban tourism. This chapter discusses the intersections between supply and demand for urban tourism in terms of *'what do people actually do in cities?'* Such a question is not as easy to answer as it may seem. As this book has already demonstrated, there are substantial gaps in our knowledge of tourist activities in urban areas while an understanding of the manner in which the city may be functionally differentiated in terms of visitor attractions is also only at a relatively early stage. At first glance this last comment may seem rather odd, given the discussion in Chapter 4 of the development of specialised tourism districts (Getz 1993a). However, while some common functions may be recognised, the exact nature of visitor flows and patterns for the tourist is rarely understood nor often differentiated between different visitor markets or differences between the behaviours of visitors and those who live in the city.

The purpose of this chapter is therefore to further develop our understanding of the different tourism function[s]
different sets of tourists and the
Arguably, over time, the urban land
of visitor demands and public and p
identified in space and in terms of
noted in Chapter 3, Burtenshaw *et*
ping functional areas in the tourist c

- the *'historic city'* (historic mon concert halls);
- the *'culture city'* (museums, art g
- the *'nightlife city'* (theatres, con light districts, cafés, restaurants)
- the *'shopping city'* (cafés, restau

Source: Wöbe

The divisions provided by Burtenshaw *et al.* (1991) provide a useful way in which to divide the activities of tourists in cities. A 'business city' may be added, which also has links with tourism because of the demands of business travellers and conference and exhibition delegates, and also 'the sports city' whereby sports facilities (such as stadia) and events are also related to functional districts and associated infrastructure (Hall *et al.* 1997). Indeed, events function as a particularly important medium in urban settings to create both visitor demand and justify specific forms of infrastructure development (C.M. Hall 1992; Roche 2000) (also see Chapters 8 and 9). The final section of the chapter analyses a neglected, but extremely significant, special case of urban tourism which is the role of capital cities which, by virtue of their status, have an important symbolic role and which also integrate a number of tourism activities discussed in this chapter.

What do people do in cities?

As noted in Chapter 3 a number of broad categories of information regarding purpose of travel exist which may provide a starting point for identifying why people travel to certain cities or parts of the cities and what they do. For example, a breakdown by main purposes of visit to 35 cities in Europe by Wöber (1997b) provides an indication of some of the different dimensions of urban tourism (Table 5.1). Wöber's (1997b) study indicates that the majority of travellers to European cities arrive for business reasons with only about 27 per cent visiting for holiday-taking. However, the different breakdown of purpose of visit for different cities will clearly depend on the form and function of individual cities (Plate 5.1).

Some of the most detailed studies of the motivations and activities of urban tourists were undertaken by Tourism Canada in the late 1980s and early 1990s. According to Tourism Canada's (1991) overview of tourism in the cities of Montreal, Toronto and Vancouver, the urban experience offered by the three cities studied was composed of such activities as:

Table 5.1　Purpose of visit in 35 European cities

Purpose	%
Business and professional	46
Leisure, recreation and holidays	27
Visiting friends and relations	8
health treatment	2
	18

(1997b: 43).

Plate 5.1 One relatively unresearched urban tourism and leisure activity is visiting markets: Granville Market, Granville Island, Vancouver, Canada

- shopping in elegant and exclusive boutiques;
- visiting museums, art galleries, zoos and botanical gardens;
- dining in chic and elegant or exotic restaurants;
- attending plays, concerts and operas;
- making the rounds of bars, nightclubs, cafés and discotheques;
- attending festivals and festivities organised by ethnic communities;
- attending sports events;
- taking part in sight-seeing tours;
- visiting an oceanside location (Vancouver);
- visiting historic sites and admiring interesting architecture;
- simply strolling around the city.

Undoubtedly some of the identified activities fit into Burtenshaw *et al.*'s (1991) functional categories but others reflect a wide range of motivations for urban tourism. However, what is apparent is that not all parts of the city can equally cater for the various motivations of urban tourists, meaning that different areas of the city will have different product characteristics. The interrelationship between motivation and function bears some similarity to recent definitions of 'special interest tourism' (SIT). For example, Derrett (2001: 3) defines SIT as 'the provision of customised leisure and recreational experiences driven by the specific expressed interests of individuals and groups'. Indeed,

Plate 5.2   The ambience of the urban environment is a key attractor of urban visits as this picture of a fountain in front of the Parliament House, Canberra, Australia shows

Schofield (2001) has discussed small business and urban tourism within the context of SIT noting the importance of the multifunctionality of cities in attracting visitors (Plate 5.2).

According to Wöber (1997a: 30), 'an urban product is what the market accepts as such', or, to paraphrase Ashworth and Voogd (1990a), every urban product is an assemblage of selected resources which are bound together through interpretation, e.g. the presentation of the product to customers through a range of communications media. A tourism product exists within particular spatial boundaries which form a nested hierarchy of individual operations and attractions, urban, regional and national supply. However, the spatial borders of the particular tourism product that the consumer is interested in will often not readily correspond to the administrative and political boundaries of the city (Plates 5.3–5.5). Indeed, the core urban tourism product may be confined to a historic core or a waterfront development, with the remainder of the city not being of interest to the majority of visitors. The administrative and political problems of urban tourism will be dealt with in more detail in Chapter 7. This chapter will highlight some of the different functional characteristics of urban tourism activities and their implications for management and marketing.

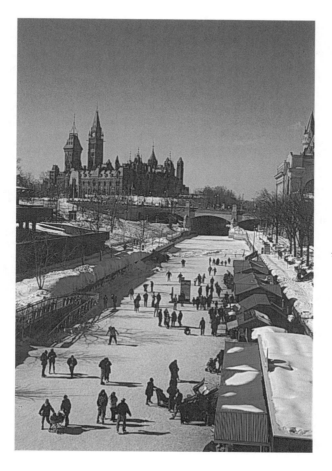

Plate 5.3 Seasonality is a vital factor in changing the appeal of the urban environment as a comparison with Plates 5.4 and 5.5 suggests of the Rideau Canal, in Ottawa, Canada in winter

Culture, heritage and the arts

The historic city and the cultural city show substantial overlap with many attractions in common. History and cultural attractions are often discussed in the context of arts and heritage tourism (Douglas *et al.* 2001). 'Culture', perhaps even more so than tourism, is an extremely difficult term to define. The term is generally used in two main ways (Tomlinson 1991; Richards 1996b). First, culture as a process, which refers to designation of 'the social field of meaning production' (Clarke 1990: 28), in other words, the manner in which

Plate 5.4   The Rideau Canal, in Ottawa, Canada in winter

Plate 5.5   The Rideau Canal in summer

people make sense of themselves and their identity in terms of social groupings such as nation, ethnicity and community. Second, culture is seen as a commercial product which is consumed. While there is substantial overlap between the two concepts, much of what is regarded as cultural tourism is aligned more closely to the latter meaning.

In an attempt to define culture more accurately for economic analysis and policy development, the Australian Statistics Working Group (1996) stated that 'the Statistical Advisory Group to the Cultural Ministers Council identified those activities which it considered were predominantly cultural in nature'. Their statistical framework defined culture to include:

- heritage;
- museums;
- zoological and botanical gardens;
- literature;
- libraries and archives;
- music;
- performing arts;
- visual arts;
- film and video;
- radio; and
- television.

All of the above influence tourism in some way in their role as tourist attractions, although the last three components of culture as well as literature also function as media influences on urban destination image as well. However, the widespread use of the term 'cultural tourism' while pointing to the marketing potential of the concept, also indicates a general failure to appreciate the complexity of the concept (Craik 2001). Indeed, Ekos Research Associates (1988) in their examination of a series of five Canadian pilot projects that attempted to integrate culture, multiculturalism and urban tourism ('Toronto for the Arts', 'Montréal Cultural Destination', 'Your Ticket to Winnipeg', 'Vancouver/Victoria Cultural Tourism Pilot Project' and the 'Highland Heart Campaign') recognised a lack of consistency in the use of the word culture:

> Both the promotional and research literature present a wide array of different usages and meanings for the key subject matters – culture, arts, culture and multiculturalism. Amidst this Babel-like confusion it is virtually impossible to make meaningful statements, since people are rarely talking about the same things when they mention the same terms. Not only does this make the accumulation of knowledge difficult, but it also renders any coherent statement of goals and strategy elusive. This has produced confusion, frustration and undoubtedly hampered the effectiveness of various efforts (Ekos Research Associates 1988: 9).

As an overarching term, 'culture' refers to the general symbol system of society. However, 'culture' contains several related elements, all of which may contribute to the touristic attractiveness of a destination. The three major components of the cultural tourism product can be identified: 'high culture', e.g. the performing arts and heritage attractions such as museums and art galleries; 'folk and popular culture', e.g. gastronomy, crafts, sport and architecture; and 'multiculturalism', which refers to cultural and racial diversity and language. Although all three dimensions of culture can be packaged as tourism products, the touristic element is greatest in high culture which can be located in specific sites and attractions as opposed to the more diffuse or non-point attractions of folk and popular culture and multiculturalism. Nevertheless, even the latter category of culture is becoming commodified through the packaging of 'lifestyles' as part of tourism promotion and through the identification of cultural precincts, such as Chinatowns or Little Italys.

As Timothy (2001) notes, few tourism researchers have studied ethnic enclaves, even though some are significant attractions, particularly in the urban context (Conforti 1996). Timothy notes that San Francisco's original Chinatown was generally considered a slum. It had a bad reputation in white American society as the dumping ground for an undesirable immigrant group (Takaki 1994). As Timothy (2001) observes, paradoxically, this very image, however, led to the development of tourism. To non-Chinese of the early twentieth century, Chinatown was a quaint and mysterious section of the city, a 'foreign colony' in America. Advertisements promised that white tourists visiting Chinatown would experience the 'sounds, the sights, and the smells of Canton'. They could imagine themselves in 'some hoary Mongolian city in the distant land of Cathay' and could 'wander in the midst of the Orient' while still in the United States, and there they would see throngs of people with 'strange faces' in the streets eating 'chop suey' (Takaki 1994: 53–4). Over time the city of San Francisco began to promote Chinatown as an exotic Chinese colony, and the dingy back alleyways were turned into picturesque little lanes. Tours began to be offered which took visitors through the curved narrow streets of Chinatown past souvenir shops, stores and restaurants. White Americans viewed the enclaves as alien districts in the heart of America – curious places to visit. In the early 1900s, tourism helped Chinese Americans survive after racial discrimination had stopped them from competing in the general labour market (Takaki 1994: 56). Around the world Chinatowns are still significant tourist destinations to this day, although social and structural conditions have improved immensely and the original social and political functions of such ghettoes have changed. For example, in San Francisco the Chinese enclave, which is home to approximately 30,000 Chinese Americans, is one of the city's most popular attractions (Abrahamson 1996).

Italian ethnic islands have also provided much of the urban lifestyle milieu that appeals to tourists, particularly in North America (Timothy 2001). Regarding the popularity of urban Italian communities, Conforti (1996: 831) claims that 'Little Italies are familiar to American tourists (and foreign visitors), usually as somewhat exotic and alien places that are quasi-foreign, where interesting food can be found, exotic people can be observed, and even a lurking danger (as the home of the Mafia) can be sensed'. Conforti (1996) also argues that tourism is a driving force for keeping the image of Little Italy alive in cities such as Baltimore, Boston and New York. It is thus 'a symbolic area with a pronounced and entrenched image shared by insiders and outsiders, an image based on the area's history and use, especially as a tourism attraction' (Conforti 1996: 836). Indeed, as Timothy (2001) observed, in some cases it is tourism that drives efforts to preserve Little Italy as a distinct ethnic enclave even after all the local Italians are gone. However, the importance of ethnic clustering in urban regions should not just be seen in a historical context: since central cities remain the commercial centre for many ethnic groups, these older centres of migration tend to be the location of first settlement for new or successive waves of migration. As Kornblum and Williams (1977: 77) observed of New York in the late 1970s, 'New York has become the capital of major streams of migration from Latin America and Asia and has a new cultural transfusion that has rejuvenated many declining neighbourhoods within the central city'.

The ease at which various aspects of culture can be packaged for tourist consumption is significant, as it has meant that what constitutes the 'culture' in cultural tourism is more often than not associated with what can be commodified. Clearly, culture is a significant aspect of the attractiveness of urban tourist destinations. Indeed, it is the very nature of the city that leads to various elements of culture, and particularly high culture, being concentrated for the consumption of tourist and local alike (Heritage Canada Foundation 1988).

The Office of National Tourism (1997) in Australia defines 'cultural tourism' as 'tourism that focuses on the culture of a destination – the lifestyle, heritage, arts, industries and leisure pursuits of the local population'. Similarly, Tighe (1985, 1986) noted that the term 'cultural tourism' 'encompasses historical sites, arts and craft fairs and festivals, museums of all kinds, the performing arts and the visual arts' and other heritage sites that tourists visit in pursuit of cultural experiences (Tighe 1986: 2). Cultural tourism was defined by the World Tourism Organization as including 'movements of persons for essentially cultural motivations such as study tours, performing arts and other cultural tours, travel to festivals and other cultural events, visits to sites and monuments, travel to study nature, folklore or art or pilgrimages' (Secretary General, WTO 1985). The range of definitions reflects the difficulties inherent in easily defining such a nebulous concept. Nevertheless, Craik (2001) notes that common elements in such definitions is the educational, experiential and communicative experience as well as the authenticity of tourist experiences and encounters (Hall and Zeppel 1990).

Although the significance of cultural tourism as a component of urban tourism is readily acknowledged, it is worth noting that a range of 'cultural' tourists exists, from the 'culturally motivated' to the 'cultural inspired' and the 'culturally attracted' tourists (Bywater 1993):

- *Culturally motivated tourists* tend to be better off financially, better educated and mainly women with substantial cultural capital in terms of their knowledge of culture (Richards 1996c). For them culture, ranging from high culture through to popular culture and multiculturalism, is the central motivation of the travel experience. In the European context, Bywater (1993) estimates that they constitute only 5 per cent of the market.

- *Culturally inspired tourists* are regarded as being inspired by a particular site (e.g. St Peters in Rome or Westminster Abbey in London) or event (e.g. a London play or Opera in the Park in Sydney). Bywater estimates that this constitutes about a third of the market, though observes, 'Culturally inspired tourists cause problems for tourist planners. They fill their day with as much as possible and frequently spend as little time and money as possible on a single destination' (Bywater 1993: 44).

- *Culturally attracted tourists* are 'incidental' cultural tourists who visit a museum, art gallery or heritage site while on holiday for other reasons. Craik (2001) refers to them as 'cultural daytrippers'. However, given that they account for approximately 60 per cent of market share, they constitute a significant segment although they pose a significant marketing challenge in that they decide to visit a cultural attraction only once they have already reached the destination.

Further evidence for this spread of motivations with respect to culture is to be found in an Australia Council for the Arts study undertaken in conjunction with Saatchi and Saatchi Australia to identify the value that Australians place on the arts. This study identified five main market arts segments in contemporary Australia (Australia Council 2000a):

- *Arts lovers* (17 per cent): who are very positive about the arts and are in favour of change.
- *Satisfied* (21 per cent): who are generally quite positive about the arts and who do not see particular reasons for the arts to change.
- *Interested* (25 per cent): who are open to a positive experience of the arts but can see ways in which the arts could change to improve their attitudes towards them.
- *Disinclined* (25 per cent): who are not particularly interested in the arts at present but can still see changes that would make them feel more positive about the arts.
- *Disengaged* (11 per cent): who have little or no interest in the arts, give them a low value and are not interested in seeing them change in the future.

However, the large number of Australians with generally positive attitudes towards the arts is obviously of significance for cultural tourism because of the extent to which arts activities, such as events, galleries, museums and arts and crafts, constitute domestic tourism activities. According to the Australia Council (2000b), 'In one year in Australia there are 12 million attendances at public art galleries, 6.7 million admissions to live theatre, 5 million admissions to musical theatre (including opera), 3.4 million attendances at dance perform-ances, 4 million attendances at classical music concerts, and 19.5 million attendances at popular music concerts'.

The growth in cultural and heritage tourism can be attributed to an increas-ing awareness of heritage, greater affluence, changed leisure patterns, greater mobility, increased access to the arts, increased levels of education and as a reaction to the demands of modern society (Brokensha and Guldberg 1992). For example, it has long been noted that in rediscovering heritage, people are looking back with a certain nostalgia at the way things used to be. According to Konrad (1982: 412), 'This increased emphasis on retrospection, whether due to a psychological need for continuity, the desire to transcend contempor-ary experience, or the urge to know one's roots, characteristically leads to some form of appreciation and concern for the past'. Urban heritage sites provide much of the focus for this psychological motive in travelling (Tunbridge and Ashworth 1996; Ashworth and Tunbridge 2000). As Lowenthal (1981: 236) observed, 'The past belongs to everyone: the need to return home, to recall the view, to refresh a memory, to trace a heritage, is universal and essential'.

However, the notion of heritage does not just refer to old buildings. At its most basic, heritage represents the things we want to keep. For example, the notion of inheritance and the responsibilities that it entails are at the heart of the World Heritage Convention. Article 4 of the Convention states that each party to the Convention recognises 'the duty of ensuring the identification, pro-tection, conservation, presentation and transmission to future generations' of the world's cultural and natural heritage' (http://www.unesco.org/whc/ heritage.htm). Therefore, heritage is the things of value that are inherited. If the value is personal we speak of family or personal heritage, if the value is communal or national we speak of 'our' heritage. More often than not, heritage is thought of in terms of acknowledged cultural values. For instance, a residence is not usually deemed as heritage unless it can be seen as part of the symbolic property of the wider culture or community, as an element of that culture's or community's identity.

The linkage between heritage and identity is crucial to understanding not only the significance of heritage as something to be valued but also the difficul-ties managers face in identifying and conserving heritage. As the Wellington City Art Gallery (1991) stated with respect to an exhibition on urban heritage in the city: 'References to heritage typically propose a common cultural her-itage. Distinguished old buildings are spoken of as being part of "our" her-itage. It is suggested that "we" metaphorically own them and that their preservation is important because they are part of our identity. But who is the we?' Issues of identity, meaning, and values therefore indicate the likelihood of their being conflicting notions of ownership attached to heritage and therefore conflicting sets of values and interests with which the manager has to contend. Indeed, the emergence of multiple perspectives on heritage has led to an expanded meaning of heritage beyond simply the things we want to keep. As Hall and McArthur (1996b: 2–3) recognised:

The identification and management of heritage is dependent on our perceptions and values. Increasingly, heritage managers realise that it is not sufficient just to manage the physical heritage resource in isolation from the people who are the 'owners' of the heritage and those who come to experience it. Particularly at a time when, more and more, heritage managers are depending on visitors to provide economic, educational and social justifications for their activities.

There is not necessarily a given, concrete thing that is intrinsically heritage. Heritage resources are an expression of appraisal and represent an entirely subjective concept. 'Resources *are* not, they *become*; they are not static but expand and contract in response to human wants and human actions' (Zimmermann 1951 in Mitchell 1979: 2). Heritage should be seen as a culturally constructed idea and set of values attached to a wide range of artefacts, environments and cultural forms. For example, the case of the regular rebuilding of temples and shrines in some Asian countries, e.g. the Ise shrine in Nara Prefecture, Japan, which is rebuilt every 20 years, indicates that the Western perception of the significance of the conservation of the original fabric of a building as being vital in terms of authenticity is culturally constructed and irrelevant in other cultures (Hall and McArthur 1998). Heritage resources are therefore defined according to individual and collective attitudes, values and perceptions, wants, technology, economics, politics and institutional arrangements. What is a heritage resource in one culture or place may be 'neutral stuff' in another. Heritage resources are subjective, relative and functional. As Tunbridge and Ashworth (1996: 6) recognised, heritage is 'a product of the present, purposefully developed in response to current needs or demands for it, and shaped by those requirements'.

Therefore, Tunbridge and Ashworth (1996) identified five different aspects of the expanded meaning of heritage:

1. A synonym for any relict physical survival of the past.
2. The idea of individual and collective memories in terms of non-physical aspects of the past when viewed from the present.
3. All accumulated cultural and artistic productivity.
4. The natural environment.
5. A major commercial activity, e.g. the 'heritage industry'.

Undoubtedly, there is significant overlap between these various conceptions of heritage. However, according to Tunbridge and Ashworth (1996: 3), 'there are intrinsic dangers in the rapidly extending uses of the word and in the resulting stretching of the concept to cover so much. Inevitably precision is lost, but more important is that this, in turn, conceals issues and magnifies problems intrinsic to the creation and management of heritage'. Ironically, the uncertainty about what constitutes heritage is occurring at a time when heritage has assumed greater importance *because* of its relationship to identity in a constantly changing world. As Glasson *et al.* (1995: 12–13) recognised, 'One reason why the heritage city is proving such a visitor attraction is that, in easily consumable form, it establishes assurance in a world which is changing rapidly'.

The implications of the subjective nature of urban heritage will be dealt with in more detail in Chapter 7 in relation to management and planning. However, in the meantime we can note the importance of commodification in identifying heritage attractions. Nevertheless, without commodification, for example through packaging and promotion and the creation of a product for which money can be exchanged, it needs to be recognised that the tourism industry as we know it would cease to exist. Yet the notion of commodification should be regarded as implying more than just a commercial exchange between consumer and producer. More often than not it has also come to imply a private rather than a public good. Indeed, one of the hallmarks of the post-industrial, postmodern city (see Chapter 2) is that many items that were once regarded as public goods, e.g. museums, art galleries, and recreational and sporting facilities, have now been privatised or corporatised with the intent of creating direct financial return to the private sector, a corporation or some form of public–private partnership. Such a situation has created its own difficulties. For example, as Uzzell (1994: 293) observes in the case of the museum sector in the United Kingdom, 'museums are increasingly subject to commercial competition from other tourism and leisure attractions'. Therefore, within the functional areas of the city which have been packaged for tourist consumption, individual institutions and attractions find themselves 'competing' not only with other institutions for visitor expenditure and numbers but also with other forms of entertainment, including video and amusement arcades, cinemas and live entertainment – 'the nightlife city' – possibly to the point where art, culture and heritage can no longer be easily differentiated from entertainment.

The nightlife city

The urban ecology of entertainment and leisure is the result of the complex interplay between political, economic, social and transport factors. Cities have long served as locations for entertainment, particularly as transport technology tended to reinforce the central place functions of urban areas. For much of the nineteenth and twentieth centuries museums and art galleries tended to be centrally located so as to allow access to the new middle classes. However, as well as providing access to high cultural entertainment, central location, particularly in relation to rail transport, was also utilised by theatres, nightclubs, restaurants and hotels. Indeed, the availability of entertainment and nightlife is clearly one of the main motivations to travel to large urban areas. Yet, in reading the tourism and urban literature it is remarkable how the importance of entertainment services (which are often temporal in nature, hence the notion of nightlife) is generally overlooked or ignored (see Ashworth *et al.* 1988 and Bianchini 1995 as notable exceptions). Such a 'blind spot' in studies of the urban environment may perhaps relate to the difficulty that some research providers have in funding something that is related to fun and entertainment, or the fact that spatial patterns have often been determined by 'moral' decisions on the part of planners and politicians that seeks to determine what is 'appropriate' in urban areas. Indeed, when entertainment districts are discussed it is often in the context of the 'symbolic economy' or the 'cultural economy' (e.g. Friedrichs 1995; Landry *et al.* 1995; Zukin 1995). Although such concepts provide useful theoretical constructs, particularly in relation to re-imaging and regeneration of cities (see Chapters 8 and 9), they fail to recognise a very important aspect of urban tourism – cities are fun! Although not everyone is able to share in such fun because of a range of significant and important sociocultural, political and economic factors, for the tourist and for many others the city is as much a site of fun as it is of social injustice.

As many readers will be aware nearly every city website in the world will have a section labelled either nightlife or entertainment. Such sections typically refer to bars, clubs, music venues, concerts, raves, casinos, restaurants and, sometimes, adult entertainment. Often entertainment and nightlife is described in relation to certain districts of the city. For example, the significance of nightlife districts such as King's Cross in Sydney or Soho in London is recognised by Ashworth and Tunbridge (1990: 65):

> Restaurants and establishments combining food and drink with other entertainments, whether night-clubs, discos, casinos and the like, have two important locational characteristics that render them useful in this context: they have a distinct tendency to cluster together into particular streets or districts . . . and they tend to be associated spatially with other tourism elements including hotels, which probably themselves offer public restaurant facilities.

As noted above there are historical reasons for such spatial association, particularly in relation to transport and regulation. The entertainment morphology of the city should therefore be seen in light of forces for centralisation and decentralisation. From a commercial perspective centralisation can often provide greater market access assuming that there are good transport connections to the central city while downtown location can also provide for easy access to tourists. Accessibility is therefore a key factor for the success of entertainment and nightlife districts. From a planning perspective the location of entertainment attractions in the inner city can serve to offset the loss of employment in 'traditional' manufacturing industries as well as the changed use of waterfront areas. Forces for decentralisation may be found in the process of suburbanisation, which often led to some entertainment, such as cinemas and bars, being located in suburban centres, while access to television and video/DVD entertainment may also serve to compete with the entertainment attractions of the central city. Overarching these factors are general changes in leisure tastes and fashions which influence leisure and tourism lifestyles (see Chapter 2 for a theoretical perspective on these locational issues).

The role of entertainment areas in cities is substantial. For example, in a study of Cologne between 1985 and 1991, Friedrichs (1995) noted that the administrative budgets for the arts and culture grew by an average 34 per cent while those for science and research declined by exactly the same percentage. Similarly, in a study of Chicago, Los Angeles and New York, Zukin (1995) indicated that between 1980 and 1990 there had been a 34 per cent increase in the employment of 'creative artists' from 202,000 in 1980 to 270,000 in 1990. With such shifts of government support and rates of growth it is therefore not surprising that such measures are an important component of the symbolic capital, which lies at the core of many 'creative cities' (Landry *et al.* 1995) that seek to attract not only visitors but employment and investment as well. However, in examining the growth of entertainment services, particularly in recent years, we are also forced to notice the connections between this and the urban restructuring and change discussed in Chapter 2. The growth of entertainment and nightlife districts is therefore as much a response to economic restructuring and deliberate urban policy decisions as it is to the tastes of the consumer.

The importance of economic restructuring as a factor in driving government support for urban entertainment services was illustrated in Hall and Hamon's (1996) study of casino development in Australia. According to Hall and Hamon (1996) casino development in Australia has gone through three waves or stages, each related to recessionary economic conditions. The first wave of casinos, built in the early 1970s at the time of the oil crisis, were small, European-style casinos developed in the small cities of Hobart and Launceston in Tasmania, and Darwin and Alice Springs in the Northern Territory. In these cases the casinos were regarded as one-off developments which it was hoped would stimulate tourism.

The 1982 recession led to the second wave of casino development, with casino licences being granted in Townsville, the Gold Coast, Adelaide and Perth. The last three were American-style high-turnover casinos. The Townsville and Gold Coast casinos were developed in already established tourist destinations. The Perth and Adelaide casinos were the first large casinos in the world to be built in large population centres that were aimed at the local market, with the tourist market being a secondary consideration (Chenoweth 1991). Perth's Burswood Casino was used to redevelop an old industrial waste dump, while the Adelaide Casino was located in an old railway station. However, neither was used as central components of a larger urban redevelopment or re-imaging strategy (see Chapter 8), although both the West and South Australian State Governments used tourism as a justification for their development. Nevertheless, as McMillan (in Chenoweth 1991: 16) observed in discussing Australian casino developments, 'They're quite obviously there for the locals, despite the rhetoric about doing it for the tourists. That notion of casinos being a honeypot and tourists flocking to them is a myth. All the specifications are for stable, local populations. Tourists are just the icing on the cake.'

The third wave of casinos was a government response to the recession of the late 1980s and early 1990s. The latest round of casino developments in Brisbane, Canberra, Melbourne and Sydney meant that, for the first time, every State and Territory capital has a legal casino. This period of casino development witnessed a new stage in the granting of casino licences whereby, in addition to traditional factors such as government increasing its tax revenue and the argument that the casinos would attract tourists, casino development became an integral component of urban redevelopment and reimaging strategies. For example, the Canberra Casino, which opened in 1994, was specifically designed to help revitalise the main downtown area, while funds from the casino licence were earmarked for arts and cultural developments in the inner-city area. The Brisbane Casino was used to provide a financial basis for the restoration of the heritage listed former Treasury building in which the casino is located. The Brisbane Casino development was also utilised by the Queensland State Government as a component of waterfront redevelopment strategies which includes the development of a major cultural, convention and leisure complex on the site of the 1988 Expo. The two largest developments of this third wave of casinos are located in Melbourne (Victoria) and Sydney (New South Wales). As these cities are by far the two largest in Australia, their casino licences were the most keenly contested and possibly the most contentious, with considerable community, legal and political debate surrounding both the bidding and the planning processes for each casino (Hall and Hamon 1996). However, in both cities the two casinos have become central components of tourism promotion and have had a major impact on the regional economy including, in the case of Melbourne, influencing retail location in the city.

Despite their importance, the city of entertainment is influenced by more than just the siting of attractions. The chapter earlier noted the importance of ethnic clusters and neighbourhoods as tourism attractions. National and ethic cultures are obviously important in identifying some neighbourhoods as tourist attractions; however, the clustering of certain lifestyle groups can also prove attractive to visitors. For example, the cities of San Francisco and Seattle in the United States have 'homosexual communities that have made tremendous contributions to the civic and leisure life available to the metropolitan population in general' (Kornblum and Williams 1977: 77). Levine (1977) argued that San Francisco's 'culture of civility' owed a great deal to the city's gay communities, while Adler and Brenner (1992) also noted the importance of the creation of gay and lesbian gendered space in attracting other gays and lesbians.

Given the degree of homophobia in certain sections of society, 'many gays will choose to travel in search of an anonymous or safe environment in which to be gay' (Hughes 1997: 5). Therefore, perhaps unsurprisingly, being a gay-friendly location acts as a significant factor in travel planning. Among American urban destinations, San Francisco rates first, with 49 per cent having visited in the past three years. Resorts such as Palm Springs and Key West also remained significant destinations. Activity- and event-related trips are also very popular among the gay community. In the previous three years, 50 per cent went to a gay pride event, 13 per cent travelled to attend a circuit party and 4 per cent participated in a 'gay ski week' event (Community Marketing 1999).

One of the world's most famous gay events, the Sydney Gay and Lesbian Mardi Gras, has substantial economic impacts. Research by the Australian Graduate School of Management (AGSM) in 1998 found that Mardi Gras contributed more than A$40 million to the Sydney economy. There were more than 5,000 international visitors to Sydney during the 1998 festivities, 3,600 of whom came specifically for the event. Of the 7,300 interstate tourists, 4,800 had Mardi Gras in mind, and AGSM also recorded 2,400 'holidays at home' (Pettafor 1999). According to Beggs (1999), the Mardi Gras attracts more international and interstate visitors than any other cultural festival in Sydney, Melbourne, Perth or Adelaide, with the festival guide carrying advertising from Hahn Ice (beer), Qantas (airline), Telstar (communications), Foxtel (satellite television), Land Rover (automobile) and other large corporations. International visitors to Mardi Gras spent an average of A$347.25 per day and stay in Australia for about 21 days, outstripping general tourist spend by 30 per cent. In relation to the effects of the 25th Mardi Gras held in 1999 the corporate manager at F.O.D. (Friends of Dorothy) Travel, Greg Miller, stated that 'One of the things people forget is that these tourists come back every year. There is very strong repeat business and when they're here, they spend' (cited in Pettafor 1999). Nevertheless, despite such financial success, gay tourists are not always welcome (Ryan and Hall 2001).

As Hughes (1997: 6) observed, 'Tourism and being gay are inextricably linked. Because of social disapproval of homosexuality many gay men are forced to find gay space. . . . Gay space is limited . . . and gays find it necessary to travel in order to enter that space' (see also Adler and Brenner 1992). The extent to which gays travel has made them a lucrative travel market has been the subject of recent debate (e.g. Holcomb and Luongo 1996; Clift and Forrest 1999). According to the 1999 report on the gay and lesbian travel industry by Community Marketing (1999) the gay and lesbian travel sector is worth approximately US$47.3 billion, or about 10 per cent of the US travel industry total. Gays and lesbians have a higher propensity to travel than the non-gay population. According to the report

- 85 per cent of gays and lesbians surveyed took a vacation in the previous 12 months, compared to a 64 per cent national average;
- 36 per cent took three or more vacations, while 45 per cent went overseas, compared to just 9 per cent of the national average.

Gay and lesbian income demographics reported in this travel survey are similar to those of other studies (e.g. Pritchard et al. 1998). Many gays and lesbians have a higher household income level. Some 75 per cent have incomes beyond US$40,000/year, and 23 per cent have an income over US$100,000/year (compared to 9 per cent of mainstream American travellers). Though one of the most significant indicators of the gay market's propensity to travel was the result that of the survey population 78 per cent held a valid passport, compared to just 29 per cent of the mainstream (Community Marketing 1999). Similarly, in Australia, *Campaign* magazine's research shows that gay men earn and spend much more than the population average. Conducted by Significant Others Marketing Consultants, the survey results reported gay men earning significantly above the national average with almost 40 per cent travelling overseas the previous year, more than half eating in a restaurant at least once a week and 23.6 per cent dining out two or more times a week (Brother Sister 1996).

Although gay-friendly areas are not red-light districts, the two types of locations do share factors in common in relation to occupying liminal space (Ryan and Hall 2001). Most significantly both areas become attractive to consumers who wish to seek concealment of their activities from those who are hostile to their behaviours and acceptance from those who are part of the location they are attracted to. Ryan and Kinder (1995), for example, stress the importance of concealment of the client. In an analysis of Auckland's red-light district they write: 'From the viewpoint of the tourist seeking a passive or active sexual entertainment . . . Fort Street represents a safe "crimogenic" place. Indeed, in many senses the term [crimogenic] is perhaps inappropriate for Fort Street. It offers a high degree of physical safety' (Ryan and Kinder 1995: 33).

Given the hedonistic nature of tourism, in many places the spatial areas of both tourist and sex worker overlap, and many hotel managers can bear witness to the fact that their premises might be regarded as both holiday accommodation and brothel (Ryan and Hall 2001). In some parts of the world the overlap becomes obvious and explicit. The 'red-light' districts of many cities are often seen as tourist attractions which attract the sensation-seeking tourist as participant or observer (Ashworth *et al.* 1988). Amsterdam's red-light district, Sydney's King's Cross and the soi of Patpong are tourist attractions for clients and onlookers alike. When conditions become too threatening or dangerous the visitor can be driven off, but where a degree of control over illegal activities is maintained, then certain tourists may be attracted. The vitality of entertainment zones is therefore quite directly linked to the social history of particular lifestyles in the city and the associated attempts by city planners, politicians and moralists to legislate for specific lifestyles. Indeed, the moralistic nature of urban planning has often sought to encourage certain types of entertainment regarded as appropriate, e.g. opera and ballet, and discourage that which is inappropriate, e.g. striptease clubs and brothels. As Kornblum and Williams (1977: 77) observed, 'The central location of commercial sex and sexually deviant groups is not regarded as a blessing by the guardians of civic virtue'. Such a perspective is well illustrated in the writings of Lewis Mumford, one of the most influential urban planners of the early twentieth century:

> Every step in relaxation from spontaneous horseplay to drunkenness, from flirtation with music to a sexual orgy, is conducted with a view toward producing a

maximum profit for the enterpriser, Saturnalia charges what the traffic will bear. Bawdiness . . . becomes itself a jaded, night-in-night-out part of a metropolitan routine; it measures its titillations and charges accordingly. And since the overt code of Western society has no place for such compensatory outbursts or moral holidays, an additional air of furtiveness hangs over these enterprises, even when they have official sanctions. Thus is formed a tie-up with the underworld of racketeers and criminals which introduces new elements of degradation into gambling and promiscuous sexual intercourse: connections between 'respectable classes' (Mumford 1938: 265–6).

The shopping city

Chapters 3 and 4 highlighted the important role that shopping plays in the urban tourist experience. This section further describes the role that tourism plays but also notes the relationship of shopping and retailing to particular modes of consumption and production strategies, most significant of which is the changing nature of the city retail centre. For example, in Dunedin in New Zealand where once there were over 70 butcher's shops in a city of just over 100,000 people, now there are 7. The main shopping street, George Street, does not have a butcher's or a greengrocer's shop but it does have many cafés, restaurants and gift shops. In Dunedin, as elsewhere around the world, the nature of urban retailing has changed.

The decline of the social and economic significance of traditional retail centres began with the rise of the automobile in the 1950s and the dominance of the suburban shopping centres and malls in the 1960s. Since that time urban and regional planners and mainstreet retailers have been grappling with the problem of revitalising the downtown area. In the 1960s and early 1970s one solution was the wholesale destruction of areas of the inner city in the name of urban renewal and the replacement of these areas by, often architect award-winning, concrete boxes, which were economic and social disasters. However, the problems of mainstreet and the downtown district did not fade away.

Throughout the 1970s and 1980s the onset of processes of gentrification led to a revival in the fortunes of many inner-city retail areas, with many small developers taking advantage of low property values to renovate old buildings. The establishment of such new businesses has had substantial implications for the revival of traditional retail districts (Smith 1972; Mattson 1983; Jansen-Verbeke 1986, 1990, 1991). As Lew (1989: 15) noted:

The gentrification process brought new ideas and energy to older retail areas at a time when the American public began to experience a nostalgia for what was perceived as the simpler values and lifestyles of a rapidly disappearing past . . . Considerable time, effort, and money have brought some remarkable changes to many inner-city landscapes, and the resulting impact in any one city is a mixture of pre-existing design elements and the ideas and innovative concepts superimposed by the new gentry.

The American experience in inner-city development has been repeated throughout the Western world. For example, in Australia and New Zealand areas such as Carlton (Melbourne), Paddington (Sydney), Fremantle (Perth), and Parnell and Ponsonby (Auckland) have all experienced a revival thanks to the inner-city migration of the middle classes. One of the main driving forces in the regeneration of older retail districts is tourism and leisure-related shopping. Potential tourist visitation can serve as a justification for the redevelopment of a downtown area or it may be a consequence of the establishment of a more attractive area which encourages increased leisure shopping by people outside the immediate community. For example, pedestrianisation of streets in retail areas is often a response to competition from suburban shopping centres through the creation of shopping areas that provide leisured space and which encourage social interaction (Roberts 1987). Either way, 'the growth of tourism as a form of economic development is having a major impact on the urban landscape of some cities, and reflects a changing attitude toward inner cities as well as a need to diversify repressed economies' (Lew 1989: 15).

Yet consumption is more than just an act of purchase. The development of inner-city areas for leisure and tourism-related shopping can also be seen as representing a particular pattern of identity and lifestyle consumption in which the goods and services that people consume effectively constitute their sense of self and other (Hebdidge 1979, 1988; Baudrillard 1988; du Gray 1996). One particular area of urban tourism and leisure which has been the subject of much research on consumption has been that of food (Cook and Crang 1996; Bell and Valentine 1997). As Gregson (2000: 321) noted, 'food and the performances accompanying its purchase, preparation, and eating are central to the expression and reconstitution of key social relations and food is also an admirable commodity to "think through", both metaphorically and in terms of material relations of power and inequality'.

Several food trends are closely connected to the role that food plays in urban tourism. First, in Western societies there is a tendency for people to eat out more (Plate 5.6). For example, in New Zealand this shift to eating away from home saw a 35 per cent increase in meals consumed in restaurants, cafés and cafeterias during 1996, which resulted in the food service industry becoming the third largest retail sector in New Zealand. That year sales reached $NZ2.2 billion (a 15 per cent increase from 1995) and the industry accounted for 124,000 full- and part-time jobs. Of an average weekly spend of NZ$25.00 per capita on food purchased away from home, NZ$15.68 was spent in restaurants and cafés and NZ$5.30 on takeaways – equating to around NZ$1.38 billion expenditure in restaurants and cafés during 1996 (Food Service Association 1997). Second, as a result of ethnic migration, travel and economic globalisation urban areas in Western cities have witnessed the increased availability of a range of different cuisines in restaurants and other commercial hospitality

Plate 5.6   Food consumption is a significant tourist activity in urban areas, reflected in this picture of the Pearl, Reykavik, Iceland, where a restaurant and interpretive complex has been built on water storage tanks

outlets. The shops on the main street near one of the authors in Dunedin, New Zealand, are as much a source of local cheeses, artisan-made pasta from northern Italy, cold pressed extra virgin olive oil from the South of France, Belgian fruit beer, Vietnamese sauces, Baltic pickled herring and anchovies from Portugal as they are a McDonald's burger or a Starbuck's coffee. Third, food has become a very significant expression of contemporary lifestyles by which interest in and consumption of food has become a form of symbolic capital. Indeed, it is ironic that while there is increasing space given in the media to food and the social and culinary practices that surround it, more and more people are becoming unfamiliar with the art of cooking and instead purchase their pre-prepared meals from the supermarket or dine out.

The production and consumption are as important to food as they are to tourism. Food becomes a significant point of difference for tourism promotion at both the regional and the urban destination level. For example, many cities, such as Singapore and Hong Kong, increasingly highlight their cuisine as a way of attracting visitors or encouraging them to stay longer. However, the relationship between food and tourism is not unidirectional: tourism can also have a substantial impact on food production and consumption. Menus may change in order to meet perceived tourist demands. For example, dog became less available in Korean restaurants during the time of the Seoul 1988 Summer

Olympics because of concerns over foreigners' perceptions. Nevertheless, while such actions may be regarded as a loss of food identity, it should also be noted that such places now have a greater selection of foodstuffs available to them than ever before, as noted in Chapter 2 in relation to the discussion of McDonaldisation (Ritzer 1996), concern over homogenisation are perceived as a 'threat' only by the person who has an immediate sense of the diversity and otherness of global cultures. For the vast majority of the world's population, who do not have the opportunity to travel widely and experience other cultures and foods, it usually does not.

The placefulness of food offers rich potential for tourism through the opportunity for place promotion through various media as well as creating tourist attractions through explicitly connecting place with certain forms of production and consumption (Hall and Mitchell 2002a, b). National and regional tourist organisations are often major sponsors and supporters of food programmes (e.g. Madhur Jaffrey's series on Asian cuisine; and Keith Floyd's travel to Australia) while advertising is also used to connect travel to the place whether it be on the media or in the supermarket through food promotions. Although such measures are perhaps as much an indicator of the lifestyle characteristics of the consumer as they are of conscious place promotion, they do draw attention to the way in which food has become a component of the tourism product at the level of both the destination and the consumption of the individual tourist. The interrelationship between food and tourism is therefore intimately tied up with the production and consumption of the cultural meaning of place and space.

According to Cook and Crang (1996: 133), such actions are used to 're-enchant' (food) commodities in order to 'differentiate them from the devalued functionality and homogeneity of standardised products, tastes and places'. Indeed, restaurants and the supermarket shelf (along with media products) are now places to experience globalisation. As Arce and Marsden (1993: 304) commented,

> Distant places of production are . . . brought together into a network where diverse environments interact . . . through the actions of a corporate food industry . . . [But the] objective is far from that of producing the homogenized 'world scene'. Rather, it is necessary to provide a whole range of differentiated food commodities as if instantly harvested from the local field for the suburban and urban platter.

The global-postmodern is therefore not marked 'by the homogenizing impacts of a material culture promoted by a monolithic transnational capitalism but by the staging and (re)construction of difference in a "globalization of diversity"' (Pieterse 1995 in Cook and Crang 1996: 133).

The global economic and cultural network in which tourism, food and cuisine are positioned is not unproblematic, though. The industrialisation of food and cuisine can lead to the loss of biodiversity as some varieties of plant and animal become favoured for properties such as keeping or their ability to produce a consistent product. For example, an American breed of potato – the Russet Burbank – is used almost universally in making French fries (Love 1986; Probyn 1998), to the exclusion of the growing of other types of potatoes. While such massification obviously has implications for the maintenance of gene pools, the obverse also exists in that specialised, rare or highly localised food products can also be attractive because they are highly differentiated and offer substantial symbolic value to the consumer (of course they may also taste good!). In addition, reaction to issues such as food homogenisation, genetic engineering of foods, food scares, decline in income for local and regional food producers, and concerns over the freshness and quality of food has also generated renewed interest in many urban centres in produce markets. Such specialised products also offer the opportunity for the development of urban visitor products through the development of produce and farmers' markets at tourist attractions, shopping and market tours, specialised restaurant menus and cooking schools. Indeed, outsider interest in local produce may serve to stimulate local awareness and interest, and not only may assist in diversification, and direct purchase from producers, but may also encourage community pride and reinforcement of local identity and economic networks (Hall and Mitchell 2002a).

The impact of the development of urban farmers' and producers' markets where farmers sell their produce direct to the public is substantial. Over 90 per cent of the approximately one million shoppers a year come to farmers' markets for the fresh produce. According to an economic impact study prepared for the Farmer's Markets of Ontario (FMO) network for every dollar spent at the market, another two dollars ripple through the provincial economy. About 27,000 people in Ontario are directly involved in preparing and selling the products at farmers' markets. In Ontario alone, annual sales at farmers' markets total almost C$500 million, leading to an overall economic impact on the Ontario economy of C$1.5 billion. Furthermore, of considerable significance for urban redevelopment projects is the notion that rather than take sales away from existing businesses, farmers' markets attract customers for them, with an estimated 60–70 per cent of market-goers visiting neighbouring businesses on their way to and from the market (Chorney 1999). Indeed, such is the success of the farmers' markets in Ontario that the FMO is extremely concerned about attracting and retaining bona-fide producer-vendors in order to maintain the original farmers' market concept.

In California the issue of authenticity of farmers' markets has been dealt with through the development of a programme of certification under state legislation. A certified farmers' market (CFM) is a location approved by the county agricultural commissioner where certified farmers offer for sale only those agricultural products they grow themselves. California certified farmers' markets are operated in accordance with regulations established in 1977 by the California Department of Food and Agriculture. Such is the interest in farmers' markets that there are now over 350 communities with CFMs in the state, with the number still growing (California Federation of Certified Farmers' Markets 2001).

Sport in the city

Sports tourism is an increasingly important component of urban tourism (Standeven and De Knop 1999). As a form of travel sport tourism falls into two categories: travel to participate in sport and travel to observe sport (Green and Chalip 1998). Therefore, sport tourism may be defined as travel for non-commercial reasons, to participate or observe sporting activities away from the home range. Additional important dimensions of sports tourism are the development of sporting infrastructure and the use of sporting events as a form of promotional vehicle for cities. This section will briefly examine these aspects of sports tourism, with particular attention being given to the role of sport in urban tourism.

Two types of tourists who travel to participate in sporting activities can be identified. First are *activity participants* who pursue sport as a form of leisure for the development and expression of skills and knowledge and for personal enrichment. Second are hobbyists who are competitive and who may be described as *players*. Players are amateurs whose participation in sporting activities is continual and systematic, and whose 'aim is to acquire and maintain the knowledge and skills enabling the individual to experience uncommon rewards from the endeavour' (Stebbins 1982: 262). However, the number of people travelling to participate in sporting events, although significant for some smaller urban destinations, is much smaller than the number travelling to observe them. Nevertheless, sport plays an important role in motivating and attracting tourist activity, particularly among domestic travellers. The role of sport in motivating people to travel in New Zealand is confirmed by Lawson *et al.* (1997). They adopt the term 'sport devotees' to describe travellers who are motivated by watching or participating in sports at any level. This segment of the travel market explains fractionally over one-fifth (20.7 per cent) of New Zealand domestic travel activity. A further 13.0 per cent of the market is motivated by 'outdoor adventures', much of which also falls within the domain of sport.

The potential attraction of sports tourism for urban areas is illustrated by Rawn's (1990) study of sports fans in Indianapolis. She describes the transition of Indianapolis from manufacturing town to international sports venue under the heading of 'smokestacks to stadiums: affluent sports fans are a clean industry'. Rawn cites an analysis of the spectators at the 1989 GTE Tennis Championships in Indianapolis, where 36 per cent of the spectators had household incomes over $75,000 (as opposed to 4 per cent of the Indianapolis population), one-third stayed in a hotel and went shopping, and 84 per cent ate in restaurants. According to Rawn such sports events have helped create service jobs in Indianapolis to help make up for employment loss in the manufacturing sector. However, in a later analysis of the investments, policies, and strategy behind Indianapolis' sports-related economic development endeavours, Rosentraub *et al.* (1994) determined that the sports strategy had little impact on development and economic growth in Indianapolis versus other mid-sized cities in the region.

The economic significance of spectating for the tourism industry is substantial. Sports events, from the Olympics to little league games, may have a major impact on regional economies and on the prestige and image of destinations (Kolsun 1988; Page 1990; Ryan and Lockyer 2001). Indeed, one of the primary justifications for the redevelopment of inner-city areas for sports and events is the perceived economic benefits of tourism (e.g. C.M. Hall 1992; Law 1993). For example, in Australia the 1986/87 America's Cup Defence was used to redevelop Fremantle in Western Australia, a Commonwealth Games bid from Victoria was used as a justification for further redevelopment of the Melbourne Docklands, with Sydney utilising the 2000 Olympic Games to similar effect (Hall 2002a). However, such large-scale redevelopments are not without their social and economic costs (Olds 1998). As Essex and Chalkley (1998: 195) noted 'As a result of the traffic congestion, administrative problems, security breaches and overcommercialization, Atlanta did not receive the kind of media attention it would ideally have liked. Its experience highlights the dangers as well as the benefits of being under the international Olympic spotlight'.

Short-term staged attractions or hallmark tourist events, otherwise referred to as mega- (Ritchie and Yangzhou 1987) or special events (Burns et al. 1986) are major festivals, expositions, cultural and sporting events which are held on either a regular or a one-off basis. Hallmark events have assumed a key role in international, national and regional tourism marketing strategies, their primary function being to provide the host community with an opportunity to secure high prominence in the tourism marketplace for a short, well-defined period of time (Ritchie 1984; C.M. Hall 1992).

The hallmark event is different in its appeal from the attractions normally promoted by the tourist industry as it is not a continuous or seasonal phenomenon. Indeed, in many cases the hallmark event is a strategic response to the problems that seasonal variations in demand pose for the tourist industry. However, the ability of an event 'to achieve this objective depends on the uniqueness of the event, the status of the event, and the extent to which it is successfully marketed within tourism generated regions' (Ritchie 1984: 2). Events can help construct a positive image and help build commercial and public awareness of a destination through the media coverage they generate (e.g. Tourism Victoria 1997a, b). For example, South Australia has for many years been known as 'The Festival State' to many Australians because of the success of the bi-annual Adelaide Festival of Arts, an image reinforced by the hosting of the Adelaide Grand Prix and associated activities. More recently, Victoria has been aggressively promoting itself as the event state, with Tourism Victoria (1997b) reporting that its research indicates that it is now recognised as the Australian city which hosts major international sporting and events, ahead of Sydney, Adelaide, Brisbane and Perth.

The high profile attached to many one-off (e.g. an Olympics) or regular (e.g. a major league club) sporting events has led many governments and municipalities to subsidise the construction and operation of stadia, arenas and associated sporting infrastructure (Lipsitz 1984; Page 1990; C.M. Hall 1992; Roche

2000), which raises a range of policy issues (Weed 2001). Okner (1974) noted several reasons why government involves itself in sports in this way:

- prestige and 'big-town' image;
- may lead to generation of new industry through relocation and establishment, and may add to the marketing power of locations;
- the possible generation of additional employment, consumer sales and tax collection that result from sporting events;
- additional recreational opportunities for community residents, especially if attendance at sporting events replaces other activities which are socially disruptive;
- beneficial effects on the morale of the citizens resulting from the presence of a successful sports team in the city; and
- encouragement of interest in sports among young.

The construction of stadia and sports facilities to promote tourism and assist in urban redevelopment is not new. The 1932 Summer Olympics and the associated construction of the coliseum in Los Angeles were designed to promote tourism (Reiss 1981), while American college football games such as the Orange Bowl (Miami), Sugar Bowl (New Orleans) and the Cotton Bowl (Dallas) were established to help revive ailing cities during the great depression (Reiss 1989). Similarly, racing was legalised in the United States (Michigan, Ohio, California, Texas, Florida) to help establish tourism (Reiss 1989).

However, much of the American literature concerning sports as economic development suggests that publicly financed stadia are not even close to a break-even proposition, and many criticise both the quantity and quality of jobs created from the presence of a professional sports team (Goodman 1979; Baade 1996). Yet it is also clear that the 'intangibles' of professional sports have a powerful sway (Quirk and Fort 1992; Chema 1996; Helyar 1996; Rosentraub 1996). Baim (1994) examined financial data from 15 subsidised stadiums in the United States and found that, with very few exceptions, the sole rational justification for stadiums built to receive or keep a sports franchise revolve around the external benefits (e.g. civic pride and leisure time options) brought to a city. However, the costs to the taxpayer varied widely depending upon the lease negotiations for each facility, noting that the smaller the market size, the more likely that the market accrued external benefits. Nevertheless, such a position could be negated because the per capita subsidy tends to be higher, and the lease terms far more generous to teams from smaller cities because of the substantial competition between medium-sized markets to attract sporting teams (Whitford 1993). For example, the Los Angeles Rams moved from Anaheim Stadium in Orange County, California – where they were losing US$6 million a year – to St Louis's new municipally funded US$276 million domed downtown stadium for the 1995 season. In exchange, the Rams organisation received a stadium lease with rent of only US$250,000 for the whole season, US$13 million in moving expenses, half of game day expenses paid by the city, a separate practice facility, all the revenues from boxes, club seats, and regular tickets, guaranteed sales of deluxe seats, most of the advertising and concession profit, and US$27 million to pay off the lease in Anaheim (Sickman 1995).

Nevertheless, the benefits of sports tourism, particularly when geared towards domestic competitions or smaller-scale sporting events that utilise existing infrastructure, may be substantial (Table 5.2). In the New Zealand context Higham (1999) argued that the economic and tourism impacts of sporting occasions that complement host city facilities and infrastructure are found to be generally positive and well in excess of the administrative costs of hosting such events. For example, the 1997 Golden Oldies Rugby competition hosted by Christchurch attracted teams from around the world to a unique sporting celebration. The duration of the event extended over two weeks during the tourist shoulder season and attracted participants with a high-spending demographic profile. Precisely the same scenario applies to the Dunedin Masters Games, a biennial sporting occasion, which attracts several thousand

Table 5.2   The tourism and economic development potential of sport: contrasts based on the scale of sport

Sporting mega-events	Regular season, domestic/regional sports
Bidding process Major costs associated with the bidding process. Public expense of bidding inflated (occasionally to crippling levels) by political corruption and sponsors' interests. Best bid not necessary successful. Furnishing political and sponsors' interests contributes to success.	Minor expenses incurred during the bidding process. In some cases the bidding process is not required at all (e.g. regular season sporting competitions). Most suitable bid usually successful.
Development issues Significant development costs associated with sporting events such as the Olympic Games, Commonwealth Games, World Cup and the America's Cup. Economic benefits associated with infrastructural developments received by business interests rather than host community.	Infrastructure generally exists. Tends to occur within the capacity thresholds of the host city. Infrastructural development costs usually appropriate to the scale of the host city.
Development legacy Legacy of underutilised and expensive facilities with associated financial debt.	The upgrading of facilities (if necessary) tends to benefit sportspeople, spectators and administrators.
Economic benefits Dominated by big business and sponsors. Local residents see comparatively little direct economic benefit. Effective means	Local community more likely to share in the positive economic benefits associated with sport.

Table 5.2   *(cont'd)*

Sporting mega-events	Regular season, domestic/regional sports
of taking money from the public purse and relocating it in private interests.	Far less burden placed on public funds and the local taxpayer.
Short-term tourism benefits Short-term upswing in tourism offset by time-switching. Displacement of tourists commonly associated with mega sporting events. 'Sports junkies' demonstrate little interest in sampling the wider tourism product at the destination.	Visitors are likely to be more frequent travellers rather than time-switchers. Less displacement of tourists occurs if sports complement the scale of host city infrastructure. Tourists likely to experience wider tourism product of the destination.
Medium-term tourism benefits Medium-term downturn in long-haul tourism associated with mega-events due to time switching.	Medium-term tourist patterns unlikely to be influenced by time switching.
Destination image Much to lose from poor publicity, capacity constraints, financial costs, political activism and terrorism.	Destination image stakes not so high. Great potential for sport tourism to act as a promotional vehicle if opportunities are recognised.
Social issues Crowding and congestion of tourism infrastructure often associated with mega-events. Local residents often excluded from participation in the event due to cost. Local lifestyles generally disrupted by mega-events and security issues.	Crowding and infrastructural congestion less likely to exist if the scale of the occasion is appropriate to host city. Greater potential for local resident involvement in the sporting occasion.
Local resident issues Displacement or removal of local residents takes place where cities are eager to capitalise on destination image. Facilities often developed in lower socio-economic areas. Host community displacements, evictions, increases in rates and rents.	Negligible impact on local residents. Often a positive impact on those who choose to be involved. Greater level of local access to sporting occasions.
Political issues Possible use of sport as a political vehicle.	Lack scale and importance to be used as a political vehicle.
Security issues Significant security cost and risks associated with sporting mega-events.	Negligible security issues and financial costs associated with domestic sporting occasions.

Source: After C.M. Hall (1992); Faulkner *et al.* (1998); Higham (1999).

high-yielding sports tourists from around New Zealand and, increasingly, from overseas. The temporal component of this event, again, contributes to mitigating a period of low domestic tourist activity in the host city (Moore 1995). Therefore, sport is a direct and indirect element of the visitor activity patterns and use of space within cities (Bale 1990) and the city-region (Fennell 1998).

Business city

Business tourism is tourism related to travel for reasons of work with the main components being short-term events such as meetings, conferences, conventions and exhibitions, which are of great economic significance to tourism (Law 1987; Hiller 1995; Wootton and Stevens 1995; Swarbrooke and Horner 2001). 'Meetings' covers all off-site gatherings, including conventions, congresses, conferences, seminars, workshops and symposiums, that bring people together for the purpose of sharing information. Major markets include the corporate and the association markets (Astroff and Abbey 1995). 'Incentive travel' is a motivational tool used by companies to encourage employees to increase their performance by rewarding increased productivity or the attainment of corporate goals. 'Exhibitions', also described as 'expositions', are designed to bring together suppliers of products, industrial equipment and services in an environment where they can demonstrate and promote their products and services (Montgomery and Strick 1995). Most major cities in the developed world have purpose-built conference and exhibition centres usually developed through government funding. Indeed, the development of such centres is usually a product of the business significance of cities and their accessibility by transport. Business tourism is attractive to cities for a number of reasons (Swarbrooke and Horner 2001):

- business travellers usually have a higher level of spending per head than other types of tourism;
- the business traveller is a core market for airlines and hotel chains; and
- the specialised nature of business travel has led to the development of a range of ancilliary services and infrastructure which generate employment and income.

Meetings and conventions offer a great deal of stability to the tourism industry as they are an integral part of business practice. Furthermore, meetings and conventions are typically booked well in advance, and larger meetings and exhibitions often have a five or ten year timespan for their development, planning and marketing. Therefore, 'they are far less vulnerable to short-term economic changes and . . . provide a buffer against short-term violent cyclical swings in . . . travel business' (Barnes 1988: 248). According to the International Congress and Convention Association (ICCA 2001), for Association meetings the average registration fee per delegate per day in 2000 was US$97 while the average fee per delegate per international meeting for the year 2000 was US$439. The average income from registration fees per international meeting in 2000 was US$357,483, based on the number of participants per meeting each specific year. The average income from fees compared with the number of meetings last year grew dramatically to US$1,024,188,957. In terms of number of participants attending international meetings ICCA figures take into account only meetings attended by between 50 and 10,000 participants. Only 11 per cent of meetings in 2000 were attended by more than 2,000 participants but that represented a gradual rise from 7 per cent in 1997. The average number of participants per meeting has been increasing since 1993 from 638 to 815 in 2000.

Meetings in North and South America have a considerably higher average attendance than meetings in other continents. However, Europe has the largest share of participants with 54 per cent; North America took 17 per cent and Asia 13 per cent (Table 5.3 records international association meetings on a city-by-city basis). In contrast the corporate meetings market is much smaller. Of the meetings included in the ICCA survey, most meetings attracted between 20 and 100 participants. The vast majority of meetings were attended by fewer than 500 people, with considerably fewer in most cases and only 7 per cent were attended by 1,000 or more delegates.

Although the meetings are themselves important it must also be realised that the business tourist also utilises other facilities and attractions visited by other market segments. Indeed, the entertainment and shopping city is often very important for business travel given the role that dining and entertainment have in establishing business networks and relationships. Owing to the high yield of the business market, numerous destinations are seeking to attract business travellers through the development of new convention and meeting centres, hotel services and improved transport connections. In the case of the latter many aviation services for the business traveller designed to ease access have been reduced since the increase in aviation security after September 2001. Nevertheless, as in the case of sports tourism the development of conference centres is usually a public sector activity in which the taxpayer underwrites such centres' losses. For example, in the case of Australia a report by the Bureau of Tourism Research (BTR) (1998) concluded that the main hindrance to growth of the MICE sector is the lack of data and research to encourage informed decision-making, particularly for investment purposes; while locations without dedicated MICE facilities believe that business could be increased if larger or more suitable facilities were available. However, they noted that this last point may be somewhat problematic, as it is debatable whether the revenue gener-ated from the additional visitors to these locations would exceed the costs of building the additional capacity, or provide the region with a fair rate of return on its investment (BTR 1998). Indeed, Chapter 7 notes the substantial sums spent by some convention bureaux in order to attract the meetings market to their cities.

Table 5.3 Number of international association meetings recorded by city 1998–2000[a]

Rank	City	1998	1999	2000
1	London	36	31	56
2	Madrid	78	49	55
	Paris	47	36	55
4	Vienna	83	64	54
5	Sydney, NSW	32	42	49
6	Stockholm	58	42	48
7	Rio de Janeiro	18	37	47
8	Amsterdam	56	42	46
9	Barcelona	44	42	40
	Helsinki	39	48	40
	Singapore	43	46	40
12	Berlin	37	43	39
	Edinburgh	35	36	39
14	Budapest	37	46	38
15	Melbourne, Vic.	28	26	35
16	Copenhagen	64	55	33
	Hong Kong	15	30	33
18	Oslo	22	24	31
19	Reykjavik	5	10	29
20	Lisbon	53	24	27
21	Prague	29	36	25
22	Montreal, PQ	24	10	24
23	Bangkok	17	24	23
	Brussels	30	24	23
25	Glasgow	15	16	22
	Munich	13	25	22
27	Beijing	15	17	21
	Buenos Aires	21	14	21
29	Bergen	9	15	20
30	Cape Town	20	12	19
	Florence	15	15	19
	Maastricht	10	13	19
33	Adelaide, S.A.	14	8	18
	Dublin	18	18	18
	Jerusalem	42	23	18
	Rome	30	29	18
	Seoul	34	40	18
38	Geneva	18	8	17
	Istanbul	14	22	17
40	Chicago, IL	9	8	16
	Manila	22	18	16
	Nice	27	16	16
	Taipei	25	23	16
44	Hamburg	18	7	15
	The Hague	10	16	15
	Tokyo	29	18	15
	Toronto, Ont.	8	17	15
	Vancouver, B.C.	21	25	15
49	Göteborg	13	16	14
	Valencia	5	13	14

[a] Included in the ICCA database are meetings that are organised on a regular basis, attract at least 50 participants and rotate between three different countries.

Source: After International Congress and Convention Association (ICCA) http://www.icca.nl/

The capital city

Capital cities represent a special case of urban tourism and integrate many of the functional and behavioural characteristics of urban tourism discussed above. As Canada's National Capital Commission (NCC) observed (2000b: 9), 'The combination of political, cultural, symbolic and administrative functions is unique to national capitals'. The capital functions as 'the political centre and symbolic heart of the country. It is the site of crucial political decision-making, yet it is also a setting for the nation's culture and history, where the past is highlighted, the present displayed and the future imagined.' Although such statements are obviously significant in political and cultural terms, the wider significance of capital city status for tourism has been grossly under-researched and, perhaps, under-appreciated. Nevertheless, capital status is important. As capitals provide an administrative and political base of government operations there will therefore be spin-off effects for business travel in terms of both those who work in the capital and those who are seeking to lobby government or influence decisions. Indeed, when Australian Prime Minister John Howard decided to make Sydney's Kirribilli House his official residence, rather than the Prime Minister's Lodge in Canberra, 'the move was interpreted as another, lamentable step in the concentration of power . . . Sydney already had the lion's share of financial and business influence, claiming the headquarters of the Reserve Bank, the Stock Exchange, about half of the top 100 companies and the regional headquarters of the majority of multinational companies' (Bradley 2000). However, Mr Howard's actions were not only significant in their effect on the symbolic status of Canberra and the location of political power but were also interpreted as having a small though significant effect on the travel behaviour of public servants and lobbyists. To a city the size of Sydney such a shift was not significant, although for Canberra its potential is, given that the city hosts approximately 300 industry and professional bodies that locate there because of the access it provides for lobbying purposes (Bradley 2000). (A discussion on tourism in Canberra is provided in Chapter 7.)

In addition to business-related travel, capital cities are also significant for tourism (Plate 5.7) because of their cultural, heritage and symbolic roles (also see Chapter 4 and the discussion of London). They are frequently home to some of the major national cultural institutions while also tending to have a significant wider role in the portrayal, preservation and promotion of national heritage, which showcase national culture (Therborn 1996). Such a concentration of arts and cultural institutions will therefore have implications for the travel and activity behaviour of culturally interested tourists as well as contributing to the image of a city as a whole. For example, Dublin Tourism's promotion states

Welcome to Ireland's capital city, steeped in history and youthful energy. Medieval, Georgian and modern architecture provide a backdrop to a friendly

Plate 5.7 The urban visitor experience and ability to understand the nature of the urban environment leads visitors to take guided tours, as shown in this sightseeing tour in London, where convenience and flexibility in an all-day ticket allows visitors to board and exit the bus at various attractions at their leisure

bustling port, where the cosmopolitan and charming converge in the delightful diversity that is Dublin. Fine museums and art galleries chronicle its long and colourful past, while the pubs and cafés buzz with traditional entertainment. Dublin's attractions are ranging from: castles, museums and art galleries to the lively spirit of Temple Bar (Dublin Tourism 2000).

According to the Austria National Tourism Office,

Vienna was and remains one of the undisputed capitals of art, music, architecture, fashion, theater, literature, intellectual pursuits, as well as a site of political and social significance in the international arena . . . Much of Vienna's cultural history is reflected in magnificent buildings and some of the glorious music created here (Austria National Tourism Office 2000).

And, in the case of Wellington, the capital of New Zealand, Tourism New Zealand promotional material states:

> The city is home to the Royal New Zealand Ballet and the New Zealand Symphony Orchestra, as well as national dance, drama, opera and musical groups. Four professional theatres operate year-round, so there are live shows every night. Wellington is also the home of much New Zealand heritage, including Te Papa, New Zealand's national, leading edge museum (Tourism New Zealand 2000).

However, while the cultural opportunities available in capital cities may be seen to be a tourist advantage, their political dimensions may not. For example, Totally Wellington, the regional tourist organisation for the city of Wellington states in its media information material:

> [Wellington] has transformed from a dull government centre into a vibrant urban destination – but Wellington's not stopping there.
> Wellington continues to outstrip Rotorua as the fourth largest visitor destination in terms of guest night national market share.
> Visitors have been lured by attractions such as Te Papa, the amazing interactive national museum of New Zealand – which had over 3.5 million visits in less than two years. Supporting Te Papa is a whole myriad of other New Zealand heritage attractions, the arts, shopping, restaurants and cafés and a plethora of events that provide an ever-changing face to Wellington (Totally Wellington 2000).

Given that designated capital cities exist in nearly every country in the world, it is 'reasonable to suppose that the capitals do have some conditions and features in common in the way they have developed, which justify their being treated as a single group' (T. Hall 1997: 2). 'Capital cities are places where authoritative and legitimate decisions are taken . . . capitals are most often the seat not only of the political institutions of government, but of administrative ones as well' (Andrew and Taylor 2000: 38). Nevertheless, Peter Hall (2000) has recognised a number of different types of capitals:

- *Multifunction capitals* – combining most of the highest national-level functions, e.g. Paris, London, Stockholm.
- *Global capitals* – representing supranational roles in politics, commercial life or both, e.g. New York, London, Tokyo.
- *Political capitals* – created as seats of government, often lacking other functions or only gaining them over time once the political function is established, e.g. The Hague, Washington, Ottawa, Canberra and Brasilia.

- *Former capitals* that have lost their role as the seat of government but that retain other historical functions, e.g. Leningrad, Philadelphia.
- *Ex-imperial capitals* – former imperial cities that have lost their empires but that may still function as national capitals or retain other functions that may also give them a pre-eminent gateway function, e.g. Lisbon, Madrid, Vienna, London (see Clark and Lepetit 1996; T. Hall 1997; Driver and Gilbert 1999).
- *Provincial/state capitals*, e.g. Montreal, Munich, Melbourne, Vancouver.
- *Super-capitals* – functioning as centres for international organisations, e.g. Brussels, Strasbourg, New York.

Peter Hall's classification does offer some insights into the function that capital cities may have, but to this list we can also add to other forms of the notion of a capital:

- Cultural capitals – particularly in Europe where a formal structure of declaring cultural capitals has been developed within the framework of the European Union.
- Brand capital – this is where a place describes itself as a capital in terms of a particular product, e.g. Zurich in Ontario as the bean capital of Canada.

The use of the notion of a capital in terms of branding and culture is significant for tourism both in terms of place promotion but also attracting high-yielding cultural tourists. Indeed, given the growth of place-marketing in an increasingly competitive global economic environment such a development is logical in terms of branding places and place competition. However, for the purpose of this discussion the notion of a capital is related primarily to political, administrative and symbolic functions which operate at a national or provincial level. Indeed, as Dubé and Gordon (2000: 6) observed, 'Planning for cities that include a seat of government often involves political and symbolic concerns that are different from those of other urban areas'. They may also be substantial in terms of scale. For example, Canada's national and provincial capital cities account for over 30 per cent of the population and 9 of the 19 largest metropolitan areas, while in Australia the figure is closer to 70 per cent of the population. Although their economic significance may be substantial, 'there is no rule that a political capital automatically attracts concomitant economic functions' (P. Hall 2000: 8), although a capital may be deliberately located so as to fulfil economic roles. For example, in the case of Brasilia, which was inaugurated as Brazil's capital in 1960, 'By transferring the federal political structure to a location in the centre of the country, it integrated the national territory at the same time that it allowed for national economic development' (Roriz 2000: 17). It should also be noted that in tourism terms the establishment of Brasilia has had a substantial impact on domestic travel flows within Brazil. Similarly, if capital status is lost it can have a significant effect on visitor numbers, as in the case of the transfer of the German national capital from

Table 5.4 Overnight stays in accommodation units[a] in selected German cities 1997–99 (millions)

City	1997	1998	1999
Berlin	7.99	8.27	9.48
Munich	6.43	6.88	7.28
Hamburg	4.35	4.51	4.65
Frankfurt upon Main	3.45	3.64	3.92
Cologne	2.74	2.81	2.96
Düsseldorf	2.19	2.32	2.29
Dresden	1.80	1.96	2.14
Stuttgart	1.69	1.95	2.03
Nuremberg	1.55	1.77	1.83
Leipzig	1.24	1.15	1.31
Bonn	1.13	1.10	1.07
Hanover	1.12	1.09	1.13
Münster	1.14	1.13	1.13
Bremen	0.91	0.97	1.04
Wiesbaden	0.90	0.93	0.98
Rostock	0.82	0.86	0.97

[a] In accommodation units with nine or more guest beds.
Source: After Federal Statistical Office of Germany (2001) *Overnights in Tourism 1: City Tourism*, http://www.destatis.de/basis/e/tour/tourtab7.htm, © Statistisches Bundesamt, Wiesbaden 1999.

Bonn to Berlin after the reunification of Germany where Berlin has witnessed a dramatic increase in overnight stays and Bonn a decline (see Table 5.4).

In addition, the historical development of capital cities may also provide them with a significant transport gateway or hub function. Particularly with respect to European imperial powers the assumption of capital status meant that capital cities were often at the centre of a web of transport networks, many of which exist to the present day. In the case of London, for example, this gateway and hub function exists to the present day and is extremely significant for international visitor arrivals. In addition, in London the hub function combines with the clustering of national institutions to give London pre-eminence in the visitor arrivals. For example, 9 of the top 20 attractions in the United Kingdom that charge for admission are located in London with a tenth, Windsor Castle, being on the outskirts of the city.

The planning of capital cities, along with the planning of tourism in capital cities, may be somewhat problematic given potentially competing agendas and demands between the national, regional and local level. As Peter Hall (2000: 6) noted, 'capital city issues dominate planning in Canberra and Brasilia, and yet are often minor concerns in London, Paris and Tokyo'. In great part this relates to the institutional arrangements established to undertake capital city planning as well as the cultural and political framework within which capital cities exist. For example, Washington, DC in the United States and Canberra in Australia have national government-mandated authorities specifically established to reinforce the capital city symbolic function, although Wellington in New Zealand does not. However, the establishment of a specific planning development body for a capital does not necessarily mean that it will embrace tourism, although arguably the creation of a specific organisation to promote national or regional identity and symbolism must have an influence on place promotion strategies and the attraction of visitors (see Chapter 7).

In a number of capital city jurisdictions, such as Canberra in Australia, tourism was actively discouraged in the past as some planners perceived it at odds with the 'cultural' aspects of the capital (Chapter 7). In contrast, more recently established bodies have actively embraced tourism because of its contribution to the symbolic status of the capital and the economic development values of the tourist dollar. For example, the Capital Commission of Prince Edward Island in Canada established in 1996 has a mandate to promote tourism and business opportunities for Charlottetown. According to Cumming (2000: 24), 'the commission has capitalised not only on the city's historical significance but on its waterfront setting, its heritage as a microcosm of Canadian immigration and settlement, its cultural diversity, its unique mixture of Georgian and Victorian architecture, and the story of its social, religious and entrepreneurial development'. One of the most important contributions that such organisations do make to tourism is the extent to which the funding they provide acts to establish tourism attractions, such as museums and galleries, in specific locations as well as providing an overall attractive environment for visitors. For example, the built and natural environments of Ottawa, 'as well as events and programs, educate, instil pride, please the senses, and enrich the quality of life for residents and visitors. They contribute to the memory of Canadians and international visitors alike, as integral parts of the Capital's symbolic image' (NCC 1998: 114). As Milroy (1993: 86) noted, 'capital cities were recognized as doubly bound to be good physical environments where people live out ordinary lives, as well as symbolically-rich cities that capture the qualities a state wishes to portray to the larger world'.

A good example of the relationship between capital city status and tourism is Ottawa in Canada. Declared capital of the new Canadian Confederation in 1867, Ottawa was then only a small city of 18,000 people covering 760 hectares. Today, the Canadian National Capital Region (NCR), located on the northwestern fringe of the Quebec City–Windsor urban corridor, covers approximately 4,660 km^2, of which 2,720 km^2 are in Ontario and 1,940 km^2 are in Quebec. The NCR is now Canada's fourth-largest metropolitan region with a population of over one million residents. Approximately 75 per cent of the NCR population are located in Ottawa–Carleton in Ontario and 25 per cent in the Outaouais in Quebec. The core area of Ottawa–Hull is the centre of NCR cultural, retail and business activities as well as the focal point for public transit systems (NCC 1998).

Ottawa is an excellent example of Gottmann's (1983) observation that 'capital cities often act as hinges between different regions of a country'. Ottawa lies at the border between French- and English-speaking Canada, a history of interaction between labour and capital, as well as being at a location where different ecological regions also coincide (NCC 1999).

Prime Minister Wilfred Laurier stated in 1896 that he wished to make Ottawa the 'Washington of the North': 'I would not wish to say anything disparaging of the Capital, but it is hard to say anything good of it. Ottawa's not a handsome city and does not appear to be destined to become one either' (1884, in NCC 1998: 2). Indeed, Laurier's comments heralded a long-standing concern with beautification in the city which lasts to the present day in both landscape and planning terms. The desire of successive Canadian governments to position Ottawa as the symbolic heart of the country and as a city of international significance has meant that Ottawa has been subject to a long history of formal planning to enhance Ottawa's status.

There are a number of primary benefits of visiting Ottawa that are unique to a capital city. In a survey conducted in 1991 85 per cent of respondents agreed that it was a good way for young people to learn about their country, while the opportunity to learn about Canada was cited as important by 57 per cent of respondents (NCC 1991). Indeed, a unique characteristic that is shared among all visitors to Ottawa–Hull is 'the desire to visit national cultural institutions and physical landmarks that symbolize and reflect all of Canada' (NCC 1991: v). According to the NCC (1999: 63): 'The function of a national cultural institution (e.g. museum) is to display, protect and explain past, present and future national phenomena and human achievements. National cultural institutions are also used to communicate social, cultural, political, scientific, technical, or other knowledge through various media'.

As noted above, one of the hallmarks of a capital city is the extent to which it enables national institutions to be clustered in a relatively small area. Table 5.5 indicates the number of visits to national institutions and attractions in Ottawa between 1992 and 1999. Parliament Hill is also one of the most visited heritage sites in Canada with 1.5 million visitors each year. Tourism now contributes well over a billion Canadian dollars to the Ottawa region economy and makes a substantial contribution to employment as well as government taxes.

The main avenue for Canadian government actions to reinforce the role of Ottawa's capital city status is the National Capital Commission (NCC), which has the mission 'To create pride and unity through Canada's Capital Region' (NCC 2000a: 5). Established in 1959 the Canadian Parliament created the NCC giving it the mandate to develop a capital that would reflect Canada as the country evolved into a modern state. The NCC is a Crown corporation governed by a national board of directors (the Commission) and reports to Parliament through the Minister of Canadian Heritage. The National Capital Act of 1958, amended in 1988, directs the NCC:

- to prepare plans for and to assist in the development, conservation and improvement of the national Capital Region in order that the nature and character of the seat of the Government of Canada may be in accordance with its national significance; and

Table 5.5   Ottawa museum and attraction attendance 1992–99 ('000s)

Attraction	1992	1993	1994	1995	1996	1997	1998	1999
Museum of Nature	242.1	281.3	343.5	267.4	282.6	258.6	260.0	278.7
Aviation Museum	135.2	150.5	157.8	139.6	145.4	158.8	160.9	162.9
National Gallery	379.8	394.6	515.4	548.8	532.2	758.3	633.6	514.0
Royal Canadian Mint	34.9	39.5	38.2	43.6	79.7	96.5	102.3	125.6
Photography Museum	48.2	36.2	35.5	39.2	43.8	43.1	36.6	44.6
Science & Technology Museum	403.7	388.0	402.5	371.6	410.5	406.5	411.8	415.0
Museum of Civilization	1,213.1	1,236.5	1,198.5	1,191.3	1,297.2	1,205.2	1,409.0	1,361.1
War Museum	337.5	111.6	189.7	232.4	111.3	114.6	145.8	115.4
Agriculture Museum	121.2	96.6	122.0	111.0	112.3	140.1	147.8	165.9
Parliament Hill	523.8	542.0	514.4	516.2	467.8	491.6	494.6	503.2
Rideau Hall	41.7	36.0	27.4	45.9	69.3	77.9	122.5	124.8
Currency Museum	18.1	20.2	20.4	23.0	28.5	24.5	26.3	37.6
Supreme Court	24.0	27.4	30.9	34.0	34.2	30.0	33.0	34.3
National Archives	27.3	24.9	20.4	19.1	12.6	11.7	9.1	8.9
National Library	9.9	9.5	16.4	15.4	13.0	7.4	11.2	5.3

Source: After Ottawa Tourism and Convention Authority (2000) *Statistical Report*, Ottawa, 86, 88, 89.

- to organise, sponsor or promote such public activities and events in the National Capital Region as will enrich the cultural and social fabric of Canada, taking into account the federal character of Canada, the equality of status of the official languages of Canada and the heritage of the people of Canada (NCC 2000a: 6)

The NCC's mandate also includes coordinating the policies and programmes of the Government of Canada with respect to the organisation, sponsorship or promotion by federal departments and agencies of public activities and events related to the NCR. In addition, it is responsible for approving the design of buildings and land use, as well as any changes in use relating to federal lands in the NCR (NCC 2000a). According to the NCC (2000b) the political function of the capital is fulfilled through the accommodation of those institutions, facilities and events that are required for the parliamentary process to function:

the cultural function of the Capital is to represent the achievements, cultural identities, customs and beliefs of the Canadian people. It has the institutions, events, attractions, symbols, landscapes, pathways and associated facilities that are required to present the nation's human and natural resources, and to display Canadian history, creativity and knowledge. It also exhibits the various cultural values, aspirations and traditions of Canadians (NCC 2000b: 10).

Although the NCC is clearly not primarily a tourist organisation, its actions and policies over the years have created both substantial tourism resources for the region in the form of attractions as well as imaging the city through its promotional and marketing campaigns. The significance of the NCC for tourism cannot be overestimated. As Tunbridge (1998: 95) observed, 'In an unmanaged state Ottawa's tourism resource would be modest: a physical environment recreationally attractive, but unexceptional in Canada; a historic ambience with distinctive elements, but weak by international standards; and an overall cultural environment which was in the 1960s the butt of jests . . . and a non-place to most further afield'.

According to the NCC it 'exists to promote national pride through the creation of a great capital for an increasingly diverse body of Canadians' (2000a: 8). A key focus of achieving its strategic goals since the early 1990s has been the theme of renewal and the development of core area vision for the NCR. In order to achieve its goals it has 'fostered the re-development of the By Ward Market, where a mix of commercial and residential uses has restored life and preserved the character of a unique heritage neighbourhood' and is looking to regenerate the Sparks Street mall area 'only a block from Parliament Hill . . . It forms the interface of the "civic" and "capital" realms. It is an expression of Ottawa and, as such, of Canada. The revitalization of Sparks Street is therefore an important symbol of Canada's commitment to a vibrant future that is solidly rooted in the past' (NCC 2000a: 3). Significantly, a future tourism focus is the development of the NCR 'as an ecodestination . . . However, to respond successfully to the needs of future travellers – not just eco-tourists, but also increasing numbers of business people, convention-goers and seniors – the NCC must support the development of new Capital services and infrastructure' (NCC 2000a: 9). In addition, the NCC has developed a series of parkways in the Ottawa region that have a historic role as recreational and leisure corridors for motorists and cyclists. The parkways also link into the transitway system and act as 'gateways' to the NCR which remain 'influencing the perception of visitors and to communicating the image and landscape of the Capital' (NCC 1998: 52).

The extent to which the NCC had made a financial commitment to urban renewal in the NCR is substantial. Until 2000 over C$109 million had been spent as part of the capital construction programme, with the NCC estimating that over C$44 million would be spent in 2001 and C$27 million in 2005 (NCC 2000a). Over C$13 million a year is allocated to promoting and animating the NCR, over C$50 million goes into real asset management and development and C$1.6 million into the planning process itself. Examples of the planning function of the NCC include development of urban land master plans, transportation planning, including contribution to a joint planning study for an interprovincial rapid transit facility, conduct of environmental impact assessments and environmental site assssessments, completing a policy for and identifying cultural landscapes in the NCR (NCC 2000a; see also Chapter 7).

Given the desire of the NCC to create a meaningful 'Capital experience' programming activities have been established in recent years, thereby creating a substantial events package for visitors. The annual Winterlude festival is now promoted internationally by the Canadian tourism industry while the annual

Canada Day celebrations have considerable national profile. For example, the televised events of the Canada Day programme in 1999 had a total of 876,000 viewers for the noon show and 1,338,000 viewers for the evening show (NCC 2000a).

Meisel (1993: 4) commented that 'capital cities are an important index to the dominant political values of their countries'; to this we should perhaps add that they are significant barometers of urban change at a global scale. Capital cities have come to be subject to the same forces of economic restructuring and reduction in government funding that has affected so many other cities in the Western world over the past 20 years. Indeed, it may be possible to argue that because of their traditional administrative functions capital cities have been even more dramatically affected by changes in the role of the state and the subsequent changes in government expenditure in some cases than many other urban centres. One clear result of this is the increased attention being given to tourism as a means of employment and revenue generation for capital city regions. This therefore leads us to Drewe's observation that the future of capital cities

> depends at least as much on their functioning regularly as cities as on their being capitals . . . it may indeed be possible to achieve a more or less balanced development; coping successfully with economic-technological change, respecting both ecological limits to urban growth and cultural imponderabilia, and reducing distributive injustice' (Drewe 1993: 368–72).

If Drewe is correct then one can anticipate that the function of tourism and place-marketing in capital cities will become even more important as capital cities seek not only to meet their symbolic functions but also to compete for capital in an increasingly competitive global place-market.

Conclusion

This chapter has highlighted some of the intersections between the demand and supply of urban tourism experiences. At the beginning of the chapter it was noted that many of the activities in this chapter bore some of the hallmarks of special interest tourism. Indeed, one of the features of urban tourism is the extent to which it is able to offer a myriad of different products – 'what the market accepts as such' – to satisfy the wide range of desires, expectations and motivations that exist in the urban marketplace. Indeed, it is this enormous range of products and therefore potential experiences that attracts people to visit cities. Simply by virtue of the agglomeration of services in the one place cities attract visitors. However, the availability and location of product are not random phenomena.

As noted both in this chapter and throughout the book different functional areas of the city can be identified and these parts of the city have certain defined attributes in which particular social and economic practices are played out. However, the chapter has also noted the role that the public sector itself plays in influencing where these practices occur either through legislation and regulation, i.e. in relation to the sex industry, or through investment and incentive programmes in order to encourage the development of desired attractions, facilities and infrastructure.

This is not to say that the urban tourism experience is deterministic. One of the great possibilities of urban tourism is the capacity of surprise, whether it be wandering around a shop or meandering through back streets. Indeed, it is the interplay between supply and demand that leads to functional differentiation of the city over time. Such areas are constantly shifting, moving and changing in reaction to the connectedness of production and consumption of contemporary lifestyles and social and economic practices. Nevertheless, cities do seek to intervene in this relationship in order to maximise their returns from tourism and it is to these points that the book will now turn.

Questions

1. From a tourism perspective what are the key features of capital cities?

2. Why are the possible advantages and disadvantages of the development of large stadia or conference centres?

3. What are the key food trends that influence urban tourism? Try to answer this question in relation to the restaurants and food suppliers where you live.

4. How might ethnic identity contribute to the development of urban tourism product?

Further reading

On issue of culture and heritage in cities see

Richards, G. (ed.) (1996). *Cultural Tourism in Europe*, Wallingford: CAB International.

Ashworth, G. and Tunbridge, J. (2000). *The Tourist-Historic City: Retrospect and Prospect of Managing the Heritage City*, Oxford: Pergamon.

Conforti, J.M. (1996). 'Ghettos as tourism attractions', *Annals of Tourism Research* 23(4): 830–42.

Gives a very useful introduction to the importance of ethnicity in the demand and supply of a certain type of urban tourist attraction.

Swarbrooke, J. and Horner, S. (2001). *Business Travel and Tourism*, Oxford: Butterworth-Heinemann.

This recent book gives a basic introduction to the field of business travel. For further information on the convention sector also see the website of the International Congress and Convention Association (ICCA) http://www.icca.nl/

Bell, D. and Valentine, G. (1997). *Consuming Geographies: We Are Where We Eat*, London: Routledge.

Provides some interesting reading on what we eat and why. For those with an interest in markets also see the US National Directory of Farmers' Markets: http://www.ams.usda.gov/farmersmarkets/ and the website of the Farmers' Markets of Ontario: http://www.fmo.reach.net/

Bianchini, F. (1995). 'Night cultures, night economies', *Planning Practice and Research* 10: 121–6.

Is a very useful introduction to the spatial and temporal dimensions of nightlife.

CHAPTER 6

The impact of urban tourism: economic, socio-cultural and environmental dimensions

Introduction

The development, expansion and operation of tourism in urban areas have both beneficial and negative effects for the city and its population: in simple terms, tourism leads to impacts in urban areas (Racine and Cosinschi 1990; Jensen and Blevins 1998; Simpson 1999). Yet this concern for the impact of tourism is not confined to urban areas: it is part of a growing concern for the impact and long-term sustainability of tourism across the world (Hall and Lew 1998). But the combination of the expansion of tourism and world population growth based in mega-cities (O'Connor 1993; Hall and Page 2000) means that in the twenty-first century, a greater emphasis is now placed on urban areas as places to work, live and visit. By understanding the impact of modern tourism, it is possible to understand how tourism actually coexists and is interdependent with other economic activities in urban areas (see Hughes 1998 on tourism and the arts) and its real contribution to the life, economy and environment of the city. As Pearce (1989) argued, research on the impact of tourism has led to varying degrees of emphasis on economic, cultural, social and environmental impacts induced by tourism and in the context of competition for visitors, destinations aggressively market their unique attributes in spite of the impacts (Rawding 2000). In the case of Amsterdam, Nijman (1999) argued that cultural globalisation and its impact on urban identities are reflected in the impact of mass tourism in cities, which has created a new identity that is not authentic as global information exchange transforms the image of localities through tourism.

One of the main criticisms of many studies of the impact of tourism is that they do not pay adequate attention to the various types of tourism that induce the impacts. All too often the studies are unable to identify and understand the processes creating the impacts. While detailed literature exists on the impact of tourism, there are no comprehensive studies that assess the diverse range of impacts of tourism in urban areas, mainly because of the methodological problems this poses: much of the research focuses on one particular type of impact. In terms of urban politics, politicians have frequently pointed to the value of developing urban tourism with its employment generating potential (Hall and Hamon 1996). However, while politicians are elected for specific time-frames, tourism operates at a different level since it is notoriously difficult to downsize an urban economy once tourism is firmly entrenched.

It is in this context that the impact of urban tourism becomes a problem for some localities where decision-makers have committed the town or city to a future economy where tourism is a significant component, often without a critical understanding of the range of impacts it can generate. Dusclaud's (1993) analysis of urban tourism in Bordeaux, France, highlighted the importance of achieving consensus among planners, administrators and local authorities to ensure tourism development projects serve the needs of the local population and economy. What Dusclaud's (1993) analysis underlines is the necessity of embedding urban tourism into the wider process of economic development, where a specific plan is developed, zones for tourism activity are identified and the public sector mobilise funds to pump-prime and develop this process. In this respect, a fundamental understanding of tourism impacts is essential to balance the community needs and economic development objectives for the locality. The purpose of this chapter is to examine the range of impacts associated with urban tourism and the different approaches used to analyse the scope and nature of specific impacts. The chapter commences with a discussion of methodological problems in assessing the impact of tourism and the constraints in developing a comprehensive approach towards impact analysis. This is followed by a detailed discussion of specific impacts which are illustrated by a range of representative case studies and the implications for the planning and management of urban tourism.

Methodological problems associated with analysing the impact of urban tourism

In any attempt to assess the impact of urban tourism, the immediate problem facing researchers and planners is the establishment of an appropriate baseline on which to measure the existing and future changes induced by tourism. This is a problem that affects all aspects of impact assessment, although it is frequently cited in Environmental Assessment (EA) (Wathern 1988; Weston 1997). Numerous studies of EA acknowledge the practical problems of establishing baseline studies and in disaggregating the impact of tourism from other economic activities in urban areas (Vetter 1985), and their different contribution to environmental impacts. Mathieson and Wall (1982) highlight the precise nature of the problem since in many tourist destinations public use has existed for long periods of time so that it is now almost impossible to reconstruct the environment minus the effects induced by tourism. However, failure to establish baseline data will mean that it will be impossible to fully assess the magnitude of changes brought by tourism (Mathieson and Wall 1982: 5).

Even when it is possible to establish a baseline of data for a specific urban destination, the problem that Pearce (1989) identifies is the extent to which pre-existing processes and changes in the physical and built environment of specific urban destinations are induced by tourism. While it is widely acknowledged that tourism is a major agent affecting the natural and built environment at a general level, isolating the precise causes or processes leading to specific impacts is difficult: is tourism the principal agent of change or is it part of a wider process of economic development in a particular destination? Mathieson and Wall (1982: 5) highlight the common problem that 'tourism may also be a highly visible scapegoat for problems which existed prior to the advent of modern tourism. It certainly is easier to blame tourism than it is to address the conditions of society and the environment'. This is compounded by the reality of impact assessment – that the complex interactions of tourism, urban areas and the built and physical environment make it virtually impossible to model or measure with any degree of precision. Even if it is possible to gauge these impacts precisely, they may not manifest themselves in a tangible form that is easily measured or gauged by survey methods. Impacts may be large scale and tangible (e.g. where a destination is saturated by visitors) and/or small scale and intangible: but how does this affect the interaction between the resident and visitor and when should one measure these impacts?

The real difficulty is in attributing cause and effect in relation to urban tourism which is not necessarily continuous in time (due to seasonality) and space (as tourism activity tends to concentrate in certain locations within cities in relation to the supply of services and facilities – see Chapter 4). Once researchers have decided on a direction to pursue in the analysis of tourism impacts in urban areas, the precise indicators chosen to represent the complex interaction of tourism and the urban destination require the establishment of a methodological framework by which to guide the impact assessment. It is not surprising, therefore, to find many general texts in tourism studies reducing the impact of tourism to costs and benefits for specific destinations, rather than entering into the complex relationships that exist for specific tourism environments such as urban areas.

Law's (1993) research monograph on urban tourism reaffirms this tendency to avoid methodological discussion of assessing the impact of tourism in large cities. For example, Law (1993: 156) states that 'the first task of any impact study is decide who is to be counted as a visitor or tourist' as a basis for calculating visitor numbers for a destination. As Chapter 3 has shown, various indicators such as accommodation can also be used to gauge demand as a baseline for estimating the magnitude of the likely impact of tourism. Where visitor surveys are undertaken, Law (1993) criticised their value as they are often undertaken at visitor attractions, to establish the nature and scale of visitors to urban destinations. Their reliability and ability to yield a representative sample or picture of what is actually happening at destinations is also questionable. It needs to be recognised that where towns and cities have visitor management projects in place, the derivation of baseline information on visitors from surveys is only one part of a more systematic attempt to recognise the impact of urban tourism from the visitor, resident and planning perspective. Nevertheless, Law (1993) did acknowledge that where visitor information is collected, it needs to be related to other forms of statistical information. In this respect, urban tourism needs to be viewed in the wider context in relation to other social, economic and environmental phenomena, so it is not examined in isolation.

Pearce (1989) presents an interesting framework for impact assessment, pointing to the stimulus from EA in North America to consider impacts, especially in relation to proposed developments. It is in this context that the work by Potter (1978) is of interest, since it provides a general methodology for impact assessment. As Figure 6.1 shows, the assessment of the impact incorporates environmental, social and economic issues, all of which can be applied to tourism. As Pearce (1989: 185) argues, the real value is in its ability to assess both the existing and proposed developments. Potter's (1978) methodology comprises a number of steps, beginning with the context of the development and proceeding through to making a decision on a particular development. Pearce (1989) moves

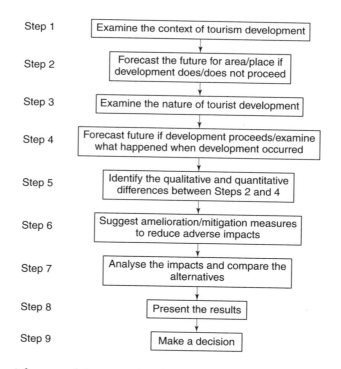

Step 1	Examine the context of tourism development
Step 2	Forecast the future for area/place if development does/does not proceed
Step 3	Examine the nature of tourist development
Step 4	Forecast future if development proceeds/examine what happened when development occurred
Step 5	Identify the qualitative and quantitative differences between Steps 2 and 4
Step 6	Suggest amelioration/mitigation measures to reduce adverse impacts
Step 7	Analyse the impacts and compare the alternatives
Step 8	Present the results
Step 9	Make a decision

Figure 6.1   A framework for assessing the impact of tourism development (source: Page 1995a)

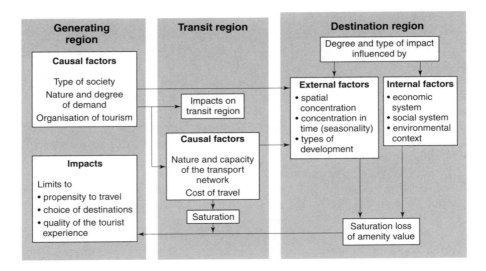

Figure 6.2 Interrelationships and causal factors and impacts associated with generating, transit and destination regions (source: Pearce 1989)

a stage further, arguing that impact studies should also consider the wider context of development rather than just the destination (i.e. the urban area). In this respect, both the origin of visitors, the processes and linkages between origin and destination area and factors influencing the outcome – the impact – need to be considered. Pearce (1989) argued that a systems model may help to provide a more holistic framework for understanding the impact of tourism. This approach is embodied in Figure 6.2 and extends the discussion of the value of a systems approach to tourism (see also C.M. Hall 2000). In fact, Figure 6.2 can be applied to urban tourism so that the relationship between the supply and demand for tourism are set in a wider geographical context, and impacts occur from tourists while in transit and also at the destination (see Page 1994b). Pearce (1989) acknowledged that the integration of both Potter (1978) and Thurot's (1980) work reinforced the significance of the contextual factors and the type of tourist development involved, as well as the range of mitigation measures necessary to reduce the range of impacts associated with tourism. Attention now turns to different aspects of tourism's impact in urban areas.

The economic impact of urban tourism

Tourism is increasingly being viewed by many national and local governments as a mechanism to aid the regeneration of the ailing economies of industrial cities (Law 1993; C.M. Hall 2000). Tourism is also being used, as Chapter 4 illustrated, as a mechanism to regenerate the historic built environment (Parlett *et al.* 1995), especially in the former Eastern Europe where monuments, historic buildings and landmarks need significant investment to ensure their upkeep. In fact, the Argentinian example of Ushuaia, which is located on the Beagle Canal in the South of Tierra del Fuego near the border with Chile, has traditionally been a frontier town since its establishment in 1884. The exodus of industries and out-migration in the late twentieth century has significantly eroded its economic rationale (Braumann and Stadel 1999). The future prospects for the town are now being linked to its 'staging post' and 'gateway' function with its proximity to Antarctica, with enhanced opportunities to service the growing tourism market. This example illustrates one of the principal reasons why tourism is being incorporated into the economic development strategies of towns and cities – it offers renewed opportunities for work, income and revenue for the local economy as places are affected by global, national and local economic restructuring. Much of the interest in tourism by local, regional and national politicians is predicated on the belief that tourism may offer a lifeline and a long-term development option for towns and cities that have seen many of its production functions rationalised or removed.

There is a prevailing perception among national and local governments that economic benefits accrue to tourism destinations, which then creates employment opportunities and stimulates the development process in resorts and localities. For the local population, it is often argued by proponents of tourism development that investment in tourist and recreational facilities provides a positive contribution to the local economy. One very controversial illustration of this can be seen in the debate on casino development in localities. There is a growing concern among urban researchers that the development of casinos, with the taxes levied from gambling, generate positive economic benefits for localities in terms of visitor spending and employment (Hall and Hamon 1996). In Auckland, New Zealand, a casino, hotel and Sky Tower were constructed in the city in the 1990s. It now acts as the city's main drawcard. The scale of the impact on the local economy can be gauged from a number of salient statistics: the casino attracts an average of 12,000 visitors a day but approximately 80 per cent of visitors are residents or New Zealanders. In April 1998, the 10 millionth customer visited the casino. In 1998, gaming revenue averaged NZ\$595,000 a day (including goods and service tax at 12.5 per cent) and the Sky Tower contributed new revenue of NZ\$13.5 million in 1998 from visitor admissions and revenue from the orbit revolving restaurant. In 1998, 700,000 people visited the Sky Tower which provides panoramic views of the city although this is somewhat short of the optimistic forecast of one million admissions in its first full year of operation. Casino operations account for 80 per cent of the revenue from the Sky Tower complex which also contains a theatre and hotel and the company employs 2,400 people. In a recent study of gaming in New Zealand, Pearce (1999a) reported the results of pre- and post-opening assessments of New Zealand's two urban casinos in Christchurch and Auckland. Pearce concluded that while these capital-intensive developments contributed to the objective of promoting tourism, other benefits have been modest. Indeed in Auckland, criticisms of the social impact in terms of gambling and the associated effects on families and low-income households have been notable negative impacts.

Assumptions about urban tourism as a stable source of income for cities are not without problems since tourists are not noted for their high levels of customer loyalty to tourism destinations. A number of features support this argument:

- Tourism is a fickle industry, being highly seasonal, and this has implications for investment and the type of employment created. Tourism employment is often characterised as being low skill, poorly paid, low status and lacking long-term stability.

- The demand for tourism can easily be influenced by external factors (e.g. political unrest, unusual climatic and environmental conditions) which are beyond the control of destination areas.

- The motivation for tourist travel to urban destinations is complex and variable and constantly changing in the competitive marketplace.

- In economic terms, tourism is price- and income-elastic (see Bull 1995), which means that it is easily influenced by small changes to the price of the product and the disposable income of consumers.

- Many cities are becoming alike, a feature Harvey (1989b) has described as *serial reproduction*. This means that once an idea for urban economic development is successful in one location, the concept diffuses to other places. The example of waterfront revitalisation is a case in point; many projects are similar in structure and character across the world, a feature discussed later in the book. For many cities seeking to harness tourism, the competition for visitors intensified in the late-1990s and new millennium as more locations compete for the same market. This was evident in Chapter 3, where many cities in Europe are seeking to harness the tourism market for short city-breaks.

Despite these underlying concerns, the growth of structural unemployment in many former industrial cities (Judd and Fainstein 1999) has led governments to promote the development of urban tourism, since it may hold many employment opportunities for cities, particularly in those redundant areas that have lost their economic rationale (see Chapters 5 and 9). As Mullins (1999: 245) argued, 'In Australia, Europe and North America, private and public investments have built unique infrastructures of consumption, both within restructured older cities and as a basis for new resort communities. The result is a distinctive sociospatial clustering of convention centres, festival shopping malls, casinos, sports stadiums and heritage areas'. In this context, tourism may offer new opportunities for cities seeking to reposition their economies to the reality of the service economy and information age (Castells 1989). However, it must be stressed that making an attempt to gauge the probable long-term benefits of tourism development in cities is complicated by the difficulty of measuring the diffuse nature of tourism as an economic activity.

In fact Pearce (1989: 192) argued that 'the objective and detailed evaluation of the economic impact of tourism can be a long and complicated task'. One immediate problem is that there is little agreement within the literature on what constitutes the tourism industry. As Chapter 4 indicated, the sectors that are usually included under the heading of the tourism industry are:

- accommodation,
- transport,
- attractions,
- the travel organisers' sector (e.g. travel agents),
- destination organisation sector,

while hospitality and ancillary services have a major role to play, as the HOTREC (2000) report indicated. Therefore, one has to agree a working definition of what to include in the category urban tourism industry.

Even once a working definition has been agreed, isolating the flow of income in the local urban tourism economy is notoriously difficult. This is because it is difficult to attribute the proportion of tourist expenditure on goods and services in relation to the total pattern of expenditure by all users of the urban area (e.g. residents, workers and visitors). In practice, one is trying to identify the different forms of tourist expenditure and how it then affects the local economy. There are a number of common factors that influence the scale of the impact in urban areas including:

- the nature of the urban area and its 'leisure product', particularly its facilities, physical characteristics and 'secondary elements';
- the volume and scale of tourist expenditure in the particular city;
- the state of the economic development and economy in the individual city;
- the size and nature of the local economy (i.e. is it dependent on services, manufacturing or is it a mixed economy?);
- the extent to which tourist expenditure circulates around the local economy and is not spent on 'imported' goods and services;
- the degree to which the local economy has addressed the problem of seasonality and extends the city's appeal to an all-year-round destination.

On the basis of these factors, it is possible to assess whether the economic impact will be beneficial to the city or if it will have a detrimental effect on its economy. In this respect, it is possible to identify some of the commonly cited economic benefits of tourism for urban areas:

- the generation of income for the local economy;
- the creation of new employment opportunities for the city;
- improvements to the structure and balance of economic activities within the locality;
- encouraging entrepreneurial activity.

In contrast, there are also a range of costs commonly associated with urban tourism and these include:

- the potential for economic overdependence on one particular form of activity;
- inflationary costs in the local economy as new consumers enter the area and potential increases in real estate prices as the tourism development cycle commences and tourism competes with other land uses;
- depending on the size and nature of the local economy, a growing dependence on imported rather than locally produced goods, services and labour as the development of facilities and infrastructure proceeds;
- seasonality in the consumption and production of tourism infrastructure and services leading to limited returns on investment;
- leakages of tourism expenditure from the local economy;
- additional costs for city authorities.

To illustrate the significance of tourism in an urban economy, the example of London highlights some of the dimensions which are readily documented in the publicly available tourism statistics.

The London tourism economy

In 1998, visitor expenditure by overseas tourists in London was estimated to be £6.7 billion and when domestic visitor expenditure is included, the figure rises to £7.8 billion, from 25.1 million international and domestic arrivals. This figure can be expanded by a further £1.7 billion if day visitor spending is also added to the total. If one then considers the economic impact of urban leisure activities by residents, 17 per cent of Londoners' weekly household expenditure was spent on leisure services and goods. A further 16 per cent was spent on eating away from home (restaurant and café meals and take-away/snack foods). Therefore, urban tourism and leisure spending are significant within the service economy, since tourism alone contributes 8 per cent to London's GDP and accounts for 200,000 jobs and 8 per cent of the capital's employment. Despite fluctuations in the volume of tourism to London, expenditure by visitors grew from £4.8 billion in 1991 to £7.8 billion in 1998 and as with many cities, it is the foreign visitor that has the greatest impact. Between 1997 and 2003, the London Tourism Board and Convention Bureau (LTBCB) forecasts predict a growth of 7 per cent in international visitor expenditure to £9.68 billion, and a modest 4.8 per cent growth in domestic visitor spending to £1.41 billion. What this snapshot of London's tourism economy illustrates is that visitor activity assumes a major role in the service sector as a source of employment, taxation for national government and as a contributor to GDP. While capital city tourism, such as that in London, is a highly developed form of activity due to historical factors and the city's gateway role, it does indicate the dimensions of the economic impacts which are cited by decision-makers who wish to promote urban tourism and leisure activity as a vehicle for local regional economic development.

Techniques and methodologies used to analyse the economic impact of urban tourism

Cooper *et al.* (1993: 115) argued that 'the measurement of the economic impact of tourism is far more complicated than simply calculating the level of tourist expenditure'. It is important to distinguish between the economic impact derived from tourist expenditure and that due to the development of tourism (e.g. the construction of facilities). While a diverse literature now exists on the economics of tourism (see Bull 1991; Sinclair and Stabler 1991), there is an absence of specific studies that review and illustrate the economic impact of tourism for the specific genre of tourist cities. Murphy (1985) points to the necessity of understanding the tourism economy of localities and the concept of economic cycles, since tourism experiences the following:

- *Short-term economic cycles*, which commonly occur within a one year time-span and reflect the seasonality in demand which destinations and their economies have to accommodate.

- *Medium-term economic cycles*, where changes in the circumstances of the tourism market may lead a destination to readjust to conditions occurring over a couple of years. For example, changes in the exchange rate and costs of producing tourism services make specific urban destinations expensive for overseas visitors.

- *Long-term economic cycles*, where long-term business cycles become important and the destination is viewed in relation to the product life-cycle concept used in marketing and subsequently applied to resort development (Butler 1980; Grabler 1997a, b). What is suggested is that the long-term economic viability of a destination may follow the growth curve of a new product where it is produced and seeks to establish an identity. If the product is a success with consumers, it gains growing acceptance leading to increased sales and peak production. However, as the number of suppliers increases, the demand for the product, patronage and sales decline and a state of low sales emerges and the product may be replaced or re-launched in a new form to stimulate sales. This principle has also been applied to resort areas to explain their evolution. It is also useful to understand the stage of development of specific urban tourism economies since it will condition the scale, volume and extent of tourist expenditure.

The key elements of the resort cycle concept are described by Butler (1980: 6) thus:

Visitors will come to an area in small numbers initially, restricted by a lack of access, facilities, and local knowledge. As facilities are provided and awareness grows, visitor numbers will increase. With marketing, information dissemination, and further facility provision, the area's popularity will grow rapidly. Eventually, however, the rate of increase in visitor numbers will decline as levels of carrying capacity are reached . . . As the attractiveness of the area declines relative to other areas, because of overuse and the impacts of visitors, the actual number of visitors may also eventually decline.

Butler's (1980) model is divided into six stages:

1. *Exploration* (e.g. only small numbers of tourists visit the destination).
2. *Involvement* (e.g. the local community provides limited facilities for tourism).
3. *Development* (e.g. rapid tourism growth occurs which corresponds with the same process in the product life cycle).
4. *Consolidation* (e.g. a slower rate of growth and visitor numbers continue to expand and marketing activity is undertaken to maintain market share and to extend the season).
5. *Stagnation* (e.g. peak numbers are reached and economic, environmental and social problems occur due to pressure on the locality by visitors).
6. *Future options* (e.g. how should the area respond to the future once stagnation has set in? Can a long-term decline be prevented by marketing the unique appeal of the city to visitors? Can a process of rejuvenation be implemented through development of new resources, such as casinos or events, in conjunction with innovative marketing, to promote the city?).

The notion of a destination product life cycle has been extremely influential in tourism research. Butler's (1980) concept of a tourist area cycle of evolution, based on some of the initial observations of Christaller (1963) and Plog, has been applied in a number of environments and settings representing the development of a destination through time and space (Cooper and Jackson 1989; Cooper 1992, 1994; Ioannides 1992). Because of its relative simplicity the concept of a destination product life cycle has emerged as a significant concept for strategic destination marketing and planning that underpins much of our understanding of urban tourism development (Grabler 1997a, b).

According to Cooper and Jackson (1989) the two most substantial managerial benefits of the life-cycle concept are its use as a descriptive guide for strategic decision-making and its capacity as a forecasting tool. As a descriptive guide the life-cycle idea implies that in the early stages of product development the focus will be on building market share while in the later stages the focus will be on maintaining that share (Rink and Swan 1979). However, the utility of the life-cycle concept as a forecasting tool relies heavily on the identification of those forces that influence the flow of tourists to a specific destination. As Haywood (1986) recognised, most models work well in their early stages but then fail in their prediction of the latter stages of the model. Haywood (1986), along with other commentators (e.g. Rink and Swan 1979; Cooper 1992; Ioannides 1992), note that there are a variety of different shaped curves with the shape of the curve depending on both supply and demand side factors. Indeed, Haywood (1986: 154) goes so far as to argue that the life-cycle approach, 'represents the supply side view of the diffusion model', by which consumers adopt new products.

According to Haywood (1986) there are six operational decisions when using the life-cycle concept:

- unit of analysis;
- relevant market;
- pattern and stages of the tourist area life cycle;
- identification of the area's shape in the life cycle;
- determination of the unit of measurement; and
- determination of the relevant time unit.

Using Haywood's insights as a basis for undertaking research on the life cycle, Grabler undertook an analysis of the destination life cycles of 43 European cities using the variables of growth data for domestic and international tourism, first-time visitor percentage, length of stay, guest-mix distribution and number of competitors. Only a small number of the variables tested proved to be significant correlates of the life cycle. According to Grabler (1997b: 69), 'A diminishing rate of first-time visitors is obvious for cities passing through later stages of the cycle. Correspondingly, the average length of stay of the guests rises . . . Competition also turned out to be a good predictor . . . Specifically, older tourism cities find themselves under strong competitive pressure'. The implications of these results are significant for city authorities as through monitoring of the variables a more strategic approach to tourism management, marketing and planning may be developed (Getz 1992). Moreover, the significance of the impacts of multiple shorter life cycles, e.g. through the addition of new products, such as waterfront developments, or new individual mega-attractions, such as a casino, or a mega-event, such as an Olympic Games, on the overall destination product life cycle may also be significant.

Although such models have limitations in terms of their application, they do assist as useful conceptual tools in establishing the state of economic development for specific urban tourist destinations. Yet how does one establish the scale and nature of economic impacts accruing from tourism within the city's economy?

Law (1993) provides a good synthesis of the ways of assessing the economic impact of tourism in large cities. He argues that expenditure information gleaned from visitor surveys together with other published data can be used to establish the following:

- *Direct expenditure* by tourists on goods and services consumed (e.g. hotels, restaurants and tourist transport services), although this is not a definitive account of expenditure due to leakage of tourist spending to areas and corporations outside the local economy.

- *Indirect expenditure* by visitors which is often estimated by identifying how many tourism enterprises use the income derived from tourist's spending. This spending is then used by enterprises to pay for services, taxes and employees which then recirculates in the urban economy. In other words, tourist expenditure stimulates an economic process which passes through a series of stages (or rounds). Specific forms of economic analysis, such as input–output analysis (see Fletcher 1989), may be used to identify the types of transaction that occur between tourism businesses to assess how indirect expenditure influences the tourism economy. Input–output analysis may illustrate how the output from each sector of the urban economy contributes to other economic activities or consumption (see Briassoulis 1991; Bull 1991). In this context, it may help to identify the role of tourism in these interactions within the local economy.

- The *induced impact* by calculating the impact of expenditure from those employed in tourism and the effect of the spending in the local economy.

On the basis of the direct, indirect and induced impacts, one can produce an estimate of the total impact of tourist spending on the urban economy. These different impacts are indicated in Figure 6.3 where the tourism economy is viewed as an open system which varies according to the degree of penetration by outside interests and amount of goods imported.

Figure 6.3 is useful as it highlights the interrelationships that exist with the tourism economy of urban areas and the flow of income within the economic system. It also introduces the concept of *leakage*, which occurs due to the taxation of income derived from tourist spending, and loss of expenditure to other areas and economies. Clearly, 'visitor expenditures represent only the first stage of economic impact on a destination community, for like other generators of basic income, tourism's contribution can multiply as the extra income passes throughout an economy' (Murphy 1985: 90).

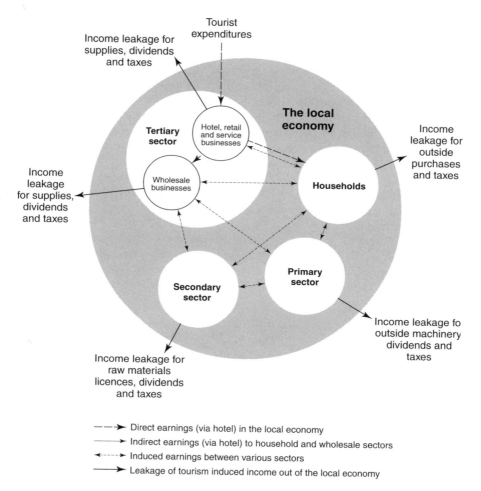

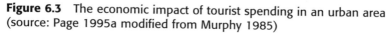

Figure 6.3 The economic impact of tourist spending in an urban area (source: Page 1995a modified from Murphy 1985)

Tourism multiplier analysis

There is a vast literature that reviews the concept of multiplier analysis (e.g. Archer 1982, 1987; Fletcher and Archer 1989; Lundberg *et al.* 1995; Tribe 1995), which Mathieson and Wall (1982: 64) define as 'the number, by which initial tourist expenditure must be multiplied in order to obtain the total cumulative income effect for a specified period'. The multiplier concept is 'based on the recognition that the various sectors which make up the economy are interdependent . . . Therefore, any autonomous change in the level of final demand will not only affect the industry which produces that final good or service, but also that industry's suppliers and the suppliers' suppliers' (Fletcher and Archer 1989: 28). The multiplier is expressed as a ratio which measures those changes, the final demand resulting from the effect of changes in variables such as economic output, income, employment, government revenue and foreign exchange flows (if appropriate). The multiplier ratio (see Cooper *et al.* 1993 for more detail on the formulae used to calculate different types of multipliers), measures the changes to the final demand resulting from the aforementioned changes and expresses the estimate of the total change in output (the output multiplier). A similar value can also be derived to estimate the total change in income (the income multiplier) to illustrate the effect of changes in demand on tourism income. These concepts help to establish the estimated changes in the direct, indirect and induced effects on the tourism economy, resulting from changes in demand.

Figure 6.4 illustrates how the multiplier concept operates from the point at which tourist expenditure is spent in the urban area on goods and services. Leakages occur where imported goods are supplied to meet tourist needs (e.g. food and beverages). Where they are not provided locally, money leaks outside

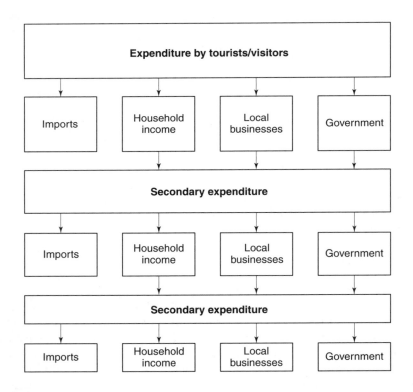

Figure 6.4   How the multiplier process operates (source: Page 1995a)

the economy and is not retained within the area. The tourist expenditure remaining after the imports are paid for is then distributed among various areas of the urban economy (e.g. as household income from employment, to local businesses or is paid to the government as taxes). The tourist expenditure then has an indirect effect on the tourism economy as secondary expenditure and the money continues to circulate through the economy and this process carries on. Thus, income that is re-spent by employers and employees as well as by government stimulates the economy once again.

The actual size of the multiplier reflects the expected economic benefit of tourism to the urban economy: the more self-sufficient a given town's economy, the greater the degree of tourist revenue that is retained in the economy. It is widely acknowledged by tourism economists that the national multipliers are larger owing to the greater propensity of the national economy to be self-sufficient compared to lower order economic systems (e.g. isolated rural areas). A number of tourism income multipliers reported in the literature are listed in Table 6.1.

Pearce (1989: 208) argues that while values vary from place to place, there is a certain amount of consistency in similar areas. For example, the higher value for Metropolitan Victoria in Canada may be attributed to the greater degree of interdependence in the regional economy and ability to retain expenditure in a diverse economic system (Var and Quayson 1985). In contrast, employment multipliers are more difficult to operationalise owing to problems in establishing the relationship between employment and its role in tourist expenditure. Employment does not necessarily expand as tourist expenditure increases because it depends on the state of the local economy, the nature of the tourism activity and degree of change in demand. Thus employment multipliers are only an indication of possible full-time employment which may result. Yet it is not just the number of jobs created, but the type and quality resulting from tourism that are important (Mathieson and Wall 1982). For example, DRV Research (1986) examined the economic impact of tourism in Merseyside and provides data on employment.

Table 6.1   Tourism income multipliers for selected urban destinations

Metropolitan Victoria British Columbia (Canada)	0.65
Edinburgh	0.35
City of Carlisle	0.40
Great Yarmouth	0.33
Kendal	0.28
Towns and Villages in Wales	0.18–0.47
UK	1.73

Source: based on Archer (1982), Murphy (1985) and Pearce (1989).

According to DRV Research (1986), leakage of expenditure in the hotel and guest-house sector reduces the beneficial effects on the hotel and guest-house sector compared with the rented self-catering sector. Nevertheless, the accommodation sector is labour intensive compared with other aspects of the tourism economy. However, it is apparent that urban tourism produces three types of employment:

1. *Direct employment* in tourism establishments.
2. *Indirect employment* in the tourism supply sector.
3. *Induced employment* or additional employment as locally employed residents spend the money earned from the results of tourism-related income circulating in the urban economy.

Although there are a range of useful studies that examine the technical aspects associated with different types of multipliers (e.g. Archer 1987) and their role in economic theory, one can summarise the significance of multipliers in the analysis of the economic impact of urban tourism thus:

- Multiplier analysis helps researchers to measure the present economic performance of the tourism industry and the effect of short-term changes in demand on the urban tourism economy.
- Multipliers may be used to assess the effects of public and private sector investment in urban tourism projects, and who are likely to be the main beneficiaries.
- Multipliers are frequently used to estimate the impact of tourist expenditure on tourism enterprises within cities together with the effect on direct, indirect and induced forms of employment and income.

The economic impact of urban tourism in Norway

The economic and employment effects of urban tourism have, not surprisingly, attracted only a limited interest from researchers and even fewer comparative studies have been conducted because of the technical expertise needed to conduct such research. This is in spite of the 'multiplier effect' of tourism in urban economies, where tourist spending stimulates the local economy in terms of sales, output and employment. As Fletcher (1989) observed, income multipliers are the most frequently used to assess the direct industry effects, direct spin-off effects, indirect effects and induced effects. According to Huse *et al.* (1998: 722–3):

> Direct effects are of two kinds: the primary tourism industry effects and associated or spin-off effects. Direct effects are related to places where the tourists

themselves spend their money. The primary tourism industry is hotels, restaurants, campgrounds, tour operators . . . Firms that experience spin-off effects include firms, institutions and individuals outside the primary industry, where the tourists themselves spend their money . . . When direct tourism income is spent locally or in the area of the study, indirect and induced effects are generated. Indirect effects occur when firms receiving tourist spending are buying supplies and services from other firms in the area. Induced effects are created when personal income from direct and indirect expenditure is spent within the area.

In Huse *et al.*'s study of Norway's small towns, secondary data on the economic impact of tourism was collected for the southern municipalities of Risør, Kvitseid, Trysil, Hol and Vinje based on published studies (Figure 6.5). Primary data were collected for a number of municipalities in northern Norway (Grong, Brønnøysund, Lenvik/Tranøy and Hammerfest) (see Figure 6.5).

Using the methodology outlined by Archer (1982), three economic effects were measured:

1. Direct industry effects (direct primary tourism industry effects).
2. Direct spin-off effects.
3. Secondary effects (indirect and induced effects).

The sales and employment multipliers can be calculated using the following formulae (Huse *et al.* 1998: 726):

$$Sales_{mT} = \frac{Sales_T}{Sales_{DI}}$$

$$Sales_{m2} = \frac{Sales_T}{Sales_{(SI+DSP)}}$$

$$Empl_{m1} = \frac{Empl_T}{Empl_{DI}}$$

$$Empl_{m2} = \frac{Empl_T}{Empl_{(DI+DSP)}}$$

$$Empl_{m3} = \frac{Empl_T}{Sales_{DI}}$$

$$Empl_{m4} = \frac{Empl_T}{Sales_{(DI+DSP)}}$$

where Sales = sales effects
    Empl = employment effects
    T = total effects or the sum of all direct and secondary effects
    DI = Direct primary tourism industry effects
    DSP = direct spin-off effects

Figure 6.5 Small towns in Norway

The results of the economic and employment effects for northern Norway
are shown in Table 6.2. This illustrates the range of tourism sales of between
US$9.1 and US$26 million, with approximately one-third of the economic
impacts due to direct industry effects, one-third a direct spin-off effect and

Table 6.2   The economic and employment effects of tourism in northern Norway small towns in 1992 (all figures in US$)

Effects	Grong	Brønnøysund	Lenvik/Tranøy	Hammerfest
Economic				
Direct industry effects	3.8	3.0	2.9	12.9
Direct spin-off effects	3.5	4.6	5.2	6.6
Secondary effects	1.8	4.4	2.6	6.5
Total effects	9.1	12.0	10.7	26.0
Employment				
Direct industry effects	45	38	36	101
Direct spin-off effects	13	25	15	27
Secondary effects	11	30	14	26
Total effects	69	93	66	154

Source: modified from Huse *et al.* (1998: 729).

one-third secondary effects. In terms of leakage, there were greater losses to employment than for economic effects. The consequence is that for some towns such as Grong, the employment effects spread to the surrounding areas because of people living in areas other than where they work. The impact of seasonal labour and seasonal demand also accounts for this difference. Other differences between the towns, including the level of economic development and the number of local businesses able to supply commodities for visitors, were important explanatory variables.

In terms of employment effects shown in Table 6.3, the total effect of direct industry impacts ranged from 1.4 to 2.4 and close to the pattern in Table 6.2 for northern Norway. Direct industry effects are around 55 per cent of the total employment although employment direct spin-off effects were lower than economic spin-off effects. The generation of tourist employment is presented in Table 6.4. This shows that US$1 million spending in the municipality created up to 12 jobs in Brønnøysund and up to 7 jobs in Risør and Vinje ($Empl_{m6}$ local). In contrast, the direct industry effects of tourist spending were 45 jobs in Risør to 12 jobs in Hammerfest per million US$ of tourist spending ($Empl_{m3}$ local).

Huse *et al.* (1998) recognised that variations to multipliers can also be attributed to the special features of tourism in each locality (i.e. type of attractions, accommodation and profile of visitors). As a result, they highlight four principal findings of value to urban tourism, albeit to a small town context (Huse *et al.* 1998: 733–5):

1. A positive correlation existed 'between the development of the local tourism industry and ratio of direct industry effects'.
2. A positive relationship was present in the size of the local economy and the secondary effects of tourism.

Table 6.3 Coefficient and multiplier comparisons in Norwegian small towns in 1992

Effects[cd]	Direct industry (%)	Direct spin-offs (%)	Secondary (%)	Multipl. 1[a] sales$_{m1}$	Multipl. 2[b] sales$_{m2}$
Economic					
Grong	41	39	20	2.4 (2.7)	1.3 (1.4)
Brønnøysund	25	38	37	4.0 (4.2)	1.6 (1.7)
Lenvik/Tranøy	27	49	24	3.7 (3.9)	1.3 (1.4)
Hammerfest	50	25	25	2.0 (2.1)	1.3 (1.4)
Kvitseid	51	16	33	2.0	1.5
Hol	65	9	26	1.5	1.4
Trysil	34	23	43	2.9	1.8
Risør	22	54	24	4.5	1.3
Vinje	59	27	14	1.7	1.2
Mean all	42	31	27	2.7	1.4
Mean northern Norway	36	38	26	3.0 (3.2)	1.4 (1.5)
Employment					
Grong	65	19	16	1.5 (2.1)	1.2 (1.7)
Brønnøysund	41	27	32	2.4 (2.6)	1.5 (1.6)
Lenvik/Tranøy	55	23	21	1.8 (2.3)	1.3 (1.7)
Hammerfest	65	18	17	1.5 (1.9)	1.2 (1.5)
Kvitseid	57	10	33	1.8	1.5
Trysil	45	14	42	2.2	1.7
Risør	2	50	18	2.4	1.2
Vinje	74	13	13	1.4	1.2
Mean all	55	22	24	1.9	1.4
Mean northern Norway	56	22	22	1.8 (2.3)	1.3 (1.6)

[a] Multiplier 1 = total effect/direct industry effects.
[b] Multiplier 2 = total effect/all direct effects.
[c] Effects for the municipality (effects for the whole region of northern Norway).
[d] All effects in the denominators are figures from the municipality.
Source: Huse *et al.* (1998: 731).

3. A strong correlation existed between self-catering tourism and direct spin-off effects.
4. A strong relationship existed between the level of tourism investment and secondary effects.

Within their study, they found that Hammerfest was the municipality with the most developed tourism industry, followed by Hol. In contrast, Lenvik/Tranøy had the least developed tourism economy with few hotels and attractions where tourists can spend money. What Huse *et al.* (1998: 734) rightly conclude in the context of urban tourism is that 'The economic impact of tourism is most beneficial in large societies because they have more diversified economic structures, and leakage effects are limited and in larger urban contexts where tourism resources exist, the economic impacts will be more beneficial to the locality'.

Table 6.4 Employment created by tourism spending (per million US$) in Norwegian small towns in 1992

Municipality	$Empl_{m3}$ local	$Empl_{m3}$ regional	$Empl_{m6}$ local	$Empl_{m4}$ regional
Grong	18	25	9	13
Brønnøysund	31	33	12	13
Lenvik/Tranøy	23	29	8	10
Hammerfest	12	15	8	10
Kvitseid	28		10	
Trysil	31		11	
Risør	45		7	
Vinje	21		7	
Mean all	26		9	
Mean northern Norway	21	25	9	12

$Empl_{m3}$ = total employment effect on economic direct tourism industry effects.
$Empl_{m4}$ = total employment effects on economic direct tourism industry effects and direct spin-off effects.
Local effects are effects for the municipality. Regional effects are effects for the region of northern Norway.
All denominators are sales in the core municipality.
Source: Huse *et al.* (1998: 733).

As Williams and Shaw (1991) recognised, if tourism is integrated in the locality so that developments are absorbed in the existing economy, it will also improve the local economic impacts. As research on industry linkages between hotels and food suppliers (see Telfer and Wall 1996) has shown, purchasing decisions by the tourism industry and its ownership structure may also stimulate secondary effects if local purchases are made. Clearly few economic sectors have such wide-ranging linkages in the local economy as tourism (Johnson and Thomas 1992; Johnson and Moore 1993). Although the form of urban tourism developed and the markets it appeals to will have a significant effect on the nature of the economic impacts that result (see Archer and Fletcher 1996; Heng and Low 1990), with excursionists versus long-stay tourists providing two divergent examples, there are also a number of variables to consider. Huse *et al.* (1998) explain many of the relationships that exist and the most significant feature of their study which is frequently overlooked in the wider public arena is that 'Effect estimations from one area, or average effects from several areas, should not be directly generalised to other areas by policymakers, and patterns of tourism impacts depend on time and various phases of development in the locality' (Huse *et al.* 1998: 735). Indeed, Saeter (1993, 1994) in other economic research on tourism conducted in Norway noted that when politicians and planners in local and regional administrations emphasise the indirect effects of tourism, there is more rhetoric than reality. Consideration should therefore at least be given to the question of whether the indirect economic effects of tourism are greater than those of other industries. For example, in his findings of a study of the impacts and integration of tourism in the economy of Roeros, a former mining town in South Troendelag county in southern Norway, near the Swedish border, Saeter (1998: 243) reported

The calculations predict that a 50 per cent increase in tourist demand will generate a modest 4 per cent increase in total employment. A very important consideration with reference to growth strategies, is that many sites can be vulnerable to the physical impacts of tourism. Therefore, there can be significant limits to growth within tourism caused by negative external effects on the product, and often produced by tourism itself. This can affect the quality of the product, in a broad sense, which can lead to lower willingness to pay, lower levels of visitor satisfaction, and an economic impact that is lower than indicated by the traffic volume.

Saeter's research, along with that of Huse *et al.* (1998), indicate that the regional economic impact of tourist development should be weighed against the economic potential of other industries. Therefore, tourism development strategies should not be disconnected from the general economic and regional planning (see Chapter 7).

More importantly, the Norwegian examples show that no simple linear relationship exists between the development of tourism and local economic impacts for the community. Again, Huse *et al.*'s (1998: 735–6) study should be compulsory reading for politicians, planners and developers because it summarises the economic effects of tourism which are relevant to urban tourism development since

> In the initial stages, tourism may create more jobs for locals. Later, with further development, both negative and positive consequences may become more apparent. Negative consequences include social and institutional impact [sic] on host government and residents, over-commitment of resources to tourism diverting investments from other sectors, congestion, pollution, in-migration of labour, and conflict with other land use, while positive consequences include the development of local infrastructures, local identities, international consciousness and social welfare.

Therefore, in view of Huse *et al.*'s comments, attention now turns to the social and cultural impacts of urban tourism.

The social and cultural impact of urban tourism

In recent years there has been a recognition by academics and community groups that the development of tourism in urban areas not only leads to economic impacts, but also results in less visible and more intangible effects (Murphy 1985). While economic impacts may be measured and quantified to identify financial and employment effects, social and cultural impacts on visitors and host communities in urban areas are often considered only when tourism development leads to local opposition. For example, in London's Central Tourism District, the effect of hotel development and tourism development in the late 1960s and 1970s, promoted by grant assistance from the

English Tourist Board, resulted in the imposition of local authority planning restraints. These were a response to local community opposition to the urban nuisances and impacts of tourists on the locality (Eversley 1977; Page and Sinclair 1989). Therefore, it is important to understand the types of social and cultural impacts that result from tourism to try to avoid negative effects and conflicts in urban areas, between the host community and visitors. Otherwise the *tourist experience* may be tainted by underlying conflicts and an unwelcoming attitude towards tourists which will ultimately erode the destination's popularity and competitive position. The attitudes of residents are a key component in identifying, measuring and analysing the impact of tourism (Ryan and Montgomery 1994). Such attitudes are also important in determining local policy, planning and management responses to the development of tourism and in establishing the extent of public support for tourism. Getz (1994) argued that resident perceptions of tourism may be one factor in shaping the attractiveness of a destination, and negative attitudes may be one indicator of an area's ability to absorb tourism. Although Getz suggests that 'identification of causal mechanisms is a major theoretical challenge, and residents can provide the local knowledge necessary to link developments with their consequences' (Getz 1994: 247), this assumes that residents are sufficiently aware, willing, perceptive and able enough to articulate their views to decision-makers and planners. But what is meant by the social and cultural impact of tourism?

According to Fox (1977), cited in Mathieson and Wall (1982: 133), 'The social and cultural impacts of tourism are the ways in which tourism is contributing to changes in value systems, individual behaviour, family relationships, collective lifestyles, safety levels, moral conduct, creative expressions, traditional ceremonies and community organisations', which they identify as 'people impacts', due to the effect of tourists on host communities and the interaction between these two groups. In other words, the analysis of social and cultural impacts of urban tourism involves the analysis of:

- *the tourist*, especially their demand for services, their attitudes, expectations and activity patterns within cities;
- *the host*, particularly their role and attitude towards the provision of services for tourists and their concerns for the impact of visitors on the traditional way of life in the locality;
- *the relationship between tourists and hosts*, and the type of contact which occurs between these two groups and the outcome for each group.

The most notable study to analyse these relationships is V. Smith's (1989) *Hosts and Guests: The Anthropology of Tourism*, which contains an interesting range of studies of the effect of imported tourist culture on host communities. For example, Smith (1989) notes that the type of tourist visiting a destination is an important precondition for their ability to adapt to local norms. Table 6.5 indicates that while certain cultural, linguistic and educational barriers inhibit

Table 6.5 Types of tourists and their adaptation to local norms

Type of tourist	Number of tourists	Adaptation to local norms
Explorer	Very limited	Accepts fully
Elite	Rarely seen	Adapts fully
Off-beat	Uncommon but seen	Adapts well
Unusual	Occasional	Adapts somewhat
Incipient mass	Steady flow	Seeks Western amenities
Mass	Continuous influx	Expects Western amenities
Charter	Massive arrivals	Demands Western amenities

Source: Based on Smith (1989) cited in Pearce (1989).

the interaction and integration of tourists into a local community, this varies according to the volume of visitors and their expectations. Although this typology has less importance to large urban areas and integrated resort complexes where visitors are effectively segregated from the local community, the expectations of service provision is a critical factor.

UNESCO (1976) focuses on the nature of tourist–host relationship where mass tourism develops which is significant for urban destinations with their capacity to absorb large numbers of mass tourists, because of the diversity of attractions and activities available for visitors. UNESCO (1976) recognises that the host–guest relationship has the following features:

- *Transitory in nature*, since most tourist visits to urban areas are short in duration which are also artificial if spent in a hotel where non-local staff are employed who are usually expected to speak the language of visitors.

- *Limited in time and space*, especially when the visitor is on a short break to an urban area which often leads to distinctive forms of visitor behaviour. For example, visitors may seek to maximise the time available by high spending on activities and tourist services. The geographical concentration of tourist accommodation and attractions in the TBD (see Chapter 3) may also isolate the visitor from interaction with local residents even though they experience the effects of tourist congestion in shopping areas used by visitors in the peak season.

- Also, as emphasised in Chapter 2, in the postmodern city, tourists may be *spatially isolated* from residents' development by high-cost attractions such as theme parks.

- *Relationships often lacking in spontaneity* in an urban context. Where package and organised itineraries are used by tourists, these lead to formal, commercialised and contractual relationships between the tourist and service providers, removing the opportunity for spontaneous interaction between visitors and the tourist service worker.

- *Unequal and unbalanced.* For the tourist, the experience of an urban destination is one based on an image of the place as a novel and exciting opportunity. Yet for the tourist worker, it is often a routine, mundane and regulated experience. There are often material differences between the affluence of visitors and the spending patterns and the relatively low levels of remuneration of workers undertaking tourism service tasks. Such relationships may lead to resentment among workers and residents in extreme cases.

Pearce (1989) examined a range of specific social and cultural impacts based on research in Spain by Figuerola (1976) which can be modified to incorporate the effects on the host population in urban areas including the following:

- The impact on the population structure of urban areas due to rural and urban migration to secure employment in service industries with the prospect of higher income levels than from rural occupations. This may often modify the age and sex structure of the destination.

- The transformation of the occupational structure of the urban area, especially with the increasing emphasis on qualifications and language skills for managerial occupations and the demand for low-paid and unskilled female labour for seasonal employment in hotels, attractions and the hospitality sector.

- The transformation of political values, where urban lifestyles among tourism workers replace more conservative rural attitudes with a greater disposition towards a new way of life. Social values also change as high levels of population turnover limits the opportunities to develop long-term social relationships. This is also complicated by the seasonal patterns of employment and the long hours and shift systems. However, for young temporary workers, this may be a positive attraction with the opportunity to live in a more cosmopolitan environment.

- The impact of gentrification in inner-city areas, as tourism and leisure-related developments (e.g. marinas in waterfront areas) lead to the local population being excluded from the local housing market (Marks 1996) or in extreme cases, mega-events lead to the eviction of residents (C.M. Hall 1992; Olds 1998), which can politicise waterfront and infrastructure development (Page 1993a, b; Doorne 1998).

- Change to the social and moral behaviour of the host population is a controversial and much debated impact in the context of prostitution, religion, crime and gambling. In the case of prostitution (Askew 1998; Ryan and Hall 2001), tourism in urban areas does not necessarily lead to its development but may change its nature. Nevertheless, it displays a distinctive urban form in tourist cities (Ashworth *et al.* 1988; see Chapter 5). For example, in the case of Auckland, New Zealand, one distinctive 'sex tourism zone'

Plate 6.1   Fort Street, downtown Auckland, with its sex tourism zone

exists in the Fort Street area (see Plate 6.1) adjacent to the recreational business district, although it does not feature as a spectacle and attraction in the same way as the red-light districts in Amsterdam, Bangkok and Hamburg. The issue of religion, however, is more complex to analyse as some forms of urban tourism have developed for spiritual reasons (see Chapter 3). In other circumstances, the Church has exploited tourism by charging admission to cathedrals, shrines and churches. Likewise, the literature on urban tourism and crime is inconclusive as to whether tourism stimulates an increase in crime against visitors (see Pizam and Mansfeld 1996; Barker *et al.* 2000). In fact, special events in New Zealand have generated a range of diverse economic (see Table 6.6), socio-cultural and environmental impacts as in the case of the hosting of the America's Cup in Auckland (Page 1999; Barker *et al.* 2000; Hall and Kearsley 2001). In fact,

Table 6.6 The economic impact of New Zealand sports events

Event	Duration	Periodicity	Estimated value (NZ$ million)
1990 Commonwealth Games	10 days	One-off	231.0
1993 Bledisloe Cup	1 day	One-off	12.8
1993/94 Whitbread Stopover	24 days	4 years	16.2
1994 Springbok Tour	7 weeks	One-off	23.7
1996 Mobil Wellington Street Race	3 days	Annual[a]	3.5[b]
1996 Masters Games	9 days	Bi-annual	4.4
2000 America's Cup	19 weeks	3 years[c]	1,300.0

[a] This event ceased in 1997.
[b] Refers to net impact.
[c] Subject to retaining the Cup; periodicity may vary.
Source: Barker *et al.* (2000).

the America's Cup did not generate the negative crime experiences in Auckland that occurred in Fremantle, Perth (Western Australia) in 1987. This illustrates the need for caution in generalising about socio-cultural impacts of urban tourism based on individual examples. Even within a New Zealand context, it is not possible to generalise on the likely socio-cultural impacts which resulted from the hosting of the events listed in Table 6.6. Each event needs to be understood in the social, cultural and urban context in which it occurred.

• The use of native language appears to experience a decline in urban areas once migrants gain employment in hotels, and where face-to-face contact with tourists requires the use of international languages such as French and English (see White 1974).

• The impact of the culture of the host population, which is the 'behaviour as observed through social relations and material artefacts . . . [and] . . . in a deeper anthropological sense, includes patterns, norms, rules and standards which find expression in behaviour, social relations and artefacts' (Mathieson and Wall 1982: 158) since culture attracts visitors to urban destinations. Examples of the attraction of culture for urban tourists includes the arts, music, history and heritage, architecture, leisure activities and festivals. Not surprisingly, certain cities have developed cultural strategies to promote these attributes (e.g. Glasgow, Sheffield and Liverpool in the UK) since culture is viewed as a symbol of civility in urban living and a necessary feature to attract the new generation of professional workers to cities (see Page 1993a). However, the exploitation of urban culture may help in urban revitalisation but the local culture may be commodified, packaged and distorted in the pursuit of mass tourist consumption. Such criticisms have been levelled at the 1980s heritage centres developed in cities in the

Plate 6.2   Jorvik Viking Centre, York

UK, such as the Canterbury Tales (Canterbury), the Jorvik Viking Centre (York) (Plate 6.2) and White Cliffs Experience (Dover) which turn local history and heritage into a form of entertainment.

- Lastly, urban tourism may require residents to modify their own patterns of consumption due to inflationary pressures induced by mass tourism or the impact of mega-events (C.M. Hall 1992), such as the America's Cup in Auckland in 1999–2000 (Hall and Page 1999; Barker *et al.* 2000).

Many of these impacts have been observed in the literature on the social and cultural impact of tourism, and a range of methodologies have been developed to analyse these impacts.

Analysing the social and cultural impact of urban tourism

As research on the impact of tourism has developed, different methodologies have been proposed to analyse social and cultural impacts (V. Smith 1989). The most commonly used approach is the social survey technique which examines the analysis, the attitudes and feelings of residents by means of closed and open-ended questions. For example, the visitor survey by Oxford City Council *et al.* (1992) employed this technique, using a sample of households and surveys undertaken at the residents' houses to gain a representative survey of all districts. While a wide range of studies have been undertaken on the social impact, few have considered the cultural implications of urban tourism. For this reason, attention focuses on two studies by Doxey (1976) and Bjorklund and Philbrick (1975).

Doxey (1976) developed his 'irridex' index of tourist irritation to illustrate how the interaction of tourists and residents may be converted into different degrees of irritation. Using observations from the West Indies and Canada, Doxey argued that residents' responses will change in a predictable manner, passing through four stages – euphoria, apathy, annoyance and antagonism (Figure 6.6). Doxey's (1976) index assumes that large numbers of visitors cause tensions and ultimately lead to antagonism. Yet it overlooks situations where such numbers of visitors does not ultimately lead to this situation (e.g. Garland and West 1985). It is also a unidirectional model that does not permit destinations to pass back to a situation where annoyance may be reduced by sensitive visitor management schemes. Garland and West (1985: 35) place resident irritation with tourists in context as 'host irritation with the presence of tourists in Rotorua is just that – irritation, and then only among small proportions of residents'. Ap and Crompton (1993) proposed an alternative model (Figure 6.7)

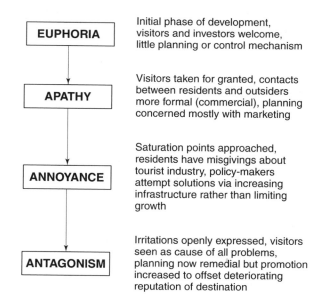

Stages of development

EUPHORIA	Initial phase of development, visitors and investors welcome, little planning or control mechanism
APATHY	Visitors taken for granted, contacts between residents and outsiders more formal (commercial), planning concerned mostly with marketing
ANNOYANCE	Saturation points approached, residents have misgivings about tourist industry, policy-makers attempt solutions via increasing infrastructure rather than limiting growth
ANTAGONISM	Irritations openly expressed, visitors seen as cause of all problems, planning now remedial but promotion increased to offset deteriorating reputation of destination

Figure 6.6   Doxey's irridex index of resident attitudes to tourism (source: Page 1995a)

Embracement:	Residents eagerly welcome tourists
Tolerance:	Residents show a degree of ambivalence towards tourism (there were elements of tourism they liked or disliked)
Adjustment:	Residents adjusted to tourism, often by rescheduling activities to avoid crowds
Withdrawal:	In this context, residents withdrew temporarily from the community

NB: All four strategies are likely to be adopted concurrently, since in any community there are going to be different reactions to tourism. The strategies and behaviour adopted by individuals and groups of residents need to be viewed in relation to thresholds and tourism impacts.

Figure 6.7   Resident attitudes to tourism (source: Page 1995a)

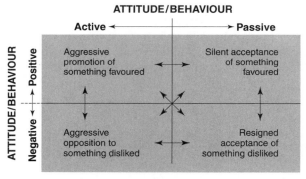

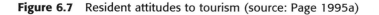

(Arrows indicate possibility of change)

Figure 6.8   Attitudinal/behavioural attributes to intercultural perception based on Bjorklund and Philbrick (source: Page 1995a modified from Bjorklund and Philbrick 1975)

to assess resident attitudes to tourism while Lankford and Howard (1994) examine a multiple item tourism impact scale to assess this issue. What Ap and Crompton illustrate is that in any urban community affected by tourism, a variety of stakeholder interests and attitudes will exist within any community as opposed to the simplified model proposed by Doxey (1976). At any one point in time, a community will be characterised by a range of views and that grouping them into a simplified model such as Doxey's does not recognise the diversity in the locality.

In contrast, Bjorklund and Philbrick's (1975) model of host attitudinal/ behavioural responses to tourism (Figure 6.8) suggests that a matrix characterises the attitudes and behaviour of the groups/individuals towards tourism. It suggests that attitudes reflect an active or passive approach and a negative or positive attitude towards tourism. Such a framework has a number of features that are useful in understanding the social impact of tourism in a locality. First, it can accommodate the diversity of the community and different interests of the local population, including the attitudes of community groups, public providers/administrators, entrepreneurs and residents. Second, it does not assume that residents and the local population will progress through a series of stages. The framework is dynamic and allows for different individuals/groups to be located at various points on the matrix depending on their views on tourism. However, as Butler (cited in Mathieson and Wall 1982: 140) notes, 'the majority of the population is likely to fall into the two passive categories, either silently accepting tourism and its impacts because of the benefits it brings or because they can see no way of reversing the trend'.

One of the most useful studies to illustrate the social and cultural (as well as the economic and environmental) impact of urban tourism is Cant's (1980) study of Queenstown, New Zealand. Although it is now rather dated, the study examines the then small town of 1,759 inhabitants which received up to 180,000 visitors a year. As part of a UNESCO project, the study examined the impact of tourism as viewed by residents in the host community, which was complemented by structural interviews and small discussion groups. Although the consensus of the community was that it had not suffered from the impact of tourism development, a number of specific pressures existed:

- the pace of life had become much quicker;
- some of the population adapted to the new pace of life and others withdrew from situations that did not suit them;
- there was a narrow range of low-cost entertainment of a suitable nature for local families;
- pressures associated with the number of people and vehicles in the central area of Queenstown in the peak season.

In addition, the study noted the existence of:

- a more transient population, making it more difficult to establish stable social relationships;
- high costs associated with the provision of public utilities reflected in the increase in property rates.

Even so, most households in Queenstown felt, on balance, that they were materially better off because of the changes induced by tourism. The study also considers attitudes to further tourism development with households more cautious about endorsing uncontrolled expansion in the future. Their consensus was that previous expansion in tourism 'had been too rapid and that future growth should be slower and more carefully planned' (Cant 1980: 96). To illustrate resident attitudes to tourism, the example of Devonport, Auckland, New Zealand, is now examined in detail.

The attitudes of residents to tourism: case study of Devonport, Auckland, New Zealand

Assessing attitudes to tourism requires a fundamental understanding of 'attitude' as a 'state of mind of the individual towards a value' (Allport 1966, cited in Getz 1994: 247) and the way in which individuals view and analyse their environment. Getz (1994) rightly recognised that attitudes are reinforced by the way individuals and groups perceive reality. However, such perceptions do not change quickly. Although research in social psychology has debated the other factors that affect attitudes, including the role of human behaviour and beliefs, McDougall and Munro (1994) recognised that attitudes may be analysed along three dimensions:

- cognitive (perceptions and beliefs);
- affective (likes and dislikes);
- behavioural (actions or expressed intent).

Attitudes will also be determined by the way in which individuals and groups view the 'real world' and synthesise the complex dimensions of reality into a mental image of a place. Therefore, attitudes can be shaped by various situational factors, though predicting behaviour based on attitudes is notoriously difficult. One additional complexity in analysing attitude is the tendency for some researchers to substitute the term 'perception', which Ap (1990) acknowledged is the meaning attributed to an object. This suggests that some people may attribute a meaning to the impact of tourism without understanding it. Consequently, it is a 'perceived view' rather than an 'attitude'. Thus various studies of resident attitudes towards tourism are probably only looking at a perceived view of tourism. The implication here is that research projects which analyse attitudes to tourism need either to explain the concept of tourism or test the respondents' understanding of tourism.

The main research on attitudes to tourism has been exploratory and descriptive in most cases (Ap 1990), with the exception of a limited number of longitudinal studies (e.g. Getz 1994). The outcome, as Ap (1990: 666) argued, is that 'there is limited understanding of why residents respond to the impacts of tourism as they do, and under what conditions they react to those impacts'. Rothman (1978) acknowledged that communities with a history of exposure to tourism adapt to accommodate its effects, so that their attitudes may change through time. This is supported by Butler's (1975) argument that communities can simultaneously hold both positive and negative attitudes towards tourism. Likewise active or passive support for tourism or opposition to it may exist at any given time, as small interest groups take political action to achieve specific aims in relation to tourism. Murphy (1985) also affirmed that a non-linear model to explain resident attitudes was appropriate, with Dogan (1989) looking at how residents may respond behaviourally to tourism, depending on their attitudes. Responses include: resistance to tourism, retreat from it, the maintenance of boundaries, revitalisation and adaptation to tourism. Ap and Crompton (1993) concluded that residents' reaction to tourism could be placed on a continuum comprising four strategies: embracement, tolerance, adjustment and withdrawal. Different residents may also use different strategies. In fact, Fredline and Faulkner's (2000) use of cluster analysis may help in identifying the response pattern of the community to tourism and the diversity of feelings, attitudes and values.

However, Ap and Crompton (1993) dispute Dogan's (1989) assertion that a cultural gap exists between residents and tourists, arguing that the strategies adopted by residents were a function of residents' reactions to tourist numbers, and the behaviour of individual tourists. Ap (1990) reviewed the contributions of Liu and Var (1986) and Milman and Pizam (1988) to help develop a better understanding of conceptual and theoretical analyses of hosts' or residents' perceptions of the impact of tourism. Their contribution is made in terms of social exchange theory which helps to explain how residents evaluate the expected benefits and costs of tourism which are exchanged in return for resources and services (Getz 1994). The outcome of Ap's (1990) research is that positive resident attitudes to tourism occur when they perceive a satisfactory balance between rewards and costs. Other needs such as 'rationality' (reward seeking), 'satisficing' (satisfying minimum aspirations), 'reciprocity' (mutual gratification) and 'justice' (fairness or equity) must also be satisfied (Getz 1994).

This case study does not set out to test the social exchange concept, but it does focus on a broader perspective of resident attitudes. To understand such attitudes and their incorporation into a community tourism plan requires some insight into how the community (i.e. the residents and business owners) understand and value the locality they live in. By explaining these values, and the patterns of how services and facilities in the locality are used, a more meaningful analysis of resident attitudes is possible. This is because the impact of tourism can be viewed in terms of the actual effects experienced by the resident population and their perceptions of the effects. The attitudes of residents to tourism can then be identified and understood in terms of how tourism affects the very qualities and features valued by residents. Such an approach has important implications for the way a community tourism plan evolves, so that tourism can be promoted and developed in sympathy with the values and attitudes of the community. Then visitors and residents can relate to each other better, giving tourists a better-quality experience.

Devonport is a suburb of Auckland, and the expansion of day-trippers in Devonport, in the absence of serviced tourist accommodation, has been facilitated by the proximity of the area to downtown Auckland by ferry, and its 'olde world' image. As a place to visit, Devonport is seen as a popular residential area with a high proportion of historic wooden houses (villas). To a certain extent this has been promoted by gentrification and the way the community sees itself as having resisted most forms of external economic development.

This small community of 16,314 receives 1.5 million visits a year from domestic, international and local Auckland-based visitors. Its location at the southern tip of Auckland's North Shore and location on a peninsula makes road access difficult, although Devonport is also accessible by ferry. Existing data on tourism in Devonport is based on unpublished reports (*The Impacts of Tourism in Devonport* 1994; Munday 1995) with a conservative estimate placing the value of tourism spending at NZ$10–15 million per annum, based on an average visitor expenditure of NZ$10, and an average length of stay of three to four hours.

Resident impact study

In May 1995, a questionnaire survey was developed in conjunction with local representatives in Devonport as a baseline study to gauge residents' attitudes to the area and the values they see in it; and the impact of tourism on these values. The study was also intended to be the first stage of a longitudinal study of resident attitudes, to be repeated in three to five years. In view of the need to develop a robust study with a wide range of responses, a random survey technique was selected and a sample of 700 households (a 4.2 per cent sample of residents) drawn from a wide cross-section of the community. To assist in generating a random geographical sample representative of the area, the three principal communities of the Old Borough, Bayswater/Belmont and the Grammar District were selected as a spatial sampling frame. To help draw the sample most efficiently over a short time, a telephone questionnaire survey was used. The elements of the survey are listed in Table 6.7.

A market research company was contracted to conduct the survey because of its ongoing research experience in tourism (it conducted the New Zealand International Visitor Survey) and state-of-the-art Computer Assisted Telephone Interviewing system (CATI). In addition, all interviewers were professionally trained, interviews were monitored to ensure consistency in the administration of the survey and up to 10 call-backs to individuals selected could be undertaken. The computer randomly selected individuals aged 18 and over on the basis of their first initials. The CATI system also had the potential to weight the data if the sample did not reflect the distribution of the population in the survey areas.

Identifying community values

The concept of community values requires some discussion, since it underpins the survey. While there is no universal agreement in the sociology literature on the definition of 'community' (Walmsley and Lewis 1993), in broad terms community 'involves an implicit sense of belonging in a taken-for-granted situation, so that any social area with agreed boundaries can constitute

Table 6.7   Elements of the questionnaire survey

- An introduction to the survey, read out by the market researcher
- A list of instructions for the market researcher to screen out certain respondents (e.g. Community Board members, North Shore City Council members and market researchers)
- An explanation of the purpose of the survey
- An outline of the time the survey would take
- Demographic details (e.g. age, sex)
- Questions on length of residence in Devonport
- A list of qualities which broadly represent community values and feelings towards Devonport
- A section that referred to the residents' use of central Devonport and their use of services and other facilities in the area
- A range of questions on their perceptions of tourism and visitors, with tourists being defined as 'anyone from other areas in Auckland, New Zealand or international visitors', using a range of statements to provoke residents' attitudes
- The future development of Devonport in relation to the expansion or need for constraint on a range of issues
- A series of statements related to the expansion of tourism in Devonport or need for constraint on its expansion
- A section to gain additional demographic data related to employment, mode of transport used to get to work and household type
- An open section to allow respondents to comment on the survey
- The name of the street in which the respondent lived

Source: Page (1995b).

a community' (Walmsley and Lewis 1993: 234). Although this concept of community contains an element of local ties, it is widely argued that in many urban contexts the concept of community is lost by the scale and nature of urban living. However, locally based communities, such as Devonport in Auckland, can survive in urban surroundings, providing an important context for local ties, support networks and reinforced by a sense of belonging. 'Urban villages' (Gans 1962), distinguished by lifestyle, class and social ties, are created by numerous social and physical factors which influence the organisation and structure of a community in an urban environment (e.g. the layout of houses may encourage social contact). Length of residence will undoubtedly deepen acquaintances and the nature of contacts, although Snaith and Haley (1999: 602) argued in the context of York, England, that 'the shorter the period of residence, the greater the likelihood of recognising both the positive and the negative impacts of tourism. This suggests that people may indeed learn to live with tourism'. But the concept of community is not necessarily synonymous with that of community values because individuals will perceive individual neighbourhoods within their locality (their home community), shaped by their identification of landmarks, and social, environmental and other physical characteristics.

Demographic profile of residents

The survey data were not weighted in any way because the profile of respondents is broadly similar to the resident population. This is reflected in two important measures: the age distribution of residents and the characteristics of their household. The 1991 census figures provided a good close approximation to the age structure of the residents in the survey looked at by area, with one or two exceptions (the 35–44 age group in Belmont and Bayswater, and the 25–34 and 45–54 age groups in the Grammar district).

In terms of household size, the sample is broadly similar (i.e. the results are within a tolerance level of ±5 per cent) to the household structure for each area based on the 1991 census, with the exception of the Grammar district. Within the Grammar district, the results are less representative of households of two and three people (Table 6.8), under- and over-representing the situation respectively. The typical respondent was drawn from a two-parent family (32.5 per cent), closely followed by those living with a partner (25.4 per cent) and those living alone (21.9 per cent). In terms of the age of respondents and their household type, the majority of those in two-parent families were aged 35–44 years (47.8 per cent), while those living alone were mainly aged over 65 years (54.2 per cent). Not surprisingly, those who stated they were flat-sharing or based in a non-family household were mainly aged 18–35 years (73.7 per cent).

Residential stability and turnover

One important indicator sometimes used to identify the existence of community spirit in an area is the degree of residential stability and turnover, since a high level of stability will contribute to a continuity of community attitudes where residents consider themselves to be stakeholders with a long-term

Table 6.8 Household size (expressed as a percentage)

Number in household	Old Borough		Area Bayswater/Belmont		Grammar	
	C	S	C	S	C	S
1	27	23.3	25	19.3	23	19.9
2	32	26.1	33	28.0	39	30.5
3	16	13.8	16	20.7	15	25.8
4	16	21.8	15	18.7	16	14.6
5	7	9.5	8	8.7	6	6.0
6 or more	2	3.5	3	3.3	1	2.0
Refused	N/A	2.0	N/A	1.3	N/A	1.3

C = household size by area based on the 1991 Census. S = household size by area based on the survey.
Source: Page (1995b).

commitment to the area. The survey indicated that the degree of residential stability of residents is particularly high, with a high proportion having lived at the same address for over six years (48.3 per cent). There is a surprisingly low level of geographical variation in the level of residential turnover by area with the average figures virtually mirrored in each district. In fact, over 32 per cent or more of residents in each area have lived at their current address for 11 or more years. Therefore, the respondents are well suited to commenting on the impact of tourism because they have lived there and seen its development and expansion in recent years.

Employment characteristics of residents

Some 48.4 per cent (339) of the residents were employed in full-time paid work with a further 14.9 per cent (104) in part-time work and 35.9 per cent (251) not employed. There was little geographical variation in the percentage of people in each category. Within the sample, proportionally more residents were employed in full-time work in the 18–54 age groups, with a noticeable 39.2 per cent in the 35–44 age group. Proportionally more residents in the 18–44 age group were represented in the part-time category. In contrast, 13.5 per cent of those not in paid employment were aged 55–64, compared to an average of 9.9 per cent in the total sample. In terms of the gender of those in full-time employment, a male : female ratio of 50.7 : 49.3 was recorded, which is in stark contrast to the 20.2 per cent of males and 79.8 per cent of females in part-time employment.

Since it is extremely difficult to ask respondents to describe something as personal as the qualities of their locality, interviewers were empowered to probe residents about three qualities they valued about their area. In some cases, a resident's comments had to be qualified so that the interviewer was aware of which category to allocate the response to. Table 6.9 lists the five most commonly cited responses. The remaining responses were recorded by 11

Table 6.9 Main qualities of Devonport

Quality	Percentage who mentioned this quality
The scenery/views/environment/beaches	63
The close community/the community spirit/friendly people	43.4
The close proximity to Devonport shops/restaurants/cinemas/village	30.1
The peace and quiet in Devonport	29.7
The historical character of the area[a]	16.4

[a] A further 9.3 per cent specifically mentioned the attractive houses and buildings.
Source: Page (1995b).

per cent or fewer residents, with only a small number of people unable to refer to three features. Residents most commonly used central Devonport two to three times a week (26.3 per cent) while 22.7 per cent visited every day, 17.9 per cent once a week and 16.4 per cent four to six times a week. This indicates a high level of usage by residents, especially among those in the Old Borough who live near to the central area.

Residents' attitudes to tourism

Within a New Zealand context, research on the social impact of tourism and resident attitudes has been limited to a number of notable studies (Cant 1980; Garland and West 1985; Evans 1994) with the most significant one published by the Ministry of Tourism (1992) examining 1,485 residents at 15 locations. Many of the statements used in the Ministry of Tourism (1992) survey were adapted for the Devonport study. Although the questions are not directly comparable it did assist in the formulation of appropriate questions to assess resident attitudes (see Table 6.10).

To assess residents' attitudes to tourism, several statements were used, inviting respondents to strongly agree, agree, disagree or strongly disagree with each item in line with the Ministry of Tourism (1992) study. The following are apparent from the findings:

Table 6.10   Resident attitudes to attributes of Devonport – future scenarios

Rating	Statements								
	A	B	C	D	E	F	G	H	I
	n	n	n	n	n	n	n	n	n
Strongly agree	97	80	236	61	38	127	109	52	117
Agree	266	172	396	207	164	407	453	138	409
Disagree	278	385	40	357	400	97	87	400	87
Strongly disagree	30	24	1	36	23	21	10	94	14
Total:	700	700	700	700	700	700	700	700	700
	(671)	(661)	(673)	(661)	(625)	(652)	(659)	(684)	(627)

Note: n = number of respondents. Responses do not total 700 because some respondents indicated that they were unsure or could not comment.
Key
A – Devonport should be preserved and maintained mainly for the benefit of local residents.
B – I would visit Devonport more often if parking was easier.
C – There is a strong community feeling in Devonport.
D – Developing tourism threatens the local environment in Devonport.
E – Shopping hours should be extended in Devonport.
F – Overall, the America's Cup will bring a positive benefit to Devonport.
G – A heritage trail would benefit Devonport.
H – Footpath congestion caused by pavement cafés is a real problem for shoppers in Devonport.
I – I think the America's Cup will be a good thing for Devonport.
Source: Page (1995b).

- There was a distinct split in residents' feelings about the preservation and maintenance of Devonport's historic character and environment mainly for residents. Nearly 52 per cent of respondents favoured such an approach, but 44 per cent disagreed.

- An overwhelming 58 per cent of respondents did not consider the lack of parking space to be a deterrent to using the town centre, but 36 per cent of the sample did consider it a problem, which indicates that parking is an issue for over a third of Devonport residents.

- To assess resident perceptions of Devonport's character as an area, respondents were asked whether a strong community feeling existed. Approximately 90 per cent of respondents agreed or strongly agreed with the assertion, indicating that it is a major factor associated with community values. In this context, the implications for tourism planning are clear: any development will need to foster and retain the community spirit. Yet, despite a strong community feeling, less than half of the respondents considered tourism a major threat to their local environment; some 56 per cent of respondents disagreed with Statement D.

Tourism and future development in Devonport

The majority of respondents were reasonably conservative in their preferences for the future development of Devonport, tending to suggest that about the same or only a little more activity and a few additional services and developments should be encouraged. For example, nearly 72 per cent of residents felt that there were enough cafés and restaurants in Devonport, with only 17 per cent believing that there were too many. Likewise, nearly 76 per cent of respondents felt there were sufficient bars or pubs. One important indicator for tourism was that 43 per cent of residents felt business development was at the right level, while 33 per cent considered that there was scope for some limited growth in this area. This is in contrast to the expectations of residents that there should be additional employment for residents. For example, 35 per cent of residents wanted a little more employment, 22 per cent would like to see a lot more jobs, and 26 per cent felt there were sufficient forms of employment for local people. Some 51 per cent of the residents perceived that there was considerable scope for expanding the market for visitors from Auckland while 38 per cent felt the existing level was sufficient. Although this does not indicate a clear consensus, there is an underlying reservation about expanding the day visitor market. This is probably a logical response to the limited economic impact which day-trip visitors make in an urban context.

There was less resentment towards an expansion of domestic tourism, with nearly 29 per cent preferring to retain this market at its existing level. In contrast, 38 per cent of residents recognised that there is scope for a limited expansion of this market, while 23 per cent believed Devonport could sustain greater growth. With regard to international tourism, 27 per cent of residents were satisfied with the existing level of visitor numbers, although 36 per cent would be prepared to see further development of this market and nearly 27 per cent would like to see a major expansion in this area. One possible explanation of the desire for a growth in international arrivals is that international tourism is a high-profile activity within the New Zealand economy, with a great deal of media coverage.

Future development scenarios for tourism in Devonport

When questioned about future scenarios for tourism development in Devonport, many respondents stated that tourist activities and attractions should be developed (44.7 per cent) and nearly 44 per cent felt the provision was adequate. Approximately 42 per cent did not see the need to expand the existing range of festivals and events in Devonport, but nearly 50 per cent felt there was scope to expand these activities. Sixty-seven per cent of residents would like to see Devonport better preserved, although nearly 28 per cent felt preservation was at the right level now.

The perceived importance of tourism and development options for Devonport

It was important to consider the degree of importance that residents attach to tourism as an economic activity because in situations where residents are inundated by visitors they may point to the costs, problems and negative aspects of tourism and minimise the benefits. In Devonport, residents perceived tourism to be important (46 per cent) or very important (37 per cent) to the local economy. When asked about the likely repercussions and effects of an increase in visitors, nearly 52 per cent of residents acknowledged that an expansion in visitor numbers would make little difference to them.

Residents were also asked about increasing visitor numbers. Some 57.2 per cent (400 residents) were in favour of an increase, while a residual, though important, minority opposed any further growth. If existing research on the impact of tourism holds true for Devonport, then one would expect residents in the Old Borough to be more dubious about expanding visitor numbers, but the survey results indicate that this is really not the case.

In terms of the degree of contact with visitors, 443 respondents were in some form of employment and 26 per cent (116) of them stated that their work was directly involved with tourists and visitors. This element of the survey was particularly significant as a potential variable that could shape resident attitudes, and so it was subjected to more detailed analysis.

It is evident that residents value highly certain attributes in the locality and are reasonably cautious about further economic development that would be detrimental to the community spirit and physical appearance of the area. The central area of the town acts as a focal point for resident activities, especially shopping and other aspects of community life. Likewise, residents' sense of place is highly developed and based on a range of tangible and sometimes intangible elements. Residents appeared to be reasonably predisposed towards visitors. A significant proportion of residents has close contact with visitors through employment or encounters in the town centre.

This interaction may not necessarily lead to more meaningful social relationships, but it does raise issues related to the endearment behaviour of tourists through their interaction with the host community (Prentice *et al.* 1994), that is, the development of a more positive attitude towards tourists because of the benefits they bring.

The environmental impact of urban tourism

The environmental dimension is assuming a growing significance as a research area in tourism studies particularly with the debate on sustainability (Hall and Lew 1998). Dowling (1992) provides a useful synthesis of how interest in the relationship between tourism and the environment has developed over the past forty years:

> In the 1950s it was viewed as being one of coexistence . . . However, with the advent of mass tourism in the 1960s, increasing pressure was put on natural areas for tourism developments. Together with the growing environmental awareness and concerns of the early 1970s the relationship was perceived to be in conflict. During the next decade this view was endorsed by many others . . . at the same time a new suggestion was emerging that the relationship could be beneficial to both tourism and the environment (Dowling 1992: 33).

The recent concern for a sustainable approach towards tourism development, to ensure its long-term viability as an economic activity, is reflected in the recent government Task Force in the UK, formed in 1990 to find solutions to the impact of tourism on the environment (English Tourist Board/Employment Department 1991). The Task Force was charged with establishing the scale and nature of environmental problems induced by mass tourism at major tourist sites. It was also required to draw up guidelines on how such problems were to be addressed while maintaining the resource-base for tourism activities. The study examined case studies of historic towns, heritage sites and resort areas that fall within the remit of urban tourism and notes common problems resulting from tourism, including: wear and tear on the urban fabric, overcrowding and social and cultural impacts between the visitors and local communities. The development of the *Journal of Sustainable Tourism* also reflects the increasing awareness that tourism needs to develop in harmony with the environment in a symbiotic manner.

Shaw and Williams (1992) provide a useful insight into the environmental implications of tourism development for urban areas. They report on the view within the literature that tourism–environment impacts have been viewed along a continuum where impacts may be minimal or positive in inner-city areas, but assume a growing negative impact as one moves through a range of other tourism environments from old coastal resorts to urban historic areas to natural coastal and rural areas. They argued that in some urban environments, where past industrial processes have damaged the environment (e.g. former inner-city and dock areas), tourism can actually enhance the environmental quality (Department of the Environment 1990) (see Plate 6.3). This is particularly the case where tourism is used to regenerate entire inner-city districts and redundant spaces in cities (Law 1993) and there is even evidence in the rhetoric for the development of sites for the Sydney 2000 Olympics of a 'green games' with sustainability and green issues on the agenda (Chalkley and Essex 1999).

Nevertheless, it is widely acknowledged that research on the environmental impact of tourism has generally neglected urban areas, although if purpose-built tourist resorts are considered as a form of urban tourism, then these localities

Plate 6.3   Carhenge, Alliance, Nebraska: this illustrates how an attraction can be used to develop a town's tourism potential with a novel development that may generate local opposition to its aesthetic qualities which ironically generate a visitor market seeking the curiosity and interest element (© Leigh Sparks)

have received a specialised treatment in the tourism literature. Much of the concern has been on *after the event* studies which consider the consequences of coastal resort development, such as that along the Mediterranean coastline or newly developed South East Asian beach resorts. Here the emphasis has been on the environmental damage and consequences of development, as the landscapes have been modified to meet the needs of the tourism industry, with urban development resulting from the economic needs of the industry to concentrate activity in urban agglomerations. Herein lie the main problems in assessing the environmental impact of tourism:

- baseline information is needed on the environment prior to, and during the development of tourism; and
- the impact attributable to tourism has to be identified and separated from non-tourism impacts, but this is less than straightforward owing to the complex interrelationships that exist between different activities within urban areas.

One useful methodology used by environmental scientists and geographers to assess the future impact of specific tourism projects is EA which, as mentioned earlier, requires the establishment of a baseline study and to monitor the effects of specific tourism projects (e.g. the impact of the Channel Tunnel on the environment in and around the main rail terminus at Waterloo and wider afield in London – see Page and Sinclair 1992 for a discussion of some of the effects of tourism). In view of the specialised nature of this environmental methodology and its increasing use in relation to major tourism projects, a number of good reviews and examples exist which explain how it is undertaken and its methodological basis (see Page 1992; Goodenough and Page 1994; Green and Hunter 1992) and need not be discussed here.

Mathieson and Wall (1982) offer a number of insights into the environmental problems associated with tourism in resort areas, which are also relevant for other urban areas. The impacts are related to:

- architectural pollution due to the effect of inappropriate hotel development on the traditional landscape;
- the effect of ribbon development and urban sprawl in the absence of planning and development restrictions (e.g. the resorts of Buggiba and Quawra on the island of Malta have now merged, forming one zone of continuous urban tourist development);
- the resort infrastructure becoming overloaded and breaking down in periods of peak usage;
- tourists becoming segregated from local residents (though this may not necessarily be a problem);
- good quality agricultural land being lost to urban tourist development because of the inflationary effect on land prices, which encourages land owners to sell to developers;

- resultant traffic congestion in urban resort areas (see Schafer 1978);
- pollution of the local ecosystem from sewage, litter and too many visitors in the peak season, which may also pose serious problems for the destination.

During the 1990s, the tourism industry recognised the potential conflicts that its activities may pose for the environment (see Pigeassou *et al.* 1999 in relation to sport tourism in Europe), since interest groups with a strong environmental debate have focused on non-urban contexts where the impact on the natural environment has been more evident. Nevertheless, the hotel sector has been concerned with a wide range of environmental issues as the International Hotels Environment Initiative (1996) has shown. The introduction of Environmental Auditing to improve the environmental performance of hospitality operations (see Goodall 1992; Ding and Pigram 1995; Stabler and Goodall 1997) has also emerged. Indeed this mirrors wider trends in the tourism sector (Goodall 1992) where the environmental performance of an organisation is subject to regular, objective and ongoing evaluation of its plant, buildings, processes and practices using environmental auditing procedures. These initiatives are very much guided by codes of conduct, best practices, accreditation schemes and approved standards (Mihalic 2000) which can have a beneficial impact on the image and marketing of the destination. In fact, Diamantis and Westlake (1997) examined the example of Molyvos, a resort on the Greek island of Mytilini where concerns with environmental elements such as waste and water use form an important element in environmental management practices. Cummings (1997) study of the Flamingo Hilton Resort and Casino in Las Vegas examined solid waste minimisation practices. What Cummings (1997) produced was a five level hierarchy for waste minimisation ranging from the most critical to least critical where:

- Level 1 – a commitment to environmental goals (e.g. conservation and environmental protection) to reduce the negative impact of tourism followed by critical sub-strategies of source reduction including levels 2 to 5;
- Level 2 – the application of eco-intelligence in the organisation's purchasing policies and activities;
- Level 3 – the application of source reduction principles of using and wasting less as well as the use of electronic communication;
- Level 4 – the reuse of resources such as refilling and repackaging of materials;
- Level 5 – recycling to avoid disposal.

Therefore, the signs are that the tourism industry in urban areas is also embracing the environmental lobby and the need for cost savings through environmental management measures.

Even where integrated tourist development occurs in a planned manner (e.g. Universal Studios in California – see Plate 6.4) many environmental problems remain as a permanent cost for developing tourism. Green and Hunter's (1992) assessment of environmental impacts caused by tourism provides a useful

Plate 6.4 Universal Studios film set location is a highly managed visitor experience which takes visitors through film sets under construction

insight into the specific environmental impacts associated with tourism. Some of the impacts associated with urban tourism *may* lead to changes in the:

- urban environment and its physical characteristics;
- visual impact of the environment;
- requirements for urban infrastructure;
- urban forms;
- restoration of specific features in the historical and cultural environment;
- competition from other urban destinations, possibly leading to a decline in the quality of the urban environment.

How do we assess whether the urban environmental quality for visitors has been eroded to such an extent that the long-term viability of tourism is threatened? One useful concept used by researchers is *carrying capacity*.

Carrying capacity

Mathieson and Wall (1982: 21) describe carrying capacity as 'the maximum number of people who can use a site [or area] without an unacceptable alteration in the physical environment and without an unacceptable decline in the quality of the experience gained by visitors'. Such a concept has been used to measure the capacity for tourism in natural and artificial tourism environments, making it suitable for use in an urban context. While the literature on carrying capacity has been extensively reviewed in other studies and need not be reiterated here (see Pigram and Jenkins 1999; Hall and Page 2002), three principal elements can be discerned in an urban context. According to van der Borg and Costa (1993: 7) the tourist carrying capacity in urban areas comprises three elements:

1. *The physical (or ecological) carrying capacity*, which is the limit at which the number of visitors can be accommodated at maximum stress. Beyond this threshold, the cultural, historical and built environment is irreparably damaged by tourism.
2. *The economic carrying capacity*, which is the limit beyond which the quality of the tourists' experience of the urban area falls and makes it less attractive to visit as a destination.
3. *The social carrying capacity*, which is the number of visitors a city can absorb without adversely affecting the other social and economic activities in the city which underpin its rationale for existence.

These components of the carrying capacity of sites or areas have become notoriously difficult to calculate. For example, what degree of environmental modification is acceptable to tourists before the visitor experience is affected? Cynics argue that the carrying capacity can only be established retrospectively, once it has been exceeded. Nevertheless, research by Canestrelli and Costa (1991) and van der Borg (1991) has attempted to establish the environmental impact of tourism in Venice using this approach.

The environmental impact of tourism in Venice

Venice is an internationally renowned tourist destination and a fine example of a small historic city, with its cultural antiquities and highly acclaimed fifteenth-century renaissance art. Venice is located on a series of islands in a lagoon, and is the capital of the Veneto region of Italy, which has experienced massive economic growth since the 1960s (Figure 6.9). However, the historic city of Venice experienced continued population loss during this period, dropping from 175,000 in 1951 to 78,000 in 1992 and receives 47,000 commuters daily

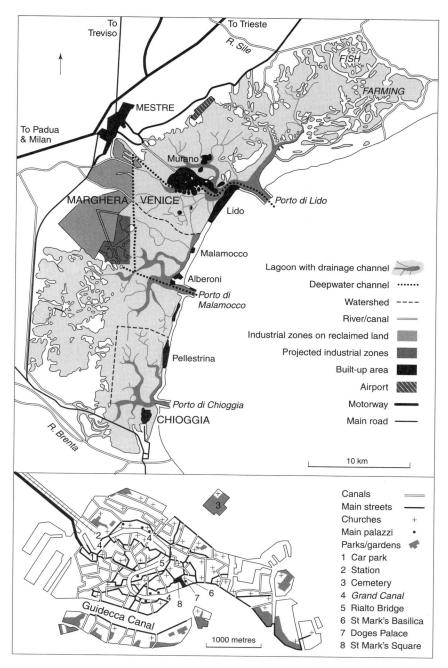

Figure 6.9 The location of Venice (source: King 1987)

(Glasson *et al*. 1995). The age and condition of many of Venice's buildings are under constant threat. The environment in Venice is suffering from:

- a sinking ground level;
- a rising sea level (Penning-Rowsell *et al*. 1998);
- pollution of the lagoon in which it is located;
- atmospheric pollution (Zilio-Grandi and Szpyrkowicz 2000).

One can also add a further category to these environmental problems – tourism.

As a tourist destination, visitor arrivals have developed from 50,000 tourists spending 1.2 million bed-nights in the historic city of Venice in 1952. By 1987 these figures had risen to 1.13 million tourist arrivals and 2.49 million bed-nights and 1.21 million arrivals and 2.68 million bed-nights in 1992. The average length of stay was 2.21 nights in 1992 (van der Borg *et al*. 1996). The number of hotel beds has grown from 20,000 in 1973 to 22,200 in 1992. These visitor numbers are swelled by a large day visitor market from other parts of Italy, especially the Adriatic beach resorts and Alpine areas. In 1992, the day-tripper market was estimated to be 6 million visitors, providing a total market in excess of 7 million visitors a year. Much of this growth in demand has been motivated by a desire to experience and understand the city's cultural heritage (Costa and van der Borg 1992; van der Borg 1994; van der Borg *et al*. 1995; van der Borg *et al*. 1996). Montanari and Muscara (1995) recognised that Venice was saturated at key times in the year (e.g. Easter) and that the police have had to close the Ponte della Liberta (leading to the mainland) when the optimum flow of 21,000 tourists a day has been greatly exceeded. The challenge posed by visitors was well illustrated in July 1989 when the pop group Pink Floyd held a concert which attracted 200,000 visitors and pushed the city's infrastructure to the limit.

Since 1987, on selected spring weekends, the land route from the mainland to Venice has been closed to visitors as an extreme form of crisis management (Montanari and Muscara 1995). Montanari and Muscara developed a nine-fold classification of tourists based on differences in their spatial behaviour, perception and spending power which can be summarised thus:

- the first-time visitor on an organised tour;
- the rich tourist;
- the lover of Venice;
- the backpacker camper;
- the worldly-wise tourist;
- the return tourist;
- the resident artist;
- the beach tourist;
- the visitor with a purpose;

reflecting the unique tourism environment (Fiorelli 1989) and the diversity of motivations for visiting the city.

What is notable in the case of Venice is the dominance of excursionists (83.1 per cent) in comparison to tourists (16.9 per cent) (van der Borg *et al.* 1996) which exhibits a very even pattern of distribution throughout the year. In the first quarter (January–March) 14 per cent of visitors arrive followed by 30 per cent (April–June), 32 per cent (July–September) and 24 per cent (October–December). The destination's accessibility has also been increased with the recent advent of low-cost airlines in Europe, following the liberalisation of air transport regulations (Mason 2000), with the growth in leisure travel noted in Chapter 3. Venice's tourist market comprises 26.3 per cent of arrivals from within Italy, 36 per cent from Europe, 17.7 per cent from the United States, 11.1 per cent from Japan and 8.8 per cent from other countries/regions. The social impact of the existing patterns of demand led van der Borg *et al.* (1996: 314) to calculate the visitor/resident (host) ratio for Venice and a number of other European heritage cities. In Venice's historical centre, a ratio of 89.4 : 1 existed while for the wider Venice municipality this dropped to 27.6 : 1. This level of visitor pressure reflects the scale of the problem facing Venice (see Costa 1990), with only Bruges recording a level of 36 : 1, in excess of Venice's municipality. Both van der Borg *et al.* (1996) and Jansen-Verbeke and Lievois (1999) refer to the term 'touristification' of the urban area, since at key points/attractions in the city, major pressure points exist where locals are greatly outnumbered by tourists and excursionists. In fact, Venice has constructed a number of hotels in the suburbs to host commuting tourists (van der Borg 1991) as one way of spreading 'tourist pressure'. While the demand and supply of urban tourism in Venice is extensively documented by van der Borg (1991) and van der Borg and Costa (1993), it is Canestrelli and Costa's (1991) attempt to calculate the carrying capacity using a mathematical model – linear programming – which offers a number of insights into the carrying capacity of Venice as a tourist destination.

Venice's carrying capacity

To assess the carrying capacity of the historic centre of Venice, Canestrelli and Costa (1991) established:

- that the historic centre of Venice comprises 700 ha, with buildings protected from alterations by government legislation;
- the resident population and extent of daily commuting into and out of the city;
- the optimal use level of the destination using a range of variables such as supporting facilities (e.g. hotels, restaurants and parking spaces) and those variables describing the nature of the users (e.g. categories of tourist);

- the local tourist-dependent and non-tourist-dependent population in the locality and the theoretical relationship that exists between tourists and these two sub-groups. Each group also seeks to maximise their own position. For example, the tourist-dependent population will seek to push the tourist carrying capacity up as they derive economic benefits from visitor spending, but residents not dependent on tourism are likely to try to minimise the number of visitors to reduce the costs of tourism.

Using a linear programming technique (see Canestrelli and Costa 1991 for full details of the mathematical model and its application), the optimal growth of Venice as a tourist destination was explored. According to Canestrelli and Costa the optimal carrying capacity for the historic city of Venice would be to admit *9,780 tourists* who use hotel accommodation, *1,460 tourists staying in non-hotel accommodation* and *10,857 day-trippers* on a *daily basis*. One important consideration is that tourism demand is seasonal, although less so for urban destinations with their all year round attractions. Nevertheless, if the 4.1 million day trippers who visit Venice were evenly spread this would still amount to 11,233 day trippers a day. In fact research has estimated that an average of 37,500 day trippers a day visit Venice in August. Canestrelli and Costa (1991) argue that a ceiling of *25,000 visitors a day* is the maximum *carrying capacity* for Venice. This has important implications for the environment and its long-term preservation if the carrying capacity is being exceeded. Obviously, the ecological and economic carrying capacity are likely to have slightly different values, but the 25,000 threshold provides an indication of the scale of tourism that is desirable in an ideal world. Yet the reality of the situation is very different: van der Borg and Costa (1993) observe that in 1987, on *156 days a year* this number was exceeded. On 22 occasions *40,000 visitors a day* visited Venice and on *6 days the visitor numbers exceeded 60,000*. So what are the implications for the future?

According to a variety of tourism forecasts produced by van der Borg (1992) for the year 2000, the critical threshold of *25,000 visitors will be exceeded on 216 days* and on *7 days the visitor numbers will exceed 100,000* if the current growth rate in arrivals continues. In fact when 100,000 visitors fill the city, the local police close Ponte della Liberta, the bridge connecting the historic centre with the mainland, for safety reasons. But the large volume of visitors that descend on Venice each year not only exceeds the desirable limits of tourism for the city, but also poses a range of social and economic problems for planners. As van der Borg (1992: 52) observes

the negative external effects connected with the overloading of the carrying capacity are rapidly increasing, frustrating the centre's economy and society . . . excursionism [day tripping] is becoming increasingly important, while residential tourism is losing relevance for the local tourism market . . . [and] . . . the local benefits are diminishing. Tourism is becoming increasingly ineffective for Venice.

Thus, the negative impact of tourism on the historic centre of Venice is now resulting in a self-enforcing decline as excursionists, who contribute less to the local tourism economy than staying visitors (Glasson *et al.* 1995: 113), supplant the staying market as it becomes less attractive to stay in the city. Ironically, changing the attitude of the city's tourism policy-makers is difficult: it is heavily influenced by the pro-tourism lobby while hotel owners have sought to get the city council to restrict the booming Eastern European day-trip market which contributes little to the tourism economy. A number of positive measures have been enacted to address the saturation of the historic city by day visitors including denying access to the city by unauthorised tour coaches via the main coach terminal.

Even so, the city continues to promote the destination, thereby alienating the local population. One also has to recognise the environmental processes which affect both the local and tourist population, namely flooding. Flooding in Venice now means that St Mark's Square, an icon for visitors, floods 40–60 times a year compared to 4–6 times a year at the beginning of the twentieth century. As a result, tourism has to be balanced with measures of environmental protection and management. A range of positive steps are needed to provide a more rational basis for the future development and promotion of tourism in the new millennium (see van der Borg 1992; Glasson *et al.* 1995 for more details). Glasson *et al.* (1995: 116) summarise the problem of seeking to manage visitors and their environmental impact in Venice:

> ... every city must be kept as accessible as possible for some specific categories of users, such as inhabitants, visitors to offices and firms located in the city, and commuters studying or working in the city. At the same time, the art city needs to be kept as inaccessible as possible to some other user categories (the excursionist/ day-trippers in particular).

What the example of Venice shows is that while tangible economic benefits accrue to the city, the social and environmental costs are very substantial. Montanari and Muscari (1995) argued that the Venice water transport plays a major role in tourism within the city which can be used to manage visitors, while the city needed to plan to separate the access, circulation and exit of the resident/commuting population and tourists.

Clearly, Venice is a small historic city under siege from a new marauding army in the early twenty-first century: the tourist and particularly the excursionist. In this case, tourism *has not* been a stimulus for urban growth, but has actually contributed to urban decline as residents have continued to leave. The excessive numbers of day-trippers have also led to a deterioration in the quality of the tourist experience. This case study is significant in that it highlights the prevailing problems affecting many historic cities around the world, especially those in Europe. But it takes political will to embark on a decision-making process that will address the pressures posed by tourism in Venice.

The carrying capacity of any tourist city needs to be carefully examined and if quantitative techniques, such as linear programming, help to establish an

independent and authoritative basis for future planning, then it is a useful starting point in helping to reach a symbiotic balance between tourism and the
urban environment. Otherwise a situation may develop that is characterised by
conflict. The management of the environment of tourist cities is equally as
important as that of sensitive rural environments even though urban areas have
attracted less attention among researchers.

Integrated impact analysis for urban tourism

The impact of tourism in urban areas, like many other aspects of tourism activity, has attracted interest in the debate on sustainability (Hall and Lew 1998).
Hinch (1996) explored the dimensions of sustainability in urban tourism in
relation to the built natural and cultural environment, considering the organisational issues in a planning and management context to implement sustainability precepts. The concern with such issues is evident from Table 6.11 which
highlights the need to address the tourism–environment interface and the
necessity of practical management approaches, which are discussed more fully
in the next chapter since this requires a clear understanding of planning and
operational issues. What this indicates is the need for a framework/model

Table 6.11   The management of tourism–environment problems

Key issues
1. Improved management information, including:
    *   Visitor surveys
    *   Site surveys (to assess carrying capacity)
    *   Systematic monitoring

2. Effective coordination, including:
    *   A partnership approach to tourism
    *   A greater emphasis on tourism development action programmes (TDAPs)
    *   Town centre management schemes

3. Adequate resourcing, including
    *   A greater integration of the public and private sector in funding tourism projects

Practical management approaches
These include:
*   The assessment of capacity
*   Tourist transport management
*   Marketing and information provision
*   Conservation and adaptation of tourist activities to suit the environment
*   A greater concern for design principles and the control of tourism development
*   A greater involvement of the local community (e.g. community planning)

Source: modified from English Tourist Board/Employment Department (1991).

which can be utilised to understand the overall impact of urban tourism to establish the point at which issues of sustainability are relevant to planning decisions. In this context, Williams and Gills's (1991) model of tourism carrying capacity as a web incorporates many of the issues and perspectives discussed in this chapter. The model incorporates both quantifiable or objective elements while qualitative or soft elements are also included. The capacity web or sub-system can be examined to establish the capacity attributes for urban tourism. As a result both the 'dimensions' of tourism carrying capacity are juxtaposed with the 'perspectives' of tourism carrying capacity so that a wide range of elements in the urban tourism system are analysed to consider the capacity levels within which tourism can operate at a sustainable level.

According to Glasson *et al.* (1995: 54), the urban tourism carrying capacity of a destination can be modelled using the following formula thus:

$$TCC = f(Ecol, Phys, Econ) \ (TC, RA, Pol)$$

since the tourist carrying capacity (TCC) is a function of:

Ecol – the ecological systems in a destination;
Phys – the physical infrastructure and level of tourist infrastructure development;
Econ – the economic characteristics of tourism investment and expenditure;
TC – tourist characteristics (socio-cultural and behavioural);
RA – residents' acceptance or tolerance of tourism activity;
Pol – the political capability and authority to make effective management decisions pertaining to urban tourism.

As a result 'It is the magnitude and direction of impacts on each of these subsystems which defines the ability of a destination to absorb tourism activity, where the marginal benefits of providing for the tourist continues to exceed, or at least equal the marginal cost' (Glasson *et al.* 1995: 55). Operationalising such a formula requires a great deal of research on each element so that baseline data and impact indicators are assembled together with systematic monitoring and evaluation before establishing the level of visitor activity an urban area can support.

Conclusion

This chapter has shown that the impact of tourism on urban destinations is far more complex than has hitherto been alluded to in the literature. Identifying the complex relationship between the costs and benefits of tourism in different cities is far from straightforward, with the economic benefits tending to overshadow the social, cultural and environmental impacts. Although there is growing evidence that some sectors of the tourism industry in urban areas are implementing environmental management measures, a more holistic assessment is needed in each locality. Even the case study of Venice illustrated that researchers tend to focus more on the economic and social carrying capacity of cities than the more complex environmental dimensions of tourism impacts. The tendency for many city authorities to hail tourism as a solution to their many economic problems may be short-term expediency, as unplanned tourism development can bring as many problems as it purports to solve. Hall's (1970: 445) prediction that 'the age of mass tourism is the biggest single factor for change in the great capitals of Europe – and in many of smaller historic cities too – in the last 30 years of this century' still remains a valid assessment of the situation now facing many urban areas at the turn of the millennium. In fact many small historic cities are now facing so many pressures from urban tourism that they are taking radical steps to try and limit tourism development and visitor numbers, often under the guise of sustainable development. As future chapters will show, visitor management strategies are key issues for many locations seeking to reduce the overwhelming impact of mass tourism. In the UK the English Tourist Board and Employment Department's (1990) *Tourism and the Environment: Maintaining the Balance* report documented many of these problems, however they are not just confined to small historic cities although the scale and magnitude of the impacts are very obvious (van der Borg *et al.* 1996; Ashworth and Tunbridge 2000). It is clear from the issues discussed in this chapter and the detailed case studies that tourism planning and development need to be carefully considered if the benefits of tourism are to be maximised and the problems minimised. For this reason, the next chapter considers the issue of tourism planning in urban areas and the objectives and goals which public sector planners have to meet in the context of tourism.

Questions

1. What are the problems associated with tourism impact analysis in urban areas? How easy is it to assemble data on these impacts?

2. To what extent can multiplier analysis be used to calculate an approximate measure of tourism's economic impact on a city?

3. How would you set out to examine resident attitudes to tourism in an urban area?

4. How would you set about developing an Action Plan for the management of tourism in Venice in the twenty-first century?

Further reading

Since this is a large chapter covering a range of impacts, the following references will be of help for specific impacts:

Ap, J. and Crompton, J.L. (1993). 'Residents' strategies for responding to tourism impacts', *Journal of Travel Research* 32(1): 47–50.
This is a very useful article which causes one to rethink the arguments put forward by Doxey and should be read in combination with P. Pearce's article listed below.
Archer, B. and Cooper, C. (1994). 'The positive and negative impacts of tourism', in W. Theobald (ed.) *Global Tourism: The Next Decade*, Oxford: Butterworth-Heinemann, 73–91.
This provides a general overview of the impacts of tourism.
Dodds, R. and Joppe, M. (2002). 'Promoting urban green tourism: the development of the *other* map of Toronto', *Journal of Vacation Marketing* 7(3): 261–7.
This paper examines how the Green Tourist Association in Toronto, Canada, has developed the concept of urban green tourism to promote environmental responsibility, local economic vitality and cultural diversity. The development of the '*other* map of Toronto', which promotes greener tourism options, is evaluated.
Mathieson, A. and Wall, G. (1982). *Tourism, Economic, Physical and Social Impacts*, London: Longman.
Although this is a dated book, it still provides one of the most comprehensive reviews of the impact of tourism.
Pearce, D.G. (1989). *Tourist Development*, London: Longman.
This book contains a good analysis of the impact of tourism in the context of tourism development and should be read in conjunction with Mathieson and Wall (1982).
Pearce, P. (1994). 'Tourism–resident impacts: examples, explanations and emerging solutions', in W. Theobald (ed.) *Global Tourism: The Next Decade*, Oxford: Butterworth-Heinemann, 103–23.
This is a useful assessment of the social and cultural impact of tourism.

Planning and managing urban tourism

CHAPTER 7

Introduction

The skill of the urban tourism planner and manager has developed from a range of influences to the point where it has become a field of specialist knowledge. The present-day urban tourism planner has to integrate skills and knowledge of policy and planning, marketing, impact assessment, and organisation and project management – all within a tourism context – in order to fulfil the requirements of destination management. The purpose of the present chapter is to outline some of the management and planning mechanisms by which cities seek to deal with tourism issues, not least of which are some of the impacts of tourism outlined in the previous chapter. For example, problems of visitation identified by the English Tourism Board and the Department of Employment (1991) include: increased risk of fire, pilferage, graffiti, accident risks for cars, atmospheric pollution, impaired ambiance, destruction of architectural and archaeological integrity, traffic congestion and parking (both private cars and _____ and crowding. Indeed, many concerns are being expressed about _____ ce but the quality of urban tourism _____ Boniface 1995). However, manage- _____ es are not value-neutral and do not _____ n of such management and planning _____ ed within the broader political and _____ themselves, points considered both _____ unt of the nature of cities in an age of _____ t chapter, where we discuss urban _____ arketing.

_____ several sections. First, it provides a _____ nships of urban tourism policy, plan- _____ sses the organisational dimension of _____ f strategic planning for urban tourism with particular emphasis on collaboration and network development. Fourth, it outlines a range of planning mechanisms for urban tourism planning and management and their operation. Finally, it provides a historical account of the changing nature of urban planning and management with respect to Canberra in Australia.

Urban tourism, policy and management

Urban tourism planning and management have developed from and been influenced by a number of different traditions. Planning for tourism has traditionally been associated with land-use zoning or development planning at the local or regional government level. Concerns have typically been focused on site development, accommodation and building regulations, the density of tourist development, the presentation of cultural, historical and natural tourist features, and the provision of infrastructure including roads and sewage. However, tourism planning at all levels of government has increasingly had to adapt in recent years to include concerns over the environmental, cultural and social dimensions of tourism and, given the changing context within which government occurs, demands for 'smaller government', particularly from some business interests which argue that self-regulation is more economically efficient than government regulation (Hall and Jenkins 1995; Davidson and Maitland 1997; C.M. Hall 2000). In a more general review of urban and regional planning, Healey (1997) also recognised several strands of planning:

- economic planning which aims to manage the productive forces of a country or region;
- the management of the physical development of towns and regions; and
- the management of public administration and policy analysis which aims to manage the efficiency and effectiveness of public agencies.

Indeed, Healey noted that most who criticise 'planning' often have the state socialist 'command and control' model of centralised economic planning in mind, rather than other forms of planning which are, in fact, in common usage in Western democratic societies. The most important characteristic of planning is that it is directed towards the future. Friedmann (1959: 334) provides an interesting list of planning characteristics that arise out of the future orientation of planning:

- It places a limit upon the time period over which projections into the future can be made without loss of practical significance for present decisions.
- It establishes the necessity for continuing planning analysis and assessment throughout the planning period and the constant re-evaluation and adjustment of means to ends.

- It suggests the use of expectational calculus in connection with statements about the future.
- It argues for the adoption of a system of framework or structural planning.
- It forces the careful consideration of flexibility in planning where the degree of flexibility introduced into a solution must be proportionate to the degree of uncertainty over future events. It is through an approach such as this that reason can come to terms with uncertainty.

Planning and policy are terms that are intimately related. According to Cullingsworth (1997: 5), 'Planning is the purposive process in which goals are set and policies elaborated to implement them'. In contrast, policy analysis is 'concerned with understanding and explaining the substance of policy content and policy decisions and the way in which policy decisions are made' (Barrett and Fudge 1981: 6), where public policy is the structure or confluence of values and behaviour involving a governmental prescription. Public policy is therefore the focal point of government activity. Tourism public policy-making is first and foremost a political activity. Public policy is influenced by the economic, social and cultural characteristics of society, as well as by the formal structures of government and other features of the political system. Policy should therefore be seen as a consequence of the political environment, values and ideologies, the distribution of power, institutional frameworks and of decision-making processes (Hall and Jenkins 1995). However, there is increasing scepticism about the effectiveness of government at all levels, and the intended consequences and impacts of much government policy, including with respect to tourism (Jenkins 1997). Nevertheless, even given demands for 'smaller government' in much of the Western world, 'market failure' still provides a number of rationales for government intervention in the urban economy including:

- improving economic competitiveness;
- amending property rights;
- enabling state decision-makers to take account of externalities;
- providing widely available public benefits;
- reducing risk and uncertainty;
- supporting projects with high capital costs and involving new technologies; and
- educating and providing information (Haughton and Hunter 1994: 263).

Such insights are extremely important as no longer can tourism planning be simply seen as an exercise solely in land-use planning. Undoubtedly, local or site level land-use planning is extremely important for urban destinations. However, such activities need to be conceived as occurring at one end of a continuum of planning-related activities which range from the local to the global and which similarly range from being land-use oriented at the site and local level to being policy oriented at the global level (C.M. Hall 2000). Indeed, it is now well recognised that planning for tourism occurs in a number of forms (e.g. development, infrastructure, land and resource use, organisation, human resource, promotion and marketing); structures (e.g. different government, quasi-government and non-government organisations); scales (international, transnational, national, regional, local, site and sectoral) and over different timescales (for development, implementation, evaluation and satisfactory fulfilment of planning objectives) (C.M. Hall 2000). Furthermore, planning is rarely exclusively devoted to tourism *per se*. Instead, planning for tourism tends to be 'an amalgam of economic, social and environmental considerations' which reflect the diversity of the factors which influence tourism development (Healey 1981: 61). A critical point arising from this consideration therefore is that urban tourism planning and management need not occur within a specifically designated tourism planning organisation. Instead, urban tourism planning and management will more typically occur within organisations that have a range of goals and objectives.

A good example of organisations that have significant roles with respect to tourism in urban destinations yet which are not tourism organisations *per se* can be found with respect to capital cities. Australia, for example, has established a National Capital Authority for Canberra:

> The Commonwealth and [Australian Capital Territory] ACT Governments share responsibility for the planning and development of Canberra. The planning and development of Canberra must achieve a balance between the interests of the nation and the interests of the local community.
>
> On behalf of the Commonwealth, the National Capital Authority administers and implements the National Capital Plan. The object of the Plan is to 'ensure that Canberra and the Territory are planned in accordance with their national significance'.
>
> The ACT Government, through the Territory Plan, is responsible for ensuring 'the planning and development of the Territory to provide the people with an attractive, safe and efficient environment in which to live and work and have their recreation'.
>
> The Territory Plan is required to be 'not inconsistent' with the National Capital Plan.
>
> The National Capital Plan and the Territory Plan are established under the Australian Capital Territory (Planning and Land Management) Act 1988.
>
> The vision of the National Capital Authority is for a National Capital which symbolises Australia's heritage, values and aspirations, is internationally recognised, and of which Australians are proud (National Capital Authority 2000).

In the United States the National Capital Planning Commission (NCPC) has been established to undertake planning and development of Washington in keeping with its capital city function. As the NCPC states, 'Washington is the seat of government and symbolic heart of the nation, and planning for the Nation's Capital is different from planning for other cities' (National Capital

Planning Commission 2001a). Indeed, its most recent strategic plan for the capital district explicitly recognises the relationship that tourism has with the political, cultural and symbolic functions of Washington's core area and the contribution it makes to economic development. The plan seeks to redefine 'Washington's Monumental Core by creating opportunities for new museums, memorials, and federal office buildings' and to preserve 'the historic character and open space of the Mall and its adjacent ceremonial corridors while accommodating growth and new development' in relation to the visitor demands that are being placed on Washington (NCPC 1997):

> The National Capital Planning Commission, working with leading planning and design professionals and with business, community, and federal and local government partners, developed the plan in response to the anticipated demands on the Nation's Capital in the 21st century. Tourism is expected to double over the next 50 years, automobile traffic could increase by a third during the next 20 years, and sites for many new memorials, museums, and federal buildings must be found.

In addition, in Washington substantial monies is being invested in urban redevelopment by the National Capital Revitalisation Corporation (NCRC) 'an independent corporate instrumentality of the District of Columbia charged with a specific mission: improving District businesses, promoting real estate development, and infusing economic development into the District of Columbia' (DCWatch 2000) as well as the NCPC itself. For example, 'The Federal Capital Improvements Program for Fiscal Years 2000–2004' contains 130 projects from 14 departments and agencies at an estimated cost of US$4.2 billion. In addition, the FCIP includes 18 other projects for future consideration by federal agencies in the region. These recommendations are intended to improve the character and quality of the region for visitors and residents (National Capital Planning Commission 2001b).

Within federal systems, planning bodies may also be established for provincial or state capitals. For example, in British Columbia in Canada the Provincial Government established a Provincial Capital Commission (PCC) for the capital of Victoria. Established in 1956 and given extra powers in 1979 (Morris 2000) the 'Commission's mandate is to protect and enhance the unique character and surroundings of British Columbia's Capital'. The scope of the Commission's powers is indicated in Section 8 of the PCC's Act in reference to its coordination powers:

> 1. The commission shall coordinate construction and development work in the Capital Improvement District in accordance with general plans approved from time to time under this Act.
> 2. Proposals for the location, erection, alteration or extension of a building or other work by or on behalf of the Province by any person on land owned, leased or otherwise controlled by the Province in the Capital Improvement District shall be referred to the commission prior to the commencement of the work.

3. No building or other work shall be erected, altered or extended by or on behalf of the Province in the Capital Improvement District unless the site, location and plans have first been approved by the commission.

4. No person shall erect, alter or extend a building or other work on land in the Capital Improvement District owned, leased or otherwise controlled by the Province unless the site, location and plans have first been approved by the commission.

5. In any case where the commission does not give its approval under this section, the Lieutenant Governor in Council may give approval.

6. This section does not apply to interior alterations in a work or building (British Columbia Provincial Capital Commission).

The above discussion highlights the need to understand the institutional arrangements surrounding urban tourism. These include not only the legal and regulatory structures that influence urban tourism but the organisations established to formulate and/or influence urban tourism policies and their respective values (Hall and Jenkins 1995).

The organisational dimension of urban tourism

Urban tourism planning, policy and management contain a strong organisational component. However, despite the centrality of organisations in the formulation of tourism planning and policy, organisations have only been subject to significant analysis over the past decade. Research on tourism organisations has tended to focus on public sector organisations at the national and regional levels and their contribution to policy and development (Pearce 1992; C.M. Hall 1994, 2000; Hall and Jenkins 1995), with only minor attention being given to the private sector. More recently, inter-organisational relationships have been given greater scrutiny (Selin and Beason 1991; Long 1997), while the role of interest groups in influencing leisure and tourism policy is also a growing area of interest (Craik 1991; Hall and Jenkins 1995).

There are almost as many different definitions of 'organisation' as there are definitions of tourism! However, for the purposes of this chapter, a working 'summary' definition of a tourism organisation is that it is a collective entity that has been established in order to achieve a goal (or set of goals) or purpose related to tourism. Organisations can be categorised in several ways; for example we describe them in terms such as private or public, voluntary or nonvoluntary or profit or non-profit driven. They may also be conceived as 'machines', 'organisms', 'cultures', 'political systems', 'instruments of domination' or other metaphors, such as a 'prison' (Morgan 1986).

Probably the central issue in trying to define the field of tourism organisations is whether we are discussing organisations that have been established specifically to further tourism-related goals or whether we also include organisations that are affected by leisure and tourism activities, issues and policies and that therefore seek to influence leisure and tourism as part of a wider mandate. The former approach may be conceptually neat but it is unfortunately extremely narrow and fails to convey the richness of the tourism field. For example, such an approach would exclude many environmental organisations, such as urban heritage and conservation organisations, which are clearly a component of the tourism field. Furthermore, the former approach might also exclude organisations that have tourism as only a minor concern in terms of their overall direction but that, for urban tourism interests, are a major concern, such as a planning ministry. Therefore, in an effort to provide a more complete picture of urban tourism planning and management, this chapter will take a broad perspective of tourism organisations.

This broad approach represents the organisational studies dimension of Leiper's (1989, 1990) concept of partial industrialisation. According to Leiper (1989: 25) partial industrialisation refers to the condition

> in which only certain organisations providing goods and services directly to tourists are in the tourism industry. The proportion of (a) goods and services stemming from that industry to (b) total goods and services used by tourists can be termed the index of industrialisation, theoretically ranging from 100 per cent (wholly industrialised) to zero (tourists present and spending money, but no tourism industry).

This situation offers one explanation for the difficulties in gaining coordination within the tourism industry, because different organisations have different degrees of tourism industrialisation and therefore different goals with respect to the industry overall. For example, although we can recognise that many segments of the urban economy benefit from tourism, it is only those organisations with a direct relationship to tourists that become actively involved in fostering tourism development or in marketing. Nevertheless, there are many other organisations such as food suppliers, petrol stations and retailers, sometimes described as 'allied industries', which also benefit from tourists but which are not readily identified as part of the tourism industry (C.M. Hall 2000).

Leiper's perspective is far more encompassing of organisations than the more narrow supply-side approach used by S.L. Smith (1988, 1991) and L.G. Smith (1992) which paid particular attention to the commodities tourism produces. From a supply-side perspective, the tourism industry may be defined as 'the aggregate of all businesses that directly provide goods or services to facilitate business, pleasure, and leisure activities away from the home environment' (S.L. Smith 1988: 183). However, a supply-side approach still means you have to draw an arbitrary line as to what constitutes direct provision. Some organisations will be included, but many would be left out. Such discussions are not just academic arguments, because the complexity of defining what we mean by tourism organisations highlights the difficulties that exist not only in developing urban tourism policies – because of the sheer range of groups and interests involved – but also in effectively analysing such policies.

Another complicating factor in studying tourism-related organisations is their sheer growth in recent years. Since the Second World War there has also been a tremendous expansion in the number and scope of interest groups (also described as pressure groups; Cigler 1991). Up until the 1960s, interest groups were primarily business association based, e.g. Chambers of Commerce. However, since the early 1960s, there has been rapid growth in Western nations in the number of citizen and public interest groups, particularly in the area of consumer and environmental concerns (Schlozman and Tierney 1986).

Tourism has not been immune from the growth in interest groups. Until the mid-1960s, tourism-related interest groups were generally confined to industry and professional associations. However, the growth of consumer, e.g. local tax- or ratepayers' associations, and environmental organisations, e.g. urban conservation organisations, extended the number of groups that had an interest in tourism issues, particularly as it related to aspects of tourism development at the local level. In the 1980s and the early 1990s, the range of groups was extended still further as social issues, such as sex tourism (Ryan and Hall 2001), and international trade became significant. Therefore, it is important to realise that tourism interest groups go well beyond those that are part of the tourism industry and include a vast array of community, public and special interest groups (Hall and Jenkins 1995).

Urban tourism organisations may be classified along a continuum, according to their degree of institutionalisation, as government and intra-governmental organisations, producer groups, non-producer groups and single interest groups (after Matthews 1976; Hall and Jenkins 1995) (Table 7.1). Government, as the dominant actor in the set of institutional arrangements that surround urban tourism, produces organisations which tend to have a high level of continuity in terms of their activities, goals and policies. Producer groups, such as business and professional organisations and labour organisations, tend to have a high level of resources, a stable membership maintained by the ability of the group to provide benefits to members, and substantial ability to gain

Table 7.1 Organisational dimensions of urban tourism

Type of organisation	Example
Government	Local government involvement in tourism provision, e.g. Tourism Dunedin; Calgary Economic and Development Authority; Tourism Vancouver
Producer	Local chambers of commerce and industry associations
Non-producer	Ratepayers and resident associations, e.g. Waikiki Improvement Association
Single interest	Single issue organisations such as a 'friends' organisation, or a group formed in order to prevent particular developments such as a hotel or airport

access to government. In non-producer groups, institutionalisation has occurred on the basis of a common interest of continuing relevance to members, e.g. organisations such as consumer and environmental groups. Single-interest groups are at the other end of the continuum from producer groups and are characterised by their limited degree of organisational permanence, as they will probably disappear altogether once their goals have been achieved or have been rendered unattainable (Hall and Jenkins 1995). Nevertheless, single issue groups are often extremely influential in urban tourism policy and planning, particularly with respect to the siting of developments or conservation campaigns to save landmarks and monuments. Indeed, all of the above organisations influence urban tourism planning and management to various degrees, both directly through their operations and actions and indirectly through their attempt to influence decision-making processes.

Nevertheless, it is important to note that organisations are not static and that they may progress through various categories. For example, local and regional conservation organisations may become nationally or even internationally based. Similarly, changes in perceptions of the role of government in tourism may also lead to organisational change. For example, in New Zealand some regional tourism organisations which at one time were fully public funded have become corporatised and now have to seek private sector funding to support their functions. In addition, the boundaries between government and producer organisations are becoming blurred as public–private partnerships, such as urban development corporations, are formed. Finally, we can note the extremely important point that cities may have more than one responsible municipal authority. The physical boundaries of a city as a destination are usually not the same as the political boundaries, thereby leading to further complication of planning measures. For example, in the case of Victoria British Columbia there are 14 municipal governments, 1 regional government, and a significant federal and provincial presence (Morris 2000), all of which have some role to play with respect to tourism. Similarly, even though it is seen by international visitors as a single destination, Auckland in New Zealand has four different local council bodies and a regional council body (Page 1999; Hall and Kearsley 2001). Such a situation therefore reinforces the need for an approach to tourism planning which is able to integrate the different stakeholders – both public and private – in effective urban tourism planning and management.

Strategic planning for urban tourism: collaboration and networks

One of the most significant developments in urban tourism planning in recent years has been the increasing emphasis on the adoption of strategic planning frameworks. Strategic urban tourism planning in its fullest sense is proactive, responsive to community needs, and perceives planning and implementation as part of a single, ongoing process (Lang 1986). Similarly, Dredge and Moore (1992: 15) highlighted the need to integrate tourism in town planning and emphasised that strategic plans need 'to be backed up by statements of implementation that guide the pattern of tourism development'.

Strategy is a means of achieving a desired end, e.g. the objectives identified for the management of urban tourism resources. In the case of urban tourism planning and management, 'the strategy' is typically developed around the use of appropriate management, marketing, management and planning practices to achieving three basic strategic objectives:

- ensuring the conservation of tourism resource values;
- enhancing the experiences of the visitors who interact with tourism resources; and
- maximising the economic, social and environmental returns to stakeholders in the host community (Hall and McArthur 1998).

However, this noted, it should also be observed that many tourism strategies are themselves tied in with broader urban strategies seeking urban redevelopment, re-imaging and place-marketing in order to be able to attract not only tourists but also capital- and employment-generating industries (see Chapter 8). Such a situation indicates that urban tourism planning is often highly complex, reflecting Peter Hall's observation that planning 'is merely an acute instance of the central problem of society' (1992: 249). By this, Hall meant that in contemporary society problems have a habit of becoming 'interconnected', in that what was initially seen as a problem in one sphere, say unemployment, may then become connected to other urban policy and planning concerns such as the environment.

Urban tourism planning often poses metaproblems. Several reasons account for this. Most significant is the nature of tourism itself, which is difficult to define, is diffuse through the urban economy and, typically, has no clear control agency. Instead, tourism tends to cut across agency boundaries. Nevertheless, planning for tourism is still regarded as important because its effects are so substantial and potentially long-standing. Indeed, concern with making tourism, along with all urban development, sustainable, has provided even greater imperative for improved tourism planning (Haughton and Hunter 1994; C.M. Hall 2000). According to Peter Hall (1992: 229), 'The old planning was concerned to set out the desired future end state in detail, in terms of land-use patterns on the ground; the new approach . . . concentrated instead on the objectives of the plan and on alternative ways of reaching them, all set out in writing rather than in detailed maps'. In the new planning 'the emphasis is on tracing the possible consequences of alternative policies, only then evaluating them against the objectives in order to choose a preferred course of action; and, it should be emphasized, this process would continually be repeated as the monitoring process threw up divergences between the planner's intentions and the actual state of the system' (P. Hall 1992: 229). The current strategic planning paradigm, which is heavily influenced by systems analysis, therefore emphasises the pattern of: goals, continuous information, projection and simulation of alternative futures, evaluation, choice and continuous monitoring.

For example, the state government tourism agency in South Australia, Tourism South Australia, developed an integrated planning model for tourism destinations in the early 1990s. Tourism South Australia (1990: 28) noted that traditional approaches to tourism planning – 'the old planning' – were 'limited because they ignore research and evaluation of tourism demand (market needs and expectations) and tourism supply (resource utilisation consistent with demand preferences and environmental sustainability)'. Therefore, in order to provide the unique, satisfying tourism experiences that differentiates urban product and destinations in the marketplace, to create long-term appeal, and to sustain the resource base on which urban tourism products and destinations are based, they argued that tourism planning must integrate market and resource driven processes. According to Tourism South Australia (1991), such an approach provides for a 'synergistic' tourism planning process which is goal oriented, integrative, market driven, resource driven, consultative and systematic.

This planning process was used in the preparation of regional tourism plans for the town of Victor Harbour in South Australia. However, while the model was well respected, particularly for the manner in which it sought to integrate sustainability issues into the planning process, its effectiveness was limited by developments at other levels. A change of government at the state level in South Australia meant that the goals of Tourism South Australia were shifted to concentrate on tourism promotion so as to encourage greater visitor numbers. In this new policy setting, long-term sustainable planning goals became secondary to short-term increases in the number of tourists. Such a situation is not unusual with respect to urban tourism planning. Indeed, within the public sphere it may even be the norm as governments, policies and institutional arrangements for tourism change. Yet such a situation also provides a valuable lesson for understanding tourism planning as it illustrates the multi-scale nature of planning, i.e. what occurs at the urban level may not be compatible with the provincial or national, and the implications of different sets of values on policy settings and planning processes (C.M. Hall 2000).

The importance of strategic planning is not only identified in relation to urban tourism overall but also particular sectors within the urban tourism product. Heritage attractions, such as museums, galleries, monuments and historic conservation areas, in particular, have had to adjust their planning approach. For example, Middleton (1994: 5) identified three aspects of management strategy for heritage resources:

- managing the heritage resource;
- managing access; and
- managing organisations.

Managing urban heritage resources, be it a collection, an historic house or park, an urban conservation area, or a traditional event, is seen, not surprisingly, as the primary duty of management for heritage bodies (Middleton 1994). Yet, as Middleton has emphasised, there is clearly a need to expand the notion of what heritage management is about in order to enable managers to respond to the changing environment in which they are operating. Middleton, as with other authors (e.g. Hooper-Greenhill 1992; Hall and McArthur 1993, 1996a; Harrison 1994), emphasised the need for managers to consider issues of access, quality, visitor demands, marketing and organisation as well as traditional urban resource conservation considerations that deal with the urban heritage resource base. Hall and McArthur (1998) observed that such a strategic approach to heritage management could only be successfully achieved by considering the primacy of stakeholders in the heritage management system and argue that the heritage manager is engaged in managing not so much a resource *per se* but the multiple attitudes, values, perceptions, interests and wants of stakeholders with respect to heritage. Such an approach represented a fundamental shift in heritage management thinking. It does not deny the importance of physical conservation and restoration of heritage. Instead, it argues that such activities need to be seen not only in a cultural context but also in the context of the, at times conflicting, demands of the various stakeholders who determine that something *is* heritage and therefore requires the development of appropriate management strategies and practice.

Middleton (1994: 10) identified a range of strategic management issues for British heritage managers which are also extremely relevant to their counterparts throughout the world:

- Recognising, through the formal adoption and operation of systematic strategic planning and monitoring procedures, that continuous change in the external environment affecting heritage is now a normal experience and not exceptional.

- Recognising that, with or without revenue objectives based on admission charges, achieving measurable satisfaction of increasingly sophisticated and frequent visitors to heritage is an essential strategic objective for sustainable heritage organisations.

- Accepting the need for setting measurable objectives and strategies, which reflect mission statements, response to identified change and visitor expectations, and aim to optimise the position for the heritage resource.

- Committing managers and trustees to the necessary disciplines of continuous systematic performance monitoring needed to assess the achievement of objectives. In practice this also means setting up information collecting procedures which are a necessary requirement of monitoring and assessment, including the use of market research as necessary, for example to measure visitor satisfaction.

- Using, supporting and helping to create networks or consortia for heritage management purposes to contribute to the tasks above and share the expertise and costs.

These strategic heritage management issues have emerged for a number of reasons that are not relevant to Britain alone. First, at a time of calls for 'smaller government' and a reduction in the size of bureaucracy, government is increasingly demanding that heritage 'pay its own way'. This has therefore meant the adoption of new financial strategies, such as the introduction, increase or expansion of visitor charges, and/or the introduction of corporate sponsorship packages as part of a philosophy of 'user-pays'. Second, there are increased demands from government, the private sector and the wider taxpaying public for accountability and responsibility for heritage funding. Third, there are greater demands for access to heritage both from the tourism industry, for whom heritage is a major attraction, and from the wider public. Fourth, there is increased concern over the conservation of heritage. Fifth, and related to the previous issues, there are widespread calls for heritage not only to be sustainable, but also to be placed within a wider framework of sustainable communities and regions and particularly in the urban context. The shift in attitudes towards heritage, called for by Hall and McArthur (1998), requires a corresponding shift in the way in which heritage management is undertaken and how it develops in the future, which parallels Peter Hall's (1992) shift from old to new planning noted earlier in the chapter. Consequently, approaches to urban heritage management need to shift from a predominantly one-dimensional outlook (one that is focused primarily on the resource), to one that is multi-dimensional and seeks to balance the concerns of stakeholders (including visitors and the community).

According to Hall and McArthur (1998), there are a number of advantages in adopting a strategic approach to heritage management:

- It provides a sense of purpose and the foundation of criteria for the formulation of new projects.
- It stresses the need for both short- and long-term objectives which can accommodate changing circumstances, e.g. a change in the level of government funding for tourism.
- It gives stakeholders a clear indication of the current and long-term level of support required for tourism management programmes.
- It provides for potential integration of stakeholder objectives into an organisational or programme strategy, thereby increasing the likelihood of success.
- It encourages strategic thinking and an increased receptiveness to opportunities in the external environment.
- It can create a sense of ownership and involvement in planning processes and outputs with a consequent likely increase in performance and level of support.

- It can make organisations more effective and efficient in attaining programme and/or organisational goals.

Furthermore, whether it be planning for heritage or for urban tourism as a whole it must be recognised that strategic planning always has an organisational focus. Even in the case of urban destination planning, for example, an organisation will still be responsible for the development, evaluation and implementation of the plan. The difficulty, of course, lies in an urban tourism organisation to be able to distinguish between a strategic plan for the organisation and a strategic plan for a destination for which it has responsibility. These are two different things. Unfortunately, the destination plan is often equated with the former (C.M. Hall 2000).

A strategic planning process is usually initiated for a number of reasons (Hall and McArthur 1998), including the following:

- *Stakeholder demands* – demand for the undertaking of a strategic plan may come from the pressure of stakeholders, e.g. the local tourism industry, urban conservation groups or municipal government.

- *Perceived need* – the lack of appropriate information by which to make decisions or an appropriate framework with which to implement legislative or regulatory requirements may give rise to a perception that new management and planning approaches are required. This factor has become extremely important with respect to the need to develop new arrangements, structures and strategies with which to develop sustainable urban tourism.

- *Response to crisis* – the undertaking of strategic planning exercises are often the result of a crisis in the sense that the existing urban management and planning system is perceived to have failed to adapt to aspects of the management environment, e.g. failure to develop an area of redundant or derelict waterfront land, failure to conserve a significant urban heritage site, or a rapid decline in the number of visitor arrivals.

- *Best practice* – urban tourism managers can be proactive with respect to the adoption of new ideas and techniques. Therefore, a strategic planning process can become a way of doing things better including benchmarking destinations or developments with competitors.

- *Adaptation, innovation and the diffusion of ideas* – individuals within an organisation can encourage strategic planning processes as part of the diffusion of ideas within and between urban tourism planning and management agencies.

The strategic planning process should be seen as being encompassed by the economic and policy environment within which tourism planning and management operate. This includes, therefore, such factors as institutional arrangements, institutional culture, and stakeholder values and attitudes as well as broader economic, social, political and economic trends. Such factors are extremely important. For example, public sector urban tourism strategic plans will be developed and written in line with the legislative and regulatory powers and organisational structures of the implementing organisation(s), broader policy settings and, in some cases, ministerial or municipal directives. However, as Hall and McArthur (1998) observed, it may also be the case that once the strategic planning process is underway, goals and objectives formulated, and the process evaluated, the institutional arrangements, including legislation and organisational structures, may be recognised as inadequate for the successful achievement of certain goals and objectives. Indeed, strategic planning for tourism at the destination level often seems to give rise to new organisational structures, such as public–private bodies, and/or responsibilities in order to try to achieve more effective implementation of planning strategies. In order to be effective, the strategic planning process also needs to be integrated with the development of appropriate organisational structures and values, yet at the urban destination level, such measures may fail if stakeholders, including the wider community, are not adequately included in the planning process. In such situations the strategic planning process is as important as its output, i.e. a plan. By having an inclusive planning process by which those responsible for implementing the plan are also those who helped formulate it, the likelihood of 'ownership' of the plan and, hence, effective implementation will be dramatically increased (Heath and Wall 1992; Hall and McArthur 1998).

Ottawa

As Chapter 5 demonstrated, capital cities have a number of significant attributes for tourism. In the case of Ottawa, the National Capital Commission (NCC) argues that 'The capital is the political centre and symbolic heart of the country' (NCC 1998: 116). The following discussion highlights the planning processes undertaken by the NCC in Ottawa. The example of Ottawa is also useful to highlight the interrelationships between planning for tourism and recreation and broader trends in urban and regional planning. Several stages to the planning of Ottawa can be identified (DeGrace 1985; Hillis 1992; Gordon 1998; Lapointe and Dubé 2000):

- The *Parks Movement* – Frederick Todd's 1903 Report to the Ottawa Improvement Commission.
- The *City Beautiful* – Edward Bennett's 1915 plan for the Report of the Federal Plan Commission on a general Plan for the Cities of Ottawa and Hull.
- *Garden Suburbs* – Thomas Adams' 1919 plan for the first federally subsidised housing project, Lindenlea.

- The *City Efficient* – Noulan Cauchon's 1922 plans for the Town Planning Commission.
- *Comprehensive Planning* – Jacque Gréber's 1950 plan for the national capital.
- *Regional Planning* – plans of the Region of Ottawa-Carleton and Communaité urbaine de l'Outaouais (1970s).
- *Urban Design* – the National Capital Commission's 1985 Confederation Boulevard plan.
- *Ecological Planning* – the NCC's 1996 Greenbelt Master Plan, and the 1998 RMOC Official Plan.
- *Cooperative Sustainable Planning* – the present day: *Plan for Canada's Capital: A Second Century of Vision, Planning and Development.*

Table 7.2 provides a more detailed history of planning for Ottawa's capital city status.

The extent to which the NCC's objectives and strategies presently influence tourism in Ottawa are indicated in Table 7.3. As the table illustrates tourism-relevant strategies cut across all the core activities of the NCC even if tourism might not be explicitly mentioned. To complicate matters further, there are a number of regional, municipal and private sector bodies that also have an interest in tourism. In one sense this also reflects Rowat's observation that 'residents of a capital city want to control decision-making in the city, while at the same time acknowledging that the amenities of the capital add to the quality of life there' (Rowat 1993: 38). But perhaps as Tunbridge (1998: 104) more

Table 7.2   A history of planning for Ottawa's capital city status

1899	Creation of Ottawa Improvement Commission.
1903	Todd Report – 'the fact that Ottawa is the Capital of an immense country whose future greatness is only beginning to unfold renders it necessary that it shall also be the centre of all those things which are an index of a man's highest intellectual attainments, and that it will be the city which will reflect the character of the nation, and the dignity, stability, and good taste of its citizens' (Frederick G. Todd).
1913	Borden Government established the Federal Plan Commission.
1915	Holt Report – recommended the creation of a powerful federal district.
1922	Cauchon Report – also recommended that a federal district be established.
1927	60th anniversary of Confederation, the Ottawa Improvement Commission was reorganised under a new name, the Federal District Commission (FDC). The FDC oversaw a considerable expansion of the region's open spaces as well as infrastructure development.
1936	Prime Minister Mackenzie King invited Jacques Gréber, the noted French town planner, to act as a planning adviser to the FDC.
1939	Gréber recommended that a master plan for capital development be undertaken and gave a broad outline for the organisation of a National Capital Planning Committee that would be responsible for the plan.

Table 7.2 (cont'd)

1945	An area of 2,330 km² was declared the 'National Capital District' and the *Federal District Commission Act* was amended to increase the responsibilities of the organisation and reinforce its national character.
1946	National Capital Planning Committee established at insistence of Gréber.
1950	*Plan for the National Capital* 'the Gréber Plan' completed.
1951	Gréber Plan submitted to Federal Parliament at a time of unprecedented prosperity allowing substantial federal plans to flow into the National Capital Region. The plan contained five main recommendations: railway relocation, extension of the parkway networks, decentralisation of federal office complexes, creation of greenbelts and expansion of Gatineau Park.
1958	Parliament passes the National Capital Act, establishing the National Capital Region and a new National Capital Commission (NCC). Region expanded to 4,660 km². The Act empowered the NCC to 'acquire, hold, administer or develop property', 'construct, maintain and operate parks, squares, highways, parkways, bridges, buildings and any other works', 'co-operate or engage in joint projects with, or make grants to, local municipalities or other authorities for the improvement, development or maintenance of property', 'administer, preserve and maintain any historic place or historic museum' and 'co-ordinate the development of public lands in the National Capital Region'. Authority and funds were made available to ensure the establishment of a greenbelt for beautification, recreation and conservation purposes.
1969	A new regional government, the Regional Municipality of Ottawa-Carleton, was created in Ontario.
1970	The Quebec legislature creates the Outaouais Regional Community and establishes the Société d'aménagement de l'Outaouais, with responsibility for industrial, commercial, tourism and recreation development.
1971	Ottawa Central Area Study conducted by NCC and the City of Ottawa recommended the establishment of measures to retain views of key public buildings.
1988	*Plan for Canada's Capital – A Federal Land Use Plan* released by NCC. The plan emphasised land use and public programming rather than land use and development. The plan also sought to improve visitor attractions, provide greater accessibility and encourage greater cooperation and partnership. *National Capital Act* amended to include the following programming activities in the NCC's mandate: 'organize, sponsor or promote such activities and events in the National Capital Region as will enrich the cultural and social fabric of Canada, taking into account the federal character of Canada, the equality of status of the official languages of Canada and the heritage of the people of Canada'.
1990	Outaouais 2050 report, a joint exercise on the future of the Outaouais region by the NCC and the Société d'aménagement de l'Outaouais, is published.
1993	NCC transferred from the portfolio of Public Works to that of Canadian Heritage.
1996	City of Ottawa and the Regional Municipality of Ottawa-Carleton approved renewed view protection measures as part of the new Official Plan.
1999	*Plan for Canada's Capital: A Second Century of Vision, Planning and Development* released by NCC.

See DeGrace (1985); Hillis (1992); Gordon (1998) and Lapointe and Dubé (2000).

Table 7.3 National Capital Commission's objectives and strategies

Objectives	Strategies
I. Promoting and animating the national capital region	
• To foster Canadian pride and contribute to awareness and understanding of, and participation in, Canada's Capital and its region	• Complete the implementation of millennial activities and develop a post-millennial plan for high-impact, four-season programming that will give Canada's Capital a higher profile among Canadians and on the world stage • Solicit continued and increased collaboration of partners and sponsors for integrated capital programming and marketing • Reach potential audiences through targeted marketing, outreach and promotional activities
II. Planning the national capital region	
• To plan the orientation, use and development of federal lands in the NCR in consultation with other planning jurisdictions, to ensure that their evolution is consistent with the image, character and quality of life in the capital	• Position the *Plan for Canada's Capital* as the overriding vision for the future development of Canada's Capital and as the framework for the completion of various supporting plans
• To coordinate development and ensure that uses, plans and designs for federal lands in the NCR are appropriate to their national significance, natural environment and heritage.	• Participate in studies led by the Region of Ottawa-Carleton and the Communauté urbaine de l'Outaouais to deal with inter-provincial transportation issues in the NCR • Implement federal plans, legislation and policies to safeguard and enhance the NCR's built and natural environment through the Federal Land Use, Design and Transaction approvals process
III. Real asset management and development	
• To provide opportunities to enhance the rich cultural heritage and natural environment of the NCR	• Protect natural lands and built assets through cost-effective maintenance, management, development and rehabilitation programmes and through the implementation of appropriate quality standards and service
• To optimise the contribution of lands and buildings in supporting the programmes and mandates of the NCC	• Manage the life cycle of NCC lands and buildings by ensuring the preservation, protection and sustainable use of natural assets in Gatineau Park and the Greenbelt, and on Capital urban lands • Manage an appropriate range of parks services and outdoor recreational facilities to enable visitors to enjoy a green Capital experience and to support the promotion and animation of the NCR

Table 7.3   *(cont'd)*

Objective	Strategies
	• Fulfil role as 'capital builder' through revitalisation of the Core Area of the Capital • Develop the recreational pathway network and associated services as a key component of the 'green Capital strategy' • Manage the payments in lieu of taxes payable by the NCC
IV. Corporate services • To provide corporate-wide strategic, financial and human resource advice, as well as technological tools and expertise, to ensure the effective and efficient operation of the NCC	• Take steps to rebuild the NCC's human resources foundation to promote a committed and motivated workforce and to develop and implement an action plan during the planning period • Exploit information technologies that provide a strategic advantage for the Corporation and facilitate effective and efficient management • Ensure that revenue generation activities allow for public access to federal lands while generating appropriate sustaining revenues • Implement measures to increase the public's awareness and appreciation of the NCC's achievements and activities • Conduct strategic and tactical research to inform decision-making for purposes of strategic planning and to support both concept testing for new programmes, services, and products and the assessment of programme effectiveness • Strengthen the federal presence throughout NCC activities, published materials, programmes and properties

Source: derived from NCC (2000a).

cogently observed, 'Locally fragmented jurisdictions create the further complication of local and regional priorities, which may be irrelevant or even contrary to the national priority or to each other. However, in practice . . . the common economic interest mutes any centrifugality and gives rise to a high degree of season-to-season cooperation'. The NCC therefore serves as a good example of some of the classic approaches to strategic planning for an organisation for which visitors act as a major stakeholder and which also has a significant spatial dimension to its planning deliberations.

As noted in Chapter 5, the NCC has several roles in the National Capital Region (NCR). 'One has to do with the physical presence of the federal government; another relates to the role of the capital in promoting Canadian identity; yet another concerns safeguarding the NCR's national symbols and its environmental integrity. The NCC balances these roles through long-term plans for federal lands in the region, through the federal approval process and through programming' (NCC 2000a: 13). 'In the absence of any statutory authority to control land use on private lands, the federal government must own, and/or plan for, all federal lands as well as other assets of Capital significance in the National Capital Region' (NCC 1999: 11). Therefore, although the NCC is the largest landowner in the NCR it has only limited direct land-use planning authority. Instead, the majority of its planning decisions have to be undertaken in conjunction with municipal, provincial and private sector partners as well as the wider resident population of the NCR. This situation therefore creates a substantial series of challenges for the NCC but which also highlights the significant role that collaboration must play in contemporary planning.

Under the 1988 federal land-use plan (NCC 1988) the development of the capital's symbolic role had been expressed in three main goals for the period 1988–98:

- to make Canada's capital a meeting place, and encourage the active participation of Canadians in the evolution of their capital;
- to use the capital to communicate Canada to Canadians to develop and highlight Canada's national identity; and
- to safeguard and preserve the nation's cultural heritage and the capital's physical assets and natural setting for future generations (NCC 1998: 46).

However, an update of the 1988 plan was required because of substantial changes in the political and economic environment not anticipated in the 1988 document:

- the impact of continued changes in the roles and size of the federal government;
- a renewed commitment by the federal government to a vital core area;
- the need to harmonise planning policies prepared by lower-tier governments and federal government agencies;
- the continuing challenge of creating a symbolic capital; and
- the influence of sustainable development on planning practice (NCC 1999: iii).

The development of a new plan for Canada's capital included a number of significant ingredients including a clear planning project management process (Table 7.4). However, one of the most important principles in the NCC process

Table 7.4   The planning project management process

Phases	Goals	Products
Initiation	Clearly define the opportunities, needs and issues that the project needs to address	Project directive
Work programme	Set up the organisational framework for the project (i.e. action plans, budget, responsibilities, communication plan)	Work plan
Planning	Examine the options available, select the best option and justify the course	Project brief, preliminary plan
Development	Fully develop the chosen option, emphasising the work required to plan its implementation	Final plan
Commissioning	Transfer the project to the client with a clear definition of implementation roles and responsibilities	Commissioning report, transfer and acceptance
Evaluation	Conduct a thorough assessment of the project and its implementation, both process and product	Close-out report

Source: NCC (2000b).

is that it starts from basics: 'The process begins with the question: "Is preparing a plan the best strategy to address the identified opportunities, needs and problems"' (NCC 1999: 16). Such a question is actually fundamental to the planning process, including that for tourism, as there is little point in initiating a resource-consuming planning process unless it is an appropriate strategy. Developing a plan at the NCC is a rigorous, integrated process that embraces environmental and heritage considerations, internal and external communication, cost benefit and feasibility analyses, and an implementation programme. This process applies to each type of plan in the NCC's planning framework which is indicated in Table 7.5. This overall planning hierarchy is important as it reflects the overall structure for planning the NCR.

The mission of the NCC is to 'make Canada's Capital Region a symbol of pride and unity for all Canadians' (2000b: 5). Three themes underlie the NCC's long-term planning and day-to-day activities:

1. Creating a meeting place for Canadians.
2. Using a capital to teach Canadians about Canada.
3. Safeguarding and preserving cultural heritage and natural treasures for future generations.

However, while this represents the organisational themes developed by the NCC it must be emphasised that they have risen out of a wider institutional

Table 7.5   The NCC's planning framework

Policy plans
- provide broad policy directions of strategies
- direct development and management of federal lands in Canada's capital region
- are approved by the NCC's Board of Directors

Example: Plan for Canada's Capital

Master plans
- develop details of PFCC policy directions and strategies
- provide development and land-use objectives for large public areas in the capital region
- are approved by the NCC's Board of Directors

Examples: Greenbelt Master Plan, Urban Lands Master Plan, Gatineau Park Master Plan

Sector plans
- refine goals and policies of the master plans for smaller geographic areas
- establish land-use priorities, rationalise property allocation and tenure among users
- define comprehensive development and conservation objectives
- are approved by the NCC's Executive Committee

Example: Core Area Sector Plan

Area plans
- identify the type and location of proposed buildings, and infrastructure and environmental features
- may establish design guidelines for the development, improvement, protection or reinstatement of specific federal properties
- are approved by the NCC's Executive Committee

Example: LeBreton Flats Plan

Source: NCC (2000b).

context for planning, including the mandate of the NCC which comes from its enabling Act as well as the wider functions of a capital city. These relationships are identified in Table 7.6, which indicates the manner in which the NCC's planning hierarchy for the capital fits together.

The vision of the current NCC plan for the NCR is to 'Imagine the heart of the Capital as a unified space for working, living and celebrating Canada' (NCC 1999: vii). The physical expression of the Capital Vision is further interpreted as goals and policies in three groupings of capital characteristics: capital settings, capital destinations and capital links. These characteristics are of great significance for tourism. For example, they lead to ensuring that the capital and its components are accessible, 'in a physical sense, accessibility means that the property is accessible to the public. In a psychological sense, accessibility means making the resource known to the public for its true heritage value, through oral, written or visual media' (NCC 1999: 49). From the perspective of heritage, interpretation and place promotion, 'The capital is a meeting place for all Canadians. It is a place that should communicate Canada to both Canadians and foreign visitors. It is also a place where the national cultural and political heritage is safeguarded and preserved' (NCC 1999: 53).

Table 7.6   The foundation of planning in the National Capital Region

Function of a capital	• national symbols • politics • culture • administration
Mandate	*National Capital Act* • prepare plans for the development, conservation and improvement of Canada's Capital Region • organise, sponsor or promote public activities and events in Canada's capital region to enrich the cultural and social fabric of Canada
Mission	To create pride and unity through Canada's Capital Region **Three key themes** *Making the capital Canada's meeting place* a common ground where Canadians can express their aspirations, appreciate diversity and celebrate those qualities that make this country unique *Communicating Canada to Canadians* as well as to visitors from around the world, while showcasing Canada's past, present and future *Safeguarding and preserving Canada's treasures* in the capital, including the numerous sites of great prestige and public interest that are held in trust for future generations of Canadians
Principles	*Sustainable development* core federal government policy which seeks to provide for 'development that meets present needs without *Capital planning* • symbolism • beautiful capital • green capital • stewardship • orientation services • safety and comfort • accessibility • transportation and communication *Regional planning* • livable region • partnerships for planning • efficiency • resource conservation • economy • the heart of the capital • transportation and communication
The planning function	*Core responsibility areas* • the NCC's planning framework • federal land-use and design approvals • heritage building and archaeological resource programme • municipal planning and development control activities • environmental assessment • corporate administration of the environment

Table 7.6 *(cont'd)*

Plans	• long-range visionary plans for the Capital Region to guide ownership, use and development of federal lands; • plans, concepts and guidelines to shape the development and management of federal lands; and • land-use and design approvals for federal lands in the Capital Region
Assets	*Land and buildings* • National Capital Greenbelt • Gatineau Park • Urban lands • Official residences
Partners	Municipal, regional, provincial and federal governments and agencies

Source: NCC (1999, 2000b: 7, 11).

Plate 7.1   The planning of urban destination is often predicated on the rediscovery of elements in the landscape that can appeal to visitors, as illustrated by Byward Markets in Ottawa, Canada

Furthermore, from the perspective of visitors, the capital plan is also conceived of in a visitor destinations goal, 'a network of visitor destinations that helps visitors explore the Capital and learn about Canada' (NCC 1999: 53) (Plate 7.1). These principles then find practical effect in the actions undertaken by the NCC. For example, with respect to arrival points to the capital the NCC notes that they influence visitor perceptions of the region and . . . of the nation. They are the visitor's first point of contact with the Capital, and are therefore significant in terms of image creation and communication of the Capital. Arrival corridors and terminals should therefore be well designed and serve to orient visitors to the region through proper landscaping, signage and related facilities.

Significantly, the NCC plan is designed to be reviewed on a five to seven year cycle, generally coincident with the plan review cycles of the three regional governments. Both the development of the plan and its components and its evaluation will be undertaken in conjunction with approaches to the capital's 'public' for comment and feedback. Stakeholders have been identified as including

- federal partners (local and national);
- NCR provincial, regional and municipal governments;
- Canada's capital cities;
- local and national interest groups (such as environmental or business groups);
- communities (local);
- professional associations (local and national);
- members of the public (local and national).

Techniques include

- workshops and charettes;
- NCC advisory committees;
- regional and local technical advisory committees;
- public meetings;
- open-house sessions;
- surveys;

with levels of involvement including:

- inform (raising awareness);
- educate (ensure understanding); and
- consult (two way communication) (NCC 1999: 17).

Significantly, the NCC (1999) also recognises that there needs to be a formal monitoring and evaluation process which should:

- be carried out on a cyclical basis;
- be cost-effective (not require significant expenditures in studies or monitoring process);
- make optimal use of existing studies or reports;
- produce useful information for project managers and decision-makers;
- be time-effective;

- be simple, relevant and easy to administer; and
- be strategic in scope and scale (with details left to Master, Sector or Area Plan monitoring and evaluation).

York

York in the United Kingdom provides an example of a city that attempted to realign its economic development and planning policies in the 1990s in an attempt to better balance the demands of the tourism industry, the wider community and its own responsibilities of city management (Meethan 1997). Although the realignment was in part related to the commencement of a new cycle of planning, a broader context also existed in relation to changing central government guidance on tourism and the growing influence of Agenda 21 and the application of principles of sustainability in urban planning.

As part of the process the city council commissioned an independent report in order to develop sustainable tourism strategies. One of the ironies of the report was that it indicated that the city had previously underestimated the importance of tourism by approximately 25 per cent. As Meethan (1997) observed, what was important here was not so much the inaccuracy of the previous figures, but the fact that they replaced accepted wisdom and could be used to justify change. Another significant component in the development of a proactive planning process was the increased cooperation between the public and private sectors, including the establishment of a Tourism Task Force, under the auspices of the Council's Economic Development Unit.

One of the main elements of the new city tourism policy was an emphasis on quality. According to Meethan (1997) this element could be interpreted in several different ways. First, it was used to describe a focus on longer-staying higher-yielding tourists and a consequent lessening of focus on the lower-spending day-tripper market. Although as Meethan cogently noted, 'such objectives do not resolve the potential for conflict between place promotion and planning . . . , nor between such factors and the needs and wishes of the city's residents. Attracting higher-spend tourists may in fact exacerbate these problems, leading to further social exclusion' (Meethan 1997: 340). The second way in which the notion of quality was used was in relation to the city and the tourism services it provides, particularly with respect to the maintenance of the heritage qualities of the city. However, the new policy noted that as well as focusing on land-use planning the council also had to convince local residents that tourism has positive as well as negative impacts in order to be able to improve the quality of services to tourists. 'In short, the selling of the city as a site for tourism has to be directed towards the inhabitants as much as to the visitors, to create an inclusive image and vision of the city in which control over space is achieved at both conceptual and strategic planning levels' (Meethan 1997: 340).

As Meethan noted, sustainability is more than just the conservation of the physical fabric of the city, as significant as that may be. To 'see sustainability in terms of extracting maximum revenue from minimum numbers by emphasising "quality" only complicates the issue, as such an approach may well benefit some in the tourism industry, but by no means all' (Meethan 1997: 341). In particular, those components of the tourism industry which rely on the day-tripping market and other relatively low-paying tourists, will be disadvantaged by a strategy that focuses on the high-yielding market segments.

The York example illustrates the complexities and difficulties of managing urban tourism destinations. Multiple industry stakeholders as well as the competing demands of the local community make the development of clearly defined sustainable tourism management policies that satisfy all the interests involved in tourism extremely difficult. A management action that 'solves' one problem may well create other, often unintended, undesirable consequences. 'Political control over such changes is clearly crucial to success in both economic and social terms, yet such control is less a case of party politics and more to do with interest-group alliances, with the local authorities acting as lead agency' (Meethan 1997: 341).

Collaboration and networks

The examples of Ottawa and York illustrate the importance of trying to develop collaborative arrangements between stakeholders. Collaboration is a highly dynamic process consisting of a number of elements:

- stakeholders are interdependent;
- solutions emerge by dealing constructively with differences;
- joint ownership of decisions is involved;
- stakeholders need to assume collective responsibility for the future direction of the domain; and
- collaboration is an emergent process.

Collaboration operates on a model of shared power which is in keeping with the idea of the existence of a shared or public interest (Wood and Gray 1991). Nevertheless, for the urban tourism planner, 'successfully advancing a shared vision, whether in the public or the private sector, requires identification and coordination of a diverse set of stakeholders, each of whom holds some but not all of the necessary resources' (Gray 1989: 9). Collaborative planning approaches have been extensively used with respect to multi-party environmental disputes, e.g. public land-use issues, and are becoming increasingly recognised as significant for tourism (Selin and Beason 1991; Selin 1993; Selin and Chavez 1994, 1995; Jamal and Getz 1995; Selin and Myers 1995, 1998; Buhalis and Cooper 1998; C.M. Hall 2000). Gray (1989) identified a number of benefits of collaboration:

- broad comprehensive analysis of the domain improves the quality of solutions;

- response capacity is more diversified;
- it is useful for reopening deadlocked negotiations;
- the risk of impasse is minimised;
- the process ensures that each stakeholder's interests are considered in any agreement;
- parties retain ownership of the solution;
- parties most familiar with the problem, not their agents, invent the solutions;
- participation enhances acceptance of solution and willingness to implement it;
- the potential to discover novel, innovative solutions is enhanced;
- relations between the stakeholders improve;
- costs associated with other methods are avoided; and
- mechanisms for coordinating future actions among the stakeholders can be established.

The emphasis on sharing power and participation means that collaborative approaches fulfil one of the social pillars of sustainability, namely the requirement for equity. As Blowers (1997: 42) noted, 'Inequality is about power relationships'. Collaboration therefore becomes a means of involving all affected parties to search for common interests and outcomes (see Table 7.7). 'Instead of trying to restrict participation, a common tactic, the professional manager gains more control over the situation by ensuring that all the necessary parties

Table 7.7 The collaborative process

Phase 1: Problem setting
- common definition of problem
- commitment to collaborate
- identification of stakeholders
- legitimacy of stakeholders in terms of both internal and external acceptance
- convenor characteristics
- resource identification and availability for participation and collaboration

Phase 2: Direction setting
- establishing ground rules
- agenda setting
- organising sub-groups, e.g. task forces
- joint information search
- exploring options
- reaching agreement and closing the deal

Phase 3: Implementation
- dealing with constituencies
- building external support
- structuring
- monitoring the agreement and ensuring compliance

Source: C.M. Hall (2000: 86); Gray (1989).

are there at the table, recognizing that parties in a dispute often engage in adversarial behaviour because no other approach is available to protect their interests' (Carpenter and Kennedy 1988: 26). Furthermore, 'joint ownership means that the participants in a collaboration are directly responsible for reaching agreement on a solution' (Gray 1989: 13). Waddock and Bannister (1991; see also Selin and Myers 1998) found the following factors to be significant predictors of partnership effectiveness:

• partners need to trust other partners;
• partner representatives need to have adequate power to make decisions for their organisations;
• appropriate partner organisations need to be identified and included in the partnership;
• partners need to sense that there will be benefits to all members of the partnership from their efforts;
• partners need to recognise that they are interdependent;
• issues being dealt with need to be salient to partners;
• partners need to feel that they add value to the partnership;
• power needs to be balanced among partners;
• objectives for the partnership should be clear and well defined;
• competent staff are required for successful implementation of the partnership;
• feedback to partners is important;
• a strong vision of the partnership must be articulated by leaders; and
• strong leadership is required to maintain the partnership.

Waddock and Bannister's (1991) observations were borne out in further research by Selin and Beason (1991) and Selin and Chavez (1994) on tourism partnerships, with the latter study also noting the significance of several organisational and operational characteristics for successful partnerships. Organisational characteristics included:

• administrative support;
• flexible protocols;
• staff continuity; and
• mediator roles;

and operational characteristics such as

• a written plan;
• meeting environment;
• cooperative agreement; and
• the setting of new goals.

Selin and Chavez (1994: 59) also observed that 'partnerships form a complex system of interrelationships between agencies and interests that is constantly changing'. Furthermore, in a wider setting, protracted conflict between stakeholders which has led to substantial mistrust, the vesting of power in elite organisations and a lack of incentives to participate may all constrain the effectiveness of collaborative strategies (Selin 1998). Indeed, this is particularly so at the community level where the central role of the 'community' in tourism planning has come to be recognised as one of the tenets of sustainable and socially responsible tourism. However, while community-based planning is an important driver in academic and bureaucratic approaches to tourism development (Murphy 1985, 1988), it is important to recognise that such an approach does not automatically lead to either sustainable urban tourism development or even a reduction in the amount of conflict surrounding urban tourism development. Instead, as C.M. Hall (2000) argued, a local focus allows for the dynamics of the planning process to possibly be altered as stakeholders face their interdependencies at a place-specific level. A key point being that we should not romanticize the concept of the local community, as so often seems to be the case in discussions of tourism planning. As Millar and Aiken (1995: 629) observed,

> Communities are not the embodiment of innocence; on the contrary, they are complex and self-serving entities, as much driven by grievances, prejudices, inequalities, and struggles for power as they are united by kinship, reciprocity, and interdependence. Decision-making at the local level can be extraordinarily vicious, personal, and not always bound by legal constraints.

Nevertheless, a community-based approach based on collaboration does provide the possibility that the necessity to consult over the use of shared resources and the needs of neighbours opens the way for resolution over conflicts over urban tourism. As Brotchie et al. (1995: 442) observed, there has been a shift in thinking in urban planning and policy theory from macro-analysis to micro-levels of analysis, 'from the notion that cities are strong, collectively organised systems to ideas that cities are composed of many groups and individuals in competition, betraying great diversity but also great adaptability, acting locally but generating organisation and order which is manifest at more global scales through the urban hierarchy'. Perhaps just as significantly, with a reduction in the extent of formal government procedures in much of the Western world as part of a push towards 'smaller government' and 'public–private partnership', a community-based process of management and conflict resolution may provide for greater informality in personal relationships between stakeholders in which trust is able to develop (C.M. Hall 2000). When examining the role of the community in tourism it is impossible to separate the social, economic and political processes which operate in a community from the conflict which occurs between stakeholders. Conflict and disagreement between members of a community over the outputs and outcomes of tourism are, in fact, the norm. As Millar and Aiken (1995: 620) commented, 'Conflict is a normal consequence of human interaction in periods of change, the product of a situation where the gain or a new use by one party is felt to involve a sacrifice or changes by others. It can be an opportunity for creative problem solving, but if it is not managed properly conflict can divide a community and throw it into turmoil'. Urban tourism planners therefore typically have to find accommodation between various stakeholders and interests in tourism development in an attempt to arrive at outcomes that are accepted by stakeholders within the wider community (C.M. Hall 2000). Indeed, much of the recent burst of activity in the tourism literature regarding cooperation and collaboration in tourism destinations is a direct response to the need to find mechanisms to accommodate the various interests that exist in tourism development (Bramwell and Lane 2000).

In a more positive vein we can also note that collaborative planning approaches also encourage planners, and others, to reflect on the manner in which planning and implementation represent two sides of the same coin. As Friedmann (1973: 359) observed, 'the kind of implementing mechanism adopted will itself influence the character of the plan and the way it is formulated. The formulation and implementation of plans are closely interdependent processes, so that the choice of one will in large measure also determine the second'. The inclusiveness of collaborative approaches may therefore help assist in dealing with some of the key problems of implementation (Ham and Hill 1994) in that many policies:

- represent compromises between conflicting values;
- involve compromises with key interests within the implementation structure;
- involve compromises with key interests upon whom implementation will have an impact; and
- are framed without attention being given to the way in which underlying economic, political and social forces will undermine them.

The importance of having those stakeholders who will be responsible for implementing the solution that emerges from the urban tourism planning process cannot be emphasised enough. It has long been recognised, though often little acted upon, that acceptance of and support for a solution is enhanced when those who must abide by it are included in designing the solution (Delbecq 1974; also see Innes, 1998; Innes and Booher 1999). For example, such a situation may be extremely important in such areas as codes of urban conservation practice for developers in historic areas of a city or other voluntary measures are sought in order to increase levels of acceptance for urban tourism decision-making and/or reduce compliance costs. Furthermore, insufficient consideration of implementation of outputs within the urban planning process, 'may result in settlements that create devastating precedents that may result in reluctance to negotiate in the future; damage interpersonal relationships; and financial, time or resource loss' (Moore 1986: 248).

Planning actions and mechanisms

So far this chapter has discussed some of the policy, organisations and relational dimensions of urban tourism management and planning. This section now introduces some of the mechanisms and actions that may be utilised in achieving urban tourism policies. As the previous chapter indicated, concerns over the capacity of urban areas to absorb tourists without degrading urban resources or lowering the quality of life for the inhabitants is a major challenge for urban planners. Traditional models of comprehensive urban land-use control are long recognised as having significant shortcomings (e.g. Altshuler 1965a, b). As Cullingsworth (1997: 125) observed, 'Local governments are severely limited in their ability to manage urban growth. The issues are essentially regional in character. Restraints in one area may simply result in development pressures moving elsewhere in the region'. In such cases resolution of growth issues then moves to another scale. In response to such problems, growth management has emerged as a highly important approach not only to urban development but to the management of tourist destinations as well (Williams and Gill 1991; Gill and Williams 1994; Gill 1998).

Growth management is a systematic impact management strategy which calls for an integrated sharing of ideas between community members and managers (Stein 1993). Such a process is not easy as it requires the identification and reconciliation of the different values of stakeholders regarding ideal conditions. As Cullingsworth (1997: 150) noted:

> Acceptability across the spectrum on interests is the key characteristic of successful growth management policies. Securing of this acceptability is difficult, enormously time consuming, and fraught with political problems. Moreover, it is an ongoing process: the determination of land uses, the timing of development, the coordination of development with the provision of infrastructure all involve continuing debate and planning, the achievement of consensus, and the provision of adequate finance. In short, growth management is a major part of the continuing process of government.

Growth management includes both the promotion of development and the protection of land against development. 'Growth management is inherently a governmental process which involves many interrelated aspects of land use. The process is essentially coordinative in character since it deals with reconciling competing demands on land and attempting to maximize locational advantages for the public benefit' (Cullingsworth 1997: 149–50). Several key components of growth management can be identified:

- consistency among government units – ensuring that different agencies share similar policy goals, values and instruments;
- concurrency – requiring infrastructure to be provided in advance or concurrent with the new development;

- containment of urban growth – the substitution of compact development for urban sprawl;
- provision of affordable housing – so as to ensure social equity;
- broadening of growth management to embrace economic development – the 'managing to grow' aspect; and
- protection of natural systems, including land, air and water; and a broadened concern for viability of the regional economy (after DeGrove and Miness 1992).

The establishment of a monitoring system is a vital aspect of growth management strategies as not only does it provide details by which progress towards desirable futures can be benchmarked, but it also details series of indicators that serve to provide a basis for informed community stakeholder debate about such futures. As Williams and Gill (1994: 184) commented, 'Community involvement in establishing desirable conditions is perhaps the single most important element of growth management'. Table 7.8 provides a number of examples of indicators of urban tourism that can be used in growth management planning strategies. The evaluation of such urban destination capacities, which is a component of growth management, parallels project-based planning which is a common feature of tourist development (Pearce 1989). Nevertheless, the selection of growth management indicators is only a part of the growth management equation as urban and municipal governments will also need to use a range of instruments, by which growth management policies can be implemented. Table 7.9 indicates such instruments, which range from no action by government as a deliberate policy measure through to voluntary measures and then on to regulatory structures that require a legislative component. There are a number of criteria by which different planning and policy instruments may be evaluated. For example, according to Haughton and Hunter (1994):

- an instrument must be capable of attaining its objective in a reliable and consistent fashion, while being adaptable to changing circumstances over time and sensitive to differences in local conditions (this is the measure of effectiveness);
- an instrument should be judged against costs (this is a measure of efficiency);
- an instrument should be equitable in its impact;
- compliance costs need to be weighed;
- an instrument must be politically acceptable, easy to operate and as transparent and understandable as possible; and
- an instrument should be compatible with other policy approaches.

Such criteria are useful in selecting an instrument or combination of instruments to achieve urban policy goals. However, as C.M. Hall (2000: 173) argued, 'it must be recognised, that there is no universally appropriate strategy available for managing growth in tourism destinations. Instead, strategies, tools and

Table 7.8   Examples of indicators of tourism impacts

Management objective	Indicators
Population stability	• out-migration levels • in-migration levels • age structure • gender structure
Employment change	• direct job creation • indirect job creation • employment levels • job retention levels • job displacement levels • job satisfaction levels • skill levels • labour force structure
Income change	• person/household income levels • inflation levels • tax revenue levels • direct economic impact • indirect economic impact
Community viability enhancement	• infrastructure levels • public service/social capital levels • housing affordability and availability • employee housing availability • resident attitudes
Welfare/social services	• health/social service/education access • services distribution • recreation activity access
Cultural enhancement	• cultural facility access • cultural event frequency • resident attitudes
Conservation improvement	• pollution levels • indicator species • measures of biodiversity • conservation practices • cultural feature damage • environmental maintenance costs
Amenity enhancement	• levels of crowding density • privacy access • visual amenity satisfaction
Tourism-specific indicators • growth in demand • capacity utilisation • competitiveness • market mix • seasonal distribution	• growth rate in total number of bed-nights, arrivals or tourist receipts • occupancy rate • market share • proportion of different markets, overnights or visits (e.g. domestic/international) monthly bed-night statistics

Source: after C.M. Hall (1992, 2000); Williams (1993); and Williams and Gill (1994).

Table 7.9   Urban tourism planning and policy instruments

Instruments	Examples
Regulatory instruments	
1. Laws	Planning laws can give considerable power to government to encourage particular types of tourism development through, e.g., land-use zoning which determines desirable and undesirable land uses.
2. Licences, permits, consents and standards	Regulatory instruments can be used for a wide variety of purposes especially at local government level, e.g., restraining undesirable uses, setting materials standards for tourism developments, or they can be used to set architectural standards for heritage streetscapes or properties.
3. Tradeable permits	Often used in the United States and, increasingly, in Europe to limit pollution or resource use. However, the instrument requires effective monitoring for it to work.
4. Quid pro quos	Government may require businesses to do something in exchange for certain rights, e.g., land may be given to a developer below market rates if the development is of a particular type or design or there is a guaranteed period of occupancy or use.
5. Removal of property rights	In order to achieve planning outcomes, such as the development of tourism infrastructure or the removal of inappropriate land uses, government may remove property rights (freehold or leasehold ownership) either on the open market or through compulsory acquisition.
Voluntary instruments	
1. Information and education	Expenditure on educating the local public, businesses or tourists to achieve specific goals, e.g., appropriate visitor or industry behaviour.
2. Volunteer associations and non-governmental organisations	Government support of community tourism organisations is very common in tourism. Support may come from direct grants, tax benefits and/or by provision of office facilities. Examples of this type of development include local or regional tourist organisations, heritage conservation groups, mainstreet groups, tour guide programmes, or the establishment of industry associations and networks, including sectoral networks, e.g., bed and breakfast, museum and gallery associations; and regional tourism operator networks.
3. Technical assistance	Government can provide technical assistance and information to businesses with regard to planning and development requirements, including the preparation of environmental and social impact statements or the preparation of business plans and strategies. In many countries business mentor programmes and business networks have been established with the support of government.

Table 7.9 (cont'd)

Instruments	Examples
4. Argument and persuasion	Government may seek the cooperation of stakeholders by persuading them that certain patterns of behaviour or conduct is appropriate for furthering the common interest of stakeholders and/or self-interest.
Expenditure	
1. Expenditure and contracting	This is a common method for government to achieve policy objectives as government can spend money directly on specific activities, this may include the development of infrastructure, such as roading, or it may include mainstreet beautification programmes. Contracting can be used as a means of supporting existing local businesses or encouraging new ones.
2. Investment or procurement	Investment may be directed into specific businesses or projects, while procurement can be used to help provide businesses with a secure customer for their products.
3. Public enterprise	When the market fails to provide desired outcomes, governments may create their own businesses, e.g., urban and regional development corporations or enterprise boards. If successful, such businesses may then be sold off to the private sector.
4. Public–private partnerships	Government may enter into partnership with the private sector in order to develop certain products, locations or regions. These may take the form of a corporation which has a specific mandate to attract business to a certain area, for example often through the provision of infrastructure or tax incentives.
5. Monitoring and evaluation	Government may allocate financial resources to monitor urban economic, environmental and socio-economic indicators. Such measures may not only be valuable to government to evaluate the effectiveness and efficiency of tourism planning and development policies and objectives but can also be a valuable source of information to the private sector as well.
6. Marketing and promotion	Government may spend money on promoting a region to visitors either with or without financial input from the private sector. Such promotional activities may allow individual businesses to reallocate their own budgets by reducing expenditures that might have been made on promotion.
7. Research	The provision of research data by government bodies transfers the cost of obtaining such data from business to the tax payer. Data may consist of market or attitudinal information which may then be utilised to decide the effectiveness of planning instruments or improve decision making.

Table 7.9   (cont'd)

Instruments	Examples
Financial incentives	
1. Pricing	Pricing measures may be used to encourage appropriate behaviour, market segments and/or to stimulate or reduce demand, e.g., use of particular attractions through variations costs.
2. Taxes and charges	Governments may use these to encourage appropriate behaviours by both individuals and businesses, i.e., pollution charges. Taxes and charges, e.g., passenger or bed taxes, may also be used to help fund infrastructure development, e.g., regional airports and public transport, or help fund regional tourism promotion.
3. Grants and loans	Seed money may be provided to businesses to encourage product development, business relocation, and/or to encourage the retention of heritage and landscape features. Grants and loans may also be used to provide for business retention in marginal economic areas or location in areas government wishes to encourage development in.
4. Subsidies and tax incentives	Although subsidies are often regarded as creating inefficiencies in markets they may also be used to encourage certain types of behaviour with respect to social and environmental externalities, e.g., heritage and landscape conservation, that are not taken into account by conventional economics. Subsidies and tax incentives are one of the most common methods to establish or retain tourism businesses, especially in economically marginal areas.
5. Rebates, rewards and surety bonds	Rebates and rewards are a form of financial incentive to encourage individuals and businesses to act in certain ways. Similarly, surety bonds can be used to ensure that businesses act in agreed ways; if they do not then the government will spend the money for the same purpose.
6. Vouchers	Vouchers are a mechanism usually used to affect consumer behaviour by providing a discount on a specific product or activity, e.g., to shop in a specific centre or street.
Non-intervention	
1. Non-intervention (deliberate)	Government deciding not to directly intervene in sectoral or regional development is also a policy instrument, in that public policy is what government decides to do and not do. In some cases the situation may be such that government may decide that policy objectives are being met so that their intervention may not add any net value to the urban development process and that resources could be better spent elsewhere.

Source: after C.M. Hall (2000: 157–9).

techniques will be selected according to local characteristics, the nature of the planning problem and the acceptability of such instruments'. Multiple instruments are often used and even these will result in 'imperfect' solutions. As Selman (1992: 10) commented with respect to environmental planning, 'this inherent variety [of instruments] is instructive . . . as it confirms that there is no single panacea . . . , but rather a menu of potential mechanisms which may be selected according to the nature of the issue at stake and their political acceptability'.

Historical dimensions of urban tourism management and policy

This final section presents an historical overview of urban tourism policy and management. Unfortunately, there are few case studies readily available that chart the changes in tourism policy and organisational structures in urban destinations over time. Such research is significant as it highlights the dynamic nature of tourism policy and management and the consequent problems in defining what urban tourism problems actually are. For the purposes of this chapter we are providing a case study of tourism in Canberra in Australia, the capital city since 1927.

The management and development of tourism in Canberra, Australia

Canberra is one of Australia's major urban tourist destinations. As the national capital, Canberra is rich in cultural and political attractions which, although not developed specifically because of tourism, have served to encourage visitation to a point at which tourism has come to represent a key element in the capital city's economic base. In addition, Canberra serves as a gateway to the rural, such as vineyards, and natural attractions of the capital city region – the Australian Capital Territory (ACT) – and of the surrounding hinterland within the state of New South Wales.

In 1993 tourism was estimated to contribute over A$500 million to the ACT economy and provide approximately 7,720 jobs representing 5 per cent of the Territory's workforce (Australian Capital Territory Tourism Commission 1993; Chief Minister's Department 1993). By 1998 it was estimated that visitation brought A$1.1 billion in direct expenditure to the ACT and an additional A$898 million in value-added economic impacts. In 1999 Canberra received 1.99 million domestic overnight visitors, 1.81 million domestic day visitors and approximately 210,000 international day and overnight visitors, with the tourism industry reported to be the largest private sector employer in the ACT, providing more than 14,000 jobs (Canberra Tourism & Events Corporation 2001a: viii).

Despite the significance attached to tourism within the present ACT Government's economic development strategies, substantial difficulties appear to have emerged in getting the 'right' promotional and development strategies in place while also establishing a suitable administrative structure. The difficulties of achieving appropriate coordination in tourism administration and a pattern of tourism development that meets the diverse needs of various stakeholders within the tourism industry is, of course, not isolated to the ACT. However, in managing tourism, the Territory government also have to overcome the various negative images of Canberra that have built up in Australia as being 'full of public servants and politicians, boring, [closed] on Sundays, hard to get around with too many roundabouts, [and] cold' (Canberra Tourism Development Bureau 1989: 26). Given the regular rounds of 'Canberra bashing' (Standing Committee on Tourism and ACT Promotion 1993), and the particular responsibilities of planning and managing the nation's capital, Canberra provides a useful example to highlight the difficulties of tourism management in an urban destination. The case study therefore provides an account of the means by which various government administrations have come to deal with issues of tourism development and the historic roots of contemporary difficulties in reconciling the various components of tourism planning and marketing in an integrative tourism strategy for the region.

Tourism development and administration in the ACT

The first report that appears to have paid attention to tourism in the ACT appears to be that of the Senate Select Committee on the Development of Canberra in 1955, which concluded that every encouragement should be given to the development of Canberra as a tourist, cultural and educational centre in keeping with its function as the nation's capital. The Committee noted that even at this stage, when Canberra was a city of only 30,000 people, it was already attracting 250,000 visitors a year and argued for the establishment of a number of national cultural institutions which would reinforce Canberra's identity in the minds of Australians. Similar issues were raised in the inquiry into the Australian Capital Territory Tourist Industry conducted in 1961 by the Joint Committee on the Australian Capital Territory. The Committee highlighted many of the same concerns that surround the ACT Tourism Industry today: the adequacy of facilities for the visitor, the adequacy of accommodation and transport links, the development and promotion of tourist attractions, and the integration of Canberra with the surrounding regions in terms of tourism promotion and marketing. In addition the report reflected many of the problems facing tourism managers and researchers in getting tourism taken seriously by politicians. For example, in a dissenting report, J.R. Fraser stated:

> I disassociate myself entirely from the report presented by the Committee . . . It is my personal belief that the time and talents of the members of the Committee

have largely been wasted on this inquiry when so many other questions bearing directly on the growth and development of the National Capital could, with benefit, have been referred to them. If the Committee is to be given no tasks more worthwhile than this it might well cease to exist as a body with any hope of contributing to thought and reality in the development of Canberra as the Seat of Government and the National Capital (Joint Committee on the Australian Capital Territory 1961: 17).

Despite the dissent from within, it is important to note that the Joint Committee laid the tourism agenda that still exists in the ACT to this day and was particularly interested in the prospects for cultural tourism and the manner in which tourism could be linked to 'fostering interest in Canberra as the Commonwealth's seat of government and the National Capital, and acceptance of it as an important symbol of Australian ideals and achievements' (Joint Committee on the Australian Capital Territory 1961: 6).

The members of the Joint Committee paid specific attention to the development of a National Library, Art Gallery and National Museum. The latter opened in 2000. In addition, the Committee recommended that consideration be given to the establishment of a hall of Aboriginal culture, a hall of New Guinea's and Territories' culture, a hall of national history, a museum of folk and social history and a national hall of photography, with the provision of indoor and open air theatres for drama, music, ballet, opera and theatre also being required.

The main thrust of the report concerned the manner in which tourism serves to reinforce national identity and national pride:

> The Committee considers that it is a legitimate function of the Federal Government to foster interest in Canberra as the seat of Government of the Commonwealth and as a symbol of Australian ideals and achievements. The capital of a nation, whether its greatest city or not, whether it has grown naturally or been brought into existence specifically to serve as the centre of administration, has been traditionally, and is to-day, a source of national pride and an inspiration for patriotic purpose. Athens, Ancient Rome and Jerusalem were such. London, Paris, Edinburgh and Washington are such to-day. In times when national cohesion is weak and patriotism a flickering flame, it is significant that there has often been no centre of political life or one which inspires no loyalty (Joint Committee on the Australian Capital Territory 1961: 9).

Undoubtedly, the report was a product of its time. Given the almost full employment of the early 1960s in Australia it should not be surprising that the employment potential of tourism received little mention in the Joint Committee's deliberations. Tourism was seen as serving primarily an educative function that would broaden Australia's understanding of the creation of the national capital and encourage a more patriotic spirit. Cultural tourism was significant, but only in terms of the imaging of a nation and the presentation of national icons.

By 1972 the picture had changed considerably. In that year the Joint Committee on the Australian Capital Territory had noted that there was still a need for the 'development of buildings and other works consistent with Canberra as the repository, and place for continuous and accessible display of matters on national importance such as art works, Australiana and the like' (1972: 42). However, it also noted that there was a need for 'co-ordination of effort of elements of the visitor industry to provide for effective development and attractive advertisement of Canberra to inform and interest Australians and other people' (Joint Committee on the Australian Capital Territory 1972: 42). The issue of coordination raised a new theme to be seen in debate on tourism in Canberra that continues to the present, that is the appropriate administrative structure and function of government in tourism. In addition, the Committee also recognised that given the dramatic growth of visitation to the ACT, tourism had the potential to become a significant source of employment for the region.

In late 1974 the National Capital Development Commission (NCDC), the Department of the Capital Territory and the Department of Tourism and Recreation commissioned Pannell Kerr Forster and Company to undertake a comprehensive study of tourism in the ACT (including the city Queanbeyan just across the border with the State of New South Wales) with the aim of providing a development strategy for the tourism industry. The first stage of the study on the economic and social impact of tourism on the ACT reported that during the study period (August 1975 to July 1976) an estimated 2,500,000 visits were made to the ACT with almost one-third of sampled visits being made by day visitors to the region. Approximately 48 per cent of visitors stayed at least one night with friends or relatives. The average length of stay for visitors staying with friends and relatives was 4.3 nights. The average length of stay for those in public accommodation was 2.2 nights. Approximately A$72 million was spent in the ACT by visitors during the study period at an average expenditure of A$32 per person/visit (Pannell Kerr Forster and Company 1977: 10).

Given a preliminary forecast of 3.75–4 million visits to the ACT in 1985, the Report recommended the immediate development of clear policy guidelines for tourism in the ACT and the development of a strategy to implement the policies that are accepted, including the preparation of an ACT 'Visitor Plan' (Pannell Kerr Forster and Company 1977: 11, 13). However, the development strategy was never completed.

In April 1979, the Minister for the Capital Territory forwarded to the Commonwealth Joint Committee on the ACT suggested terms of reference for an inquiry into tourism in the ACT. The Committee had a wide brief for the inquiry with particular attention to be paid to the desirable role for tourism in the future development of the ACT. The changed economic and political climate since the Joint Committee Report of 1961 was indicated in that the primary focus of the report was on the potential economic and employment benefits of tourism and the use of tourism as a mechanism for regional economic development. Although mention was also made of the potential of tourism to serve educational functions and strengthen tourist's consciousness of the national and cultural heritage (Joint Committee on the Australian Capital Territory 1980: 20). The Committee concluded

> that while tourism should not be seen as a remedy for all the future economic problems that might confront the A.C.T. it is able to play a desirable role in the future development of the A.C.T. by contributing to the economic and social growth of the Territory because:
> (a) it can broaden the economic base of the A.C.T.;
> (b) it is a growth industry which has scope for increasing employment opportunities within the A.C.T.;
> (c) it can contribute to the development of the growing inter-dependence of the A.C.T. and the surrounding region;
> (d) it can lead to the development of tourist facilities and attractions which will enhance the every-day life of local residents;
> (e) it can contribute to the development and diversification of particular areas in the A.C.T. such as Civic, the City Centre, and
> (f) it can foster the recognition of Canberra's role as the national capital and seat of government and strengthen a sense of national pride and identity.
> (Joint Committee on the Australian Capital Territory 1980: 23)

Furthermore, the Committee concluded that whether the substantial potential for the development of tourism in the ACT was to be realised would 'depend on the promotion of existing and future attractions on both the domestic and international markets and the development of additional tourist attractions in the A.C.T.' (Joint Committee on the Australian Capital Territory 1980: 30). Since the report, attractions such as the Telecommunications Tower on Black Mountain, the High Court, the National Gallery, the New Parliament House and the National Museum have all been completed. Indeed, Canberra is now rich in built cultural and heritage resources and is increasingly developing tourist events, such as Floriade, the Canberra Festival and the National Theatre Festival, in order to add an extra dimension to the cultural touristic attractiveness of the region.

Natural attractions such as park and rural areas within the Territory, including the Tidbinbilla National Park, were also recognised as significant tourist attractions, although not of the same scale as the city's cultural sites. The Committee also concluded that the most effective way of promoting the ACT would be to establish an ACT Tourist Commission which 'would operate along the lines of the Australian Tourist Commission but would continue to have day-to-day involvement in the marketplace through the operation of information and service centres which would provide travel services to both tourists and local residents' (Joint Committee on the Australian Capital Territory 1980: 116).

In addition to the report of the Joint Committee, the NCDC, then the statutory authority responsible for the planning, development and construction of

Canberra, also reported on tourism in the ACT as 'planning for tourism requires a comprehensive approach which takes into account the various aspects of tourism as they interact within, and form part of, the community' (National Capital Development Commission 1981: 85). The NCDC had no direct responsibility for the administration or promotion of tourism in the ACT. However, the Commission did have a major involvement in tourism through its land-use policies and its influence on the location and scale of attractions, facilities and infrastructure. Under the NCDC's Tourism Subject Plan 1978/88 tourism accommodations and attractions were concentrated in a series of zones: the city centre and the central area, town centres, northern approach zone (Barton and Federal Highways), southern approach zone (Jerrabomberra and Canberra Avenues) and other Canberra (primarily rural) areas (National Capital Development Commission 1981).

The definition of zone boundaries by the NCDC reflected the distribution of commercial accommodation in 1978. 'As a result, the delineation of zones has precluded the development of a concentration of accommodation at a specific location. This may have created an effective barrier to the development of associated tourist facilities (e.g. entertainment) in conjunction with accommodation' (National Capital Development Commission 1981: 90–91). Indeed, the NCDC went on to note that their locational policies in terms of memorials, national cultural and political sites, and other built attractions, 'necessitate a level of mobility by the tourist which is not necessarily required to the same extent in alternative tourist destinations' (1981: 103). The impacts of the NCDC policies on tourism development remains to the present day and provides the physical framework within which tourism in the urban areas of the ACT have to operate. The problems that previous management and planning strategies have created for present-day management are clearly expressed in the following observations from the NCDC:

> In creating a framework in which tourism operates within the A.C.T., the Commission's policies partially mitigate against the future development of a successful tourist industry.
>
> The accommodation policies contained in the Tourism Subject Plan, particularly through the delineation of zones, have precluded the development of a concentration of accommodation at a specific location.
>
> Such a concentration is intrinsic and vital to a successful tourist industry. Moreover, accommodation policies have been formed without due consideration of related tourist activities and resources . . .
>
> The tourist attraction base is principally provided by the Commission through its catering for national Capital functions. The spatial distribution of attractions is dispersed requiring private motor vehicle transport to facilitate movement. Also their location does not readily relate to accommodation, entertainment, etc. . . .
>
> Overall, Commission policies although determining the character of tourism in the A.C.T. and providing a wide range of resources both natural and man-made for visitor use, have also created a dispersal of resources. The location of tourism resources bear little relationship to each other and ideally should form

part of a total comprehensive planning framework for tourism which is not just limited to a small number of types (National Capital Development Commission 1981: 121–2).

Given the NCDC's own comments regarding tourism development and planning in the ACT it was not surprising that it noted the need for a tourism development strategy for the ACT. However, what was perhaps most surprising was its failure to recognise the role of planning in effective tourism development. Instead, it concluded, 'The key to development of the tourist industry in Canberra is effective marketing and promotion which, on the basis of experience elsewhere is likely to be best achieved if it is administered by an adequately autonomous body whose functions are specifically directed towards this end' (National Capital Development Commission 1981: 163).

The imperative for the development of a tourism development plan remained throughout the 1980s, particularly given the opportunities presented by the opening of the new Parliament House and the bicentennial of European settlement celebrations of 1988 and concerns at the range of major problems perceived as besetting tourism in the ACT. According to the Joint Committee on the Australian Capital Territory (1986: 6), 'complaints ranged from inadequate promotion, insufficient funding, unsatisfactory marketing, poor and uncoordinated collection of visitor statistics and inappropriate administrative arrangements'.

In 1986 the Joint Committee on the Australian Capital Territory in a review of the hospitality industry recommended 'that the NCDC, in consultation with representatives of the tourist and hospitality industry, should prepare a tourist development plan for the ACT aimed at achieving positive development of the plan from 1988 onwards' (1986: ix). The provision of a development plan was a direct response to the fragmented nature of tourism planning under the NCDC and the need for improved policy and planning coordination. In addition, the Joint Committee recommended a further restructuring of tourism administration in the ACT. They recommended 'that an ACT Development Board incorporating the present Canberra Tourist Bureau and the Canberra Development Board be established to promote, develop and provide economic assistance to tourism and hospitality in the ACT' (1986: ix). The new tourism authority was regarded as being necessary in order 'to coordinate tourism and economic developments in an effective manner', with the new organisation also being required to 'focus on the development of local opportunities and industries rather than being primarily concerned with activities outside the Territorial border as is the case at present' (1986: 4).

In July 1988, the Canberra Development Board released its tourism strategy which represented the first attempt to provide a comprehensive development plan for tourism in the ACT. The plan reflected the increasing desire of government to provide greater economic development for Canberra through tourism. The aim of the plan was 'to assist in promoting growth and diversification of the local economy by encouraging the private sector to develop tourism opportunities, while remaining sympathetic to the unique environment of Canberra and its character as the national capital' (Canberra Development Board 1988: 1). The objectives of the plan were

- to help the tourism industry maintain and improve its viability, for example by encouraging visitors –
  - to come to Canberra in greater numbers
  - to spend more time and money in the area, including through optimal use of its facilities
  - to leave with favourable impressions, leading to repeat visits and appropriate word-of-mouth publicity
- to encourage activities which will help the local economy by providing more jobs and increases in incomes/revenues
- to facilitate tourism development which takes appropriate account of environmental and other local community interests as well as those of visitors (Canberra Development Board 1988: 1).

Strategies designed to achieve the above objectives included the encouragement of private sector tourism product development, provision of relevant infrastructure and facilities for visitors, and improved marketing and promotion of Canberra as a visitor destination and convention centre. Greater awareness by the NCDC of visitor needs to a more coordinated approach to the development of tourist-oriented areas in the civic centre, Lake Burley Griffin and the Gold Creek area was matched by the identification of development opportunities in a rural outdoor focus, history (arts and heritage tourism), and improvements to the entertainment industry in Canberra.

A more strategic approach to tourism planning and the provision of tourism product in the ACT was also apparent in the development of a tourism marketing strategy by the then Canberra Tourism Development Bureau (1989). The strategy paid specific attention to matching the unique attractions of the Canberra region with relevant domestic and international market segments through product development, price considerations, distribution channels and promotional activities and served as a clear blueprint for tourism marketing in the Territory. Of particular interest in the marketing strategy was the focus on a number of 'key result areas' (1989: 10) which were considered as being of crucial importance in the marketing of Canberra's tourism product. These included

- a campaign to improve the image of Canberra as a holiday and meetings destination ('Canberra – The Natural Capital');
- a focus on special events and the conventions industry;
- pursuing a multicultural marketing strategy;
- target promotion of the short-break market from Sydney and Melbourne; and
- the targeting of the special interest tourism market, particular sports and cultural groups.

Plate 7.2 In planning the future vision of tourism in an urban environment, the reuse of former historic buildings can add value to the visitor experience, where a new function is added to the building. This is shown in the Old Parliament House, Canberra, Australia which now houses a museum and gallery

To a substantial extent, the focus of the 1989/90 strategy still serves as the basis of Canberra's tourism marketing, although the current marketing focus has grown to include the role of the Canberra casino, cultural tourism (Plate 7.2) and Canberra's relationship with the surrounding region, including the wine industry.

Since the coming of self-government in the early 1990s the ACT is still trying to find an appropriate formula for tourism planning and development. The need to be more cost-effective in promotion and marketing runs parallel to the desire of the ACT government to broaden the economic base of the Territory and create more employment opportunities. Given the chequered history of government and administrative debate over tourism in the ACT it should therefore not be surprising that a further inquiry into tourism was conducted by the Standing Committee on Tourism and ACT Promotion of the Legislative Assembly for the ACT (1993). Again, not surprisingly given the outputs of the various other inquiries into tourism in the ACT over the past 30 years, the Standing Committee noted that there was 'a degree of uncertainty in sectors of the industry about its long and short term goals', although they did go on to observe, 'this may well reflect an industry involving a wide range of large and small enterprises as well as governmental institutions' (Standing Committee on Tourism and ACT Promotion 1993: 9). Nevertheless, they believed that it was imperative that the ACT Tourism Commission (ACTTC), in consultation with the tourism industry, develop 'an integrated tourism strategy for the ACT which incorporates regional factors and interdependence' (Standing Committee on Tourism and ACT Promotion 1993: 10).

A key element in the new tourism strategy was a greater degree of coordination with the New South Wales government and regional shires in promoting a regional economic strategy which includes tourism. However, while the ACTTC was to act as the catalyst for the tourism industry, the degree of successful tourism promotion which can be done in cooperation with the NSW Tourism Commission may be more problematic given that state's shift from regional promotion towards Sydney (Standing Committee on Tourism and ACT Promotion 1993: 23).

Another important element in the successful promotion and development of tourism in the ACT was regarded as the integration of national institutions and national capital characteristics into a unique Canberra tourist product. Nevertheless, significant problems emerge in such a strategy, as while national institutions are a significant tourist drawcard to the ACT, 'it is regrettable that a number of them do not appear to regard themselves as part of the tourism industry' and do not appropriately cater to the needs of visitors, particularly during the summer months (Standing Committee on Tourism and ACT Promotion 1993: 22).

The relationship between national institutions and the tourism industry lies at the heart of the difficulties of developing an integrated tourism strategy for the ACT. Undoubtedly, Canberra is a cultural tourism destination *par excellence*, but the divide between public and private sector goals, and national and ACT government objectives are extremely hard to reconcile, given long-standing organisational cultures that have only recently been made aware of responsibilities towards visitor needs. For example, one of the stated objectives of the National Capital Planning Authority (NCPA) (the organisational heirs to the NCPC following self-government) is to ensure that it remains and develops as an organisation 'which fosters a greater appreciation and understanding of the National Capital's role and its special character, through promoting Canberra as a major tourist and visitor attraction and through information and education programs' (National Capital Planning Authority 1992: 5). The National Capital Planning Authority's role in Canberra is similar to the reduction in scope of the National Capital Commission in Ottawa (see Chapter 5 and this chapter), but without the extensive programming activity (Gordon 2000).

The NCPA is potentially important for tourism as it attempts to foster an awareness of the national capital through provision of the secretariat to the National Capital Attractions Association, research on the awareness of the national capital, community events, promotion of the National Capital Exhibition, educational tourism and in its planning role of ensuring that the Territory Plan of the ACT government is 'not inconsistent' with the National Capital Plan of the NCPA. Nevertheless, the NCPA's contribution to tourism in the ACT is problematic and appears to be measured by that organisation solely in terms of how many people visit the National Capital Exhibition on the shores of Lake Burley Griffin rather than in the broader context of how the parliamentary triangle and other areas under its charge contribute to the broader development of tourism. Indeed, the NCPA in its submission to the Standing Committee on Tourism and ACT Promotion's inquiry, noted factors such as car parking, signage, improved landscaping and lighting as factors which would improve Canberra's attractiveness as a tourist destination (Standing Committee on Tourism and ACT Promotion 1993: 11). This is not to say that these factors are not important. However, they are the very same factors that the 1961 Joint Committee inquiry noted as being important! Despite 30 years of advances in tourism planning and development and calls for better integration of planning, marketing and promotion functions in the ACT the NCPA had arrived at where the management of tourism in the ACT had more or less started from.

Following self-government and the need of the ACT government to broaden the Territory's economic and employment base, tourism has become an important component of the regional development strategy. Despite the establishment of the new Canberra Tourism and Events Corporation (CTEC) in July 1997, the development of a new comprehensive holiday package, the construction of a new visitor centre (Canberra Tourism 1997) and the development of yet another strategic masterplan (CTEC 2001a), tourism development still remains in, at least, a partially confused state. This is partly as a result of disagreements between different industry sectors over the direction of tourism in the ACT. Yet it is also a reflection of deep-seated differences in perception over the role of those national institutions that make up such an important part of Canberra's tourism product, image and identity. Indeed, the new Masterplan noted that 'Canberra's national capital status and proliferation of national institutions overshadow the ACT as a leisure destination and visitors often overlook attractions outside the Parliamentary Triangle'. In short, there exists a potential conflict in the eyes of some between the form and function of Canberra as a national capital and Canberra as a tourist destination.

CTEC was established to market the ACT as a tourism and events destination. However, the new organisation had a different structure from previous Canberra tourism authorities and was the ACT's first statutory corporation and the first Australian tourism authority to be created in this form. Under the Canberra Tourism and Events Corporation Act 1997, CTEC has entered into a service level agreement with the ACT Chief Minister's Department, with the Office of Business, Tourism and the Arts performing the role of purchaser of tourism outputs and outcomes (CTEC 2001b).

CTEC is required to operate within core functions defined by the Canberra Tourism and Events Corporation Act 1997. They are to:

- market the Territory to local, interstate and international travellers;
- identify tourism opportunities for the Territory;
- encourage the ecologically sustainable development of the tourist and travel industry;

- establish and operate tourist events and festivals;
- construct and operate tourist facilities;
- provide tourism and travel information and booking services;
- advise the tourism and travel industry on reducing the environmental impact of tourism-related activities;
- undertake activities in cooperation with other persons where appropriate for the purpose of discharging its other functions; and
- advise the Minister on matters relating to tourism and the tourism industry of the Territory.

The recently completed masterplan is regarded by CTEC (2001a: viii) as articulating 'future directions for tourism in the ACT which, when implemented, is intended to deliver four key outcomes':

1. Strengthening appeal of the ACT as a destination.
2. Increasing the number of visitors and tourism yield.
3. Strengthening industry by improving links within the tourism industry.
4. Ensuring sustainability of ACT tourism by sound planning and policy development.

Significantly, the executive summary notes that several common threads run through the masterplan (CTEC 2001a). These are the need for:

- better information on which to base business decisions;
- improved communications within and between industry sectors;
- quality of products and services;
- a well-integrated industry that achieves its optimum critical mass;
- more effective marketing by both CTEC and industry which improves the ACT's identity and appeal and a common branding to all advertising;
- improved support to new business investment;
- more viable businesses within the industry.

Interestingly, to a great extent these are the same threads that have run through plans for tourism in the ACT since the early 1970s. New organisational structures and institutional arrangements have been put in place by different political masters; however, the basic core goals have remained very similar. Such a situation clearly raises a number of significant questions regarding the effectiveness of such organisations and even the strategies themselves, particularly when issues such as coordination and marketing effectiveness arise time and time again. Despite consistent calls for stakeholders to work together it appears that effective collaboration has been hard to come by. The Canberra case study therefore indicates a number of significant items to examine in urban tourism management and planning not only with respect to the goals of strategies and evaluating their effectiveness but also the institutional arrangements which are put in place to implement them.

Conclusion

This chapter has provided a review of some of the key trends and issues in urban tourism planning and management (Plate 7.3). It has highlighted the significance of understanding the interrelationships of the various layers of urban tourism management from policy through to planning and then to the actual strategies and actions themselves. Of key importance in understanding urban tourism planning and management is the role that collaboration plays in achieving the goals of strategic urban tourism planning which may be regarded as part of the 'new planning' or 'relational planning' in the broader field of urban and regional planning (C.M. Hall 2000).

The chapter also provided two detailed case studies of urban tourism planning in the cities of Canberra in Australia and Ottawa in Canada: although both cities are the capital of their respective countries, there are clearly different planning processes and structures in place. Finally, this chapter also highlighted the range of different instruments that are available to achieve urban tourism planning goals, particularly with respect to the concept of growth management. The next chapter examines one potential instrument, namely promotion and marketing, and continues to relate such mechanisms to broader

Plate 7.3 Sport and its association with tourism are reflected in the development of venues to host hallmark events, such as the construction of this Olympic Stadium in Sydney, Australia

changes in the economic and political environment which affects tourism in cities and its relationship to broader development goals.

Questions

1. What are the similarities and differences between urban tourism planning in Canberra and Ottawa?
2. What are the most significant aspects of growth management?
3. What criteria should be used to evaluate the selection of urban tourism management instruments?
4. What difficulties exist in developing more collaborative relationships between stakeholders in urban tourism destinations?

Further reading

Influential general texts on urban and regional planning theory are

Hall, P. (1992). *Urban and Regional Planning*, 3rd edn, London and New York: Routledge.

Healey, P. (1997). *Collaborative Planning: Shaping Places in Fragmented Societies*, Basingstoke: Macmillan Press.

The latter is well complemented by

Innes, J.E. and Booher, D.E. (1999). 'Consensus building as role playing and bricolage: toward a theory of collaborative planning', *Journal of the American Planning Association* 65(1): 926–40.

On tourism planning and policy see

Hall, C.M. (2000). *Tourism Planning*, Harlow: Prentice Hall.

Hall, C.M. and Jenkins, J.M. (1995). *Tourism and Public Policy*, London: Routledge.

An excellent recent edited book on issues of collaboration in tourism is

Bramwell B. and Lane, B. (eds) (2000). *Tourism Collaboration and Partnerships: Politics, Practice and Sustainability*, Clevedon: Channel View Publications.

The Ottawa National Capital Commission's website is http://www.capcan.ca/

The Canberra Tourism and Events Corporation's Australia's website is http://www.canberratourism.com.au/. At the time of writing the masterplan was available for downloading.

Marketing urban tourism

CHAPTER 8

Introduction

The urban landscape – which includes the built environment and its material and social practices, as well as their symbolic representation (Zukin 1991: 16) – may be read as a text (McBride 1999). Based on the premise that 'landscapes are communicative devices that encode and transmit information' (Duncan 1990: 4), the 'tropes' – signs and symbols into which various meanings are condensed – that communicate this information including items in and of the built and physical environment, such as buildings, monuments and public spaces as well as signs, slogans, relationships and brands, have become increasingly important to the languages of consumption associated with specific urban places (Jackson and Taylor 1996; T. Hall 1997). As a conceptual tool reading the urban landscape not only illustrates the ideology of the landscape (Cosgrove 1984: 15), but it can also illuminate the way it may 'reproduce social and political practices' (Duncan 1990: 18).

Issues of ideology, identity and representation have therefore become central to much analysis of the manner in which the city has come to be packaged as a product to be sold (e.g. Kearns and Philo 1993). This chapter therefore seeks to discuss the way in what at one level may be perceived as a purely technical issue, that of marketing the city, actually has other political and cultural layers to it, thereby further highlighting the complexity of urban tourism management. The chapter is divided into four main sections. The first examines the concept of place-marketing; the second considers the issues associated with the differentiation of space with respect to what the nature of place-marketing is. The third section discusses the nature of urban reimaging strategies with particular attention to the role of culture and heritage, while the final section discusses how place-marketing should be contextualised within notions of the ideology of place.

Place-marketing

A consideration of place-marketing is a natural extension of the process of urban management and planning, which requires public authorities to consider the market context and competitive position of the city, especially in terms of tourism and leisure markets. It is significant as there is a recognition within the tourism literature that tourists select particular place products (i.e. destinations) in their holiday decision-making process which normally involves the selection of a limited set of place products, often on the basis of limited knowledge of the destination and available options (see Kent 1990). As Goodall (1990: 260) observes, the holiday may be as much the place as the place is the holiday for the tourist. In contrast, the various businesses and organisations associated with tourism focus on specific aspects of the place product (e.g. an attraction or facility). The organisation charged with marketing the city will tend to adopt a composite view of the city and its place product in selling the destination to potential visitors. Yet this also illustrates one of the major problems associated with the marketing of places: place-marketers adopt a composite view of the place product without little real understanding of the diversity of the services and products being sold by the tourism industry within the locality. This can lead to a more generalised image of the urban tourism destination and the way in which it is constructed and sold to visitors by agencies responsible for marketing and promotion.

The term place-marketing (Madsen 1992), selling places (Burgess 1982) or geographical marketing (Ashworth and Voogd 1987) in an urban context is based on the principle that the city is a place product that can be marketed and promoted to potential customers. Even so, certain critics have questioned its role in the local authority planning (Clarke 1986). In 'marketing terminology, a customer purchases the core product (set of valued attributes) by acquiring the tangible product' (Ashworth and Voogd 1990a: 69–70). This is based on the premise that marketing is a process whereby individuals and groups obtain the types of products or goods they value (Kotler and Armstrong 1991). These goods are created and exchanged through a social and managerial process which requires a detailed understanding of consumers, their wants and desires so that products can be effectively and efficiently delivered to the customer.

In place-marketing, the 'place has a certain amount of resources (infrastructure, houses, castles, parks, people, museums, etc.). It is only through an interpretation of these resources that a place product and a place image' (Madsen 1992: 633) are derived. This involves organisations engaging in each of the three areas of marketing activity. Consequently, the process of place-marketing requires urban managers and planners to engage in:

- product development to improve the physical resources of the city;
- the promotion of the city as a place by producing and enhancing people's image of the city as a place to visit.

As Madsen (1992: 633) observes 'the promotion of a place-image becomes a matter of commodifying it through a rigorous selection from its many characteristics'.

The concept of place-marketing: marketing influences

The science of marketing has evolved from the practices of the private sector with its pursuit of profit and exchange of goods and services. Yet as Ashworth and Voogd (1990a) explain, the concept of place-marketing is an amalgam of three different traditions in marketing: marketing in non-profit organisations, social marketing and image marketing. The process of place-marketing is described by Ashworth and Voogd (1988: 68) as one:

> whereby urban activities are as closely as possible related to the demands of targeted customers so as to maximise the efficient social and economic functioning of the area . . . [which] can be applied at many spatial scales and thus city marketing can be viewed as part of a broader geographical marketing alongside regional or even national marketing.

This involves the recognition of the relationships that exist between customer and producers, requiring an understanding of the spatial and organisational structure of the city in relation to its product. It also requires an understanding of the demand for the product in terms of the characteristics, market behaviour and needs of its customers. In a marketing context, these relationships are normally achieved through the 'marketing mix'.

In terms of city-marketing, Ashworth and Voogd (1988: 68) note that 'it is appropriate to develop a geographical marketing mix that is distinctly spatial'. As part of the process of marketing, cities will need to devise a strategy in which its policy towards marketing the city is outlined. As discussed in Chapter 7, strategy and plan formulation is an important and lengthy process and will also need to be applied to marketing the city. Kotler *et al.* (1993: 18) argue that

> place-marketing at its core embraces four activities:
> - designing the right mix of community features and services
> - setting attractive incentives for the current and potential buyers and users of its goods and services
> - delivering a place's products and services in an efficient, accessible way
> - promoting the place's values and image so that potential users are fully aware of the place's distinctive advantages.

This requires a policy and Ashworth and Voogd (1988: 69) identify four types commonly used:

1. A consolidation or defensive policy, whereby the existing range of services are maintained for current consumers.

2. A quality-oriented policy, whereby the effort is placed upon enhancing a better quality of facilities for consumers.
3. An expansionist policy, whereby towns and cities with an attractive portfolio of historic buildings or resources seek to develop a marketing strategy to promote urban heritage tourism.
4. A diversification policy, whereby new markets are targeted for a new range of services it is providing, such as Sheffield's cultural and sport strategy following the infrastructure that was available after the World Student Games (Roche 1992).

But who is responsible for place-marketing?

Local authority marketing

In many cities, this is one additional function adopted by the local municipal authorities. But this is a relatively recent feature for many such bodies, which is reflected in what has been termed minimal marketing, the belief that the product actually sells itself without promotion, though there are examples of aggressive marketing where cities have over-invested without regard to the market. In some cases the local authority has created a new organisation to promote this function or added it to the existing function of a tourist board.

An effective marketing strategy for a city will include the following stages:

- Auditing the market, which is the systematic analysis of the market position of a city in relation to its external environment, including issues that cannot be influenced by planning, and internal issues within organisations. This is often expressed as a Strengths, Weaknesses, Opportunities and Threats analysis (SWOT analysis). The external audit will help to shape the policies required to shape the product to meet the needs of users. For example, how do users perceive the city and its products? Have past policies met the needs of users and how effective are the current organisation and management of the city and resources to deliver these products?

- Identifying the target market, which will need to be identified by market segmentation, a process discussed at length in Chapter 2. This may also incorporate information on the spatial behaviour of users and the consumer decision-making process on the consumption of product within the city.

- Identifying the qualities of the city, which will need to use complex quantitative multi-criteria evaluation techniques such as competition analysis and potency analysis (see Ashworth and Voogd 1990a: 53–64 for a detailed discussion) to establish how the city's product compares to other cities.

- Developing the city product, which needs to be shaped to meet the needs of the market.

- Constructing the image of the city, which needs to be transmitted to the target market through the process of promotion. This may require extensive efforts in relation to image building.

The application of these principles to selling cities as urban tourism destinations raises one important question: *Can places be sold for tourism?* (Ashworth and Voogd 1990b). To examine this contention, it is useful to consider a number of issues such as whether a tourism destination is a product and whether the tourist is a place customer, drawing on the seminal study by Ashworth and Voogd (1990b).

Marketing urban tourism places: the city as a tourism place product

The discussion of tourism supply issues in Chapter 4 highlighted the concept of the city as a leisure product that is a bundle of products consumed by the tourist as part of their urban tourism experience. The issue here is whether these can be sold as a commodity even though many elements of the tourist experience are services. The fundamental difference between a marketable service or good compared to a tourism destination is the way in which it is consumed. The service or good is purchased and consumed directly by the tourist. The place product is rather more complex to understand as Jansen-Verbeke (1988) noted in her concept of the tourist recreation product (TRP). The TRP is both a complex product representing the city as well as being the commodities of which it is composed (Ashworth and Voogd 1990b: 7). Furthermore, Ashworth and Voogd (1990b) also note the following issues which affect the extent to which a tourist destination constitutes a product:

- Defining and delimiting a tourist city as a product (Ashworth 1987) pose practical problems in terms of the spatial extent of the city as well as more complex conceptual issues. For example, urban tourism destinations contain both facilities and attractions as well as other elements which are both the product and the containing context for the bundle of products.

- Many aspects of the services and products sold to the tourist are consumed as packages which are determined by the producer of the services or the intermediaries in the tourism industry. This means that the destination marketing agencies are unable to market a precise product in view of all the possible permutations and variants available to the tourist.

- The scale at which the city is marketed to tourists is often arbitrarily constructed, since local government boundaries may not reflect the real range of experiences or products available to the tourist.

- Cities marketed by local authorities may be multi-sold, meaning that the city as a product is simultaneously sold to different customers with different needs and motives for visiting, unlike the marketing of goods. For example, the tourist-historic city (see Ashworth and Tunbridge 1990) may be sold to one group of tourists while at the same time, the city may be marketed as a desirable location for leisure shopping. This can lead to planning or resource conflicts if physical planning does not recognise the potential conflicts that may arise from multi-selling the city product.

Furthermore, assuming that the tourist is a place customer also requires some qualification as the following factors imply:

- The tourist is a sophisticated consumer, with different and varied patterns of behaviour, which need to be recognised and analysed. Research by Crompton (1979) is interesting in this context as it found that individual tourists' perceptions of the same product can vary, which needs to be recognised in dealing with tourists as customers.

- The tourist product is not only multi-sold but multi-bought and therefore the product is being simultaneously consumed by tourists, residents, workers, shoppers and other visitors. Each of these users needs to be recognised so that the product can be targeted to each group. Yet as Ashworth and Voogd (1990b: 11) argue 'the tourist is logically a place consumer but the identification and measurement of this market will pose particular difficulties' as the tourist can only usually be identified at the point of consumption. Therefore, how do cities differentiate themselves on the basis of place?

The local state and place-marketing: issues in the differentiation of place

The local state is 'the set of institutions charged with the maintenance and protection of social relations at the sub-national level' (Johnston *et al.* 1986: 263). The sub-national level of course is not a single level of territoriality. Government may include several levels at the sub-national level including provinces or states, regional government and municipal and local government. However, within the globalised economy, the local state, in its various forms, is almost universally seen as having increased importance (Know 1997). As noted in Chapters 1 and 2, the political, social and geographical transformations which are now being brought about through the international restructuring of capitalist economies and the consequent changes to the nature and role of cities as they seek to attract ever more mobile investors

has created new centres and peripheries, and also new territorial hierarchies. It has produced new relational contexts and configurations . . . beyond this, there is the overarching global context: 'regional differentiation becomes increasingly organised at the international rather than national level; sub-national regions increasingly give way to regions of the global economy' (Smith 1988 in Robins 1991b: 24).

Moreover, government and industry have also focused on the concept of place within the context of regional development and promotion, reflecting Kotler *et al.*'s dictum: 'In a borderless economy, [places] will emerge as the new actors on the world scene' (Kotler *et al.* 1993: 346).

Tourism is intimately connected to the regional differentiation of places in the global economy because of the way in which it is often used as a focus for urban redevelopment, revitalisation, marketing and promotion strategies in order to attract economic and cultural capital. Within the tourism and marketing literature, the interrelated concepts of 'place-marketing' (e.g. Madsen 1992) also sometimes described as 'selling places' (e.g. Burgess 1982; Kearns and Philo 1993), 'geographical marketing' (e.g. Ashworth and Voogd 1988, 1990a), 'place advertising' (Burgess and Wood 1989) or 'reimaging strategies' (Roche 1992; Hall 1994), have all come to receive significant attention in recent years. As Ashworth and Voogd (1988: 65) argue, the process of place-marketing reflects a

New paradigm structuring the way the complex functioning of cities is viewed . . . [as] . . . many urban activities operate in some kind of a market . . . in which a planned action implies an explicit and simultaneous consideration of both the supply-side and the demand-side . . . [and] . . . such an approach has implications for . . . the way the cities are managed.

Within this new paradigm the competitive ethos of the marketplace has therefore became translated into a burgeoning 'place market' (Sadler 1993). 'The primary goal of the place marketer is to construct a new image of the place to replace either vague or negative images previously held by current or potential residents, investors and visitors' (Holcomb 1993: 133), in order to effectively compete with other places within the constraints of a global economy for a share of mobile international capital (Harvey 1989a). 'This marketing operation involved the construction or selective tailoring of particular images of place, which enmeshed with the dynamics of the global economy and legitimised particular conceptions of what were 'appropriate' state policy responses' (Sadler 1993: 175). Nevertheless, within the context of globalisation, local place-promotional messages are both a product of global economic forces, which provide an extrinsic stimulant for the growth of tourism, and an articulation of a search for local identity, which provides an intrinsic interest in using tourism as a means to articulate identity (Schollmann *et al.* 2000). The new rhetoric of 'the local' therefore has to be seen as deeply embedded in processes of global accumulation, in a 'fragmented mosaic of uneven development in which competitive places try to secure a lucrative development niche' (Swyngedouw 1989: 31).

The notion of rapidly circulating international capital within the global economy is also implicit in the work of Kotler *et al.* (1993) which comes from within the mainstream empiricist marketing tradition (also see Porter 1997). According to Kotler *et al.* (1993: 18) a central proposition of *Marketing Places: Attracting Investment, Industry, and Tourism to Cities, States, and Nations*, was that the 'marketplace shifts and changes occur far faster than a community's capacity to react and respond. Buyers of the goods and services that a place can offer (i.e. business firms, tourists, investors, among others) have a decided advantage over place sellers (i.e. local communities, regions, and other places that seek economic growth)'.

Kotler *et al.* (1993: 18) refer to the need for places to adopt a process of 'strategic place-marketing' for urban and regional revitalisation in order to design a community 'to satisfy the needs of its key constituencies' which embraces four core activities:

1. Designing the right mix of community features and services.
2. Setting attractive incentives for the current and potential buyers and users of its goods and services.
3. Delivering a place's products and services in an efficient, accessible way.
4. Promoting the place's values and image so that the potential users are fully aware of the place's distinctive advantages (1993: 18).

Nevertheless, while Kotler *et al.* (1993) and others (e.g. Porter 1997) recognise the importance of globalisation, the response to the issue of place competition has been substantially different from those who are interested in the cultural and political bases on which place-marketing rests. A cursory glance through most of the major tourism and marketing journals suggests that the influence of the empiricist or 'technical' approach to place-marketing has been extremely strong in academic research on place promotion, whereas, for the most part, discussion on the cultural and political domain has been limited more to the urban geography and cultural studies literature. For example, Mazanec (1997b: xv) argues that marketing an urban destination to tourism generation countries is 'not fundamentally different from marketing a branded product to consumer target groups'. According to Mazanec, the managers of a municipal tourist board are like other colleagues in the service sector in that 'they have to decide on which urban tourism products should be offered to which segments of international tourist demand. This implies analytical and subsequent planning exercises called 'product positioning' and 'market segmentation' (Mazanec 1997b: xv). Such an observation raises numerous questions about the nature of marketing urban destinations in terms of both processes and techniques as well as the base assumptions which underlie urban tourism marketing. Undoubtedly positioning and market segmentation issues are strategic decision issues that need to be seen within the wider context of what cities are trying to achieve through tourism as well as being more 'technical' concerns in relation to the design of individual marketing instruments and accompanying actions. However, even from within an empiricist or technical approach to issues of place-marketing, strategic marketing cannot function without a major investment into market research and data analysis. However, good tourism statistics at the city level are often difficult to locate, with the exception of some of the recent developments in the harmonisation of European city tourism statistics (Wöber 1997a, 2000; see also Chapter 3), therefore often making it difficult to effectively utilise secondary data sources. Although various cities may hold accommodation statistics, conduct visitor surveys, as well as utilise other statistical sources, such as the international visitor surveys conducted by a national tourism organisation, there are often substantial differences in methodology and approach.

Whereas a discussion of the re-imaging dimensions of place-marketing (see below) highlights the local people as paramount in the research question, much of the marketing literature remains more interested in the visitor (C.M. Hall 2000). For example, a significant component of urban tourism marketing is the assessment of visitor satisfaction of the urban experience. Many individual businesses, particularly within the accommodation sector, conduct their own assessment of their customers' satisfaction with their experience. However, it is only in recent years that urban tourism organisations have conducted evaluations of visitor satisfaction with the destination as a whole. Satisfaction may be conceived as a transaction-specific 'short-term and ephemeral state of evaluation connected with one particular service encounter'. By contrast, 'attitudes' are then understood to be stable and long-term states of mind rendering a 'cumulative conceptualization' of 'satisfaction' (Mazanec 1997c: 77). In a study of the 1994/95 Austrian national guest survey, Mazanec (1997c) investigated the satisfaction levels of visitors to major urban areas. Thirteen items in the survey related to the major ingredients of a leisure trip to an urban destination:

- landscape and cityscape;
- peace and quiet;
- furnishing and pleasantness of accommodation;
- service in the accommodation;
- cuisine and catering;
- friendliness of staff in restaurants and inns;
- friendliness of the local people;
- cultural life;
- scope for excursions;
- entertainment, sports and shopping facilities;
- opening hours of shops;
- walking and hiking paths;
- offers for families with children.

An additional seven items in the survey were indicative of how visitors judged the urban experience in terms of value for money and price:

- drinks;
- meals;
- accommodation;
- sports facilities;
- cultural offers and entrance fees;
- entertainment facilities;
- public transport.

A number of different market segments were identified in the analysis of the survey data. Table 8.1 highlights the most typical ratings out of the list of 23 satisfaction items for each of the four satisfaction segments. The significance of the market segmentation exercise undertaken by Mazanec lies not so much on his results, as useful as they might be for understanding Austrian urban tourism, but rather it serves as an example of the utility of such research for understanding the urban tourism market.

Similarly, substantial research is undertaken with respect to positioning. Positioning may be conceived as the visualisation of consumer perceptions. The core idea of positioning is the comparison of one product within its competitors. Grabler's (1997a) study of the perceptual map and positioning of six European tourist cities (Barcelona, Budapest, Paris, Prague, Venice and Vienna) observed that for the German respondents the ambience of the city and the attractiveness of price levels were the most important factors when going on a city trip. Less important for the German market were the shopping and entertainment facilities. In comparison, for the British respondents the most important factor was the quality of the food and beverages, followed by the ambience and the cultural resources. Shopping and entertainment facilities were the least important for the British. Grabler (1997a) reported that for three of the six cities (Vienna, Prague and Budapest) there was a distinctly different position for the two geographical segments, with the difference probably due

Table 8.1 Summarising results for the Austrian urban tourism satisfaction segments

Type	Percentage	Rating
1	16	Dissatisfied with everything except landscape and cityscape, cultural events and walking paths; extremely dissatisfied with the level of prices for beverages, meals and accommodation.
2	40	Moderately satisfied with all tourist services except opening hours of shops; no criticism for the level of prices
3	23	Highly satisfied with all tourist services except opening hours of shops; no criticism for the level of prices
4	21	Highly satisfied with everything including the level of prices

Source: Mazanec (1997c).

to the better product knowledge of the Germans due to their close geographical proximity. In contrast Barcelona, Paris and Venice had a much more stable image in the two markets.

The results of Grabler's research were significant, as mentioned in Chapter 3, in that they indicated that the image appeal of a city appears to be the main pull factor for potential city tourists (also see Bramwell and Rawding 1996). 'Both price/friendliness and infrastructure can be regarded as 'hygiene factors' that must not drop below a certain limit. However, they do not heavily influence the liking of the cities. Nevertheless, they strongly determine the perception of the cities . . . The perceptions of the cities are relatively homogeneous' (Grabler 1997a: 111–12). Therefore, in the European case individual segments did not perceive cities as being significantly different. Such a finding has substantial implications for urban tourism marketing strategies as tourism promotion organisations will need 'to detect those segments for which the city offers the attributes which fit the needs of customers' (Grabler 1997a: 112) if they are to be effective in their marketing.

As the previous chapter argued, such urban marketing research is an extremely important tool for urban tourism management and planning. Indeed, if well-conducted, place-marketing can have positive effects for cities and even countries in the development of place brands, which can have a flow or 'halo effect' to other products from that place, especially when consumers have limited familiarity with the destinations (Shimp *et al.* 1993). However, for all the successful place brands many more have failed. Therefore, place-marketing needs to be seen as much within the wider context of the politics of place as it is within a technical dimension of urban marketing.

Re-imaging

Roche (1992, 1994) and Hall (1994) have also described such place-marketing activities under the rubric of re-imaging strategies. Contemporary urban imaging strategies are typically policy responses to the social and economic problems associated with deindustrialisation and globalisation and associated issues of economic restructuring, urban renewal, multiculturalism, social integration and control. The principal aims of urban imaging strategies are to

- attract tourism expenditure;
- generate employment in the tourist industry;
- foster positive images for potential investors in the region, often by 're-imaging' previous negative perceptions; and
- provide an urban environment which will attract and retain the interest of professionals and white-collar workers, particularly in 'clean' service industries such as tourism and communications (C.M. Hall 1992).

Plate 8.1   Key urban facilities such as the Crown casino in Melbourne, Australia, are used to market the city's appeal to visitors who would like to gamble and are part of a wider re-imaging of the city as a business tourism destination, with the nearby conference and convention facilities and sporting venues

Urban imaging processes are characterised by some or all of the following:

- the development of a critical mass of visitor attractions and facilities, including new buildings/prestige/flagship centres (e.g. shopping centres, stadia, sports complexes and indoor arenas, convention centres, casino development; Plate 8.1);

- the hosting of hallmark events (e.g. Olympic Games, Commonwealth Games, the America's Cup and the hosting of Grand Prix) and/or hosting major league sports teams;

- development of urban tourism strategies and policies often associated with new or renewed organisation and development of city marketing (e.g. 'Absolutely, Positively Wellington', Sheffield City of Steel, Cutlery and Sport); and

- development of leisure and cultural services and projects to support the marketing and tourism effort (e.g. the creation and renewal of museums and art galleries and the hosting of art festivals, often as part of a comprehensive cultural tourism strategy for a region or city).

As noted above, re-imaging and place-marketing began to be recognised as significant urban phenomena from the early 1980s on, at a time when globalisation started to be seen as economically, politically and socially significant and when substantial changes in the nature of consumption and production also occurred. Indeed, it is no coincidence that in this time of dramatic shifts in the character of contemporary capitalism that the 1980s were characterised as the decade in which consumers were taught 'how to desire' (Bocock 1993; York and Jennings 1995: 44; Pawson 1997: 17). For producers, an essential means of achieving this has been by 'romancing the product' through the use of brands (Pawson 1997). Branding is a way of seeking to add value to commodities including services and places. A successful brand creates distinctiveness in the marketplace, including the highly competitive place marketplace. As Pawson (1997: 17) notes, 'It is an investment in product quality at the same time as seeking to create more illusory associations to appeal to specific groups of consumers in the local spaces of globalised capitalism. Both branding and advertising are inherently spatial practices, used by producers in the expansion and differentiation of markets'. In the case of urban re-imaging, marketing practices, such as branding, rely upon the commodification of particular aspects of place, exploiting, reinventing or creating place images in order to sell the place as a destination product for tourists or investment. Through this process the ways of living of a place may become commoditised in order to make them a commercial product or a specific dimension of place promotion that can be experienced by the consumer.

Hall (2002b) recently argued that urban imaging strategies are conscious attempts by places to 'seduce', as they seek not only to develop something that is attractive but in so doing they aim to package specific representations of a particular way of life or lifestyle for consumption. Hall (2002b) compared the Australian cities of Melbourne and Sydney and observed that their mutual desire to 'place themselves on the map' as a 'world city' was tied in to the broader processes of globalisation and localisation as well as historical competition for capital. In the marketing of these two cities economic conditions have had a major impact on re-imaging strategies, with greater attention being given to attractions such as events, casinos and waterfront development proposals at times of economic recession than during periods of economic growth (Hall and Hamon 1996). For example, Melbourne's unsuccessful bid for the 1996 Olympic Games was followed by Sydney's successful bid for the 2000 Summer Olympics. In the case of Melbourne, the bid was tied to the redevelopment of the Melbourne Dockland area, while the key feature of the Sydney bid was the redevelopment of the former industrial site and waste dump at Homebush Bay on Sydney Harbour as the main Games stadium complex. In both cities the bidding for events by state governments and city authorities was integrated into the development of new cultural, leisure and tourism policies which focused on attracting visitors to the city and broader urban redevelopment programmes which seek to develop cultural, housing, leisure and entertainment complexes in waterfront areas (Hall 1998).

Similarly, in the late 1980s Sydney and the New South Wales State Government undertook to redevelop the run-down inner-city Darling Harbour dockland area as a waterfront tourism, retail, leisure and entertainment complex while Melbourne and the Victorian State Government undertook to develop the derelict industrial south bank of the River Yarra in a similar fashion (Hall and Hamon 1996; Hall 1998). To walk through the cities of Melbourne and Sydney is therefore to witness the physical representation of both attempts to seduce capital and visitors as well as the results of such seduction (Hall 2002b).

Therefore, representations of culture are intimately connected to place-marketing. Whether we are using culture in the sense of being indicative of a 'particular way of life, whether of a people, a period, a group, or humanity in general' or 'as a reference to the works or practices of intellectual and especially artistic activity' (Williams 1983: 90), culture is becoming commodified and bought and sold in the global marketplace. Cultural policies are used to generate artistic and 'high' cultural activity in order to attract visitors and to make the city an attractive place to live for the middle-class, white-collar workers and business that places seek to attract, while wider notions of cultural identity are also being used to attract investment, visitors and employment.

Ley (1989: 57) suggests that the desire to incorporate the arts into urban redevelopment strategies must be seen as the postmodern project of the 'new cultural class'. This class, he argues, has emerged from the radicalism of the 1960s to be the advocate of an urban design that seeks to reconstruct as meaningful the dehumanising modernist spaces of the city. The cultural class claims that the challenge for planning and architecture is to use both the expressive arts and the aesthetics of design to rebuild (inner) cities as places that are grounded in the history and the culture of the people who use them. Ley (1989: 53) goes on to describe this postmodern project as being an attempt to achieve the 're-enchantment of the built environment' or, as Robins (1991a: 2) suggests, the postmodern city is 'about an attempt to re-imagine urbanity: about recovering a lost sense of territorial identity, urban community and public space. It is a kind of return to (mythical) origins'. Indeed, heritage plays a central role within postmodernist ideas of place and representation. Similarly to Ley (1989), Bianchini and Schwengel (1991: 227) argue that when cities have a crisis in terms of both urbanity and social cohesion which place-marketing may seek to correct, heritage then represents 'a feeble attempt to reconstruct some common identity in the face of potentially explosive social tensions and conflicts'.

The loss of historically rooted places, including the attempt to depoliticise them 'decontextualising them and sucking out of them all political controversy – so as to sell . . . places . . . to outsiders who might otherwise feel alienated or encounter encouragements to political defiance' (Philo and Kearns 1993: 24) is commonplace in tourism. Heritage centres and historical anniversaries typically serve to flatten and suppress contested views of history. For example, in the case of Britain's museums, Hewison (1991: 175) argued

this pastiched and collaged past, once it has received the high gloss of presentation from the new breed of 'heritage managers', succeeds in presenting a curiously
unified image, where change, conflict, clashes of interest, are neutralized within a
single seamless and depthless surface, which merely reflects our historical anxi-
eties . . . There seem to be no winners, and especially no losers. The open story of
history has become the closed book of heritage.

Of significance to the manner in which heritage and urban tourism are developed Hewison went on to argue (1991: 175) that 'the time has come to argue
that commerce is *not* culture, whether we define culture as the pursuit of music,
literature or the fine arts, or whether we adopt Raymond Williams's definition
of culture as "a whole way of life". You cannot get a whole way of life into a
Tesco's trolley or a V & A Enterprises shopping bag'. Such arguments are
important because they run counter to the notions of commodification of place
and culture as product intrinsic to place-marketing. Furthermore, they run
counter to both the macro-political narratives of postmodernism and post-
Fordism and the (related) micro-political actions of actors within the policy-
making process. 'The assertion of moral values, over against those commodity
values which are not merely the theoretical result of the cultural logic of late
capitalism, but the very practical result of the political and economic logic of
the contemporary Conservative government' (Hewison 1991: 176). Therefore,
Hewison concluded, there is a need for 'a version of the past that does not
exclude conflict and change (the hidden agenda of Heritage being to exclude
these irritants), and which admits the existence of contingency, the possibility
of accident, and the reality of winners and losers' (Hewison 1991: 176).

However, the presentation of one-dimensional views of the past to the
tourist and the community is also encountered at the destination level. In her
excellent study of tourism, history and ethnicity in Monterey, Norkunas
(1993) argues that the rich and complex ethnic history of Monterey is almost
completely absent in the 'official' historical tours and the residences available
for public viewing. In Monterey, as in many other parts of the world, heritage
is presented in the form of the houses of the aristocracy or elite. 'This synopsis
of the past into a digestible touristic presentation eliminates any discussion of
conflict; it concentrates instead on a sense of resolution. Opposed events and
ideologies are collapsed into statements about the forward movement and
rightness of history' (Norkunas 1993: 36). Narratives of labour, class and ethnicity are typically replaced by romance and nostalgia. Overt conflict, whether
between ethnic groups, classes or, more particularly, in terms of industrial and
labour disputes, are either ignored or glossed over in 'official' tourist histories.
The overt conflict of the past has been reinterpreted by local elites to create a
new history in which heritage takes a linear, conflict-free form. In the case of
Monterey, the past is reinterpreted through the physical transformation of the
canneries. 'Reinterpreting the past has allowed the city to effectively erase from
the record the industrial era and the working-class culture it engendered.

Commentary on the industrial era remains only in the form of touristic inter-pretations of the literature of John Steinbeck' (Norkunas 1993: 50–51).

City Centres, City Cultures (Fisher and Worpole 1988), a collaborative work published by the Centre for Local Government Strategies in Britain, has been extremely influential in setting the agenda for city-based cultural planning schemes. The over-arching aim of the initiatives outlined in this publication is to link the development of a comprehensive local policy for the arts and cul-tural activity with the objective of improving the 'quality' of urban life (Fisher and Worpole 1988: 10). 'Quality of life', here, is an expansive concept dis-cussed with reference to such diverse matters as the crime rate, public transport systems, the standard of roads, street lighting and the like. However, significantly such cultural measures are related to the importance of re-imaging and revitalising urban space in order to attract capital and people rather than just undertaking such measures for the people who already live in urban areas.

The use of heritage and cultural images (Plates 8.2 and 8.3) to attract visitors is not new. It has been around for as long as tourism. However, the effects of place-marketing may be pervasive within specific places targeted for consump-tion, because the notion of selling places implies not only trying to affect demand through the representation of cultural images, but also the manipula-tion and management of the supply-side, e.g. those things that make up a com-munity's life, into a package which can be 'sold'. Such actions clearly have implications not only for how the external consumer sees places, but also for how those people who constitute place are able to participate in the making of their collective and individual identity and the structures that sell place (Hall and Hodges 1997).

All of this has substantial implications for the actions and institutional arrangements of the local state and, indeed, of the nation-state. In commodify-ing place as a product that can be revitalised, advertised and marketed, places are presented not so much 'as foci of attachment and concern, but as bundles of social and economic opportunity *competing* against one another in the open (and unregulated) *market* for a share of the capital investment cake (whether this be the investment of enterprises, tourists, local consumers or whatever)' (Philo and Kearns 1993: 18). The 'terrain of thinking' about local economic policies and political forms and the role of the local state is therefore being shifted (Duncan and Goodwin 1985a,b, 1988), with the result that a range of local institutions 'now internalise the idea that the interests of a place are best served by lifting the "dead hand" of regulation and by opening it to the sway of market forces' (Philo and Kearns 1993: 19). Similarly, Kotler *et al.* (1993: 25) state: 'The public sector, being largely monopolistic in character, often lags behind the private sector in being responsive to the needs and service require-ments of its citizens'. Almost nine years later as some of the most inefficient of ineffective examples of privatisation are being reregulated or examined by gov-ernments in various parts of the world at great expense, such as the railway sys-tem in the UK, the notion that the private sector is more responsive no longer has such sway. Nevertheless, there is clearly a role for the private sector in

Plate 8.2   In terms of positioning a destination, the popularity of the heritage and global brand of a city such as London is reflected in this enormous queue for entrance to a paid attraction – the London Dungeon on an Easter weekend. This also reflects a growing fascination with the darker aspects of urban life which has been labelled 'dark tourism'

urban management and in infrastructure and facility provision, though the exact nature of the relationship between the public and the private sectors will vary on a situation by situation basis.

Theories are clearly also policies (Hall and Jenkins 1995). Academic, government and industry arguments as to the role of the local state and the functions and tasks they should fulfil are intimately related. The period 1980–95 witnessed the re-emergence of political structures and ideologies that were based around the notions of privatisation and deregulation, twin processes that supposedly promote the unfettered operation of so-called 'market forces'

Plate 8.3 Icons such as the Tower of London are widely used in the marketing of destinations because of their memorable and easily recognisable nature in promotional literature

(Cloke 1992). Despite public reservations, the infrastructure of urban government is still being privatised, and the ideologies and discourses of regeneration and revitalisation remain highly significant (see Chapter 9). 'Where public agencies were once seen as an essential part of the solution to any urban crisis, they are now viewed as part of the problem itself' (Goodwin 1993: 148). Indeed, it is ironic that nowhere in Kotler *et al.*'s (1993) discussion of strategic place-marketing is the means by which the citizenry can actually participate in the place-marketing process to decide how their city should be presented to consumers, if at all (T. Hall 1997). Within this context, normative assumptions often exist about equal individual access to power and decision-making processes within the local state. Yet, clearly, individuals do not have equal access to power and decision-making. As Hall and Jenkins (1995) argued, business interest groups dominate the place-marketing and tourism policy-making process, while Harvey (1988) highlighted the role of growth coalitions in urban redevelopment. Similarly, Lowe (1993: 211) commented on 'the potential power of the "regional entrepreneur" in moulding the contemporary urban landscape':

> A person of vision, tenacity and skill (such as a charismatic mayor, a clever city administrator, or wealthy business leader) to put a particular stamp upon the

nature and direction of urban entrepreneurialism, perhaps to shape it even, to particular political ends' (Harvey 1989b: 7).

Therefore, to return to a question that haunted much urban geography and planning in the late 1960s and early 1970s, in whose interests are cities, places and regions being constructed, promoted and revitalised? Or are we witnessing the creation and promotion of places in the gaze of North American marketing academic middle-class notions of what constitutes civil society (T. Hall 1997)?

Place-marketing and the ideology of place

Under the enterprise economy, 'the ideology of locality, place and community becomes central to the political rhetoric of urban governance which concentrates on the idea of togetherness in defence against a hostile and threatening world of international competition' (Harvey 1989a: 14). One of the great ironies therefore, given the enterprise culture of place-marketing which extols the virtues of competition and choice, is the manner in which debate over representation and redevelopment of place is denied within and by the local state. Throughout much of the Western world, in order to ensure that regional, often urban, development projects are carried out, 'local authorities have had planning and development powers removed and handed to an unelected institution. Effectively, an appointed agency is, in each case, replacing the powers of local government in order to carry out a market-led regeneration of each inner city' (Goodwin 1993: 161). Harvey recognised that 'the new entrepreneurialism has, as its centrepiece, the notion of a "public–private partnership" in which a traditional local boosterism is integrated with the use of local government powers to try [to] attract external sources of funding, new direct investments, or new employment sources' (1989b: 7). However, the partnership does not include all members of a community, those who do not have enough money, are not of the right lifestyle, or simply do not have sufficient power, are ignored. As Mommaas and van der Poel (1989: 263) observe, the development of a more economically oriented regional development policy style has led to 'projects, developed in public–private partnerships, [which] are meant not for the integration of disadvantaged groups within society, but for servicing the pleasures of the well-to-do'. For example, referring to Derwentside in the United Kingdom for example, Sadler (1993: 190) argued,

> The kind of policy which had been adopted – and which was proving increasingly ineffective even in terms of its own stated objectives – therefore rested not so much on a basis of rational choice, but rather was a simple reflection of the narrow political and intellectual scope for alternatives. This restricted area did not come about purely or simply by chance, but had been deliberately encouraged and fostered.

Similarly, in the case of the Sydney bid for the 2000 Summer Olympics the former New South Wales State Premier, Nick Greiner, argued that 'The secret of the success was undoubtedly the creation of a community of interest, not only in Sydney, but across the nation, unprecedented in our peacetime history' (1994: 13). The description of a 'community of interest' is extremely apt, as such a phrase indicates the role of the interests of growth coalitions in mega-event proposals (C.M. Hall 1996). In particular, the Sydney media played a critical role in creating the climate for the bid. As Greiner stated:

> Early in 1991, I invited senior media representatives to the premier's office, told them frankly that a bid could not succeed if the media played their normal 'knocking role' and that I was not prepared to commit the taxpayers' money unless I had their support. Both News Ltd and Fairfax subsequently went out of their way to ensure the bid received fair, perhaps even favourable, treatment. The electronic media also joined in the sense of community purpose (Greiner 1994: 13).

The use of public–private partnerships is increasingly being extolled within much of the tourism literature, either implicitly or explicitly (Bramwell and Lane 2000). However, many members of the public of the local state are actually being excluded from the new corporatist, public–private, set of institutional arrangements which are supposedly there to benefit them. Policy visions, whether they be for places or for the tourism industry, typically fail to be developed in the light of oppositional or critical viewpoints. Place visions tend to be developed through the activities of industry experts rather than the broad populace. Perhaps because the vision of the wider public for a place may not be the same as some segments of business, community involvement is undertaken through opinion polls, surveys or SWOT analyses rather than through participatory measures (C.M. Hall 2000; see also Chapter 7).

As with production and consumption, globalisation and localisation cannot be separated (C.M. Hall 1997). Globalisation is about the achievement of a new global–local relationship. 'Globalization is like putting together a jigsaw puzzle: it is a matter of inserting a multiplicity of localities into the overall picture of a new global system' (Robins 1991b: 35). Nevertheless, as Robins argues, we should not idealise the local. 'We should not invest our hopes for the future in the redemptive qualities of local economies, local cultures, local identities. It is important to see the local as a relational, and relative, concept. If once it was significant in relation to the national sphere, now its meaning is being recast in the context of globalization' (Robins 1991b: 35). But 'local' in this sense does not correspond to any specific territorial configuration. 'Local' should not be mistaken for 'locality'. The 'local' should be seen as a fluid and relational space, constituted only in and through its relation to the global. For the global corporation, the local might, in fact, correspond to different regional spheres of activity depending on the product and the constituency of the market.

However, place-marketers have equated place with the local state. Cities are positioning themselves in an attempt to gain access to scarce international mobile capital in order to redevelop themselves, with the help of architects, as postmodern cities of pastiche and image. So they can, again, go in search of economic and cultural capital with which then to compete against other places.

> Whether it is to attract a new car factory or the Olympic Games, they go as supplicants. And, even as supplicants, they go in competition with each other: cities and localities are now fiercely struggling against each other to attract footloose and predatory investors to their particular patch. Of course, some localities are able successfully to 'switch' themselves in to the global networks, but others will remain 'unswitched' or even 'plugged'. And, in a world characterized by the increasing mobility of capital and the rapid recycling of space, even those that manage to become connected in to the global system are always vulnerable to the abrupt withdrawal of investment and to [partial] disconnection from the global system (Robins 1991b: 35–6).

Conclusion

This chapter has emphasised the multilayered nature of one of the key dimensions of urban tourism management – place-marketing. It has illustrated that place-marketing should not be seen as solely a technical marketing issue but rather there are significant political and cultural dimensions to the concept.

The chapter has also highlighted the way in which culture and heritage are tied into place-marketing (see also Chapter 5) and the connections between place-marketing and postmodernity (see also Chapter 2) through the 'flattening' of history through place promotion and imaging. Significantly, the chapter has also noted the way in which place-marketing needs to be seen within the context of globalisation and place competition, a point returned to in the final chapter. The next chapter examines urban redevelopment as a specific component of urban reimaging strategies.

Questions

1. To what extent is place-marketing a response to globalisation?
2. What are the relationships between place-marketing and postmodernism?
3. Is there anything inherently wrong with seeing place-marketing as purely a technical exercise?
4. What are the four main forms of urban re-imaging strategies?

Further reading

Although slightly dated Kearns and Philo (1993) provide an excellent account of the social, economic and political issues surrounding place-marketing:

Kearns, G. and Philo, C. (eds) (1993). *Selling Places: The City as Cultural Capital, Past and Present*, Oxford: Pergamon Press.

The approach of Kearns and Philo (1993) should be contrasted with the influential work of Kotler *et al.*:

Kotler, P., Haider, D.H. and Rein, I. (1993). *Marketing Places: Attracting Investment, Industry, and Tourism to Cities, States, and Nations*, New York: The Free Press.

A useful recent case study of place-marketing is:

Schollman, A., Perkins, H.C. and Moore, K. (2000). 'Intersecting global and local influences in urban place promotion: the case of Christchurch, New Zealand', *Environment and Planning A* 32(1): 55–76.

A more extensive read is:

Rutheiser, C. (1996). *Imagineering Atlanta: The Politics of Place in the City of Dreams*, New York: Verso.

CHAPTER 9

Tourism and urban regeneration

Introduction

Rediscovering a lost urban experience is one of the central themes of the contemporary discourse of the city. A telling indicator of its centrality is the extensive use of the prefix 're' in the language of urban planning and development. The literature is littered with examples, such as re-enchantment, re-construction, re-creation, re-juvenation and re-generation, perhaps indicating the cyclical nature of much postmodernist theory and/or the desire to reclaim or reconstruct a (mythical) urban past in a city that never actually existed. The use of such language therefore clearly demands analysis of the assumptions and values implicit in urban development and its strong relationship to tourism.

The present chapter serves to discuss the manner in which tourism has been integrated as a key component of urban regeneration programmes and of the wider place-marketing and re-imaging strategies of which they are a part. The chapter first discusses the nature of regeneration and its relationship to tourism. It then goes on to examine the manner in which mega-events are tied into urban regeneration. The chapter then concludes by posing the question as to whether or not we are entering a stage of seemingly permanent urban regeneration.

Urban regeneration

Following the economic restructuring of many regions and the subsequent loss of heavy industry in many industrial and waterfront areas in the 1970s and 1980s, tourism has been perceived as a mechanism to regenerate urban areas through the creation of leisure, retail and tourism space. This process appears almost universal in the developed world. Such a situation led Harvey (1988,

Plate 9.1 In the regeneration and redevelopment of localities, malls and their associated facilities, such as this recreational rink at Edmonton Mall, Canada, can have a major economic impact on the locality

cited in Urry 1990: 128) to ask 'How many museums, cultural centres, convention and exhibition halls, hotels, marinas, shopping malls, waterfront developments can we stand?' Similarly, Zukin (1991) observed that the city is a site of spectacle, a 'dreamscape of visual consumption'.

Law (1993) noted that such measures were part of physical regeneration policies, particularly with respect to the reuse of transport lands (railways or waterfronts or both): 'many of these lands were previously cut off from public access and dock walls and buildings obscured the view of the water, but they can be reclaimed by the community . . . the juxtaposition of land and water is appealing to most people and these waterside zones have been reused for a variety of purposes, including prestige offices, upmarket housing involving gentrification, and tourism activities' (Law 1993: 131). Indeed, Law's comments highlight the fact that regeneration is an activity spatially concentrated on areas of derelict industrial land, often on waterfronts affected by the raise in container shipping; inner-city areas and other points of severe social deprivation (Plates 9.1–9.3).

Tourism has become critical to regeneration in waterfront and core urban areas (e.g. Gospodini 2001; Hoyle 2001) but not in the suburbs. As noted throughout this book, in the urban core tourism has become a key component of urban policies tied in to place-marketing and urban re-imaging strategies which detailed:

Plate 9.2   Former industrial buildings, such as this gasworks in Hobart, Tasmania can be reused to attract tourists to urban areas

- emphasis on economic policies;
- emphasis on obtaining private investment;
- emphasis on property investment;
- public sector investment in the infrastructure;
- public sector 'anchors', e.g. convention centres, museums;
- focus on the city centre;
- public–private partnership;
- semi-autonomous public agencies
- flagship projects;
- image.

Such policy settings are firm fixtures in North America, Europe and Australasia. The extent to which cities are seeking to utilise place-marketing

Plate 9.3   Former dock areas, such as Chatham Dockyards, Kent, England, have a long maritime history and this can be incorporated into the re-theming and re-imaging of such areas during the regeneration process to build on strengths in heritage products

strategies is well illustrated in the Canadian context. The following provides a snapshot of what Canada's provincial cities are undertaking with respect to place-marketing and revitalisation in 2000:

- St John's, Newfoundland – has set aside a heritage conservation area; currently developing a downtown strategy for economic development and heritage preservation (O'Brien 2000).

- Fredricton, New Brunswick – a heritage and waterfront revitalisation scheme (Forbes and DeGrace 2000).

- Halifax, Nova Scotia – Halifax Tourism Culture and Heritage is seeking to make Halifax a major entertainment, tourism and cultural centre and trying to become a year-round destination by positioning it as the 'entertainment capital' of Atlantic Canada. Halifax is being promoted as one of the 'cultural capitals' of North America and the City Council in conjunction with the province has launched a 'New Tourism' initiative, which emphasises community heritage, natural heritage resources and heritage cultures between 2000 and 2006. 'The objectives here are twofold: (1) to reinforce the value that the communities place on heritage; and (2) to link the same resources to revenue-producing streams, in order to foster self-sustainability among the groups and communities that manage heritage-based, cultural and natural resources' (Norris and Patterson 2000: 26).

- Montreal, Quebec – the Commission de la capitale nationale du Québec has sought to position Montreal as the grand port entrance to North America with this being tied in with waterfront redevelopment and heritage. In addition, the activities of the Commission are related to the continuing efforts of the Quebec provincial government to seek cultural and political independence from Canada, a factor that means that Montreal has placed enormous efforts on place promotion strategies (Fillion 2000).

- Toronto, Ontario – Toronto has been subject to ongoing redevelopment of the waterfront since the early 1980s in order to attract tourist, leisure and retail development. In addition, it has also made two bids to host the Summer Olympic Games with both bids seeking to use the Olympics as a catalyst for further waterfront development (see below).

- Winnipeg, Manitoba – the provincial government has led the development of a capital region strategy in order to try to revitalise the downtown area of the city (Wight 2000).

- Regina, Saskatchewan – the provincial government has undertaken a number of initiatives to try to redevelop the inner city with emphasis on cultural developments. In addition the city is seeking to enhance its historic links with the Royal Canadian Mounted Police (RCMP) given that the Mounties are one of Canada's most well-known icons. 'New policies have been proposed to benefit both the RCMP and the city by increasing the visibility of the force, using its presence to promote tourism and civic identity, and reinforcing understanding of the role played by Regina and the RCMP in the history of Western Canada' (Braitman 2000: 32).

- Edmonton, Alberta – the city and the province have developed a capital city downtown plan as a response to the loss of retail functions in the inner city. The focus of the plan is in creating cultural, tourism and recreational opportunities in relationship with the development and attraction of new retail outlets (Duncan 2000).

- Victoria, British Columbia – British Columbia's Provincial Capital Commission is responsible for enhancing the capital for the benefit of visitors and the people of the province. Within the inner harbour area it has taken a lead on new hotel, heritage and cultural projects as well as beautification programmes to improve and maintain the inner-city environment.

- Yellowknife, North West Territories – is positioning itself as the diamond capital of North America as well as developing a Great Slave Lake waterfront management plan in order to help undertake tourism-related development (Smyth 2000).

What is remarkable in the above list is the extent to which the interrelationship of tourism with urban regeneration is such a common phenomenon. However, even world cities such as London are seen by government as requiring regeneration strategies in order to enable them to compete effectively. The Department of the Environment, Transport and the Regions (DETR) (1996) reported that for London the factors which matter most in creating and maintaining a competitive edge are:

- physical improvement in the centre;
- facilities and attractions;
- internal, national and international transport links;
- competitive regulations;
- education and training;
- image/market research/marketing.

Significantly, such factors were related to the visitor and capital rather than the local community with the Department stating:

> Government needs to maintain the right economic climate for business and trade to prosper, and encourage investment in public transport, the environment and flagship facilities and attractions to accommodate and entertain the international businessperson and tourist of the future . . . The factors which will determine success in the future are those which make it easy and enjoyable to network and to conduct business – access, openness, urban ambience, hotels and cultural and entertainment facilities.

Undoubtedly, in London the role of government has been substantial. A final evaluation of the London Docklands Development Corporation (LDDC), which was commissioned by the DETR, reported that 'When all projects are completed the total public sector cost of regenerating Docklands will be of the order of £3,900 million, 48% incurred by the LDDC, 25% by London Transport and 27% by the Isle of Dogs Enterprise Zone. Almost half the public sector cost of regenerating Docklands was devoted to transport infrastructure' (DETR 1998). In contrast, private sector investment in Docklands was estimated at £8,700 million by March 1998. The evaluation concluded that every £1 million of public sector cost generated net additional benefits in the Urban Development Authorities of 23 jobs, 8,500 m^2 of office floorspace, 7.8 housing units plus many other diverse and intermediate benefits, including substantially more varied housing tenure, new housing stock for an additional 45,000 population, a three-fold increase in employment and a fivefold increase in the number of firms (Table 9.1).

Nevertheless, the above discussion raises substantial questions about the nature of regeneration. To what extent is it physical, i.e. concerned with architecture and image; or social, i.e. concerned with improving the quality of life of those who already live in the areas that government has sought to regenerate?

Table 9.1   Changes in key baseline indicators in the UDA

	1981	1998	End state forecast
Population ('000s)	39	84	115
Employment in UDA ('000s)	27	84	168
Stock of housing units ('000s)	15	36	50
of which privately owned (%)	5	44	52
Number of firms in UDA	1,014	2,600	5,000
Number of residents working in UDA	5,200	10,500	13,000

Source: DETR (1996).

Such a distinction reflects the spatial split noted above as well as the comments regarding the delivery of urban regeneration in *Towards an Urban Renaissance: The Report of the Urban Task Force Chaired by Lord Rogers of Riverside* for the British Government (DETR 2000a):

> There are neighbourhoods where regeneration can only be achieved through comprehensive packages of measures to tackle not just the physical environment, but also the economic and social needs of local people. These areas include inner-urban ex-industrial districts with large amounts of derelict, vacant and under-used land and buildings; and more built-up areas, including many publicly owned housing estates, suffering from concentrated social deprivation.

Yet how successful has such an approach been? A review conducted of urban regeneration policies in the United Kingdom provides interesting insights into the success of such initiatives. The DETR-sponsored evaluation defined 'regeneration' as broadly consisting of Area Based Initiatives (ABIs) mainly introduced by the Department of the Environment and/or DETR, in England, since 1990. Such ABIs were introduced to address cumulative, social, economic and physical problems in disadvantaged areas. In the 1980s and early 1990s, many regeneration measures were oriented towards land and property led economic regeneration. Initiatives included projects such as City Challenge and the Single Regeneration Budget Challenge Fund (SRB) which placed a stronger emphasis on comprehensive regeneration through partnership working, and the more recent New Deal for Communities (NDC) projects which target substantial resources at deprived neighbourhoods of 1,000–4,000 households. Although the evaluation reported that the schemes have made improvements to areas on some indicators, substantial issues remain, particularly with assisting those who live in such areas. Indeed, it concluded that 'Physical regeneration has, in many cases, played an important role in improving neighbourhood identity and external image, and in attracting employment opportunities into the area – although most jobs have not been secured by residents of deprived neighbourhoods' (DETR 2000b).

Arguably, as the discussion below with respect to the impacts of events highlights, the UK experience with regeneration is not unique. Most significantly it forces the reader to critically consider what urban regeneration projects mean and for who or what they are actually for.

Mega-events and urban regeneration

Mega-events have long been regarded as playing a significant role in urban regeneration strategies. As Law (1993: 107) noted, mega-events act

> as a catalyst for change by persuading people to work together around a common objective and as fast track for obtaining extra finance and getting building projects off the drawing board. This is not without its problems, since some would argue that it gives priority to development issues over those of welfare. The physical aspect of this strategy is that it has been linked with inner city regeneration and in particular with that of the city centre.

However, the majority of studies have focused on the hosting of events in the developed rather than the less-developed world. Hiller's (1997, 1998, 2000) studies on the Cape Town 2004 Olympic bid provide a notable exception to the dominant focus in the event literature. Cape Town's bid for the 2004 Olympic Games was unsuccessful but was nevertheless significant as it explicitly linked the hosting of a mega-event to the social and economic development needs of a city in a less-developed country. Indeed, Hiller (2000) noted that the bid from Rio de Janiero for the same Summer Olympics included only one sentence that indicated that improving the living conditions in the slum neighbourhoods of the city would be a priority and, as Hiller commented in a footnote, 'It was considered that this was a late addition prior to publication rather than being a keystone idea in the bid'. In contrast, the Cape Town bid document sought to add a fourth 'pillar' to the Olympic Movement's pillars of sport, culture and the environment, which was that of 'human development'. The Bid Book argued that every aspect of hosting the Olympics 'should contribute to the upliftment and quality of life of the people of the city . . . we place special emphasis on our disadvantaged communities' (Hiller 2000: 441).

The Cape Town Olympic bid was therefore designed to be transformative in a much wider sense than had hitherto been the case. Rather than merely focus on urban regeneration through the provision of new infrastructure and increase in city profile the Cape Town bid sought to be transformative in a social as well as economic sense. Therefore, the Cape Town bid introduced two innovative ideas into the role of hosting the Olympics. First, the Olympics would serve as a catalyst for improving the social and economic conditions of the historically disadvantaged. Second, they would act to redesign the apartheid city and create new linkages between people and cultures. The bid aimed to achieve these objectives through a number of measures (Hiller 2000):

- *A transformational catalyst accelerating change* – using the Olympics as a mechanism to effect immediate short-term change in the physical and social well-being of the city as well as longer-term impacts.

- *The construction of facilities in disadvantaged areas* – of the 42 activity sites for competitions in the Cape Town region, seven were planned for disadvantaged areas. However, 66 of the 77 proposed training sites were planned for disadvantaged areas, thereby creating a substantial permanent resource in those urban areas most substantially impacted by the legacy of apartheid.

- *Facilities as 'kick-start' initiatives* – the development of new facilities and the upgrading of some existing ones was seen as a mechanism for community revitalisation as part of a wider redevelopment strategy to attract new housing, retailing and investment to disadvantaged areas.

- *Quality sports facilities supporting community sports programmes* – sport and recreation provision was seen as a means of improving the quality of life as well as reducing crime and improving community pride.

- *A human resource opportunity* – it was projected that 90,000 permanent jobs would be created in South Africa as a result of hosting the Olympics.

- *Contribution to the stock of affordable housing* – it was expected that the Olympic developments, including the athletes and media accommodation, would make a small though significant contribution to the housing stock in Cape Town.

- *Support for small business* – the bid explicitly sought to assist small businesses through an economic empowerment policy which offered 50 per cent of its business transactions to enterprises from previously marginalised communities.

- *Urban integration of the transport system* – 70 per cent of the transport system development funds were earmarked for projects that would directly benefit disadvantaged areas by linking those areas more effectively into the wider urban structure.

- *Community consultation* – the Olympic bid group explicitly sought to involve the community in the bid process through a variety of mechanisms including local Olympic Steering Committees, a Community Olympic Forum, and a Strategic Environmental Assessment process.

As Hiller (2000: 455) noted, 'the idea of harnessing a mega-event to a broader urban agenda that moves beyond the interests of finance capital, developers, inner-city reclamation and the tourist city is a relatively new idea. This is especially so given the preoccupation with winning IOC [International Olympic Committee] votes internationally and the minimization of local costs and dissent'. However, it is notable that Cape Town did not win its bid (coming third in the final vote) and that, subsequently, South Africa missed out to Germany in a bid to host the 2006 World Cup Soccer. Therefore, the Cape

Town Bid Company's argument that in awarding the bid to Cape Town, the International Olympic Committee would have demonstrated that the Olympic Movement was not 'beholden to gigantism and commercial exploitation' and was instead 'devoted to the progress of all people and must therefore also offer opportunity to those still struggling for their place in the economic sun' (Olympic Bid Company 1996: 38 in Hiller 2000: 442) holds considerable weight in judging why mega-events are located where they are. Nevertheless, what is also significant in the Cape Town bid is that it demonstrated that the hosting of mega-events can be utilised as much as an oppositional strategy for the broader public good as it is a characteristic of the postmodern city where events are tied for the regeneration of city centres as places of consumption, entertainment and leisure (Hannigan 1995; see also Chapter 2). As Hiller (2000: 455) observed: 'When local people in the millions lack adequate housing, food and other subsistence needs, preparing for a "circus" when people need "bread" will always appear inappropriate. But the Cape Town bid raises some new options for consideration that could give mega-events new humanitarian urban value'.

The Cape Town bid, as with the earlier bid of Toronto for the 1996 Summer Olympics, also reflects the growing recognition that the hosting of mega-events, as perhaps with all large-scale urban regeneration projects, need to be perceived as part of a broader social contract in which public debate and argument are an exercise of social democracy and the development of public commitment (Kidd 1992). Indeed, as authors such as Cox (1998) and Olds (1998) have argued, there is a real need to connect the hosting of mega-events with human and social rights, particularly given that human rights conventions have a marked resemblance to the arrays of social indicators used in social impact assessment. For example, the Organisation for Economic Cooperation and Development's (OECD) list of social concerns on which their social indicator programme (OECD 1986) was developed includes:

- a healthy life;
- employment and quality of working life;
- personal economic situation;
- individual development through education;
- shelter and security of housing;
- personal safety and protection from crime;
- social opportunity and participation;
- pursuit of culture and leisure activities; and
- a satisfactory physical environment.

Indeed, as Cox (1998: 177) records, 'rather than being a separate assessment, human rights is one perspective of social assessment: it implies a reference to legal instruments as well as ethical principles in grounding and justifying impact management and mitigation measures'. That human rights and development could be grounded in urban regeneration strategies has been demonstrated by the Cape Town bid for the Olympics noted above. However, the history of using events as part of urban redevelopment is not a happy one with respect to human rights. As Cox (1998: 182) argues, 'the human rights dimension of hallmark events indicates a recurrent series of impacts on the homeless and other marginalised groups. The motivations behind hallmark events – to show off the city – directly result in the sanitising of public areas, through street sweeps, inappropriate use of legislation and arrest powers, or other means'.

The post-industrial urban environment associated with contemporary hallmark events often has a major impact on the lower socio-economic groups that occupy the inner-city areas which are usually those designated for renewal. Mega-events that involve substantial infrastructure development may have a considerable impact on housing and real-estate values, particularly with respect to their 'tendency to displace groups of citizens located in the poorer sections of cities' (Wilkinson 1994: 29). At worse, this tends to lead to a situation in which residents are forced to relocate because of their economic circumstances (Olds 1998). The creation of a 'desirable' middle-class environment invariably leads to increased rates and rents, and is accompanied by a corresponding breakdown in community structure, including ethnicity, as families and individuals are forced to relocate (C.M. Hall 1992). Moreover, the people who are often most impacted by hallmark events are those who are least able to form community groups and protect their interests. This tends to lead to a situation in which residents are forced to relocate because of their economic circumstances. For example, in the case of the 1986 Vancouver Expo, six hundred tenants were evicted (Olds 1989), including long-term, low-income residents from hotels near the Expo site (O'Hara 1986; White 1986). Similarly, the 1987 America's Cup and the 1988 Brisbane Expo also led to substantial resident dislocation (Day 1988; Hall 1989b, c).

In a study of the potential impacts of the Sydney Olympics on low-income housing, Cox *et al.* (1994) concluded that previous mega-events often had a detrimental effect on low-income people who are disadvantaged by a localised boom in rent and real-estate prices, thereby creating dislocation in extreme cases. The same rise in prices is considered beneficial to home owners and developers. Past events have also shown that this has led to public and private lower-cost housing developments being pushed out of preferred areas as a result of increased land and construction costs (e.g. Cox *et al.* 1994; Olds 1998). In the case of the Barcelona Games 'the market price of old and new housing rose between 1986 and 1992 by 240% and 287% respectively' (Brunet 1993 in Wilkinson 1994: 23). A further 59,000 residents left Barcelona to live elsewhere between the years of 1984 and 1992 (Brunet 1993 in Cox *et al.* 1994).

Housing impacts can also be substantial in smaller centres. In the case of the 1980 Lake Placid Winter Olympics, tenant eviction increased dramatically for the two months of the Games (January, February). 'The amount of evictions is not recorded but the fact that a citizens' rental coalition was formed gives some indication of the severity of the problem. Tenant turnover of rentals increased 20–30%, as many landlords rented to outside groups at high rental costs during the Games' (Wall and Guzzi 1987 in C.M. Hall 1992). However, the eviction of tenants due to the hosting of hallmark events is not isolated to the West. For example, the Asian Coalition for Housing Rights (1989: 92) noted that South Korea's preparations for the 1988 Olympic Games led to the 'rehabilitation' and 'beautification' of numerous areas of Seoul, whereby 'many communities were evicted from sites, simply because they were next to the path along which the Olympic torch was to be carried and the public authorities did not want these communities to be visible to the reporters and television cameras following the path of the torch'. According to Levinson (1993) this was done to ensure that Olympic guests to the city would not 'suffer the discomfort of seeing a single poor person in Seoul' (as quoted from an official Seoul Olympic publication).

In the United States the Olympic Games have also been related to civil and human rights abuse. In the Los Angeles Olympics of 1984, Levinson reports that homeless people were detained without charge for up to 22 hours and were arrested for jaywalking and other selectively enforced offences. Similarly, with respect to the 1996 Atlanta Olympics the Atlanta Task Force for the Homeless estimated that 'around 9,000 arrests of homeless persons occurred in the lead up to the Atlanta Games, with many arrests being without just cause and with police exceeding their authority in dealing with the homeless' (Cox 1998). Given the above discussion of the problematic manner in which mega-events may be integrated with urban regeneration projects it could be expected that lessons could be learned from the experience in order to ensure that the wider public good is being met. However, this rarely appears to be the case because of the predominance of growth coalitions and boosters in the urban redevelopment process.

In pro-growth ideologies, business interests are always equated with the well-being of the community as a whole (Judd and Collins 1979; Schimmel 1995), the assumption being that the benefits of urban regeneration programmes will trickle-down to the population as a whole. However, this assumption would appear to be substantially flawed. As Schimmel (1995) argued, economic growth associated with urban redevelopment strategies such as stadium development, may actually make life more difficult for low-income residents, and that many of the employment opportunities which are created will be of a low-paid, casual and part-time nature. Some of these issues are raised in the following case study of Toronto's bid to host the 2008 Olympic Games.

Toronto: 'the biggest and most costly mega-project in the history of Toronto'

Toronto's bid to host the 2008 Summer Olympic Games, as with its previously unsuccessful bid for the 1996 Games, is built on a waterfront redevelopment strategy which seeks to revitalise the harbour area through the development of

an integrated sports, leisure, retail and housing complex. One of the most strik-
ing features of the Toronto bid is the extent to which information on the bid is
either unavailable or provides only limited detail on the costs associated with
hosting the event. However, Toronto has been fortunate to have a non-profit
public interest coalition, Bread Not Circuses (BNC), actively campaigning for
more information on the bid proposal and for the municipal, provincial and
federal governments to address social concerns.

BNC argues that given the cost of both bidding for and hosting the
Olympics, the bidding process must be subject to public scrutiny. 'Any
Olympic bid worth its salt will not only withstand public scrutiny, but will be
improved by a rigorous and open public process' (Bread Not Circuses 1998a),
and also argued that Toronto City Council should make its support for an
Olympic bid conditional on the following:

- The development and execution of a suitable process that addresses financial, social and environmental concerns, ensures an effective public participation process (including intervenor funding), and includes a commitment
to the development of a detailed series of Olympic standards. A time-frame
of one year from the date of the vote to support the bid should be set to
ensure that the plans for the participation process are taken seriously.
- A full and open independent accounting of the financial costs of bidding
and staging the Games.
- A full and open independent social impact assessment of the Games.

The other key elements of a public participation process include:

- a full, fair and democratic process to involve all of the people of Toronto in
the development and review of the Olympic bid;
- an Olympic Intervenor Fund, similar to the fund established by the City of
Toronto in 1989, to allow interested groups to participate effectively in the
public scrutiny of the Toronto bid;
- an independent environmental assessment of the 2008 Games, and strategies should be developed to resolve specific concerns;
- the development of a series of financial, social and environmental standards
governing the 2008 Games, similar to the Toronto Olympic Commitment
adopted by City Council in September of 1989 (Bread Not Circuses 1998a).

In addition to the factors identified by BNC it should also be noted that the
city's previous experiences with stadiums and events raise substantial questions about the public liability for any development. For example, in 1982, the
then Metropolitan Toronto Chairman Paul Godfrey promised that Toronto's
SkyDome, a multipurpose sports complex used for baseball and Canadian
football could be built for Can.$75 million, with no public debt. However, the
final price of the development was over Can.$600 million, with taxpayers

having to pay more than half. BNC also noted that even the previous Toronto bid costs were 60 per cent over budget, 'with a great deal of spending coming in the final, overheated days of the bidding war leading up to the International Olympic Committee (IOC) Congress. There was no public control, and little public accountability, over the '96 bid', while 'There was virtually no assessment of the social, environmental and financial impact of the Games until Bread Not Circuses began to raise critical questions. By then, it was too late to influence the bid' (Bread Not Circuses 1998c).

BNC lobbied various city councillors in terms of their decision of whether or not to support a bid. However, only 1 councillor out of 55 voted against the Olympic bid proposal even though they had only a 20 page background document to the proposal in terms of information. When city councillors voted on the project, they did not have:

- an estimate of the cost of bidding for the Games;
- a list of the names of the backers of 'BidCo', the private corporation that is heading up the Olympic bid;
- a reliable estimate of the cost of staging the Games;
- a plan for the public participation process, the environmental review process or the social impact assessment process;
- a detailed financial strategy for the Games.

Such a situation clearly has public interest organisations, such as BNC, very worried as to the economic, environmental and social costs of a successful bid. Clearly, the history of mega-events such as the Olympic Games indicates that such a situation is not new (e.g. C.M. Hall 1992; Cox 1998; Olds 1998). The IOC has already sought to ensure that the Games are environmentally friendly. As Cox (1998) and Hiller (2000) have argued it would also be appropriate to ensure they meet a wider notion of the public good and build wider assessment of the social impacts of the Games into the planning process as a mandatory component of the Olympic bidding process. In this vein BNC, in a letter to the IOC President requested 'that the IOC, which sets the rules for the bidding process, take an active responsibility in ensuring that the local processes in the bidding stage are effective and democratic' and specifically address concerns regarding the 'financial and social costs of the Olympic Games' and proposed:

(1) an international network be created that includes COHRE, the HIC Housing Rights Subcommittee, academics, NGOs (including local groups in cities that have bid for and/or hosted the Games);

(2) a set of standards regarding forced evictions, etc., would be developed and adopted by the network;

(3) a plan to build international support for the standards, including identification of sympathetic IOC, NOC and other sports officials, would be developed and implemented;

(4) the IOC would be approached with the request that the standards be incorporated into the Olympic Charter, Host City Contracts and other documents of the IOC (Bread Not Circuses 1998b).

Such a social charter for the Olympics would undoubtedly greatly assist in making the Games more place-friendly and perhaps even improve the image of the IOC. However, even as the IOC visited Toronto in March 2001 to evaluate the city's bid, the Toronto bid had still not been opened for full public scrutiny. Neither had there been any adequate response to the proposal for creation of a set of social standards for the Olympics. Indeed, when IOC delegates tried to make the point that Toronto's homeless problem was a 'pre-existing condition' that ought not to be a factor in evaluating Toronto's bid for the 2008 Games, the activists from BNC 'argued that the inability of governments at all levels in Canada to solve the homeless problem should cause the IOC to question their ability to stage an undertaking such as the Olympics' (Campbell 2001: A22). Some would argue that the failure of the Toronto bid to win the rights to host the Olympics means that the problem has gone away. Yet this would be misleading. Instead the issues associated with the Toronto bid need to be seen within the ongoing role that urban growth coalitions play within urban regeneration strategies.

Continuous regeneration?

The revitalisation of urban places requires more than just the development of product and image. The re-creation of a sense of place is a process that involves the formulation of urban design strategies based on conceptual models of the city which are, in turn, founded on notions of civic life and the public realm and the idea of planning as debate and argument (Bianchini and Schwengel 1991). As Smyth (1994: 254) recognised

> This needs to be undertaken in a frank way and in a forum where different understandings can be shared, inducing mutual respect, leading to developing trust, and finally conceiving a development which meets mutual needs as well as stewarding resources for future generations . . . This proposes a serious challenge to the public sector as well as to the private sector, for authorities have undermined the well-being of their local populations by transferring money away from services to pay for flagship developments . . .

However, as Brand (1997, p.18) records, 'Slow is healthy. Much of the wholesome evolution of cities can be explained by the steadfast persistence of Site'. The pattern of ownership of land and property is extremely important for the way in which places change. Small lots allow for ongoing fine change as

Plate 9.4   In creating a number of internationally renowned icons, such as Singapore's Raffles Hotel in its refurbished state, a major attraction and visitor drawcard has been created in the urban environs

opposed to the sudden wholesale change that can occur with large parcels of land. The more owners, the more gradual and adaptive will be the change.

> Small lots will support resilience because they allow many people to attend directly to their needs by designing, building and maintaining their own environment. By ensuring that property remains in many hands, small lots bring important results: many people make many different decisions, thereby ensuring variety in the resulting environment. And many property owners slow down the rate of change by making large-scale real estate transactions difficult (Moudon 1986:188).

Such an observation has many significant implications for the way in which tourism development is managed, particularly in urban areas (Plates 9.4 and 9.5). Appropriate tourism development may well mean relatively gradual small-scale change with the inclusion of large numbers of stakeholders as opposed to large-scale developments with limited numbers of 'owners' of the project. The large-scale project may well be a grand gesture that politicians and boosters support by virtue that they are seen to be 'doing something'. The more unspectacular gradual change is likely to be more sustainable. For example, in the case of Vancouver in British Columbia, Canada, the gradual redevelopment

Plate 9.5   The Singapore river environment illustrates how a leisure environment can be juxtaposed with the business environment, which is transformed in the evening into a major food and entertainment district

of Granville Island as a mixed use area which maintained associations with traditional waterfront businesses, e.g. chandlers, boat repairs and moorings, as well as providing for new uses such as a hotel, markets, bookshops and theatres, has proven to be a far more sustainable development than the large-scale development of other parts of the former dock area through the hosting of the 1986 Expo. Over a decade later many parts of the former Expo site were still undeveloped.

Unfortunately, such ideas have only limited visibility within the place-marketing and imaging realms as tourism and place planning is often poorly conceptualised with respect to participatory procedures. The institutional arrangements for many of the so-called partnerships for urban redevelopment actually exclude community participation in decision-making procedures while also seeking to achieve a 'quick fix' solution for complex urban problems. Indeed, one of the most significant aspects of large-scale urban regeneration strategies, such as mega-events and waterfront redevelopment, is that they exclude participation from urban social democracy while at the same time requiring such large public investments that if they do not work as revitalisation strategies then their actual and opportunity costs are substantially modified. Reflecting Law's (1993: 23) observation, 'Urban policies are concerned with both winning economic growth for a city and regenerating the core areas, goals which may not always be coincident'.

Significantly, Harvey (1993, 2000) noted that resistance by members of some communities has not checked the overall process of place competition. A mixture of coercion and co-optation centred around maintenance of real-estate values, assumptions regarding employment and investment generation, and an assumption that growth is automatically good, has led to the creation of local growth coalitions in many communities. 'Coercion arises either through inter-place competition for capital investment and employment (accede to the cap-italist's demands or go out of business; create a "good business climate" or lose jobs) or more simply, through the direct political repression and oppression of dissident voices, from cutting off media access to the more violent tactics of the construction mafias in many of the world's cities' (Harvey 1993: 9).

Whether it be in the developed world or in the less-developed countries tourism development has tended to be dominated by sectional interests and by an institutional ideology that inherently represents tourism as a 'good' form of economic development. As has been argued above, such a process is inherently political. As Harvey (1993: 8) asked, 'The question immediately arises as to why people accede to the construction of their places by such a process'. In many cases they, of course, do not: communities may resist the change inher-ent in tourism development. For example, 'political battles between residents and specially created redevelopment authorities have punctuated the urban renewal of Australian waterfronts' (Kelly and McConville 1991: 91). However, while short-term opposition did save the physical fabric of many Australian inner-city communities, it is worthwhile noting that the social fabric has been changed through gentrification and touristification of many areas, leaving only heritage facades. Surely a community is more than a collection of buildings? This is an issue to which we turn in the final chapter.

Questions

1. To what extent is it possible to distinguish between different forms of regeneration?

2. Why is the regeneration such a common issue in cities in developed countries?

3. How do mega-events affect urban regeneration strategies?

Further reading

A useful journal article on urban regeneration and its relationship to events is
Whitson, D. and Macintosh, D. (1996). 'The global circus: international sport, tourism, and the marketing of cities', *Journal of Sport and Social Issues* 23: 278–95.

Two edited books provide some interesting case studies on issues surrounding regeneration:

Judd, D. and Fainstein, S. (eds) (1999). *The Tourist City*, New Haven: Yale University Press.

Tyler, D., Guerrier, Y. and Robertson, M. (eds) (1998). *Managing Tourism in Cities: Policy, Process and Practice*, Chichester: Wiley.

The website of the Department of Transport, Local Government and Regions provides access to British research and government policy on urban regeneration http://www.regeneration.detr.gov.uk/index.htm

CHAPTER 10

The future of urban tourism

Introduction

In the twenty-first century urban places have become increasingly valued as places of consumption, requiring an emphasis on the physical and cultural aesthetics and qualities of the urban landscape. What the urban environment exhibits is both continuity in the nature of the place as a containing context for tourism and leisure activities, but also change in the nature of the product offering and what is consumed. Cities are not a new phenomenon for tourism and leisure consumption. Their very essence throughout history has been focused on productive activities, supported by service functions such as tourism and leisure. What is now evident is that many of the precursors of urban development – the productive activities (i.e. markets in towns based on exchange and trade) and the impact of industrialisation – have waned and tourism and leisure have replaced them as the economic rationale or a substantial element of what makes the place exist economically, socially and culturally. As a consequence, towns and cities have adapted, as they have throughout their specific histories (e.g. Canterbury, UK; Page 1992), to develop new rationales which help them retain their urban function. In a more theoretical context, this has manifest itself, as this book has discussed, through re-imaging and place-marketing strategies: places have sought to utilise tourism and leisure as a component of assigning symbolic and aesthetic value to urban areas, often in terms of their heritage or urban regeneration. In the highly changing global environment, places reposition themselves, their offerings and their appeal to business and visitors alike. While the emergence of tourism and leisure is not a new phenomenon in towns and cities, the influence of globalisation and the power of visitor spending is now more embracing than in the past (Plate 10.1). The outcome is that many towns and cities now have tourism strategies, cultural industries strategies and a public awareness of the tourism and leisure phenomenon. As a consequence, representations and redevelopment of

Plate 10.1   With globalisation now a pervasive element in the urban environment, particularly in consumptive activities, this Starbucks Coffee shop in Auckland's downtown location could conceivably be in any city in the world as a global brand

place have therefore become a key component of local and even national economic development strategies in order to attract investment, migration and capital, as well as generating increased tourism activity. For example, in relation to such concepts as the development of 'creative cities':

> The creative city is an ambitious agenda. It should be. Three-quarters of the European population live in urban areas, much of which is blighted, in both image and reality, by poverty, poor ł degradation. The need for cities to – many cities are anachronistic gi industrial past and urgent action is n of this new economy is based upon and 'knowledge economy' and some industries have a key role to play in t

However, as writers such as Britto the specificity of places cannot be processes involved in the production of tourism within urban areas need and local forces, which both affect a urban.

The enlarge
emerging tech
increasing mobil
that urbanites will
spatial patterns of the
disparate, less and less tie

are no
in
commer

Perhaps most significant of these forces is the role of economic and cultural globalisation in substantially affecting not only the value of urban cores and industrial and inner-city space, but its influence on contemporary lifestyles and the desirability of urban areas. In addition, globalisation provides the context for place competition and hence place-marketing in order to attract economic and cultural capital as well as the tourist. Undoubtedly, globalisation will continue to be a dominant force in shaping the patterns and flows of urban tourism for the foreseeable future (Know 1997). However, the exact nature of its effect on urban tourism is still to be fully clarified. Globalisation is a complex, chaotic, multiscalar, multitemporal and multicentric series of processes operating in specific structural and spatial contexts (Jessop 1999). Globalisation should be seen as an emergent, evolutionary phenomenon that results from economic, political, socio-cultural and technological processes on many scales rather than a distinctive causal mechanism in its own right. Indeed, 'a key element in contemporary processes of globalisation is not the impact of "global" processes upon another clearly defined scale, but instead the relativisation of scale' (Kelly and Olds 1999: 2). Such relativities occur in relation to both 'space–time distantiation' and 'space–time compression'. The former refers to the stretching of social relations over time and space, e.g. through the utilisation of new technology such as the Internet, so that they can be coordinated or controlled over longer periods of time, greater distances, larger areas and on more scales of activity. The latter involves the intensification of 'discrete' events in real time and/or increased velocity of material and non-material flows over a given distance, again this is related to technological change, including communication technologies, and social technologies (Jessop 1999). Such observations are important because at the same time that there operate forces for the deconcentration of metropolitan areas, other counterveiling elements continue to maintain urban cores. Such debates have been well anticipated.

The coming of the 'nonplace urban realm'

Webber (1963, 1964) argued for the coming of the 'nonplace urban realm'. Nonplace urban realms are communities with shared activities and exchange of formation which are analogous to urban regions but are not the same, as they t spatially determined. Instead, they are determined by interaction. As he ted:

d freedom to communicate outside one's place community that the ological and institutional changes promise, coupled with an ever-ty and ever-greater degrees of specialization, will certainly mean eal with each other over greater and greater distances. The interactions with others will undoubtedly be increasingly d to the place in which they reside or work, less and less marked by the unifocal patterns that marked cities in an earlier day (Webber 1964: 146).

Webber's observation certainly strikes a present-day chord in light of the debates over the influence of communications technology, such as the Internet, on cities and their relationship to new urban forms such as the 'Edge City' (Garreau 1991), or to new nodes in what used to be regarded as the rural periphery (Müller 1999). However, urban cores still remain significant for activities that require social or face-to-face contact and, as Peter Hall (1996: 12) recognised, 'if anything these are growing in importance: they include not merely financial and business services, but the increasingly important service sectors of education, culture, entertainment, and the media. As Webber himself pointed out, these tend to be highly localized in a few urban cores, because of agglomeration economies'. Tourism can also be added to the list of such service sectors, particularly because of its overlap with the service sectors which Peter Hall described above, but also because:

> There is also a huge range of jobs, involving varied levels of skills, performing personal services in restaurants and hotels and transport, which serve the new informational economy and which also remain locked in the cities where that economy is located. This is the new international division of labour, and as usual it combines some elements of geographical agglomeration and some of geographical diffusion (P. Hall 1996: 13)

Fascinatingly, the attractiveness of urban areas to tourists becomes not just a contributor to increased temporary mobility but also a means to reinforce the centrality of urban nodes – albeit in substantial competition (as noted in Chapter 9). In order to attract investment cities seek to reinvent themselves. For example, Totally Wellington, the city council funded body charged with promoting tourism, asserts that an 'intense inner-city experience' is critical for urban tourism development (Coventry 2000: 66). This assumes not only a practical dimension, since visitor activities and their search space often begin with inner-city or downtown locales (Page 1989a, 1991; Lawton and Page 1997). But more importantly, it is the differentiating feature of the experience that enables the globalised to retain its localised elements in an environment of substantial competition for the urban visitor spend. It is not surprising that the 1980s and 1990s witnessed a number of massive inner-city redevelopment schemes globally, at a time of economic restructuring and employment loss: tourism and leisure functions have, in some successful cases, filled these empty, redundant and historic spaces.

Zukin (1998: 832) notes that the fastest growing metropolitan areas in the United States, Las Vegas, Nevada and Orlando, are also 'major tourist destinations', a point also taken up in Hannigan's (1998) notion of the 'Fantasy City' (see Chapter 2). Therefore, the desire of urban regimes to retain the centrality of their cities in an interconnected world serves only to reinforce the role that tourism plays in the urban environment. As much of this book has demonstrated, the attraction of the city for tourists is the possibility for enhanced interaction for a given period of time. If you want to minimise interaction you go to a wilderness area or to rural areas, if you want to maximise interaction you go to the city. As Schneider (1963: 318) commented, 'enjoying the crowds, the satisfaction of "being there", feeling oneself a part of that power complex which is called city . . . all that is the attraction of the city'. A point borne out, for example, in a survey of why visitors travelled to Toronto in Canada for leisure (Table 10.1) (David-Peterson Associates 1992) (see also Jansen-Verbeke and Lievois 1999 and Chapters 3 and 5). Tourism is therefore being both impacted by and is impacting upon the nature of the city. The future of the urban tourism must therefore be seen in the context of interaction and the implications that this has for urban places. As Webber (1964: 147) argued, 'it is interaction, not place, that is the essence of the city and city life'.

Indeed, one of the interesting by-products in considering the development of nonplace realms is the extent to which some urban and rural places have become closely bound through the capacity of some individuals to have multiple homes, often with one in the city and a second home (or more) in an area with high amenity values. P. Hall (1996: 12) suggests the development of increasingly polycentric urban systems: 'More and more people are residing for all or part of the week in these peripheral locations, further increasing the probability that they will bypass the cores altogether on some or all days each week'. The pattern of second home ownership therefore needs to be seen in relation to the links between rural and metropolitan areas and the lifestyles of the owners. Second homes provide a complement to the owners' urban everyday life and therefore, comfortable accessibility is crucial. Hence, second homes are often located within the metropolitan areas' leisure peripheries, allowing frequent visits and ease of access in both directions. Urban growth and the restructuring of the economy thereby influence second home location by pushing the recreational zone further from the urban areas and at the same time creating new second home areas. The relative attraction of which will be

Table 10.1   Reasons for leisure travel to Toronto

• experiencing the city/atmosphere	• lots to see and do/variety
• sight-seeing	• architecture/buildings
• culture in general	• theatre/musical performances
• arts	• museums
• food/varied dining/restaurants	• history
• education	• shopping
• sports events	• nightlife/dancing
• big events/festivals	• new people to see and meet
• diversity of people	• gambling

Source: derived from David-Peterson Associates Inc. (1992).

a function of accessibility, property prices and amenity landscape (Lündgren 1974; Müller 1999).

Such 'networks of places' invariably generate circulation flows. These new forms of mobility both constitute and are the results of globalisation (Held 2000) which, as now widely acknowledged, serve to enhance rather than diminish place differences. The places locked together by these new forms of mobility are not, of course, the outcome of a random spatial lottery but are those with particular place features, whether these be amenity- or interaction-based. Moreover, places may actively promote themselves in the global marketplace on the bases of these new forms of mobility. However, as Williams and Hall (2000, 2002) argue, data constraints, together with a weak theoretical base in the face of the need for an holistic approach, have contributed to the overall lack of research on circulation and temporary mobility related to tourism.

Given that interaction and interconnection are now recognised as being so important for contemporary economy and society, the fundamental issue faced by urban tourism managers is then how to create the nodes that facilitate such interaction. Many governments have sought to create or recreate such interaction through regeneration strategies. As Judd (1995: 75) recorded, 'In their attempts to attract tourists, cities have been aggressively reconstructing their physical environment'. Yet, as the previous chapter indicated, architectural regeneration, while making some urban spaces attractive to the wealthier elements of society, fails to deal with the social issues of regeneration and instead displaces problems. Displacement was both a controversial feature of regeneration and a component of contested landscapes for tourists, embodied in the 1980s in London Docklands with vivid graffiti as a means of local expression in the absence of democratic mechanisms to question the fundamental question in urban redevelopment schemes: who benefits? (Page 1987, 1988a, b; Page and Fidgeon 1988; Page 1989a, b). This is vividly conveyed in the tourism and leisure landscapes arising from investment in consumptive activities, where massive socio-economic contrasts exist juxtaposed to each other. As Chatterton (2001) discusses in relation to the notion of the creative city

> In many ways, the creative city is a rhetorical device which can placate the hearts and minds of local councillors and politicians that they are actually doing something whilst doing hardly anything at all. In many ways, to be creative is simply to do something in a new way and rather than being strategic, then, the agenda is opportunistic. The toolkit which is offered is laden with buzz words: 'innovation matrix', 'holism', and 'creative lifecycles'. The danger is that prevailing structures of power remain intact and cities are successfully rebranded and rewritten to wash over persistent problems. Experiences of Glasgow and Manchester and increasingly Newcastle testify to this.

Even where towns and cities have identified the market and future for their locality based on tourism (e.g. Dover in the UK – see Page and Piotrowski 1991 for a discussion of these points), these issues have become politicised when short-term failures in attraction development have arisen. This has contributed to debates on the efficacy of tourism-led urban regeneration schemes where a cluster of activity and development has not achieved the scale of growth envisaged in feasibility studies that predate the development.

As Meethan (1997: 341) observed, 'power over place is exercised through the ability of interest groups to impose or appropriate a vision of the city'. In the current set of values within which urban tourism operates, social and environmental goals take second place to those of economic growth, or are at least termed in relation to their potential to contribute to economic development. Although tourism may appear to be an 'obvious' solution to problems of urban development, it is not without its negative impacts on at least some of the people who live in the tourist city. Arguably this is because the focus has been on the physical infrastructure of tourism in terms of attractions, convention centres, museums and waterfront developments rather than the social infrastructure of tourism and the wider urban society. The problems have therefore been defined in terms of space rather than the more inclusive notion of place. Interestingly, some of the original work undertaken on the use of tourism as a means to regenerate areas associated with industrial and manufacturing decline, such as Bradford, Glasgow and Manchester, was posited as 'tourism in difficult areas' (Buckley and Witt 1985, 1989). This is possibly interpreted as meaning 'unattractive to the middle class'. In these projects the primary attention was being given to the development of new spaces of consumption and the attraction of the middle class in the belief that it would 'trickle down' or 'enlarge the size of the economic pie' rather than directly reskilling and assisting those workers and their families most impacted by structural economic change (Kearns and Philo 1993). The development of new spaces for the middle class – whether to live or visit – therefore often constitutes a planned intervention in order to gentrify parts of the city: 'a process of the middle class replacing the working class; increasing property values; alteration in the built environment and the emergence of a new urban style of life' (Savage and Warde 1993: 80). The importance of the development of such lifestyles has been profound for tourism (Meethan 1996, 2001). As Zukin (1998: 825) recognised, gentrification, the development of spaces for consumption and new urban lifestyles and identities are inextricably linked to 'new patterns of leisure, travel and culture'. Indeed, many urban areas have evolved into 'centres of consumption' (Rowe and Stevenson 1994: 180).

The problem that urban managers and researchers face is clear.

Any fundamental change in the use of space within the urban arena is bound to impact on the daily lives of the inhabitants, opening up the possibility of social exclusion through producing a city vision that caters for outside or sectional interests only. Selling change must therefore be directed towards the population as a whole as much as to any interest group, for policies that focus on the centre – in terms of both location and influence – run the risk of creating a socially and economically isolated periphery (Meethan 1997: 341).

Yet such changes in space, place and identity are not uncontested. Local claims to uniqueness are an expression of the current political and social relationships that are in place in a community. The construction of selective histories of the past are based on ideas of the present that are linked to articulations of identity at both the local and the national levels (C.M. Hall 1997; Thorns 1997). Therefore, local senses of place, as constructed in place-promotion imagery, are constantly reviewed and reflected in changing social relationships in urban places and through time (Schollmann *et al.* 2000). For example, Singapore's Little India historic district is such a contested landscape, particularly between insider and outsider groups. The relationship between insiders and outsiders takes a number of forms including the relationship between tourists and locals, ethnic tensions between the Indian and the Chinese communities, and the relationship between planners and users of the area. Different people have different levels of attachment to place (Chang 2000).

The central concerns of politics and power are sometimes apparent in tourism at the community level, but more often they are not. Ideology and power relations are inscribed not only in space through the uneven development of the qualities of places (Lefebvre, 1991; Harvey 1993, 2000; C.M. Hall 2000), but also through their representation. This is particularly so in relation to tourism promotion and imaging and heritage. As Norkunas (1993: 97) described with respect to heritage tourism in Monterey:

> The ruling class carefully controls the form and content of historical re-creations and tourist landscapes, legitimizing itself by projecting its own contemporary sociocultural values upon the past. This struggle, the tension between groups with power and groups with varying but lesser degrees of power, is replayed in the many spheres in which the public enactment of identity is staged. The erection or non-erection of statuary is a physical manifestation of that tension; nostalgic reinterpretations of socially condemnatory fiction, which results in a humorous caricature of poverty is yet another manifestation of this struggle. Dominance is expressed not in terms of physical coercion but as rhetoric.

Will things change?

In the era of globalisation greater interconnections exist within and between each level of the state. Local states, particularly with an urban base, are now international actors in tourism not only in terms of their advertising and promotional campaigns to attract tourists but also in terms of their attempts to attract investment and events. The restructuring of the institutional arrangements for tourism at the local state level is an essential element in such reimaging strategies (Roche 1992, 1994, 2000; C.M. Hall 1994, 2000) (Chapter 8). Cultural policies and tourism policies are becoming almost inextricably entwined, while funding for the arts, culture, sports and recreation and amenity

Plate 10.2   What is the future for a small town such as Paihai in the Bay of Islands, Northland, New Zealand in an increasingly globalised society? Its future will depend not only upon good access to the major gateway – Auckland – but being interconnected with the rest of the world through technology and a differentiated product that is based on the global–local nexus

improvements are usually justified primarily in terms of the contribution they will make in economic attractiveness via tourism rather than their social contribution to all the inhabitants of a region (Plates 10.2 and 10.3). In this light the institutional arrangements for tourism are perhaps best understood as instrumental arrangements of the local state which serve a narrow range of global and local interests, what may otherwise be described as 'urban regimes' (Harvey 1989b; Hall and Hubbard 1998; Painter 2000).

A marked change is therefore needed in the way in which cities involve themselves in tourism. Public tourism policy and planning have traditionally been fragmented with a top-down bias whereby governments or agencies, often in partnership with the private sector, promote and develop tourist destinations. There is increasing emphasis by government at all levels on the supremacy of the market, state involvement through public–private partnerships, reduced budget deficits, international trade expansion (especially in growth industries such as tourism), employment growth and lower levels of direct central government intervention; local communities (including their locally elected representatives, namely, local government) will be left to ponder what might or should be and how to get there (Jenkins and Hall 1997).

Plate 10.3 What is the future for small historic cities such as Canterbury, England that have had to implement visitor management measures at its major attraction – the Cathedral?

The local state, as the immediate and critical receptor for local development plans and development on behalf of its constituents, will be required to conduct its functions in increasingly dynamic environments and perhaps with less direct assistance from higher levels of government, but at the same time being strongly urged by central government and other interests to take up tourism opportunities, especially opportunities associated with large-scale developments or events. However, the decision-making process for local communities can be confusing. It is therefore difficult to see how tourism-specific policies, and especially those of small, under-resourced local governments:

> . . . can counter processes in which place prosperity is largely determined by exogenous events like changing lifestyle preferences, infrastructure investment,

technological innovation, currency movements (a major factor affecting farm profitability and the flow of overseas tourists), interest rates, taxation, the length of the working week, labour costs, and so on (Sorenson 1990: 59).

The interactional world in which we live has enormous consequences. While some of us, the authors included, have the means and capacity to operate in such a world, many do not. We see this in 'the emergence of wide zones of structural decline and physical decay and social malaise between the traditional centre and outlying nodes. These are the areas that have failed to make the transition, so far, to the new international economy . . . with tragic consequences . . . the people the Americans have called the urban underclass and the French now refer to as *les exclus* – the excluded' (P. Hall 1996: 14). Urban tourism management is therefore not just about attracting tourists but also making sure the benefits of tourism are maximised for the wider population and not just a select few who share the new urban lifestyles. While it may sound clichéd, tourism must be regarded as a means to an end. The most appropriate policy and institutional response to the global environment will be one that sees tourism as part of an integrated inclusive development strategy, rather than as a single end in itself. The central problem of urban tourism, just as Clawson (1971) observed about American suburbia, is not the phenomenon, since most people like it, but the fact that some of them cannot join in the fun.

Questions

1. What is a nonplace urban realm?
2. To what extent is it true to say that the development of second homes in rural areas is an urban phenomenon?
3. How has globalisation influenced the development of entrepreneurial cities?
4. Is the attraction of the city for tourists the possibility of enhanced interaction?

Further reading

Although not specifically urban in focus for contemporary discussions on issues of circulation and mobility and their relationship to tourism see
Meethan, K. (2001). *Tourism in Global Society: Place, Culture, Consumption*, Basingstoke: Palgrave
and
Hall, C.M. and Williams, A.M. (eds) (2002). *Tourism and Migration: New Relationships Between Consumption and Production*, Dodtrecht: Kluwer.
On the entrepreneurial city see
Hall, T. and Hubbard, P. (eds) (1998). *The Entrepreneurial City*, Chichester: Wiley.

Bibliography

Abrahamson, M. (1996). *Urban Enclaves: Identity and Place in America*, New York: St. Martin's Press.

Adler, S. and Brenner, J. (1992). 'Gender and space: lesbians and gay men in the city', *International Journal of Urban and Regional Research* 16: 24–34.

Allcock, J. (1994). 'Seasonality', in S. Witt and L. Mountinho (eds) *Tourism Marketing and Management Handbook*, 2nd edn, Hemel Hempstead: Prentice Hall, 86–92.

Altshuler, A. (1965a). *The City Planning Process: A Political Analysis*, Ithaca, New York: Cornell University Press.

Altshuler, A. (1965b). 'The goal of comprehensive planning', *Journal of the American Institute of Planners* 31(3): 186–97.

Andrew, C. and Taylor, J. (2000). 'Capital cities, special cities: how to ensure their successful development', *Plan Canada* 40(3): 38–39.

Anon. (1994). *The Impacts of Tourism in Devonport: A Study Identifying Environmental, Economic and Social Impacts of Tourism in Devonport*, report prepared for the Devonport Community Board, Auckland: Massey University, Albany.

Ap, J. (1990). 'Residents' perception research on the social impacts of tourism', *Journal of Travel Research* 32(1): 47–50.

Ap, J. and Crompton, J. (1993). 'Residents' strategies for responding to tourism impacts', *Journal of Travel Research* 32(1): 47–50.

Arbel, A. and Pizam, A. (1977). 'Some determinants of hotel location: the tourists inclination', *Journal of Travel Research* 15(Winter): 18–22.

Arce, A. and Marsden, T. (1993). 'The social construction of international food: a new research agenda', *Economic Geography* 69(3): 293–311.

Archer, B. (1982). 'The value of multipliers and their policy implications', *Tourism Management* 3: 236–41.

Archer, B. (1987). 'Demand forecasting and estimating on', in J.R.B. Ritchie and C.R. Goeldner (eds) *Travel, Tourism and Hospitality Research: A Handbook for Managers*, New York: Wiley, 77–85.

Archer, B. and Fletcher, J. (1996). 'The economic impact of tourism in the Seychelles', *Annals of Tourism Research* 23: 32–47.

Ashworth, G.J. (1987). 'Marketing the historic city: the selling of Norwich', in R.C. Riley (ed.) *Urban Conversation: International Comparisons*, Occasional Paper No. 7, Portsmouth: Department of Geography, Portsmouth University, 51–67.

Ashworth, G.J. (1989). 'Urban tourism: an imbalance in attention', in C.P. Cooper (ed.) *Progress in Tourism, Recreation and Hospitality Management* Volume 1, London: Belhaven, 33–54.

Ashworth, G.J. (1992a). 'Is there an urban tourism?', *Tourism Recreation Research* 17(2): 3–8.

Ashworth, G.J. (1992b). 'Planning for sustainable tourism: a review article', *Town Planning Review*, 63(3): 325–9.

Ashworth, G.J. (1993). 'Culture and tourism, conflict or symbiosis in Europe?', in W. Pompl and D. Lavery (eds) *Tourism in Europe*, London: Mansell, 13–35.

Ashworth, G.J. and de Haan, T.Z. (1986). 'Uses and users of the tourist-historic city', *Field Studies* 10, Groningen: Faculty of Spatial Sciences.

Ashworth, G.J. and Tunbridge, J.E. (1990). *The Tourist-Historic City*, London: Belhaven.

Ashworth, G.J. and Tunbridge, J.E. (2000). *The Tourist-historic City: Retrospect and Prospect of Managing the Heritage City*, Oxford: Pergamon.

Ashworth, G.J. and Voogd, H. (1987). 'Geografische marketing, een brunikbare invalshoek voor onderzoek en planning', *Stedebouw and Volkhuisvesting* 3: 85–90.

Ashworth, G.J. and Voogd, H. (1988). 'Marketing the city: concepts, processes and Dutch applications', *Town Planning Review* 59(1): 65–80.

Ashworth, G.J. and Voogd, H. (1990a). *Selling the City: Marketing Approaches in Public Sector Urban Planning*, London: Belhaven Press.

Ashworth, G.J. and Voogd, H. (1990b). 'Can places be sold for tourism?' in G.J. Ashworth and B. Goodall (eds) *Marketing Tourism Places*, London: Routledge, 1–16.

Ashworth, G.J., White, P.E. and Winchester, H. (1988). 'The redlight district of the West European city: a neglected aspect of the urban landscape', *Geoforum* 19: 201–12.

Asian Coalition for Housing Rights (1989). 'Evictions in Seoul, South Korea', *Environment and Urbanization* 1: 89–94.

Asian Development Bank (1998). *The Development and Management of Asian Megacities*, Manila: Asian Development Bank.

Askew, M. (1998). 'City of women, city of foreign men: working spaces and re-working identities among female sex workers in Bangkok's tourist zone, Singapore', *Journal of Tropical Geography* 19(2): 130–50.

Astroff, M.T. and Abbey, J.R. (1995). *Convention Sales and Services*, 4th edn, Cranbury: Waterbury Press.

Australia Council (2000a). *Australians and the Arts*, Surry Hills: Australia Council for the Arts & Saatchi and Saatchi.

Australia Council (2000b). *The Arts in Australia – Some Statistics*, Surry Hills: Australia Council for the Arts, http://www.ozco.gov.au/resources/snapshots/statistics.html

Australian Capital Territory Tourism Commission (1993). *1992–93 Annual Report*, Canberra: Chief Minister's Department.

Austria National Tourism Office (2000). Vienna Gloriosa, http://www.anto.com/vienna.html, accessed 14 December 2000.

Baade, R.A. (1996). 'Professional sports as catalysts for metropolitan economic development', *Journal of Urban Affairs* 18(1): 1–17.

Baim, D.V. (1994). *The Sports Stadium as a Municipal Investment*, Westport: Greenwood Press.

Bale, J. (1989). *Sport and Place*, London: E and F N Spon.

Barker, M. (2000). *An Empirical Investigation of Tourist Crime in New Zealand: Perceptions, Victimisation and Future Implications*, unpublished Ph.D. thesis, Dunedin: University of Otago.

Barker, M., Page, S.J. and Meyer, D. (2002). 'Evaluating the impact of the 2000 America's Cup on Auckland, New Zealand', *Event Management* 7(2): 79–92.

Barnes, C. (1988). 'Bureaux – the marketing professionals', in J. Blackwell (ed.) *The Tourism and Hospitality Industry*, Sydney: International Magazine Services, 245–50.

BarOn, R. (1975). *Seasonality in Tourism*, London: Economist Intelligence Unit.

BarOn, R. (1999). *The Measurement of Seasonality and Its Economic Impacts*, World Tourism Organization Conference on the Measurement and Economic Impact of Tourism, Nice, June.

Barrett, J.A. (1958). *The Seaside Resort Towns of England and Wales*, unpublished Ph.D. thesis, London: University of London.

Barrett, S. and Fudge, C. (1981). *Policy and Action*, London: Methuen.

Baudrillard, J. (1988). 'Consumer culture', in M. Poster (ed.) *Jean Baudrillard: Selected Writings*, Cambridge: Polity Press.

Baum, T. and Lundtorp, S. (eds) (2001). *Seasonality in Tourism: An Exploration of Issues*, Oxford: Pergamon Press.

Beer, A. (1995). 'Regional cities in Australia's changing urban system', *Geographica Polonica* 66: 33–49.

Beggs, Z. (1999). 'Lesbian and gay rights: is Mardi Gras enough?', *Green Left Weekly* 24 February.

Bell, D. and Valentine, G. (1997). *Consuming Geographies: We Are Where We Eat*, London: Routledge.

Bentley, T., Meyer, D., Page, S.J. and Chalmers, D. (2001). 'Recreational tourism injuries among visitors to New Zealand: an exploratory analysis using hospital discharge data', *Tourism Management* 22(4): 373–81.

Bianchini, F. (1995). 'Night cultures, night economies', *Planning Practice and Research* 10: 121–6.

Bianchini, F. and Schwengel, H. (1991). 'Re-imagining the city', in J. Corner and S. Harvey (eds) *Enterprise and Heritage: Crosscurrents of National Culture*, London: Routledge, 212–34.

Bitner, M.J., Booms, B. and Tetrant, M. (1990). 'The service encounter: diagnosing favourable and unfavourable incidents', *Journal of Marketing* 71–84.

Bjorklund, E.M. and Philbrick, A.K. (1975). 'Spatial configuration of mental processes', in M. Belanger and D.G. Janelle (eds) *Building Regions for the Future, Notes et Documents de Documents du Recherche No. 6*, Quebec: Department de Geographie, Universite Laual, 57–75.

Blank, U. and Petkovich, M. (1987). 'Research on urban tourism destinations', in J.R.B. Ritchie and C.R. Goeldner (eds) *Travel, Tourism and Hospitality Research: A Handbook for Managers*, New York: Wiley, 165–77.

Blowers, A. (1997). 'Environmental planning for sustainable development: the international context', in A. Blowers and B. Evans (eds) *Town Planning Into the 21st Century*, London: Routledge, 34–53.

Bocock, R. (1993). *Consumption*, London: Routledge.

Boniface, P. (1995). *Managing Quality Cultural Tourism*, London: Routledge.

Bordieu, P. (1984). *Distinction*, London: Kegan and Paul.

Bradley, S. (2000). 'Mr Howard goes to Sydney – is it goodbye Canberra?', *The Age* 11 December.

Braitman, B. (2000). 'Regina: division and reintegration', *Plan Canada* 40(3): 31–2.

Bramwell, B. (1998). 'User satisfaction and product development in urban tourism', *Tourism Management* 19(1): 35–48.

Bramwell, B. and Lane, B. (eds) (2000). *Tourism Collaboration and Partnerships: Politics, Practice and Sustainability*, Clevedon: Channel View Publications.

Bramwell, B. and Rawding, L. (1996). 'Tourism marketing images of industrial cities', *Annals of Tourism Research* 23(2): 201–21.

Brand, S. (1997). *How Buildings Learn: What Happens After They're Built*, London: Phoenix Illustrated.

Braumann, V. and Stadel, C. (1999). 'Boom town in transition? Development process and urban structure of Ushuaia, Tierra des Fuego, Argentina', *Conference of Latin Americanist Geographers Yearbook* 25: 33–44.

Bread Not Circuses (1998a). *Bread Alert!* (E-mail edition) 2(2) 20 February.

Bread Not Circuses (1998b). *Bread Alert!* (E-mail edition) 2(3) 26 February.

Bread Not Circuses (1998c). *Bread Alert!* (E-mail edition) 2(8) 8 April.

Bread Not Circuses (1999). *The REAL Olympic Scandal: The Financial and Social Costs of the Games*, Media Advisory, 17 March.

Briassoulis, H. (1991). 'Methodological issues: tourism input–output analysis', *Annals of Tourism Research* 18: 485–95.

British Columbia Provincial Capital Commission (2000). http://www.bcpcc.com/index.html, accessed 15 December.

British Tourist Authority (1993). *Guidelines for Tourism to Britain 1993–97*, London: British Tourist Authority.

Britton, S. (1991). 'Tourism, capital and place: towards a critical geography of tourism', *Environment and Planning D: Society and Space* 9: 451–78.

Brokensha, P. and Guldberg, H. (1992). *Cultural Tourism in Australia*, A study commissioned by the Department of the Arts, Sport, the Environment and Territories, Australian Government Publishing Service, Canberra.

Brokensha, P. and Tonks, A. (1985). *An Interim Report on the Economic Impact of the 1984 Adelaide Festival of Arts*, a report prepared for the South Australian Department for the Arts, Adelaide: Graduate Studies Centre, Elton Mayo School of Management, South Australian Institute of Technology.

Brotchie, J., Batty, M., Blakely, E., Hall, P. and Newton, P. (eds) (1995). *Cities in Competition: Productive and Sustainable Cities for the 21st Century*, South Melbourne: Longman Australia.

Brother Sister (1996). 'Pink dollar hot again', *Brother Sister – Queer News From Downunder* 122, 26 December.

Buckley, P.J. and Witt, S.F. (1985). 'Tourism in difficult areas I: case studies of Bradford, Bristol, Glasgow and Hamm', *Tourism Management* 6(3): 205–13.

Buckley, P.J. and Witt, S.F. (1989). 'Tourism in difficult areas II: case studies of Calderdale, Leeds, Manchester and Scunthorpe', *Tourism Management* 10(2): 138–52.

Buhalis, D. and Cooper, C. (1998). 'Competition or co-operation? Small and medium sized tourism enterprises at the destination', in E. Laws, B. Faulkner and G. Moscardo (eds) *Embracing and Managing Change in Tourism: International Case Studies*, London: Routledge, 324–46.

Bull, A. (1991). *The Economics of Travel and Tourism*, London: Pitman.

Bull, A. (1995). *The Economics of Travel and Tourism*, 2nd edn, Harlow: Longman.

Bull, P. (1997). 'Tourism in London: policy changes and planning problems', *Regional Studies* 31(1): 82–5.

Bull, P. and Church, A. (1994). 'The hotel and catering industry of Great Britain during the 1980s: sub-regional employment change, specialisation and dominance', in C.P. Cooper and A. Lockwood (eds) *Progress in Tourism, Recreation and Hospitality Management*, Volume 5, Chichester: Wiley, 248–69.

Bull, P. and Church, A. (1996). 'The London tourism complex', in C. Law (ed.) *Tourism in Major Cities*, London: International Thomson Business Press, 155–78.

Bureau of Tourism Research (1998). *The Australian MICE Sector*, Canberra: Bureau of Tourism Research.

Burgess, E. (1925). 'The growth of the city', in R. Park, E. Burgess and R. McKenzie (eds) *The City: Suggestions of Investigations of Human Behaviour in the Urban Environment*, Chicago: University of Chicago Press, 47–62.

Burgess, J. (1982). 'Selling places: environmental images for the executive', *Regional Studies* 16: 1–17.

Burgess, J. and Wood, P. (1989). 'Decoding docklands: place advertising and decision-making strategies in the small firm', in J. Eyles and D.M. Smith (eds) *Qualitative Methods in Human Geography*, Oxford: Polity Press.

Burns, J.P.A., Hatch, J.H. and Mules, F.J. (eds) (1986). *The Adelaide Grand Prix: The Impact of a Special Event*, Adelaide: Centre for South Australian Economic Studies.

Burtenshaw, D., Bateman, M. and Ashworth, G.J. (1991). *The European City: A Western Perspective*, London: David Fulton Publishers.

Butler, R. (1975). 'Tourism as an agent of social change', in *Tourism as a Factor in National and Regional Development*, Occasional Paper 4, Peterborough: Department of Geography, Trent University, 85–90.

Butler, R. and Mao, B. (1997). 'Seasonality in tourism: problems and measurement', in P. Murphy (ed.) *Quality Management in Urban Tourism*, Chichester: Wiley, 9–24.

Butler, R. and Waldbrook, L. (1991). 'A new planning tool: The Tourist Opportunity Spectrum', *Journal of Tourism Studies* 2(1): 2–14.

Butler, R.W. (1980). 'The concept of a tourist area cycle of evolution, implications for management of resources', *Canadian Geographer* 24(1): 5–12.

Bywater, M. (1993). 'The market for cultural tourism in Europe', *Travel and Tourism Analyst* 6: 30–46.

Caffyn, A. and Lutz, J. (1999). 'Developing the heritage tourism product in multi-ethnic cities', *Tourism Management* 20(2): 213–21.

Calatone, R., di Benedetto, I., Hakam, A. and Bojanic, B. (1989). 'Multiple multi-dimensional tourism positioning using correspondence analysis', *Journal of Travel Research* 28: 25–32.

California Federation of Certified Farmers' Markets (2001). *What is a Certified Farmers' Market?*, http://farmersmarket.ucdavis.edu/docs/about.html

Campbell, M. (2001). 'IOC panel sees city's other side', *Globe and Mail* 10 March: A22.

Canberra Development Board (1988). *The Canberra Tourism Strategy*, Canberra: Canberra Development Board.

Canberra Tourism (1997). *Target Tourism*, Winter.

Canberra Tourism and Events Corporation (CTEC) (2001a). *ACT Tourism Masterplan 2001–2005: Developing Our Tourism Capital. Another Face of Our National Capital*, Canberra: Canberra Tourism and Events Corporation and Tourism Industry Council ACT and Region.

Canberra Tourism and Events Corporation (CTEC) (2001b). *Annual Report 2000–2001*, Canberra: Canberra Tourism and Events Corporation.

Canberra Tourism Development Bureau (1989). *1989/90 Marketing Strategy*, Canberra: Canberra Tourism Development Bureau.

Canestrelli, E. and Costa, P. (1991). 'Tourist carrying capacity: a fuzzy approach', *Annals of Tourism Research* 18(2): 295–311.

Cant, G. (1980). 'The impact of tourism on the host community – the Queenstown example', in D.G. Pearce (ed.) *Tourism in the South Pacific: The Contribution of Research to Development and Planning*, MAB report No. 6, Christchurch: New Zealand National Commission on UNESCO, 87–96.

Carpenter, S.L. and Kennedy, W.J.D. (1988). *Managing Public Disputed: A Practical Guide to Handling Conflict and Reaching Agreements*, San Francisco: Jossey-Bass.

Carr, N. (2001). 'An exploratory study of gendered differences in young tourists' perception of danger within London', *Tourism Management* 22(5): 565–70.

Castells, M. (1989). *The Informational City: Information Technology, Economic Restructuring and the Urban–Regional Process*, Oxford: Blackwell.

Castells, M. (1996a). *The Rise of the Network Society*, Oxford: Blackwell.

Castells, M. (1996b). 'European cities, the informational city and the global economy', in R. LeGates and F. Stout (eds) *The City Reader*, 2nd edn, London: Routledge, 557–67.

Cazes, G. and Potier, F. (1996). *Le Tourisme Urbain*, Paris: Presses Universitaires de France.

Chalkley, B. and Essex, S. (1999). 'Sydney 2000: the green games?', *Geography* 84(4): 299–307.

Chang, T.C. (2000). 'Singapore's Little India: a tourist attraction in a contested landscape', *Urban Studies* 37(2): 343–66.

Chang, T.C. and Yeo, B. (1999). ' "New Asia – Singapore": communicating local cultures through global tourism', *Geoforum* 30(2): 101–15.

Chang, T.C., Milne, S., Fallon, D. and Pohlmann, C. (1996). 'Urban heritage tourism: the global–local nexus', *Annals of Tourism Research* 23(2): 284–305.

Chatterton, P. (2001). 'The creative city: creative for who, by who?', *Urban and Regional Regeneration Bulletin*, http://www.ncl.ac.uk/curds/urrb/

Chema, T.V. (1996). 'When professional sports justify the subsidy, a reply to Robert A. Baade', *Journal of Urban Affairs* 18(1): 19–22.

Chenoweth, N. (1991). 'Casino boom: You can bet on it', *Australian Business* 29 May: 14–18.

Chief Minister's Department (1993). *Canberra Visitors Survey: A Summary of the Main Findings for 1992/93*, Canberra: Strategic Research Section, Chief Minister's Department.

Chorney, R. (1999). *Introduction, Come for the Tradition*, http://www.fmo.reach. net/intro.html

Christaller, W. (1963). 'Some considerations of tourism location in Europe: the peripheral regions – underdeveloped countries – recreation areas', *Regional Science Association Papers* 12: 95–105.

Christiansen, E. and Brinkerhoff-Jacobs, J. (1995). 'Gaming and entertainment: an imperfect union', *Cornell Hotel and Restaurant Quarterly*.

Cigler, A.J. (1991). 'Interest groups: a subfield in search of an identity', in W. Crotty (ed.) *Political Science: Looking to the Future, Vol. 4, American Institutions*, Evanston: Northwestern University Press.

Clark, N., Clift, S. and Page, S.J. (1993). *A Safe Place in the Sun? Health Precautions of British Tourists in Malta*, Travel, Lifestyles and Health Working Paper No. 1, Canterbury: Christ Church College of Higher Education.

Clark, P. and Lepetit, B. (1996). *Capital Cities and Their Hinterlands in Early Modern Europe*, Aldershot: Scolar Press.

Clark, R.N. and Stankey, G.H. (1979). *The Recreation Opportunity Spectrum: A Framework for Planning, Management and Research*, USDA Forest Service, General Technical Report PNW-98.

Clarke, A. (1986). 'Local authority planners or frustrated tourism marketers?', *The Planner* 72(5): 23–6.

Clarke, J. (1990). 'Pessimism versus populism: the problematic politics of popular culture', in R. Butsch (ed.) *For Fun and Profit: The Transformation of Leisure into Consumption*, Philadelphia: Temple University Press, 28–44.

Clave, S. (1998). 'Residential tourism development. From the conquest of travel to the restructuring of tourist cities', *Documents d'Analisi Geografica* 32: 17–43.

Clawson, M. (1971). *Suburban Land Conversion in the United States: An Economic and Governmental Process*, Baltimore: John Hopkins University Press.

Clift, S. and Forrest, S. (1999). 'Gay men and tourism: destinations and holiday motivations', *Tourism Management* 20: 615–25.

Cloke, P. (ed.) (1992). *Policy and Planning in Thatcher's Britain*, Oxford: Pergamon.

Cockerell, N. (1997). 'Urban tourism in Europe', *Travel and Tourism Analyst* 6: 44–67.

Cohen, E. (1972). 'Towards a sociology of international tourism', *Social Research* 39: 164–82.

Commons, J. and Page, S.J. (2001). 'Managing seasonality in peripheral tourism regions: the case of Northland, New Zealand', in T. Baum and S. Lundtorp (eds) *Seasonality in Tourism: An Exploration of Issues*, Oxford: Pergamon, 153–72.

Community Marketing (1999). *Annual Gay & Lesbian Travel Survey*, San Francisco: Community Marketing.

Conforti, J. (1996). 'Ghettos as tourism attractions', *Annals of Tourism Research* 23(4): 830–42.

Cook, I. and Crang, P. (1996). 'The world on a plate: culinary cultures, displacement and geographical knowledges', *Journal of Material Culture* 1(2): 131–53.

Cooper, C. (1992). 'The life cycle concept and tourism', in P. Johnson and B. Thomas (eds) *Choice and Demand in Tourism*, London: Mansell, 145–60.

Cooper, C. (1994). 'Product lifecycle', in S.F. Witt and L. Moutinho (eds) *Tourism Marketing and Management Handbook*, Englewood Cliffs: Prentice Hall, 145–60.

Cooper, C. and Jackson, S. (1989). 'Destination life cycle: the Isle of Man case study', *Annals of Tourism Research* 16: 377–89.

Cooper, C., Fletcher, J., Gilbert, D. and Wanhill, S. (1993). *Tourism: Principles and Practice*, London: Pitman.

Cosgrove, D. (1984). *Social Formation and Symbolic Landscape*, London: Croom Helm.

Costa, P. (1990). 'Tourism in Venice until the year 2000: main results', *Nota di Lavoro – Dipartimento di Scienze Economiche, Università degli Studi di Venezia*, No. 90.07, 49pp.

Costa, P. (1991). 'Managing tourism carrying capacity of art cities', *The Tourist Review* 4: 8–11.

Costa, P. and van der Borg, J. (1992). 'The management of tourism in cities of art', *Vriji Tijd en Samenleving* 10(2/3): 45–57.

Coventry, N. (2000). 'Wellington gets a life!', *Journal of Management* 66.

Cox, G. (1998). 'Faster, higher, stronger . . . but what about our rights? Human rights and hallmark events', *Impact Assessment and Project Appraisal* 16(3): 175–84.

Cox, G., Darcy, M. and Bounds, M. (1994). *The Olympics and Housing: A Study of Six International Events and Analysis of Potential Impacts*, Sydney: University of Western Sydney.

Craik, J. (1991). *Resorting to Tourism: Cultural Policies for Tourist Development*, Sydney: Allen & Unwin.

Craik, J. (2001). 'Cultural tourism', in N. Douglas, N. Douglas and R. Derrett (eds) *Special Interest Tourism*, Brisbane: John Wiley, 113–39.

Crompton, J.L. (1979). 'An assessment of the image of Mexico as a vacation destination', *Journal of Travel Research* 17(Fall): 18–23.

Cullingworth, B. (1997). *Planning in the USA: Policies, Issues and Processes*, London: Routledge.

Cumming, J. (2000). Charlottetown: Canada's birthplace, *Plan Canada* 40(3): 24.

Cummings, L. (1997). 'Waste minimisation supporting urban tourism sustainability: a mega-resort case study', *Journal of Sustainable Tourism* 5(2): 93–108.

Cybriwsky, R. (1999). 'Changing patterns of urban public space: observations and assessments from the Tokyo and New York metropolitan areas', *Cities: The International Journal of Urban Policy and Planning* 16(4): 223–31.

Dahles, H. (1998). 'Redefining Amsterdam as a tourism destination', *Annals of Tourism Research* 25(1): 55–69.

Dalyrymple, T. (1999). 'An amusement arcade masquerading as a museum', *New Statesman* 12 February, http://www.newstatesman.co.uk/199902120027.htm, accessed 28 April 1999.

David-Peterson Associates Inc. (1992). *Toronto as a Tourist Destination*, prepared for KPMG-Peat Marwick Stevenson and Kellog on behalf of Metropolitan Toronto Convention and Visitors Association, Ontario Ministry of Tourism, Recreation and Industry Science, Technology Canada, Toronto: David-Peterson Associates.

Davidson, R. and Maitland, R. (1997). *Tourism Destinations*, London: Hodder and Stoughton.

Davis, S. (1999). 'Space jam: media conglomerates build the entertainment city', *European Journal of Communication* 14(4): 435–59.

Day, P. (1988). *The Big Party Syndrome: A Study of the Impact of Special Events and Inner Urban Change in Brisbane*, St. Lucia: Department of Social Work, University of Queensland.

DCWatch (2000). National Capital Revitalisation Plan, http://www.dcwatch.com/ncrc/001207.htm III accessed 15 December.

Dear, M. (1994). 'Postmodern human geography: a preliminary assessment', *Erdkunde* 48(1): 2–13.

Dear, M. (1999). 'The relevance of post modernism', *Scottish Geographical Magazine* 115(2): 143–50.

Dear, M. and Flusty, S. (1998). 'Postmodern urbanism', *Annals of the Association of American Geographers* 88(1): 50–72.

Dear, M. and Flusty, S. (1999). 'Engaging postmodern urbanism', *Urban Geography* 20(5): 412–16.

DeGrace, W. (1985). 'Canada's capital 1900–1950: five town planning visions', *Environments* 17(2): 45–57.

DeGrove, J.M. and Miness, D.A. (1992). *The New Frontier for Land Policy: Planning and Growth Management in the States*, Cambridge: Lincoln Institute of Land Policy.

Delbecq, A.L. (1974). 'Contextual variables affecting decision-making in program planning', *Journal of the American Institute for Decision Sciences* 5(4): 726–42.

Department of the Environment (1990). *Tourism and the Inner City*, London: HMSO.

Department of the Environment, Transport and the Regions (DETR) (1996). *Four World Cities: A Comparative Study of London, Paris, New York and Tokyo* (Urban Research Summary No. 7), http://www.regeneration.detr.gov.uk/rs/00796.htm

Department of the Environment, Transport and the Regions (1998). *Regeneration Research Summary: Regenerating London Docklands* (No. 16), http://www.regeneration.detr.gov.uk/rs/01698/index.htm

Department of the Environment, Transport and the Regions (2000a). *Towards an Urban Renaissance: The Report of the Urban Task Force Chaired by Lord Rogers of Riverside*, http://www.regeneration.detr.gov.uk/utf/renais/index.htm

Department of the Environment, Transport and the Regions (2000b). *Regeneration Research Summary: A Review of the Evidence Base for Regeneration Policy and Practice* (No. 39), http://www.regeneration.detr.gov.uk/rs/03900/index.htm

Derrett, R. (2001). 'Special interest tourism: starting with the individual', in N. Douglas, N. Douglas and R. Derrett (eds) *Special Interest Tourism*, Brisbane: John Wiley, 1–28.

Devas, N. and Rakodi, C. (eds) (1993). *Managing Fast Growing Cities: New Approaches to Urban Planning and Management in the Developing World*, Harlow: Longman.

Diamantis, D. and Westlake, J. (1997). 'Environmental auditing: an approach towards monitoring the environmental impacts in tourism destinations, with reference to the case of Molyvos', *Progress in Tourism and Hospitality Research* 3(1): 3–15.

Dick, H. and Rimmer, P. (1998). 'Beyond the third world city: the new urban geography of South East Asia', *Urban Studies* 35(12): 2303–21.

Dicken, P. (1998). *Global Shift: Industrial Change in a Turbulent World*, London: Paul Chapman.

Dicken, P. and Lloyd, P. (1978). *Location in Space*, Harper Row: London.

Ding, P. and Pigram, J. (1995). 'Environmental audits: an emerging concept in sustainable tourism development', *Journal of Tourism Studies* 6(2): 2–10.

Dixon, C. and Smith, D. (eds) (1997). *Uneven Development in South East Asia*, Aldershot: Ashgate.

Dogan, H. (1989). 'Forms of adjustment: sociocultural impacts of tourism', *Annals of Tourism Research* 16(2): 216–36.

Doorne, S. (1998). 'Power, participation and perception: an insider's perspective on the politics of the Wellington waterfront redevelopment', *Current Issues in Tourism* 1(2): 129–66.

Douglas, N., Douglas, N. and Derrett, R. (eds) (2001). *Special Interest Tourism*, Brisbane: John Wiley.

Douglass, M. (1995). 'Global interdependence and urbanisation: planning for the Bangkok mega-urban region', in T. McGee and I. Robinson (eds) *The Mega-urban Regions of Southeast Asia*, Vancouver: UBC Press, 45–77.

Dowling, R.K. (1992). 'Tourism and environmental integration: the journey from idealism to realism', in C.P. Cooper and A. Lockwood (eds) *Progress in Tourism, Recreation and Hospitality Management*, Volume 4, London: Belhaven, 33–44.

Doxey, G.V. (1975). 'A causation theory of visitor-resident irritants: methodology and research inferences', *Proceedings of the Travel Research Association 6th Annual Conference*, San Diego: California, 195–8.

Dredge, D. and Moore, S. (1992). 'A methodology for the integration of tourism in town planning', *Journal of Tourism Studies* 3(1): 8–21.

Drewe, P. (1993). 'Capital cities in Europe: directions for the future', in J. Taylor, J.G. Legellé and C. Andrew (eds) *Capital Cities: International Perspectives/Les capitales: Perspectives internationales*, Ottawa: Carleton University Press.

Driver, F. and Gilbert, D. (eds) (1999). *Imperial Cities: Landscape, Display and Identity*, Manchester: Manchester University Press.

DRV Research (1986). *An Economic Impact Study of the Tourist and Associated Arts Development in Merseyside*, Bournemouth: DRV Research.

Dubé, P. and Gordon, G. (2000). 'Capital cities: perspectives and convergence', *Plan Canada* 40(3): 6–7.

Dublin Tourism (2000). Things to See and Do in Dublin, http://www.visitdublin. com/attract.htm, accessed 14 December 2000.

du Gray, P. (1996). *Consumption and Identity at Work*, London: Sage.

Duncan, B. (2000). 'Edmonton: doing things right', *Plan Canada* 40(3): 33.

Duncan, J. (1990). *The City as Text: The Politics of Landscape Interpretation in the Kandyan Kingdom*, Cambridge: Cambridge University Press.

Duncan, S.S. and Goodwin, M. (1985a). 'Local economic policies: local regeneration or political mobilisation', *Local Government Studies* 11(6): 75–96.

Duncan, S.S. and Goodwin, M. (1985b). 'The local state and local economic policy: why the fuss?', *Policy and Politics* 13: 247–53.

Duncan, S.S. and Goodwin, M. (1988). *The Local State and Uneven Development*, Cambridge: Polity Press.

Dusclaud, M. (1993). 'Tourisme urbain intercommunal dans l'agglomeration bordelaise', *Espaces* 121: 14–18.

Echtner, C. and Ritchie, J.B. (1993). 'The measurement of destination image: an empirical assessment', *Journal of Travel Research* 31: 3–13.

Ekos Research Associates Inc. (1988). *Culture, Multiculturalism and Tourism Pilot Projects and Related Studies: A Synthesis*, prepared for Communications Canada, Secretary of State Tourism Canada in the context of the Conference on Tourism, Culture and Multiculturalism.

English Historic Towns Forum (1992). *Retailing in Historic Towns: Research Study 1992*, London: Donaldsons.

English Tourist Board/British Tourist Authority (1985). *English Hotel Occupancy Survey*, London: English Tourist Board.

English Tourist Board/Department of Employment (1991). *Tourism and the Environment: Maintaining the Balance*, London: English Tourist Board.

Essex, S. and Chalkey, B. (1998). 'Olympic Games: catalyst of urban change', *Leisure Studies* 17(3): 187–206.

Evans, G. (1999). 'Networking for growth and digital business: local urban tourism SMTEs and ICT', in D. Buhalis and W. Schertler (eds) *Information Communication and Technologies in Tourism 1999*, Vienna: Springer Verlag, 376–87.

Evans, T.R. (1994). 'Residents' perceptions of tourism in selected New Zealand communities: a segmentation study', unpublished MCom thesis, Dunedin: University of Otago.

Eversley, D. (1977). 'The ganglion of tourism', *The London Journal* 3(2): 186–211.

Faulkner, B. and Ryan, C. (1999). 'Innovations in tourism management research and conceptualisation', *Tourism Management* 20(1): 3–6.

Faulkner, B., Tideswell, C. and Weston, A.M. (1998). *Leveraging Tourism Benefits from the Sydney 2000 Olympics*. Keynote Address, Sport Management: Opportunities and

Change. Fourth Annual Conference, Sports Management Association of Australia and New Zealand (SMAANZ), 26–28 November 1998, Gold Coast, Australia.

Feng, K. and Page, S.J. (2000). 'An exploratory study of the tourism, migration–immigration nexus: travel experiences of Chinese residents in New Zealand', *Current Issues in Tourism* 3(3): 246–81.

Fennell, D. (1998). 'The economic impact of hockey in Saskatchewan: a rural–urban comparison', *Great Plains Research* 8(2): 315–33.

Figuerola, M. (1976). 'Turismo de masa y sociologia: el caso espanol', *Travel Research Journal*: 25–38.

Fillion, S. (2000). 'La capitale nationale du Québec', *Plan Canada* 40(3): 27–8.

Finn, A. and Erdem, T. (1995). 'The economic impact of a mega-multi mall: estimation issues in the case of West Edmonton Mall', *Tourism Management* 16(5): 367–73.

Fiorelli, F. (1989). 'Venezia e il turismo', *Revista Geografica Italiana*.

Fisher, M. and Worpole, K. (eds) (1988). *City Centres, City Cultures: The Role of the Arts in the Revitalisation of Towns and Cities*, Manchester: Centre for Local Government Strategies.

Fletcher, J. (1989). 'Input–output analysis and tourism impact studies', *Annals of Tourism Research* 16: 514–29.

Fletcher, J.E. and Archer, B.H. (1989). 'The development and application of multiplier analysis', in C.P. Cooper (ed.) *Progress in Tourism, Recreation and Hospitality Management*, Volume 1, London: Belhaven, 28–47.

Food Service Association (1997). *Vital Statistics 1997: Foodservice Facts*, http://www.hhes.co.nz/fanz/html/vital_stats.html

Forbes, A. and DeGrace, B. (2000). 'Two hundred years of planning in Fredericton', *Plan Canada* 40(3): 25.

Forer, P. and Page, S.J. (1998). 'Tourism in Tai Tokerau: general patterns and Maori perspectives. Part 1: Tourism demand in Tai Tokerau', a report for *FoRST Project Sustainable Maori tourism for Tai Tokerau*, Department of Geography, University of Auckland, July, p. 40.

Forer, P. and Page, S.J. (1999). 'Spatial modelling of tourist flows in Northland/Tai Tokerau', paper presented at the New Zealand Tourism and Hospitality Research Conference, 1–4 December, Akaroa, New Zealand.

Forer, P. and Pearce, D.G. (1984). 'Spatial patterns of package tourism in New Zealand', *New Zealand Geographer* 40: 34–42.

Fredline, E. and Faulkner, B. (2000). 'Host community reactions: a cluster analysis', *Annals of Tourism Research* 27(3): 763–84.

Friedmann, J. (1959). 'Introduction', *International Social Science Journal* 11(3): 327–34.

Friedmann, J. (1973). 'A conceptual model for the analysis of planning behaviour', in A. Faludi (ed.) *A Reader in Planning Theory*, Oxford: Pergamon Press, 344–70.

Friedrichs, J. (1995). 'Cologne: a creative city', *European Planning Studies* 3: 441–64.

Fyfe, N. and Bannister, J. (1996). 'City watching: closed circuit television surveillance in public places', *Area* 28: 37–46.

Gans, H.J. (1962). *The Urban Villagers: Groups and Class in the Life of Italian–Americans*, New York: Free Press.

Garland, B.R. and West, S.J. (1985). 'The social impact of tourism in New Zealand', *Massey Journal of Asian and Pacific Business* 1(1): 34–9.

Garreau, J. (1991). *Edge City: Life on the New Frontier*. New York: Doubleday.

Garrod, B. and Fyall, A. (2000). 'Managing heritage tourism', *Annals of Tourism Research* 27(3): 682–708.

Gartner, W. (1989). 'Tourism image: attribute measurement of state tourism products using multidimensional scaling techniques', *Journal of Travel Research* 28: 16–20.

Gastellars, R.v.E. (1988). 'Revitalising the city and the formation of metropolitan culture: rivalry between capital cities in the attraction of new urban elites', in A. de Swann *et al.* (eds) *Capital Cities as Achievement: Essays*, Amsterdam: Centrum voor Grootstedelijk Onderzook, University of Amsterdam, 38–43.

Gertler, M. (1997). 'Globality and locality: the future of geography', in P. Rimmer (ed.) *Pacific Rim Development: Integration and Globalisation in the Asia-Pacific Economy*, St. Leonards: Allen and Unwin, 12–33.

Getz, D. (1991). *Festivals, Special Events and Tourism*, New York: Van Nostrand Reinhold.

Getz, D. (1992). 'Tourism planning and destination life cycle', *Annals of Tourism Research* 19: 752–70.

Getz, D. (1993a). 'Planning for tourism business districts', *Annals of Tourism Research* 20: 583–600.

Getz, D. (1993b). 'Tourist shopping villages: development and planning strategies', *Tourism Management* 14(1): 15–26.

Getz, D. (1994). 'Residents' attitudes towards tourism: a longitudinal study in Spey Valley, Scotland', *Tourism Management* 15(4): 247–58.

Gilbert, D. and Clark, M. (1997). 'An exploratory examination of urban tourism impacts, with reference to residents' attitudes in the cities of Canterbury and Guildford', *Cities: The International Journal of Urban Policy and Planning* 14(6): 343–52.

Gilbert, E.W. (1949). 'The growth of Brighton', *Geographical Journal* 114: 30–52.

Gill, A. (1998). 'Local and resort development', in R. Butler, C.M. Hall and J. Jenkins (eds) *Tourism and Recreation in Rural Areas*, Chichester: Wiley, 97–111.

Gill, A. and Williams, P.W. (1994). 'Managing growth in mountain tourism communities', *Tourism Management* 15(3): 212–20.

Gladstone, D. (1998). 'Tourism urbanisation in the United States', *Urban Affairs Review* 34(1): 3–27.

Glasson, J., Godfrey, K. and Goodey, B. with Absalom, H. and van der Borg, J. (1995). *Towards Visitor Impact Management: Visitor Impacts, Carrying Capacity and Management Responses in Europe's Historic Towns and Cities*, Aldershot: Avebury.

Gold, J. and Gold, M. (1995). *Imagining Scotland: Tradition, Representation and Promotion in Scottish Tourism since 1750*, Aldershot: Scholar.

Gold, J. and Ward, S. (eds) (1994). *Place Promotion: The Use of Publicity and Marketing to Sell Towns and Regions*, Chichester: Wiley.

Goldberger, P. (1996). 'The rise of the private city', in J. Vitullo Martin (ed.) *Breaking Away: The Future of Cities*, New York: The Twentieth Century Fund.

Goodall, B. (ed.) (1989). 'Tourism accommodation', *Built Environment* 15(2): 72–158.

Goodall, B. (1992). 'Environmental auditing for tourism', in C. Cooper and A. Lockwood (eds) *Progress in Tourism, Recreation and Hospitality Management, Vol. 4*, London: Belhaven Press, 60–74.

Goodenough, R. and Page, S.J. (1994). 'Evaluating the environmental impact of a major transport infrastructure project: the Channel Tunnel High Speed Rail-Link', *Applied Geography* 14(1): 26–50.

Goodman, R. (1979). *The Last Entrepreneurs: America's Regional Wars for Jobs and Dollars*, New York: Simon and Schuster.

Goodrich, J. (1978). 'The relationship between preferences for and perceptions of vacation destinations: application of a choice model', *Journal of Travel Research* 17: 8–13.

Goodwin, M. (1993). 'The city as commodity: the contested spaces of urban development', in G. Kearns and C. Philo (eds) *Selling Places: The City as Cultural Capital, Past and Present*, Oxford: Pergamon Press, 145–62.

Gordon, D. (1998). 'A city beautiful plan for Canada's capital', *Planning Perspectives* 13: 275–300.

Gordon, D. (2000). 'Planning Canberra and Ottawa: more differences than similarities', *Plan Canada* 40(3): 20–21.

Gottmann, J. (1983). 'Capital cities', *Ekistics* 50: 88–93.

Gospodini, A. (2001). 'Urban waterfront redevelopment in Greek cities: a framework for redesigning spaces', *Cities: The International Journal of Urban Policy and Planning* 18(5): 285–95.

Grabler, K. (1997a). 'Perceptual mapping and positioning of tourist cities', in J. Mazanec (ed.) *International City Tourism: Analysis and Strategy*, London: Pinter, 101–13.

Grabler, K. (1997b). 'Cities and the destination life cycle', in J.A. Mazanec (ed.) *International City Tourism: Analysis and Strategy*, London: Pinter, 39–53.

Grabler, K., Mazanec, J. and Wöber, K. (1996). 'Strategic marketing for urban tourism: analysing competition among European tourist cities', in C.M. Law (ed.) *Tourism in Major Cities*, London: International Thomson Business Publishing, 23–51.

Graefe, A.R. and Vaske, J.J. (1987). 'A framework for managing quality in the tourist experience', *Annals of Tourism Research* 14(3): 390–404.

Graham, B., Ashworth, G. and Tunbridge, J. (2000). *A Geography of Heritage*, London: Edward Arnold.

Gray, B. (1989). *Collaborating: Finding Common Ground for Multiparty Problems*, San Francisco: Jossey-Bass.

Green, C. and Chalip, L. (1998). 'Sport tourism as the celebration of subculture', *Annals of Tourism Research* 25(2): 275–91.

Gregson, N. (2000). 'Family, work and consumption: mapping the borderlands of economic geography', in E. Sheppard and T.J. Barnes (eds) *A Companion to Economic Geography*, Oxford: Blackwell, 311–24.

Greiner, N. (1994). 'Inside running on Olympic bid', *The Australian* 19 September: 13.

Gunn, C. (1972). *Vacationscape: Designing Tourist Regions*, Austin: University of Texas.

Hall, C.M. (1989a). 'Hallmark tourist events: analysis, definition, methodology and review', in G.J. Syme, B.J. Shaw, D.M. Fenton and W.S. Mueller (eds) *The Planning and Evaluation of Hallmark Events*, Aldershot: Avebury, 3–19.

Hall, C.M. (1989b). 'Hallmark events and the planning process', in G.J. Syme, B.J. Shaw, D.M. Fenton and W.S. Mueller (eds) *The Planning and Evaluation of Hallmark Events*, Aldershot: Avebury, 20–39.

Hall, C.M. (1989c). 'The politics of hallmark events', in G.J. Syme, B.J. Shaw, D.M. Fenton and W.S. Mueller (eds) *The Planning and Evaluation of Hallmark Events*, Aldershot: Avebury, 219–41.

Hall, C.M. (1989d). 'The definition and analysis of hallmark events', *GeoJournal* 19(3): 263–8.

Hall, C.M. (1992). *Hallmark Tourist Events: Impacts, Management and Planning*, London: Belhaven.

Hall, C.M. (1994). *Tourism and Politics*, Chichester: John Wiley & Sons.

Hall, C.M. (1996). 'Mega-events and their legacies', in P. Murphy (ed.) *Quality Management in Urban Tourism*, New York: John Wiley, 77–89.

Hall, C.M. (1997). 'Geography, marketing and the selling of places', *Journal of Travel and Tourism Marketing* 6(3/4): 61–84.

Hall, C.M. (1998). 'The politics of decision making and top-down planning: Darling Harbour, Sydney', in D. Tyler, M. Robertson and Y. Guerrier (eds) *Tourism Management in Cities: Policy, Process and Practice*, Chichester: John Wiley & Sons, 9–24.

Hall, C.M. (2000). *Tourism Planning*, Harlow: Prentice Hall.

Hall, C.M. (2002a). *Tourism in Australia*, South Melbourne: Pearson Education.

Hall, C.M. (2002b). 'Seducing global capital: reimaging and the creation of seductive space in Melbourne and Sydney', in C. Cartier and A. Lew (eds) *Seductions of Place: Geographies of Touristed Landscapes*, New York: Routledge.

Hall, C.M. and Hamon, C. (1996). 'Casinos and urban redevelopment in Australia', *Journal of Travel Research* 34(3): 30–36.

Hall, C.M. and Hodges, J. (1997). 'Sharing the spirit of corporatism and cultural capital: the politics of place and identity in the Sydney 2000 Olympics', in M. Roche (ed.) *Sport, Popular Culture and Identity*, Chelsea School Research Centre Edition, Vol. 5, Aachen: Meyer & Meyer Verlag, 95–112.

Hall, C.M. and Jenkins, J.M. (1995). *Tourism and Public Policy*, London: Routledge.

Hall, C.M. and Kearsley, G.K. (2001). *Tourism in New Zealand: An Introduction*, Melbourne: Oxford University Press.

Hall, C.M. and Lew, A. (eds) (1998). *Sustainable Tourism Development: Geographical Perspectives*, Harlow: Longman.

Hall, C.M. and McArthur, S. (eds) (1993). *Heritage Management in New Zealand and Australia*, Auckland: Oxford University Press.

Hall, C.M. and McArthur, S. (eds) (1996a). *Heritage Management in Australia and New Zealand: The Human Dimension*, Melbourne: Oxford University Press.

Hall, C.M. and McArthur, S. (1996b). 'Introduction: the human dimension of heritage management: different values, different interests . . . different issues', in C.M. Hall and S. McArthur (eds) *Heritage Management in Australia and New Zealand: The Human Dimension*, Melbourne: Oxford University Press, 2–21.

Hall, C.M. and McArthur, S. (1998). *Integrated Heritage Management*, London: HMSO.

Hall, C.M. and Mitchell, R. (2000). 'We are what we eat: food, tourism and globalisation', *Tourism, Culture and Communication* 2(1): 29–37.

Hall, C.M. and Mitchell, R. (2002a). 'Tourism as a force for gastronomic globalisation and localisation', in A. Hjalager and G. Richards (eds) *Tourism and Gastronomy*, London: Routledge.

Hall, C.M. and Mitchell, R. (2002b). 'The changing nature of the relationship between cuisine and tourism in Australia and New Zealand: from fusion cuisine to food networks', in A. Hjalager and G. Richards (eds) *Tourism and Gastronomy*, London: Routledge.

Hall, C.M. and Page, S.J. (1999). *The Geography of Tourism and Recreation: Environment, Place and Space*, 1st edn, London: Routledge.

Hall, C.M. and Page, S.J. (2000). 'Introduction: tourism in South and Southeast Asia: region and context', in C.M. Hall and S.J. Page (eds) *Tourism in South and South-East Asia: Critical Perspectives*, Oxford: Butterworth-Heinemann, 3–28.

Hall, C.M. and Page, S.J. (2002). *The Geography of Tourism and Recreation: Environment, Place and Space*, 2nd edn, London: Routledge.

Hall, C.M. and Williams, A.M. (eds) (2002). *Tourism and Migration: New Relationships Between Consumption and Production*, Dordtrecht: Kluwer.

Hall, C.M. and Zeppel, H. (1990). 'Cultural and heritage tourism: the new grand tour?', *Historic Environment* 7(3–4): 86–98.

Hall, C.M., Jenkins, J. and Kearsley, G. (1997). 'Tourism planning and policy in urban areas: introductory comments', in C.M. Hall, J. Jenkins and G. Kearsley (eds) *Tourism, Planning and Policy in Australia and New Zealand: Issues, Cases and Practices*, Sydney: Irwin Publishers, 198–208.

Hall, P. (1970). 'A horizon of hotels', *New Society* 15, 389–445.

Hall, P. (1992). *Urban and Regional Planning*, 3rd edn, London and New York: Routledge.

Hall, P. (1996). 'Revisiting the nonplace urban realm: have we come full circle?', *International Planning Studies* 1(1): 5–15.

Hall, P. (1997). 'Modelling the post-industrial city', *Futures* 29(4/5): 311–22.

Hall, P. (1999). 'The future of cities', *Computers, Environment and Urban Systems* 23: 173–85.

Hall, P. (2000). 'The changing role of capital cities', *Plan Canada*, 40(3): 8–12.

Hall, T. (1997). *Planning Europe's Capital Cities*, London: E & FN Spon.

Hall, T. and Hubbard, P. (eds) (1998). *The Entrepreneurial City*, Chichester: Wiley.

Ham, C. and Hill, M.J. (1994). *The Policy Process in the Modern Capitalist State*, New York: Simon and Schuster.

Hannigan, J. (1995). 'The postmodern city: a new urbanisation', *Current Sociology* 43(1): 151–217.

Hannigan, J. (1998). *Fantasy City: Pleasure and Profit in the Postmodern Metropolis*, London: Routledge.

Harrison, R. (ed.) (1994). *Manual of Heritage Management*, Oxford: Butterworth-Heinemann.

Hartmann, R. (1986). 'Tourism, seasonality and social change', *Leisure Studies* 5(1): 25–33.

Harvey, D. (1988). 'Voodoo cities', *New Statesman and Society*, 30 September, 33–35.

Harvey, D. (1989a). *The Urban Experience*, Oxford: Blackwell.

Harvey, D. (1989b). 'From managerialism to entrepreneurialism: the transformation in urban governance in late capitalism', *Geografiska Annaler* 71B: 3–17.

Harvey, D. (1993). 'From space to place and back again: reflections on the condition of postmodernity', in J. Bird, B. Curtis, T. Putnam, G. Robertson and L. Tickner (eds) *Mapping the Future: Local Cultures, Global Change*, London: Routledge, 3–29.

Harvey, D. (2000). *Spaces of Hope*, Berkeley: University of California Press.

Haughton, G. and Hunter, C. (1994). *Sustainable Cities*, Regional Policy and Development Series 7, London: Jessica Kingsley.

Haywood, K.M. (1986). 'Can the resort-area life cycle be made operational?', *Tourism Management* 7: 154–67.

Healey, J. (1981). 'Planning for tourism in Britain', *Town Planning Review* 52: 61–79.

Healey, P. (1997). *Collaborative Planning: Shaping Places in Fragmented Societies*, Basingstoke: Macmillan Press.

Heath, E. and Wall, G. (1992). *Marketing Tourism Destinations: A Strategic Planning Approach*, New York: John Wiley & Sons.

Hebdidge, D. (1979). *Subculture: The Meaning of Style*, London: Methuen.

Hebdidge, D. (1988). *Hiding in the Light*, London: Comedia.

Held, D. (ed.) (2000). *A Globalizing World? Culture, Economics, Politics*, London: Routledge.

Helyar, J. (1996). 'A city's self-image confronts tax revolt in battle on stadiums', *The Wall Street Journal* 19 March: A1.

Heng, T. and Low, L. (1990). 'The economic impact of tourism in Singapore', *Annals of Tourism Research* 17: 246–69.

Herbert, D. (ed.) (1995). *Heritage, Tourism and Society*, London: Mansell.

Heritage Canada Foundation (1988). 'A new tourism for Canada: can we meet the challenge?', paper presented at National Conference on Tourism, Culture and Multiculturalism, 17–19 April, Montreal.

Heung, V. and Qu, H. (1998). 'Tourism shopping and its contribution to Hong Kong', *Tourism Management* 19(4): 383–6.

Hewison, R. (1987). *The Heritage Industry: Britain in a Climate of Decline*, London: Methuen.

Hewison, R. (1991). 'Commerce and culture', in J. Corner and S. Harvey (eds) *Enterprise and Heritage: Crosscurrents of National Culture*, London: Routledge, 162–77.

Higham, J. (1999). 'Sport as an avenue of tourism development: an analysis of the positive and negative impacts of sport tourism', *Current Issues in Tourism* 2(1): 82–90.

Hiller, H. (1995). 'Conventions as mega-events: a new model for convention–host city relationships', *Tourism Management* 16(5): 375–81.

Hiller, H. (1997). 'And if Cape Town loses? Mega-events and the Olympic candidature', *Indicator South Africa* 14: 63–7.

Hiller, H. (1998). 'Assessing the impact of mega-events: a linkage model', *Current Issues in Tourism* 1: 47–57.

Hiller, H. (2000). 'Mega-events, urban boosterism and growth strategies: an analysis of the objectives and legitimations of the Cape Town 2004 Olympic bid', *International Journal of Urban and Regional Research* 24(2): 439–58.

Hillis, K. (1992). 'A history of commissions: threads of an Ottawa planning history', *Urban History Review* 21(1): 46–60.

Hinch, T. (1996). 'Urban tourism: perspectives on sustainability', *Journal of Sustainable Tourism* 4(2): 95–110.

Holcomb, B. (1993). 'Revisioning place: de- and re-constructing the image of the industrial city', in G. Kearns and C. Philo (eds) *Selling Places: The City as Cultural Capital, Past and Present*, Oxford: Pergamon Press, 133–43.

Holcomb, B. and Luongo, M. (1996). 'Gay tourism in the United States', *Annals of Tourism Research* 23(3): 711–13.

Holloway, J.C. and Plant, R.V. (1989). *Marketing for Tourism*, London: Pitman.

Hooper-Greenhill, E. (1992). *Museums and the Shaping of Knowledge*, London: Routledge.

HOTREC (2000). 'Facts and figures on the hotel, restaurant and café sector in Europe', www.hotrec.org, accessed 8 August 2000.

Houinen, G. (1995). 'Heritage issues in urban tourism: an assessment of new trends in Lancaster County', *Tourism Management* 16(5): 381–8.

Hoyle, B. (2001). 'Lamu: Waterfront revitalisation in an East African port-city', *Cities: The International Journal of Urban Policy and Planning* 18(5): 297–313.

Hoyle, B.S. and Pinder, D. (eds) (1992). *European Port Cities in Transition*, London: Belhaven.

Hughes, H. (1997). 'Holidays and homosexual identity', *Tourism Management* 18(1): 3–9.

Hughes, H. (1998). 'Theatre in London and the interrelationship with tourism', *Tourism Management* 19(5): 445–52.

Hughes, H. (2000). *Arts, Entertainment and Tourism*, Oxford: Butterworth-Heinemann.

Huse, M., Gustaven, T. and Almedal, S. (1998). 'Tourism impact comparisons among Norwegian towns', *Annals of Tourism Research* 25(3): 721–38.

Industry Commission (1995). *Tourism Accommmodation and Training*, Melbourne: Industry Commission.

Innes, J.E. (1998). 'Information in communicative planning', *Journal of the American Planning Association* 64(1): 52–63.

Innes, J.E. and Booher, D.E. (1999). 'Consensus building as role playing and bricolage: toward a theory of collaborative planning', *Journal of the American Planning Association* 65(1): 926–40.

INRETS (1996). *Le Tourisme Urbain – Les Pratiques des Francais*, Report no. 208, Paris: Institut National de Recherche sur les Transports et leur Sécurité.

International Congress and Convention Association (ICCA) (2001). *Statistics 2000*, Amsterdam: International Congress and Convention Association.

International Hotels Environment Initiative (1996). *Environmental Management for Hotels: The Industry Guide to Best Practice*, Oxford: Butterworth-Heinemann.

Ioannides, D. (1992). 'Tourism development agents: the Cypriot resort cycle', *Annals of Tourism Research* 19: 711–31.

Jackowski, A. and Smith, V.L. (1992). 'Polish pilgrim tourists', *Annals of Tourism Research* 19(1): 92–106.

Jackson, P. (1999). 'Postmodern urbanism and the ethnographic void', *Urban Geography* 20(5): 400–402.

Jackson, P. and Taylor, J. (1996). 'Geography and the cultural politics of advertising', *Progress in Human Geography* 20(3): 356–71.

Jakle, J.A. (1985). *The Tourist: Travel in Twentieth-Century North America*, Lincoln: University of Nebraska Press.

Jamal, T.B. and Getz, D. (1995). 'Collaboration theory and community tourism planning', *Annals of Tourism Research* 22: 186–204.

Jansen-Verbeke, M. (1986). 'Inner-city tourism: resources, tourists and promoters', *Annals of Tourism Research* 13: 79–100.

Jansen-Verbeke, M. (1988). *Leisure, Recreation and Tourism in Inner Cities*, Explorative Case Studies, Amsterdam/Nijmegen: Netherlands Geographical Studies 58.

Jansen-Verbeke, M. (1990). 'Leisure + shopping = tourism product mix', in G. Ashworth and B. Goodall (eds) *Marketing Tourism Places*, London: Routledge, 128–37.

Jansen-Verbeke, M. (1991). 'Leisure shopping: a magic concept for the tourism industry?', *Tourism Management* 11(1): 9–14.

Jansen-Verbeke, M. (1995). 'Urban tourism and city trips', *Annals of Tourism Research* 22(3): 699–700.

Jansen-Verbeke, M. (1996). 'Cultural tourism in the 21st Century', *World Leisure and Recreation* 1: 6–11.

Jansen-Verbeke, M. (1997). 'Urban tourism: Managing resources and visitors', in S. Wahab and J. Pigram (eds) *Tourism, Development and Growth*, London: Routledge, 237–56.

Jansen-Verbeke, M. (1998). 'Touristification of historic cities: a methodological exercise', *Annals of Tourism Research* 25(2).

Jansen-Verbeke, M. and Ashworth, G.J. (1990). 'Environmental integration of recreation and tourism', *Annals of Tourism Research* 17(4): 618–22.

Jansen-Verbeke, M. and Lievois, E. (1999). 'Analysing heritage resources for urban tourism in European cities', in D.G. Pearce and R. Butler (eds) *Contemporary Issues in Tourism Development*, London: Routledge, 81–107.

Jansen-Verbeke, M. and Rekom, J. (1996). 'Scanning museum visitors: urban tourism marketing', *Annals of Tourism Research* 23(2): 364–75.

Jefferson, A. and Lickorish, L. (1991). *Marketing Tourism: A Practical Guide*, Harlow: Longman.

Jenkins, C.L. and Henry, B.M. (1982). 'Government involvement in tourism in developing countries', *Annals of Tourism Research* 9(4): 499–521.

Jenkins, J. (1997). 'The role of the Commonwealth Government in rural tourism and regional development in Australia', in C.M. Hall, J. Jenkins and G. Kearsley (eds) *Tourism Planning and Policy in Australia and New Zealand: Cases, Issues and Practice*, Sydney: Irwin Publishers, 181–91.

Jenkins, J. and Hall, C.M. (1997). 'Tourism planning and policy in Australia', in C.M. Hall, J. Jenkins and G. Kearsley (eds) *Tourism, Planning and Policy in Australia and New Zealand: Issues, Cases and Practice*, Sydney: Irwin Publishers, 35–46.

Jensen, K. and Blevins, A. (1998). *The Last Gamble: Betting on the Future in Four Rock Mining Towns*, Tucson: University of Arizona Press.

Jessop, B. (1999). 'Reflections on globalisation and its (il)logic(s)', in K. Olds, P. Dicken, P.F. Kelly, L. Kong and H.W. Yeung (eds) *Globalisation and the Asia-Pacific: Contested Territories*, Warwickshire Studies in Globalisation Series, London: Routledge, 19–38.

Johnson, P. and Thomas, B. (1992). *Tourism, Museums and the Local Economy*, Aldershot: Edgar Elgar.

Johnson, R. and Moore, G. (1993). 'Tourism impact estimation', *Annals of Tourism Research* 20: 279–88.

Johnston, R.J. (1981). 'Urbanisation', in R. Johnston, D. Gregory, P. Haggett, D. Smith and D. Stoddard (eds) *The Dictionary of Human Geography*, Oxford: Blackwell, 363–4.

Johnston, R.J. (1991). *Geography and Geographers: Anglo-American Human Geography Since 1945*, 4th edn, London: Edward Arnold.

Johnston, R.J., Gregory, D. and Smith, D.M. (eds) (1986). *The Dictionary of Human Geography*, 2nd edn, Oxford: Basil Blackwell.

Joint Committee on the Australian Capital Territory (1961). *Report on the Australian Capital Territory Tourist Industry*, Canberra: Parliament of the Commonwealth of Australia.

Joint Committee on the Australian Capital Territory (1972). *Report of the Joint Committee on the Australian Capital Territory on Employment Opportunities in the A.C.T.*, Canberra: Parliament of the Commonwealth of Australia.

Joint Committee on the Australian Capital Territory (1980). *Tourism in the A.C.T., Report of the Joint Committee on the Australian Capital Territory Tourist Industry*, Canberra: Australian Government Publishing Service.

Joint Committee on the Australian Capital Territory (1986). *Hospitality in the ACT*, Canberra: Commonwealth of Australia.

Jones, E. (1966). *Towns and Cities*, Oxford: Oxford University Press.

Jones Lang Wooten (1989). *Retail, Leisure and Tourism*, London: English Tourist Board.

Judd, D. (1995). 'Promoting tourism in US cities', *Tourism Management* 16(3): 175–87.

Judd, D. and Fainstein, S. (eds) (1999). *The Tourist City*, New Haven: Yale University Press.

Judd, D.R. and Collins, M. (1979). 'The case of tourism: political coalitions and redevelopment in central cities', in G. Tobin (ed.) *The Changing Structure of the City*, Thousand Oaks: Sage.

Kearns, G. and Philo, C. (1993). 'Preface', in G. Kearns and C. Philo (eds) *Selling Places: The City as Cultural Capital, Past and Present*, Oxford: Pergamon Press, ix–x.

Kelly, M. and McConville, C. (1991). 'Down by the docks', in G. Davidson and C. McConville (eds) *A Heritage Handbook*, North Sydney: Allen & Unwin, 91–114.

Kelly, P.F. and Olds, K. (1999). 'Questions in a crisis: the contested meanings of globalisation in the Asia-Pacific', in K. Olds, P. Dicken, P.F. Kelly, L. Kong and H.W. Yeung (eds) *Globalisation and the Asia-Pacific: Contested Territories*, Warwickshire Studies in Globalisation Series, London: Routledge, 1–15.

Kent, P. (1990). 'People, places and priorities: opportunity sets and consumers' holiday choice', in G.J. Ashworth and B. Goodall (eds) *Marketing Tourism Places*, London: Routledge, 42–62.

Kent, W. (1983). 'Shopping: tourism's unsung hero(ine)', *Journal of Travel Research* Fall: 2–4.

Keown, C. (1989). 'A model of tourists' propensity to buy: the case of Japanese visitors to Hawaii', *Journal of Travel Research* Winter: 31–4.

Kidd, B. (1992). 'The Toronto Olympic commitment: towards a social contract for the Olympic Games', *Olympika: The International Journal of Olympic Studies* 1: 154–67.

King, R. (1987). *Italy*, London: Paul Chapman Publishing.

Know, P. (1997). 'Globalization and urban economic change', *The Annals of the American Academy of Political and Social Science* 551: 17–27.

Kolsun, J. (1988). 'The Calgary Olympic visitor study', *The Operational Geographer*, 16 (September): 15–17.

Konrad, V.A. (1982). 'Historical artifacts as recreational resources', in G. Wall and J. Marsh (eds) *Recreational Land Use: Perspectives on its Evolution in Canada*, Ottawa: Carleton University Press, 393–416.

Kornblum, W. and Williams, T. (1977). 'Lifestyle, leisure and community life', in David Street and Associates (eds) *Handbook of Contemporary Urban Life*, San Francisco: Jossey-Bass, 58–89.

Kotler, P. and Armstrong, G. (1991). *Principles of Marketing*, 5th edn, New Jersey: Prentice Hall.

Kotler, P., Haider, D.H. and Rein, I. (1993). *Marketing Places: Attracting Investment, Industry, and Tourism to Cities, States, and Nations*, New York: The Free Press.

KPMG (1993). *Toeristiche Concurrentie postie van Amsterdam ten opzichte van tien andere Europese steden*, Amsterdam: Klynveld Management Consultants.

Lake, R. (1999). 'Postmodern urbanisation?', *Urban Geography* 20(5): 393–5.

Lambooy, J.G. (1988). 'Global cities and the world economic system: rivalry and decision making', in A. de Swann *et al.* (eds) *Capital Cities as Achievement: Essays*, Amsterdam: Centrum voor Grootstedelijk Onderzook, University of Amsterdam, 44–51.

Landry, C., Bianchini, F., Ebert, R., Gnad, F. and Kunzmann, K. (1995). *The Creative City in Britain and Germany*, London: Anglo-German Foundation.

Lang, R. (1986). 'Achieving integration in resource planning', in R. Lang (ed.) *Integrated Approaches to Resource Planning and Management*, Calgary: University of Calgary Press, 27–50.

Langton, J. (1978). 'Industry and towns 1500–1730', in R. Dodgshon and R. Butlin (eds) *An Historical Geography of England and Wales*, London: Academic Press, 173–98.

Lankford, S.V. and Howard, D.R. (1994). 'Developing a tourism impact scale', *Annals of Tourism Research* 21(1): 121–39.

Lapointe, F. and Dubé, P. (2000). 'A century of urban planning and building in Canada's capital region', *Plan Canada* 40(3): 18–19.

Lashley, C. and Morrison, A. (eds) (2000). *In Search of Hospitality: Theoretical Perspectives and Debates*, Oxford: Butterworth-Heinemann.

Latham, J. (1989). 'The statistical measurement of tourism', in C.P. Cooper (ed.) *Progress in Tourism, Recreation and Hospitality Management* Vol. 1, London: Belhaven, 57–76.

Law, C.M. (1988). 'Conference and exhibition tourism', *Built Environment* 13(2): 85–92.

Law, C.M. (1992). 'Urban tourism and its contribution to economic regeneration', *Urban Studies* 29(3/4): 599–618.

Law, C.M. (1993). *Urban Tourism: Attracting Visitors to Large Cities*, London: Mansell.

Law, C.M. (ed.) (1996a). *Tourism in Major Cities*, London: International Thomson Business Press.

Law, C.M. (1996b). 'Introduction', in C. Law (ed.) *Tourism in Major Cities*, London: International Thomson Business Press, 1–22.

Law, C.M. (2002). *Urban Tourism: The Visitor Economy and the Growth of Large Cities*, 2nd edn, London: Continuum.

Laws, E. (1991). *Tourism Marketing*, Cheltenham: Stanley Thornes.

Lawson, R., Thyne, M. and Young, T. (1997). *New Zealand Holidays: A Travel Lifestyle Study*, Dunedin: Marketing Department, University of Otago.

Lawton, G. and Page, S.J. (1997). 'Analysing the promotion, product and visitor expectations of urban tourism: Auckland New Zealand as a case study', *Journal of Travel and Tourism Marketing* 6(3/4): 123–42.

Lawton, R. (1978). 'Population and society 1730–1900', in R. Dodgshon and R. Butlin (eds) *An Historical Geography of England and Wales*, London: Academic Press, 313–66.

Lefebvre, H. (1991). *The Production of Space*, Oxford: Blackwell.

Leiper, N. (1989). *Tourism and Tourism Systems*, Occasional Paper No. 1, Department of Management Systems, Palmerston North: Massey University.

Leiper, N. (1990). 'Partial industrialization of tourism systems', *Annals of Tourism Research* 17: 600–605.

Levine, M.P. (1977). 'Gay ghetto', paper presented to the Annual Meeting of the American Sociological Association, September, Chicago.

Levinson, H. (1993). *Misplaced Priorities: Atlanta, the '96 Olympics and the Politics of Urban Removal*, Atlanta: Atlanta Task Force for the Homeless.

Lew, A.A. (1985). 'Bringing tourists to town', *Small Town* 16: 4–10.

Lew, A.A. (1987). 'A framework for tourist attraction research', *Annals of Tourism Research* 14(4): 553–75.

Lew, A.A. (1989). 'Authenticity and sense of place in the tourism development experience of older retail districts', *Journal of Travel Research* 27(4): 15–22.

Ley, D. (1989). 'Modernism, post-modernism and the struggle for place', in J. Agnew and J. Duncan (eds) *The Power of Place*, Winchester: Unwin Hyman.

Li, Y. (2000). 'Geographical consciousness and tourism experience', *Annals of Tourism Research* 27(4): 863–83.

Limburg, B. (1998). 'City marketing: a multi attribute approach', *Tourism Management* 16(5): 475–8.

Lipsitz, G. (1984). 'Sports stadia and urban development: a tale of three cities', *Journal of Sport and Social Issues* 8(2): 1–18.

Liu, J. and Var, T. (1986). 'Resident attitudes towards tourism impacts in Hawaii', *Annals of Tourism Research* 13(2): 193–214.

Lloyd, P. and Dicken, P. (1977). *Location in Space: A Theoretical Approach to Economic Geography*, 2nd edn, London: Harper and Row.

London Arts Board (1994). *Capitalising on Creativity – Prospects for the Arts in London*, London: Mimeo.

London Tourist Board and Convention Bureau (LTBCB) (1993). *Tourism Strategy for London Action Plan 1994–1997*, London: London Tourist Board and Convention Bureau.

Long, P.E. (1997). 'Researching tourism partnership organizations: from practice to theory to methodology', in P. Murphy (ed.) *Quality Management in Urban Tourism*, Chichester: John Wiley & Sons.

Love, J.F. (1986). *McDonald's: Behind the Arches*, Toronto: Bantam.

Lowe, M. (1993). 'Local hero! An examination of the role of the regional entrepreneur in the regeneration of Britain's regions', in G. Kearns and C. Philo (eds), *Selling Places: The City as Cultural Capital, Past and Present*, Oxford: Pergamon Press, 211–30.

Lowenthal, D. (1981). 'Conclusion: Dilemmas of preservation', in M. Binney and D. Lowenthal (eds) *Our Past Before Us, Why Do We Save It?*, London: Temple Smith, London, 213–37.

Lundberg, D., Drishnamoorthy, M. and Stavenga, M. (1995). *Tourism Economics*, New York: Wiley.

Lündgren, J.O.J. (1974). 'On access to recreational lands in dynamic metropolitan hinterlands', *Tourist Review* 29: 124–31.

MacCannel, D. (1976). *The Tourist: A New Theory of the Leisure Class*, London: Macmillan.

Madsen, H. (1992). 'Place-marketing in Liverpool: a review', *International Journal of Urban and Regional Research* 16(4): 633–40.

Manete, M., Minghetti, V. and Celotto, E. (2000). Artist (Agenda for Research on Tourism by Integration of Statistics/Strategies for Transport) Work Package 2: Final Report, Venice: CISET, University Ca' Foscari of Venice (unpublished), 27 January.

Manrai, L. and Manrai, A. (1993). 'Positioning European countries as brands in a perceptual map: an empirical study of determinants of consumer perceptions and preferences', *Journal of Euromarketing* 2: 101–29.

Mansfeld, J. (1999). 'Consuming spaces', in R. Le Heron, L. Murphy, P. Forer and M. Goldstone (eds) *Explorations in Human Geography: Encountering Place*, Auckland: Oxford University Press, 318–43.

Mansfeld, Y. (1992). 'Industrial landscapes as positive settings for tourism development in declining industrial cities – the case of Haifa, Israel', *GeoJournal* 28(4): 457–63.

Marketpower (1991). *A Report on the Structure of the UK Catering Industry*, London: Marketpower Ltd.

Marks, R. (1996). 'Conservation and community: the contradictions and ambiguities of tourism in the Stone Town of Zanzibar', *Habitat International* 20(2): 265–78.

Mason, K. (2000). 'The propensity of business travellers to use low cost airlines', *Journal of Transport Geography* 8(2): 107–19.

Mathieson, A. and Wall, G. (1982). *Tourism: Economic, Physical and Social Impacts*, London: Longman.

Matthews, T. (1976). 'Interest group access to the Australian government bureaucracy', in *Royal Commission on Australian Government Administration: Appendixes to Report, Volume Two*, Canberra: Australian Government Publishing Service.

Mattson, R. (1983). 'Store front remodeling on main street', *Journal of Cultural Geography* 3: 41–55.

Mazanec, J. (ed.) (1997a). *International City Tourism: Analysis and Strategy*, London: Pinter.

Mazanec, J.A. (1997b). 'Introduction: information requirements for the strategic management of city tourism', in J.A. Mazanec (ed.) *International City Tourism: Analysis and Strategy*, London: Pinter, xv–xvi.

Mazanec, J.A. (1997c). 'Satisfaction tracking for city tourists', in J.A. Mazanec (ed.) *International City Tourism: Analysis and Strategy*, London: Pinter, 75–100.

McBride, B. (1999). 'The (post)colonial landscape of Cathedral Square: urban redevelopment and representation in the "cathedral city" ', *New Zealand Geographer* 55(1): 3–11.

McDougall, G. and Munro, H. (1994). 'Scaling and attitude measurement in travel and tourism research', in J.R.B. Ritchie and C. Goeldner (eds) *Travel, Tourism and Hospitality Research: A Handbook for Managers and Researchers*, 2nd edn, Chichester: Wiley, 115–30.

McGee, T. (1979). 'The changing cities', in R. Hill (ed.) *South-East Asia: A Systematic Geography*, Kuala Lumpur: Oxford University Press, 180–91.

McGee, T. (1995). 'Metrofitting the emerging mega-regions of ASEAN: an overview', in T. McGee and I. Robinson (eds) *The Mega-Urban Regions of Southeast Asia*, Vancouver: UBC Press, 3–26.

McGee, T. and Greenberg, C. (1992). 'The emergence of metropolitan regions in ASEAN', *ASEAN Economic Bulletin* 9(1): 5–12.

McNeill, D. (1999). 'Globalisation and the European city', *Cities: The International Journal of Urban Policy and Planning* 16(3): 143–7.

Meethan, K. (1996). 'Consumed (in) in civilised city', *Annals of Tourism Research* 32(2): 322–40.

Meethan, K. (1997). 'York: managing the tourist city', *Cities: The International Journal of Urban Policy and Planning* 14(6): 333–42.

Meethan, K. (2001). *Tourism in Global Society: Place, Culture, Consumption*, Basingstoke: Palgrave.

Meisel, J. (1993). 'Capital cities: What is a capital?', in J. Taylor, J.G. Legellé and C. Andrew, (eds) *Capital Cities: International Perspectives/Les capitales: Perspectives internationales*, Carleton University Press, Ottawa.

Meyer-Arendt, K. (1990). 'Recreational business districts in Gulf of Mexico seaside resorts', *Journal of Cultural Geography* 11: 39–55.

Middleton, V.T.C. (1988). *Marketing in Travel and Tourism*, Oxford: Heinemann.

Middleton, V.T.C. (1994). 'Vision, strategy and corporate planning: an overview', in R. Harrison (ed.) *Manual of Heritage Management*, Oxford: Butterworth-Heinemann.

Mihalic, T. (2000). 'Environmental management of a tourist destination: a factor of tourism competitiveness', *Tourism Management* 21(1): 65–78.

Mill, R.C. and Morrison, A.M. (1992). *The Tourism System. An Introductory Text*, 2nd edn, New Jersey: Prentice Hall.

Millar, C. and Aiken, D. (1995). 'Conflict resolution in aquaculture: a matter of trust', in A. Boghen (ed.) *Coldwater Aquaculture in Atlantic Canada*, 2nd edn, Moncton: Canadian Institute for Research on Regional Development, 617–45.

Milman, A. and Pizam, A. (1988). 'Social impacts of tourism on central Florida', *Annals of Tourism Research* 15(2): 191–204.

Milroy, B.M. (1993). 'What is a capital?', in J. Taylor, J.G. Legellé and C. Andrew (eds) *Capital Cities: International Perspectives/Les capitales: Perspectives internationales*, Ottawa: Carleton University Press.

Ministry of Tourism (1992). *Residents' Perceptions and Acceptance of Tourism in Selected New Zealand Communities*, Wellington: Ministry of Tourism.

Mitchell, B. (1979). *Geography and Resource Analysis*, London: Longman.

Mommaas, H. and van der Poel, H. (1989). 'Changes in economy, politics and lifestyles: an essay on the restructuring of urban leisure', in P. Bramham, I. Henry, H. Mommaas and H. van der Poel (eds) *Leisure and Urban Processes: Critical Studies of Leisure Policy in Western European Cities*, London: Routledge, 254–76.

Montanari, A. and Muscara, C. (1995). 'Evaluating tourist flows in historic cities: The case of Venice', *Tijdschrift voor Economische en Sociale Geografie* 86(1): 80–87.

Montgomery, R.J. and Strick, S.K. (1995). *Meetings, Conventions, and Expositions: An Introduction to the Industry*, New York: Van Nostrand Reinhold.

Moore, C.W. (1986). *The Mediation Process: Practical Strategies for Resolving Conflict*, San Francisco: Jossey-Bass.

Moore, N.S.R. (1995). *National Mutual Masters Games, Economic Impact Assessment, Dunedin, February 5th–13th*, unpublished dissertation thesis, Dunedin: University of Otago.

Morgan, G. (1986). *Images of Organization*, Newbury Park: Sage.

Morris, D. (2000). 'British Columbia's Provincial Capital Commission: its role in shaping the image of Victoria', *Plan Canada* 40(3): 34.

Moscardo, G. (1996). 'Mindful visitors: heritage and tourism'. *Annals of Tourism Research* 23: 376–97.

Moudon, A.V. (1986). *Built for Change*, Cambridge: MIT Press.

Moutinho, L. (1987). 'Consumer behaviour in tourism', *European Journal of Marketing* 21(10): 3–44.

Moutinho, L., Rita, P. and Curry, B. (1996). *Expert Systems in Tourism Marketing*, Routledge: London.

Müller, D.K. (1999). *German Second Home Owners in the Swedish Countryside: On the Internationalization of the Leisure Space*, Östersund: European Tourism Research Institute.

Mullins, P. (1991). 'Tourism urbanization', *International Journal of Urban and Regional Research* 15(3): 326–42.

Mullins, P. (1994). 'Class relations and tourism urbanisation: the regeneration of the petite bourgeoisie and the emergence of a new urban form', *International Journal of Urban and Regional Research* 18(4): 591–607.

Mullins, P. (1999). 'International tourism and the cities of Southeast Asia', in D. Judd and S. Fainstein (eds) *The Tourist City*, New Haven: Yale University Press, 245–60.

Mumford, L. (1938). *The Culture of Cities*, New York: Harcourt Brace Jovanovich.

Munday, S. (1995). *A Study of Tourism Trends in Devonport*, report prepared for North Shore City Council, Auckland: Massey University, Albany.

Murphy, L. (1999). 'Visioning of cities', in R. Le Heron, L. Murphy, P. Forer and M. Goldstone (eds) *Explorations in Human Geography: Encountering Place*, Auckland: Oxford University Press, 289–317.

Murphy, P. (1985). *Tourism: A Community Approach*, London: Methuen.

Murphy, P. (ed.) (1997). *Quality Management in Urban Tourism*, Chichester: Wiley.

Murphy, P.E. (1988). 'Community driven tourism planning', *Tourism Management* 9(2): 96–104.

Myerscough, J. (1988). *The Economic Importance of the Arts in Britain*, London: Policy Studies Institute.

Nagy, L. (1999). 'Velence megovasa az arvitzol', *Vizugyi Kozlemenyek* 81(2): 295–310.

National Capital Authority (2000). http://www.nationalcapital.gov.au/fs-planning.html, accessed 15 December.

National Capital Commission (1988). *Plan for Canada's Capital – A Federal Land Use Plan*, Ottawa: National Capital Commission.

National Capital Commission (1991). *NCR Visitor Survey, Volume 1 – Analysis of Findings*, conducted for the National Capital Commission by Gallup Canada, Ottawa: National Capital Commission.

National Capital Commission (1998). *A Capital in the Making*, Ottawa: National Capital Commission.

National Capital Commission (1999). *Plan for Canada's Capital: A Second Century of Vision, Planning and Development*, Ottawa: National Capital Commission.

National Capital Commission (2000a). *Summary of the Corporate Plan 2000–2001 to 2004–2005*, Ottawa: National Capital Commission.

National Capital Commission (2000b). *Planning Canada's Capital Region*, Ottawa: National Capital Commission.

National Capital Development Commission (1981). *Assessment of ACT Tourist Industry Structure*, Canberra: National Capital Development Commission.

National Capital Planning Authority (1991). *National Capital Plan, Amendment No. 2*, Canberra: Australian Government Publishing Service.

National Capital Planning Authority (1992). *Annual Report 1991–92*, Canberra: Australian Government Publishing Service.

National Capital Planning Commission (NCPC) (1997). *Extending the Legacy: Planning America's Capital for the 21st Century*, Washington, DC: National Capital Planning Commission, http://www.ncpc.gov/planning_init/legacy.html, accessed 26 February 2001.

National Capital Planning Commission (2001a). About NCPC, http://www.ncpc.gov/about.html, accessed 26 February.

National Capital Planning Commission (2000b). Federal Capital Improvements Program, http://www.ncpc.gov/planning_init/fcip.html, accessed 26 February.

Nijman, J. (1999). 'Cultural globalisation and the identity of place: the reconstruction of Amsterdam', *Ecumene* 6(2): 146–64.

NIPO (1996). *Survey of City Trips of the Dutch Population*, Amsterdam: Nederlands Instituut Publicksonderzoek.

Nolan, M.L. and Nolan, S. (1992). 'Religious sites as tourism attractions in Europe', *Annals of Tourism Research* 19(1): 68–78.

Norkunas, M.K. (1993). *The Politics of Memory: Tourism, History, and Ethnicity in Monterey, California*, Albany: State University of New York Press.

Norris, D. and Patterson, L. (2000). 'The revitalization of Halifax', *Plan Canada*, 40(3): 26.

O'Brien, K. (2000). 'St. John's: the Atlantic entrance to the New World', *Plan Canada*, 40(3): 23.

O'Conner (1993). 'World population concentrating in mega-cities', *The Independent* 13 December.

Office for National Statistics (2000). *Focus on London 2000*, London: The Stationery Office.

Office of National Tourism (1997). *Cultural Tourism*, Tourism Facts No. 10, May, http://www.tourism.gov.au/new/cfa/cfa_fs10.html, accessed 31 December 1997.

O'Hara, J. (1986). 'The grand design of a world's fair: special report/Expo '86', *Macleans* 99 (17 March): 16–23.

Okner, B.A. (1974). 'Subsidies of stadiums and arenas', in R.G. Noll (ed.) *Government and the Sports Business*, Washington, DC: The Brookings Institution, 325–48.

Olds, K. (1989). 'Mass evictions in Vancouver: the human toll of Expo '86', *Canadian Housing* 6(1): 49–53.

Olds, K. (1998). 'Urban mega-events, evictions and housing rights: the Canadian case', *Current Issues in Tourism* 1(1): 2–46.

Olympic Bid Company (1986). *Policy Framework*, Cape Town: Cape Town 2004 Olympic Bid Company.

Oppermann, M., Din, K. and Amri, S. (1996). 'Urban hotel location and evolution in a developing country', *Tourism Recreation Research* 21(1): 55–63.

Organisation for Economic Cooperation and Development (OECD) (1986). *The OECD List of Social Indicators*, Paris: OECD.

Owen, C. (1990). 'Tourism and urban regeneration', *Cities: The International Journal of Urban Policy and Planning* August: 194–201.

Oxford City Council, The Thames and Chilterns Tourist Board and the Oxford and District Chamber of Trade (1992). *Oxford Visitors Study 1990–91: Final Report*, Oxford: Oxford Centre for Tourism and Leisure Studies, Oxford Brookes University.

Page, S.J. (1987). 'London Docklands: Redevelopment schemes in the 1980s', *Geography* 72(1): 59–63.

Page, S.J. (1988a). 'Tourists arrive in the Docks', *Town & Country Planning* 57(6): 178–9.

Page, S.J. (1989a). 'Tourist development in London Docklands in the 1980's and 1990's, policies and the Docklands experience', *GeoJournal* 19(3): 291–5.

Page, S.J. (1989b). 'Tourism planning in London', *Town and Country Planning* 58(3): 334–5.

Page, S.J. (1989c). *Tourism Accommodation in London in the 1980s and 1990s: A Review of the Main Trends and Activities in the London Hotel Market*, Consultant's Report for the Spanish National Tourism Plan, Tourism Research Centre, Canterbury Business School.

Page, S.J. (1990). 'Arena development in the UK and urban regeneration in London Docklands', *Sport Place: An International Journal of Sports Geography* 4(1): 2–15.

Page, S.J. (1991). 'Tourism in London: The Docklands' connection', *Geography Review* 4(3): 3–7.

Page, S.J. (1992). 'Managing tourism in a small historic city', *Town and Country Planning* 61(7/8): 208–11.

Page, S.J. (1993a). 'Perspectives on urban heritage tourism in New Zealand: Wellington in the 1990s', in C. M. Hall and S. McArthur (eds) *Heritage Management in New Zealand and Australia: Visitor Management, Interpretation and Marketing*, Auckland: Oxford University Press, 218–30.

Page, S.J. (1993b). 'Urban tourism in New Zealand: the National Museum of New Zealand Project', *Tourism Management* 14: 211–17.

Page, S.J. (1994a). 'Waterfront revitalisation in London: market-led planning and tourism in London Docklands', in S. Craig-Smith and M. Fagence (eds) *Urban*

Waterfront Development and Planning: An International Survey, New York: Praeger.

Page, S.J. (1994b). 'Tourism and peripherality: a review of tourism in the Republic of Ireland', in C. Cooper (ed.) *Progress in Tourism, Recreation and Hospitality Management*, Volume 5, Chichester: Wiley, 26–53.

Page, S.J. (1995a). *Urban Tourism*, London: Routledge.

Page, S.J. (1995b). *Devonport Residents Survey*, Consultant's Report for North Shore City Council and Devonport Community Board, Auckland.

Page, S.J. (1997). 'Urban tourism: analysing and evaluating the tourist experience', in C. Ryan (ed.) *The Tourist Experience: A New Introduction*, London: Cassell, 112–36.

Page, S.J. (1999). *Transport and Tourism*, Harlow: Addison Wesley Longman.

Page, S.J. (2000). 'Urban tourism', in C. Ryan and S.J. Page (eds) *Tourism Management: Towards the New Millennium*, Oxford: Pergamon, 197–202.

Page, S.J. (2001). 'Gateways, hubs and transport interconnections in South east Asia: implications for tourism development in the Twenty First century', in P. Teo, T. Chang and H. Chong (eds) *Interconnected Worlds: Tourism in Southeast Asia*, Oxford: Pergamon.

Page, S.J. and Fidgeon, P. (1989). 'London Docklands: a tourism perspective', *Geography* 74(1): 66–8.

Page, S.J. and Hardyman, R. (1996). 'Place marketing and town centre management: a new tool for urban revitalisation', *Cities: the International Journal of Urban Policy and Planning* 13(3): 153–64.

Page, S.J. and Piotrowski, S. (1991). 'Tourism and regeneration: the Dover experience', *Town and Country Planning* 60(1): 24–6.

Page, S.J. and Sinclair, M.T.C. (1989). 'Tourism accommodation in London: alternative policies and the Docklands experience', *Built Environment* 15(2): 125–37.

Page, S.J. and Sinclair, M.T.C. (1992). 'The channel tunnel: an opportunity for London's tourism industry', *Tourism Recreation Research* 17: 57–70.

Page, S.J., Forer, P. and Lawton, G. (1999). 'Small business development and tourism: *terra incognita?*', *Tourism Management* 20(4): 435–60.

Page, S.J., Brunt, P., Busby, G. and Connell, J. (2001). *Tourism: A Modern Synthesis*, London: Thomson Learning.

Painter, J. (2000). 'State and governance', in E. Sheppard and T.J. Barnes (eds) *A Companion to Economic Geography*, Oxford: Blackwell, 359–76.

Pannell Kerr Forster & Company (1977). *The Economic and Social Impact of Visitors on the ACT*, a report prepared by Pannell Kerr Forster & Company for National Capital Development Commission, Department of the Capital Territory, Department of Industry and Commerce, Sydney: Pannell Kerr Forster & Company.

Parlett, G., Fletcher, J. and Cooper, C. (1995). 'The impact of tourism on the old Town of Edinburgh', *Tourism Management* 16(5): 355–60.

Patmore, J.A. (1983). *Recreation and Resources*, Oxford: Blackwell.

Pawson, E. (1997). 'Branding strategies and languages of consumption', *New Zealand Geographer* 53(2): 16–21.

Pearce, D.G. (1987). *Tourism Today: A Geographical Analysis*, London: Longman.

Pearce, D.G. (1989). *Tourism Development*, 2nd edn, Harlow: Longman.

Pearce, D.G. (1992). *Tourist Organizations*, Harlow: Longman.

Pearce, D.G. (1995). *Tourism Today: A Geographical Analysis*, 2nd edn, London: Longman.

Pearce, D.G. (1998). 'Tourism development in Paris: Public intervention', *Annals of Tourism Research* 25(2): 457–76.

Pearce, D.G. (1999a). 'Assessing the impact of urban casinos on tourism in New Zealand', *Tourism Economics* 5(2): 141–59.

Pearce, D.G. (1999b). 'Tourism districts in Paris: structure and functions', *Tourism Management* 19(1): 49–66.

Pearce, P. (1982). *The Social Psychology of Tourism*, Oxford: Pergamon.

Pearce, P. (1993). 'The fundamentals of tourist motivation', in D.G. Pearce and R. Butler (eds) *Tourism Research: Critiques and Challenges*, London: Routledge, 113–34.

Pearce, P.L. (1991). 'Analysing tourist attractions', *Journal of Tourism Studies* 2: 46–55.

Penning-Rowsell, E., Winchester, P. and Gardiner, J. (1998). 'New approaches to sustainable hazard management for Venice', *Geographical Journal* 164(1): 1–18.

Pettafor, E. (1999). 'Mardi Gras kiss of life to the economy', *Australian Financial Review* 27 February.

Philo, C. and Kearns, G. (1993). 'Culture, history, capital: a critical introduction to the selling of places', in G. Kearns and C. Philo (eds) *Selling Places: The City as Cultural Capital, Past and Present*, Oxford: Pergamon Press, 1–32.

Pigeassou, C., Vanreusel, B., Miranda, J. and Monserrat, S. (1999). 'Les conflits entre tourisme sportif et environnement dans quelques pays europeens: une situation preoccupante', *Cahiers Espaces* 62: 12–20.

Pigram, J. and Jenkins, J. (1999). *Outdoor Recreation Management*, London: Routledge.

Pizam, A. and Mansfeld, Y. (eds) (1996). *Tourism, Crime and International Security Issues*, Chichester: Wiley.

Porter, M.E. (1997). 'New strategies for inner-city economic development', *Economic Development Quarterly* 11(1): 1–19.

Postman, N. (1985). *Amusing Ourselves to Death*, New York: Viking.

Potter, A.F. (1978). 'The methodology of impact analysis', *Town and Country Planning* 46(9): 400–4.

Pratt, A. (1998). 'The cultural industries production system: a case study of employment change in Britain, 1984–91', *Environment and Planning D* 29: 1953–74.

Prentice, R. (1993). *Tourism and Heritage Places*, London: Routledge.

Prentice, R., Witt, S. and Wydenbach, E. (1994). 'The endearment behaviour of tourists through their interaction with the host community', *Tourism Management* 15(2): 117–25.

Pritchard, A. and Morgan, N. (2000). 'Privileging the male gaze – gendered tourism landscapes', *Annals of Tourism Research* 27(4): 884–905.

Pritchard, A., Morgan, N.J., Sedgely, D. and Jenkins, A. (1998). 'Reaching out to the gay tourist: opportunities and threats in an emerging market segment', *Tourism Management* 19(3): 273–82.

Probyn, E. (1998). 'McIdentities: food and the familial citizen', *Theory, Culture & Society* 15(2): 155–73.

Quirk, J. and Fort, R.D. (1992). *Pay Dirt: The Business of Professional Team Sports*, Princeton: Princeton University Press.

Racine, J. and Cosinschi, M. (1990). 'Les espaces urbains. Des villes, des espaces et des hommes', *Nouvelle Geographie de la Suisse et des Suissees* 2: 409–76.

Ravenscroft, N., Reeves, J. and Rowley, M. (2000). 'Leisure, property, and the viability of town centres', *Environment and Planning A* 32(8): 1359–74.

Rawding, C. (2000). 'Tourism in Amsterdam: marketing and reality', *Geography* 85(2): 167–72.

Rawn, C.D. (1990). 'From smokestacks to stadiums: affluent sports fans are a clean industry in Indianapolis', *American Demographics* October: 49–50.

Reid, L. (1994). *London Tourism*, London: London Pride Partnership (mimeo).

Reiss, S.A. (1981). 'Power without authority: Los Angeles' elites and the construction of the coliseum', *Journal of Sport History* 8: 50–65.

Reiss, S.A. (1989). *City Games: the Evolution of American Urban Society and the Rise of Sports*, Urbana: University of Illinois Press.

Richards, G. (ed.) (1996a). *Cultural Tourism in Europe*, Wallingford: CAB International.

Richards, G. (1996b). 'The scope and significance of cultural tourism', in G. Richards (ed.) *Cultural Tourism in Europe*. Wallingford: CAB International, 19–45.

Richards, G. (1996c). 'Production and consumption of European cultural tourism', *Annals of Tourism Research* 23(2): 261–83.

Rimmer, P. (ed.) (1997). *Pacific Rim Development: Integration and Globalisation in the Asia-Pacific Economy*, St. Leonards: Allen and Unwin.

Rink, D.R. and Swan, J.E. (1979). 'Product life cycle research: literature review', *Journal of Business Research* 78: 219–42.

Rinschede, G. (1986). 'The Pilgrimage town of Lourdes', *Journal of Cultural Geography* 7(1): 21–34.

Rinschede, G. (1990). 'Religious tourismus', *Geographische Rundschau* 42(1): 14–20.

Ritchie, J.B.R. (1984). 'Assessing the impact of hallmark events: conceptual and research issues', *Journal of Travel Research* 23(1): 2–11.

Ritchie, J.B.R. and Yangzhou, H. (1987). 'The role and impact of mega-events and attractions on national and regional tourism: a conceptual and methodological overview', paper prepared for presentation at the 37th Annual Congress of the International Association of Scientific Experts in Tourism (AIEST), Calgary, Canada.

Ritzer, D. (1996). *The McDonaldisation of Society*, revised edn, Pine Forge: Thousand Oaks.

Roberts, J. (1987). 'Buying leisure', *Leisure Studies*, 6(1): 87–91.

Robertson, K. (1995). 'Downtown redevelopment strategies in the United States: an end of century assessment', *Journal of the American Planning Association* 61(4): 429–37.

Robins, K. (1991a). 'Prisoners of the city: whatever could a postmodern city be?', *New Formations* 15(Winter): 1–22.

Robins, K. (1991b). 'Tradition and translation: national culture in its global context', in J. Corner and S. Harvey (eds) *Enterprise and Heritage: Crosscurrents of National Culture*, London and New York: Routledge, 21–44.

Roche, M. (1992). 'Mega-events and micro-modernization: on the sociology of the new urban tourism', *British Journal of Sociology* 43(4): 563–600.

Roche, M. (1994). 'Mega-events and urban policy', *Annals of Tourism Research* 21(1): 1–19.

Roche, M. (2000). *Mega-Events and Modernity: Olympics and Expos in the Growth of Global Culture*, London: Routledge.

Rojek, C. (1993). *Ways of Escape: Modern Transformations in Leisure and Travel*, Basingstoke: Macmillan.

Roriz, J.D. (2000). 'Brasilia: a national project for development and integration', *Plan Canada* 40(3): 16–17.

Rosentraub, M.S. (1996). 'Does the emperor have new clothes? A reply to Robert A. Baade', *Journal of Urban Affairs* 18(1): 3–31.

Rosentraub, M.S., Swindell, D., Przybliski, M. and Mullins, D. (1994). 'Sport and downtown development strategy: if you build it, will jobs come?', *Journal of Urban Affairs* 16(3): 221–39.

Rothman, R. (1978). 'Residents and transients: community reaction to seasonal visitors', *Journal of Travel Research* 16(4): 8–13.

Rowat, D. (1993). 'Ways of governing federal cities', in J. Taylor, J.G. Legellé and C. Andrew (eds) *Capital Cities: International Perspectives/Les capitales: Perspectives internationales*, Ottawa: Carleton University Press.

Rowe, D. and Stevenson, D. (1994). ' "Provincial paradise": urban tourism and city imaging outside the metropolis', *Australian and New Zealand Journal of Sociology* 30(2): 178–93.

Rutheiser, C. (1996). *Imagineering Atlanta: The Politics of Place in the City of Dreams*, New York: Verso.

Ryan, C. (1991). *Recreational Tourism: A Social Science Perspective*, London: Routledge.

Ryan, C. (1995). *Researching Tourist Satisfaction*, London: Routledge.

Ryan, C. (ed.) (1997). *The Tourist Experience*, London: Cassell.

Ryan, C. and Hall, C.M. (2001). *Sex Tourism: Marginal People and Liminalities*, London: Routledge.

Ryan, C. and Kinder, R. (1995). 'The deviant tourist and the crimogenic place', in A. Pizam and Y. Mansfield (eds) *Tourism Crime and International Security Issues*, Chichester: Wiley, 23–36.

Ryan, C. and Kinder, R. (1996). 'Sex, tourism and sex tourism: fulfilling similar needs?', *Tourism Management* 17(7): 507–18.

Ryan, C. and Lockyer, T. (2001). 'An economic impact case study: the South Pacific Masters' Games', *Tourism Economics* 7(3): 267–76.

Ryan, C. and Montgomery, D. (1994). 'The attitudes of Bakewell residents to tourism and issues in community responsive tourism', *Tourism Management* 15(5): 358–70.

Ryan, C. and Page, S.J. (2000). 'Preface', in C. Ryan and S.J. Page (eds) *Tourism Management: Towards the New Millennium*, Oxford: Pergamon, ix–xi.

Sadler, D. (1993). 'Place-marketing, competitive places and the construction of hegemony in Britain in the 1980s', in G. Kearns and C. Philo (eds) *Selling Places: The City as Cultural Capital, Past and Present*, Oxford: Pergamon Press, 175–92.

Saeter, J.A. (1993). *Local Economic Impacts of Tourism – A Case Study of the Municipalities Risoer, Roeros, Vaagan and Bykle in Norway* (in Norwegian, title translated), report 17/1993, Lillehammer: Eastern Norway Research Institute.

Saeter, J.A. (1994). *Tourism Related Employment in the Municipalities Risoer, Roeros, Vaagan and Bykle in Norway* (in Norwegian, title translated), paper 04/1994, Lillehammer: Eastern Norway Research Institute.

Saeter, J.A. (1998). 'The significance of tourism and economic development in rural areas: a Norwegian case study', in R.W. Butler, C.M. Hall and J. Jenkins (eds) *Tourism and Recreation in Rural Areas*, Chichester: John Wiley, 235–46.

Sant, M. and Waitt, G. (2000). 'Sydney: all day long, all night long', in J. Connell (ed.) *Sydney: The Emergence of a World City*, Melbourne: Oxford University Press.

Savage, M. and Warde, A. (1993). *Urban Sociology, Capitalism and Modernity*, Basingstoke: Macmillan.

Sawicki, D. (1989). 'The festival marketplace as public policy, *Journal of the American Planning Association* Summer: 347–61.

Schafer, U. (1978). 'Traffic problems in holiday resorts', *Tourist Review* 33(2): 9–15.

Schimmel, K.S. (1995). 'Growth politics, urban development, and sports stadium construction in the United States: a case study', in J. Bale and O. Moen (eds) *The Stadium and the City*, Keele: Keele University Press.

Schlozman, K.L. and Tierney, J.T. (1986). *Organized Interests and American Democracy*, New York: Harper and Row.

Schneider, W. (1963). *Babylon Is Everywhere: The City as Man's Fate*, New York: McGraw-Hill.

Schofield, P. (1996). 'Cinematographic images of a city: alternative heritage tourism in Manchester', *Tourism Management* 17(5): 333–40.

Schofield, P. (2001). 'Urban tourism and small business', in N. Douglas, N. Douglas and R. Derrett (eds) *Special Interest Tourism*, Brisbane: John Wiley, 432–54.

Schollman, A., Perkins, H.C. and Moore, K. (2000). 'Intersecting global and local influences in urban place promotion: the case of Christchurch, New Zealand', *Environment and Planning A* 32(1): 55–76.

Scottish Executive (2000). *A New Strategy for Scottish Tourism*, Edinburgh: Scottish Executive.

Selin, S. (1993). 'Collaborative alliances: new interorganizational forms in tourism', *Journal of Travel and Tourism Marketing* 2(2/3): 217–27.

Selin, S. (1998). 'The promise and pitfalls of collaborating', *Trends* 35(1): 9–13.

Selin, S. and Beason, K. (1991). 'Interorganisational relations in tourism', *Annals of Tourism Research* 18: 639–52.

Selin, S. and Chavez, D. (1994). 'Characteristics of successful tourism partnerships: a multiple case study design', *Journal of Park and Recreation Administration* 12(2): 51–62.

Selin, S. and Chavez, D. (1995). 'Developing a collaborative model for environmental planning and management', *Environmental Management* 19(2): 189–96.

Selin, S. and Myers, N. (1995). 'Correlates of partnership effectiveness: the coalition for unified recreation in the Eastern Sierra', *Journal of Park and Recreation Administration* 13(4): 38–47.

Selin, S. and Myers, N. (1998). 'Tourism marketing alliances: member satisfaction and effectiveness attributes of a regional initiative', *Journal of Travel and Tourism Marketing* 7(3): 79–94.

Selman, P. (1992). *Environmental Planning: The Conservation and Development of Biophysical Resources*, London: Paul Chapman Publishing.

Shaw, G. and Williams, A. (1992). 'Tourism, development and the environment: the eternal triangle', in C.P. Cooper and A. Lockwood (eds) *Progress in Tourism, Recreation and Hospitality Management*, Volume 4, London: Belhaven.

Shaw, G. and Williams, A. (1994). *Critical Issues in Tourism: A Geographical Perspective*, Oxford: Blackwell.

Shimp, T.A., Samiee, S. and Madden, T.J. (1993). 'Countries and their products: a cognitive structure perspective', *Journal of the Academy of Marketing Science* 21: 323–30.

Sickman, P. (1995). 'Sports pork', *The American Enterprise* 6(3): 80–82.

Simpson, F. (1999). 'Tourist impact in the historic centre of Prague: resident and visitor perceptions of the historic built environment', *The Geographical Journal* 165(2): 173–83.

Sinclair, M.T. (ed.) (1997). *Gender, Work and Tourism*, London: Routledge.

Sinclair, M.T. and Stabler, M. (1991). 'New perspectives in the tourism industry', in M.T. Sinclair and M.J. Stabler (eds) *The Tourism Industry: An International Analysis*, Oxford: CAB International: 1–14.

Sinclair, M.T. and Stabler, M. (1997). *The Economics of Tourism*, London: Routledge.

Smith, A. (1972). 'The future of downtown retailing', *Urban Land* 31: 3–10.

Smith, L.G. (1992). 'From condescension to conflict resolution: adjusting to the changing role of the public in impact assessment', in *Proceedings of an International Symposium on Hazardous Materials/Waste: Social Aspects of Facility Planning and Management*, Toronto: Institute for Social Impact Assessment, 96–101.

Smith, S.L.J. (1983). 'Restaurants and dining out: geography of a tourism business', *Annals of Tourism Research* 10(4): 515–49.

Smith, S.L.J. (1988). 'Defining tourism: a supply-side view', *Annals of Tourism Research* 15: 179–90.

Smith, S.L.J. (1989). *Tourism Analysis*, Harlow: Longman.

Smith, S.L.J. (1991). 'The supply-side definition of tourism: reply to Leiper', *Annals of Tourism Research* 18: 312–18.

Smith, S.L.J. (1993). 'Return to the supply side', *Annals of Tourism Research* 20: 226–9.

Smith, V. (ed.) (1989). *Hosts and Guests*, Philadelphia: University of Pennsylvania Press.

Smyth, H. (1994). *Marketing the City: The Role of Flagship Developments in Urban Regeneration*, London: E & FN Spon.

Smyth, J. (2000). 'Yellowknife: diamond capital of North America', *Plan Canada* 40(3): 8–35.

Snaith, T. and Haley, A. (1999). 'Resident opinions of tourism development in the historic city of York, England', *Tourism Management* 20(5): 595–603.

Soja, E. (1989). *Postmodern Geographies: The Reassertion of Space in Critical Social Theory*, Verso: London.

Soja, E. (1996). 'Los Angeles 1965–1992: the six geographies of urban restructuring', in A. Scott and E. Soja (eds) *The City: Los Angeles and Urban Theory at the End of the Twentieth Century*, Los Angeles: University of California Press, 426–62.

Sorensen, A.D. (1990) 'Virtuous cycles of growth and vicious cycles of decline: regional economic decline in northern New South Wales', in D.J. Walmsley (ed.) *Change and Adjustment in Northern New South Wales*, Armidale: Department of Geography and Planning, University of New England.

Sorkin, M. (ed.) (1991). *Variations on a Theme Park: The New American City and the End of Public Space*, New York: Hill and Wang.

Spoonley, P. (2000). 'The city and city life', in G. McLennan, A. Ryan and P. Spoonley (eds) *Exploring Society: Sociology for New Zealand Students*, Auckland: Longman, 172–90.

Stabler, M. and Goodall, B. (1997). 'Environmental awareness, action and performance in the Guernsey hospitality sector', *Tourism Management* 18(1): 19–33.

Stanback, T. (1985). 'The changing fortunes of metropolitan economies', in M. Castells (ed.) *High Technology, Space and Society*, Beverly Hills, CA: Sage.

Standeven, J. and De Knop, P. (1999). *Sport Tourism*, Champaign, IL: Human Kinetics.

Standing Committee on Tourism and ACT Promotion (1993). *ACT and Region Tourism, Legislative Assembly for the Australian Capital Territory*, Canberra: The Standing Committee on Tourism and ACT Promotion.

Stansfield, C.A. (1964). 'A note on the urban-nonurban imbalance in American recreational research', *Tourist Review* 19(4): 196–200.

Stansfield, C.A. and Rickert, J.E. (1970). 'The recreational business district', *Journal of Leisure Research* 2(4): 213–25.

Statistics Working Group of the Cultural Ministers Council (1996). *Australia's Balance of Trade in Culture*, Canberra: Department of Communication and the Arts.

Stebbins, R.A. (1982). 'Serious leisure a conceptual statement', *Pacific Sociological Review* 25(2): 251–72.

Stein, J.M. (ed.) (1993). *Growth Management: The Planning Challenge of the 1990s*, Newbury Park: Sage.

Swarbrooke, J. and Horner, S. (2001). *Business Travel and Tourism*, Oxford: Butterworth-Heinemann.

Swyngedouw, E. (1989). 'The heart of the place: the resurrection of locality in an age of hyperspace', *Geografiska Annaler* 71B: 31–42.

Takaki, R. (1994). *Ethnic Islands: The Emergence of Urban Chinese America*, New York: Chelsea House Publishers.

Tang, M. and Thant, M. (1994). *Growth Triangles: Conceptual Issues and Problems*, Economics Staff Paper No. 54, Manila: Asian Development Bank.

Telfer, D. and Wall, G. (1996). 'Linkages between tourism and food production', *Annals of Tourism Research* 23(3): 635–53.

Teo, P., Chang, T. and Chong, H. (eds) (2001). *Interconnected Worlds: Tourism in Southeast Asia*, Oxford: Pergamon.

Therborn, G. (1996). *Monumental Europe: The National Years of the Iconography of European Capital Cities*, Gothenberg: University of Gothenberg.

Thorns, D.C. (1997). 'The global meets the local: tourism and the representation of the New Zealand City', *Urban Affairs Review* 33: 189–208.

Thrift, N. (1997). 'Cities without modernity, cities with magic', *Scottish Geographical Magazine* 113: 138–49.

Thurot, J.M. (1980). *Capacite de Charge et Production Touristique*, Etudes et Memoires No. 43, Aix-en-Provence: Centre des Hantes Touristique.

Tighe, A.J. (1985). 'Cultural tourism in the USA', *Tourism Management*, 6(4): 234–51.

Tighe, A.J. (1986). 'The arts/tourism partnership', *Journal of Travel Research*, 24(3): 2–5.

Timothy, D. (2001). 'Tourism and the growth of urban ethnic islands', in C.M. Hall and A.M. Williams (eds) *Tourism and Migration: New Relationships Between Consumption and Production*, Dordrecht: Kluwer.

Timothy, D. and Wall, G. (1996). 'Tourist accommodation in an Asian historic city', *Journal of Tourism Studies* 6(2): 63–73.

Tomlinson, J. (1991). *Cultural Imperialism: A Critical Introduction*, Baltimore: John Hopkins Press.

Totally Wellington (2000). Wellington Media Kit, http://www.wellingtonnz.co.nz/media/mediakit.asp, accessed 18 December 2000.

Touche Ross (1988). *London Tourism Impact Study*, London: Touche Ross.

Touche Ross: Greene Belfield-Smith Division (1991). *Survey of Tourist Offices in European Cities*, London: Touche Ross.

Tourism Canada (1991). *Inventory of Studies Conducted in Canadian Cities Montreal, Toronto and Vancouver Overview*, Canada: Industry, Science and Technology Canada – Tourism, Products and Services.

Tourism New Zealand (2000). Wellington, http://www.purenz.com/IndRegion.cfm?region=Wellington, accessed 15 December 2000.

Tourism South Australia (1990). *Planning for Tourism: A Handbook for South Australia*, Adelaide: Tourism South Australia.

Tourism South Australia (1991). *Making South Australia Special: South Australian Tourism Plan 1991–1993*, Adelaide: Tourism South Australia.

Tourism Victoria (1997a). *Annual Report 1996–97*, Melbourne: Tourism Victoria.

Tourism Victoria (1997b). *Strategic Business Plan 1997–2001: Building Partnerships*, Melbourne: Tourism Victoria.

Towner, J. (1996). *An Historical Geography of Recreation and Tourism in the Western World 1540–1940*, Chichester: Wiley.

Trew, J. (1999). 'London', *City Reports* 2: 37–63.

Tribe, J. (1995). *The Economics of Leisure and Tourism: Environments, Markets, Impacts*, Oxford: Butterworth-Heinemann.

Tufts, S. and Milne, S. (1999). 'Museums: a supply side perspective', *Annals of Tourism Research* 26(3): 613–31.

Tunbridge, J. (1998). 'Tourism management in Ottawa, Canada: nurturing in a fragile environment' in D. Tyler, Y. Guerrier and M. Robertson (eds) *Managing Tourism in Cities: Policy, Process and Practice*, London: Wiley, 91–108.

Tunbridge, J.E. and Ashworth, G.J. (1996). *Dissonant Heritage: The Management of the Past as a Resource in Conflict*, Chichester: Wiley.

Turner, L. and Reisinger, Y. (2001). 'Shopping satisfaction for the domestic tourist', *Journal of Retailing and Customer Services* 8(1): 15–27.

Tyler, D., Guerrier, Y. and Robertson, M. (eds) (1998). *Managing Tourism in Cities: Policy, Process and Practice*, Chichester: Wiley.

UNESCO (1976). 'The effects of tourism on socio-cultural values', *Annals of Tourism Research* 4: 74–105.

United Nations (1998a). *Human Development Report*, New York: United Nations.

United Nations (1998b). *Population of Capital Cities and Cities of 100,000 and more Inhabitants*, New York: United Nations.

Urry, J. (1990). *The Tourist Gaze: Leisure and Travel in Contemporary Societies*, London: Sage.

Urry, J. (1991). 'The sociology of tourism', in C. Cooper (ed.) *Progress in Tourism, Recreation and Hospitality Management, Vol. 3*, London: Belhaven.

Urry, J. (1995). *Consuming Places*, London: Routledge.

Uysal, M. (1998). 'The determinants of tourism demand: a theoretical perspective', in D. Ioannides and K. Debbage (eds) *The Economic Geography of the Tourist Industry: A Supply Side Analysis*, London: Routledge, 79–96.

Uysal, M., Oh, H. and O'Leary, J. (1995). 'Seasonal variation in propensity to travel in the US', *Journal of Tourism Systems and Quality Management* 1(1): 1–13.

Uzzell, D. (1994). 'Heritage interpretation in Britain four decades after Tilden', in R. Harrison (ed.) *Manual of Heritage Management*, Oxford: Butterworth-Heinemann, 293–302.

van den Berg, L., van der Borg, J. and van der Meer, J. (1995). *Urban Tourism: Performance and Strategies in Eight European cities*, Aldershot: Avebury.

van der Borg, J. (1991). *Tourism and Urban Development: The Impact of Urban Tourism Development*, thesis, Amsterdam: Tinberg Institute Research.

van der Borg, J. (1992). 'Tourism and urban development: the case of Venice, Italy', *Tourism Recreation Research* 17(2): 45–56.

van der Borg, J. (1994). 'Demand for city tourism', *Tourism Management* 15: 66–9.

van der Borg, J. and Costa, P. (1993). 'The management of tourism in cities of art', *Tourist Review* 2–11.

van der Borg, J., Costa, P. and Gotti, G. (1996). 'Tourism in European heritage cities', *Annals of Tourism Research* 23(2): 306–21.

Var, T. and Quayson, J. (1985). 'The multiplier impact of tourism in the Okanagan', *Annals of Tourism Research* 12(4): 497–514.

Veal, A.J. (1992). *Research Methods for Leisure and Tourism: A Practical Guide*, Harlow: Longman.

Vetter, F. (ed.) (1985). *Big City Tourism*, Berlin: Dietrich Verlag.

Waddock, S.A. and Bannister, B.D. (1991). 'Correlates of effectiveness and partner satisfaction in social partnerships', *Journal of Organizational Change Management* 4(2): 74–89.

Walmesley, D.J. and Jenkins, J. (1992). 'Tourism cognitive mapping of unfamiliar environments', *Annals of Tourism Research* 19(3): 268–86.

Walmsley, D.J. and Lewis, G.J. (1993). *People and Environment: Behavioural Approaches in Human Geography*, 2nd edn, London: Longman.

Ward, S. (1998). *Selling Places: The Marketing and Promotion of Towns and Cities 1850–2000*, London: E & FN Spon.

Warf, B. (2000). 'New York: The Big Apple in the 1990s', *Geoforum* 31: 487–99.

Wathern, P. (ed.) (1988). *Environmental Impact Assessment: Theory and Practice*, London: Unwin Hyman.

Webber, M.M. (1963). 'Order and diversity: community without propinquity', in L. Wingo *et al.* (eds) *Cities and Space: The Future Use of Urban Land*, Baltimore: John Hopkins University Press, 23–54.

Webber, M.M. (1964). 'The urban place and the nonplace realm', in M.M. Webber *et al.* (eds) *Explorations into Urban Structure*, Philadelphia: University of Pennsylvania Press.

Weed, M. (2001). 'Towards a model of cross-sectoral policy development in leisure: the case of sport and tourism', *Leisure Studies* 20(2): 125–41.

Wellington City Art Gallery (1991). *Inheritance: Art, Heritage and the Past*, Wellington: Wellington City Art Gallery.

Wells, W.D. and Gubar, G. (1986). 'Life cycle concept in marketing research', *Journal of Marketing Research* 355–63.

Weston, J. (ed.) (1997). *Planning and Environmental Impact Assessment in Practice*, Harlow: Longman.

White, C.A. (1986). 'Evictions no room at the inn', *Canada and the World* 51: 4.

White, P.E. (1974). *The Social Impact of Tourism on Host Communities: A Study of Language Change in Switzerland*, Research Paper No. 9, Oxford: School of Geography, Oxford University.

Whitford, D. (1993). *Playing Hardball: The High-stakes Battle for Baseball's New Franchises*, New York: Doubleday.

Whitson, D. and Macintosh, D. (1996). 'The global circus: international sport, tourism, and the marketing of cities', *Journal of Sport and Social Issues* 23: 278–95.

Wight, I. (2000). 'Capitalizing on provincial capital status: a novel strategy for Winnipeg', *Plan Canada* 40(3): 30.

Wilkinson, J. (1994). *The Olympic Games: Past History and Present Expectations*, Sydney: NSW Parliamentary Library.

Williams, A. and Shaw, G. (eds) (1991). *Tourism and Economic Development*, London: Belhaven.

Williams, A.M. and Hall, C.M. (2000). 'Tourism and migration: new relationships between production and consumption', *Tourism Geographies* 2(1): 5–27.

Williams, A.M. and Hall, C.M. (2002). 'Tourism, migration, circulation and mobility: the contingencies of time and place', in C.M. Hall and A.M. Williams (eds) *Tourism and Migration: New Relationships Between Consumption and Production*, Dordrecht: Kluwer.

Williams, M.V. (1993). 'Growth management in community tourism planning', unpublished research project for the Master of Natural Resource Management, School of Resource and Environmental Management, Simon Fraser University, Burnaby.

Williams, P.W. and Gill, A. (1991). *Carrying Capacity Management in Tourism Settings: A Tourism Growth Management Process*, Vancouver: Centre for Tourism Policy and Research, Simon Fraser University.

Williams, P.W. and Gill, A. (1994). 'Tourism carrying capacity management issues', in W. Theobald (ed.) Global Tourism: The Next Decade, Oxford: Butterworth-Heinemann, 174–87.

Williams, R. (1983). *Keywords*, London: Fontana.

Witt, S.F., Brooke, M.Z. and Buckley, P.J. (1991). *The Management of International Tourism*, London: Unwin Hyman.

Wöber, K. (1997a). 'Introducing a harmonization procedure for European city tourism statistics', in J.A. Mazanec (ed.) *International City Tourism: Analysis and Strategy*, London: Pinter, 26–38.

Wöber, K. (1997b). 'International city tourism flows', in J.A. Mazanec (ed.) *International City Tourism: Analysis and Strategy*, London: Pinter, 39–53.

Wöber, K. (2000). 'Standardising city tourism statistics', *Annals of Tourism Research* 27(1): 51–68.

Woo, K. and Page, S.J. (1999). 'Case study: tourism demand in East Asia Pacific – the case of the South Korean outbound market and activity patterns in New Zealand', in C.M. Hall and S.J. Page (eds) *The Geography of Tourism and Recreation: Environment, Place and Space*, London: Routledge, 70–75.

Wood, D.J. and Gray, B. (1991). 'Toward a comprehensive theory of collaboration', *Journal of Applied Behavioral Science* 27(2): 139–62.

Wootton, G. and Stevens, T. (1995). 'Business tourism: a study of the market for hotel-based meetings and its contribution to Wales's tourism', *Tourism Management* 16(4): 305–15.

World Tourism Organization (WTO) (1985). *The State's Role in Protecting and Promoting Culture as a Factor of Tourism Development and the Proper Use and Exploitation of National Cultural Heritage of Sites and Movements for Tourism*, Madrid: WTO.

Yacoumis, J. (1980). 'Tackling seasonality: the case of Sri Lanka', *Tourism Management* 1(2): 84–98.

York, P. and Jennings, C. (1995). *Peter York's 80's*, London: BBC Books.

Zelinsky, W. (1973). *The Cultural Geography of the United States*, Englewood Cliffs, NJ: Prentice Hall.

Zelinsky, W. (1994). 'Conventionland USA: the geography of a latter day phenomenon', *Annals of the Association of American Geographers* 84: 68–86.

Zilio-Grandi, F. and Szpyrkowicz, L. (2000). 'The survey of acid rains in the Venice region', *Pollution Research* 19(1): 1–29.

Zukin, S. (1991). *Landscapes of Power: From Detroit to Disney World*, Berkeley: University of California Press.

Zukin, S. (1995). *The Culture of Cities*, Oxford: Blackwell.

Zukin, S. (1998). 'Urban lifestyles: diversity and standardisation in spaces of consumption', *Urban Studies* 35(5/6): 825–40.

Index